Beginning Structured COBOL

Brooks/Cole Series in Computer Science

Beginning BASIC
D. K. Carver

Beginning Structured COBOL
D. K. Carver

BASIC: An Introduction to Computer Programming, Second Edition
Robert J. Bent and George C. Sethares

Business BASIC
Robert J. Bent and George C. Sethares

FORTRAN with Problem Solving: A Structured Approach
Robert J. Bent and George C. Sethares

Beginning

Structured

COBOL

D. K. Carver

Brooks/Cole Publishing Company
Monterey, California

Brooks/Cole Publishing Company
A Division of Wadsworth, Inc.

Printed in the United States of America

10   9   8   7   6   5   4   3

Library of Congress Cataloging in Publication Data

Carver, D. K.
    Beginning structured COBOL.

    Includes index.
    1. COBOL (Computer program language)   2. Structured
programming.   I. Title.
QA76.73.C25C36   001.64′24   81-10236
ISBN 0-8185-0463-3   AACR2

Subject Editor: James F. Leisy, Jr.

Manuscript Editor: Dex Ott

Production Editor: Cece Munson

Interior Design: Design Office, Bruce Kortebein

Cover Design: Stanley Rice

Illustrations: Art by Ayxa

Typesetting: Graphic Typesetting Service
                   Los Angeles

Acknowledgment

Preface

COBOL is the predominant computer language of the business world, and it can be learned without any previous programming experience. Its major advantage over other computer languages is its close similarity to the English language—a feature that makes COBOL self-documenting and easy to learn.

All the major concepts and topics necessary for a beginning course in COBOL are presented in this book. The reader is led gradually through the learning steps, since each lesson builds upon the material presented in the previous chapters. Another major feature of this book is the "Common Errors" section found in each chapter. Here, examples of errors beginning programmers tend to make are discussed in detail: how and why they are made and how they can be avoided. A third major feature, also found in each chapter, is the section "Problem Solving Techniques," where practical advice is given on how to go about solving programming problems. Finally, the book offers the section "Self-Study: Questions and Answers" at the end of each chapter. Don't skip over this part! It contains typical student questions (and answers) that the author has encountered in one form or another during many years of COBOL instruction.

A variety of problems are presented, analyzed, coded, and run so that the reader can see the exact sequence of steps the programmer must go through in order to achieve the proper output. The sample problems are short and relate to the subject matter of their respective chapters. The author feels that short, concise examples are better than long, multi-page programs that might cause the reader more problems than they solve. The programming exercises at the end of each chapter usually start with some minor variations or changes on sample programs that were contained in the chapter. Each succeeding exercise then gets progressively more complex.

Every program is written in a top-down, structured manner—an idea that is being adopted by more and more job shops today. As an aid to understanding the nature of program structure, the problem analysis is developed through the use of top-down design charts, pseudocode charts, and program flowcharts. In addition, the text also covers another diagramming method rapidly becomming popular: Warnier/Orr diagrams. Several of the more complex programs throughout the text are diagrammed using this method in addition to standard flowcharting and/or pseudocode. This side-by-side comparison should be extremely useful for the beginning programmer.

The general problem-solving process required for the solution of any computer program is covered extensively in Chapter 1. This presentation is immediately followed by a discussion of top-down design and structured programming techniques, including Warnier/Orr diagrams and a sample COBOL program. Chapters 2 through 6 cover the fundamentals of COBOL programming: the nature of the language, the basic statements, and programming techniques.

Starting with Chapter 8, specific storage media and common types of problems are presented. Chapter 8, for example, discusses the makeup and creation of a magnetic tape file. Chapter 9 covers in greater detail the handling of tape files: updating, matching, and merging of tape records. Single- and multiple-level control breaks plus group indication methods are extremely common business jobs and are discussed in detail in Chapter 10. Tables—both one- and two-dimensional—are the topic of Chapter 11. Here the reader will learn how to create tables and manipulate the data elements using two different sets of COBOL statements. Chapter 12 goes one step further in the use of tables by showing how data within a table are sorted for later use in the program. Finally, Chapter 13 discusses the magnetic disk and the creation and use of both sequential and indexed sequential files.

My thanks go to the following people who provided constructive criticism and advice on technical matters during the production of the text: Bela A. Banathy, Monterey Peninsula College; James L. Beug, California State Polytechnic University; Charles P. Downey, University of Nebraska, Omaha; James C. Hershauer, Arizona State University; William A. Jones, Modesto Junior College; Marilyn Meyers, California State University, Fresno; and Charles Saxon, Eastern Michigan University.

Finally, a special word of thanks is due my wife, June, for typing through several revisions in order to bring the text to fulfillment.

Keith Carver

Contents

Chapter 7   The Procedure Division— Part II   160

Chapter 8   Magnetic Tape Processing   196

Beginning Structured COBOL

Chapter 1

Computers and Problem Solving

The computer is an incredibly complex marvel of electronic and mechanical parts, and yet it is relatively easy to control. Very quickly you will learn how to write computer programs, using a programming language called COBOL (*CO*mmon *B*usiness *O*riented *L*anguage), that direct the machine to solve a wide variety of problems. However, before getting into a discussion of problem solving on the machine, we had better take a look at the makeup of a typical computer.

A computer system

Any computer system, whether large or small, consists of certain identifiable parts, as shown in Figure 1-1. As you can see, the heart of a computer system is the Central Processing Unit (or CPU), which normally is comprised of the Control Unit, Memory (sometimes called Main Storage), and the Arithmetic/Logic Unit (ALU). Various types of Input Devices (such as card readers) and Output Devices (such as printers) are attached to the CPU to provide paths for the entry of programs and data and the output of results of computations.

FIGURE 1-1

Schematic of a Computer System

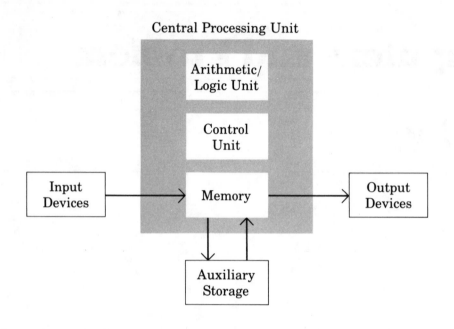

The other major part of a computer system (the term *system* means that it has more than one part) is the auxiliary storage. It is here that we have the capability of storing millions of characters of information in the form of *records* of data. Although the topic is discussed more thoroughly later, a record of data consists of all the required information concerning a single transaction.

The two most common forms of auxiliary storage are magnetic tape and magnetic disk. On tape storage devices the data are recorded in the form of individual records strung along the length of the tape, whereas magnetic disk devices store information on tracks on the surface of platters that resemble stacked phonograph records. Both of these devices are discussed in detail in later chapters, where you will learn the actual COBOL instructions that are used to activate the magnetic tape and the disk units as well as the card reader and the printer. Figure 1-2 shows the central processing unit and operator console of a large computer system. Figure 1-3 shows a printer and several magnetic tape drives that are typical on large systems.

FIGURE 1-2. *Large Computer System showing CPU and Operator Console.*
(Courtesy of International Business Machines Corporation.)

FIGURE 1-3. *Printer and Magnetic Tape Storage Units.*
(Courtesy of International Business Machines Corporation.)

Figure 1-4 shows another computer system on which the component parts are, to a great extent, hidden behind removable panels. In this figure one of the operators is changing the removable disk pack on the disk drive at the left.

FIGURE 1-4. *Computer System with Magnetic Disk Storage Units.*
(Courtesy of International Business Machines Corporation.)

The problem-solving process

How do we go about solving problems in our lives? What is the process we use in order to find a solution to a problem we have encountered? Well, the steps used in "real life" problem solving are very much the same as those used in programming.

In one way, programming the solution to a problem on the computer may be much easier than solving the same problem in the outside world. The reason this statement can be made is that in a particular programming language you are limited to a very specific set of instructions or statements that the machine can understand. As the programmer, you must solve the problem within the limitations imposed by the computer hardware and by the particular programming language. In real life you may not be so severely constrained and, therefore, may have almost too many possibilities from which to choose.

The general problem-solving process involves several distinct steps, which you have used all your life. Later sections in the book go into more detail on each of the following steps.

1. Analyzing the problem.
2. Designing a solution.
3. Trying the solution.

Analyzing the problem

The term *analyzing the problem* really means that you have to study the problem until you understand its nature completely. The key word is "completely." To do this you will have to break down the problem into its smallest components. (Remember that we are talking about *any* kind of problem you may face—not just problems for solution on the computer.) Most beginning programmers are not willing to devote the time to this most crucial step. They are often too eager to get to the "fun" part of the process—coding or writing the actual COBOL statements. This same criticism of impatience may be applied to a great many of our everyday problems as well.

If the problem is too large to grasp and seems insurmountable, break it down into smaller, more manageable parts. Keep doing this until you feel comfortable with the parts. For example, the task of building an entire house may seem impossible to you, and, if asked, you would say "No, I couldn't do it."

The process, however, can be broken into small steps—such as laying the foundation, putting in the subfloor, framing, roofing, and so on. If the step of "laying the foundation" is still too large to grasp, it can be further broken down into the substeps of laying out the foundation site, digging the trenches, building foundation walls, pouring the cement, and so on.

Computer problems should be approached in exactly the same way. As indicated earlier, they usually are easier to solve because the computer is designed to handle problems that have a definite pattern or structure to them. The computer's power lies in its ability to perform repetitive tasks, particularly those in which the relationships of all the elements in the problem are understood. Payroll, inventory, and accounting activities are typical of problems that are easily solvable on the computer. In a way, these problems are much like mathematical problems: they contain input data of some type that must be processed in order to turn out answers (output data). As you will see throughout the text, the steps of input, processing, and output are the three basic building blocks of any computer program.

Designing a solution

Theoretically, by the time you get to this second step, you have analyzed or defined all the components of the problem and understand their relationship. You are now ready to design a solution, which the analysis process itself will often suggest. Over the years, your analysis of problems has indicated that certain types of problems can be grouped into categories and that a similar approach can be applied to each of these. Problems involving conversion—pounds to kilograms, ounces to pounds, inches to feet, and so on are typical examples. Summation, or totalling, problems are yet another category that you identified early in your life.

With the computer, almost every problem must involve the three steps mentioned earlier: (a) inputting the data (because you cannot possibly work on the data until it has entered the machine), (b) processing the data, and (c) outputting the results (which can only take place after the processing step). Generally, the best approach to take on a problem you intend to solve on the computer is to determine how you would do it at the human level. Ultimately, your computer solution may vary from the human solution, but this is an excellent starting point.

Consider the following example. You have just completed six months of work at ABC company, and you now wish to look at your pay stubs to determine how much you earned during that time and what the average pay was per month. This is, of course, a very simple problem, but let's analyze it and propose a solution.

The input data is the net pay figure on the pay stubs—12 stubs if one assumes you were paid every two weeks. The output is to be two figures: (a) a total net pay figure and (b) the average pay per month. To achieve the output you want from the input available, you will have to do at least two things: (a) add together or sum up the 12 net pay amounts and (b) divide this total by 6 to get the average monthly net pay amount. So far, so good.

Suppose the two of us were talking about the problem, and I asked "How would you go about solving it?" Probably your answer would be "Simple. Just add the values and divide by 6."

And you would be correct in terms of the human solution, but you would not be exactly correct in terms of the computer solution! The reason for this is that humans have complex mental abilities that cannot be duplicated by a computer. In COBOL, one cannot "just add the values and divide by 6." The computer is an incredibly simple machine that can only respond to a limited number of very specific instructions. There simply is no instruction that says "add all the numbers together." Although there are wide ranges of differences from machine to machine and language to language, you must instruct the machine to:

Add the first number to the second (to get an initial total).

Add the third number to the previous total (to get a new total).

Add the fourth number to the previous total (to get a new total).

Etc.

Divide by 6 (to get the average).

You can now see that the design of a computer solution involves a careful analysis of the problem. Perhaps the best way to approach the design phase is to start with the most general action required in the program and then proceed to more and more specific functions. This is the top-down approach discussed in detail in the next chapter.

As indicated earlier, a computer is a machine that follows the detailed instructions of the programmer. These instructions, collectively known as a program, are written in a specific computer language that the machine has been built to "understand." Thus, a computer program is a detailed set of instructions (actually, they are called "statements") that direct the computer to solve a specific problem. There are relatively few statements in COBOL, and we will only consider the more basic ones in this beginning text. Learning how to program is a different matter entirely. It is not hard, but it does require some thought as to the exact sequence in which the instructions must be executed.

Since a computer executes instructions, or statements, sequentially—that is, one after another—extreme care must be taken to put them in the right order. This sequence of steps represents your design for the solution of the problem and must be determined *before* writing the program. Actually, you use plans for every task you perform all day long. In most cases, however, you have had so many years of practice at these repetitive tasks that the sequence of steps is extremely well known to you.

For example, it is doubtful that you have to consciously plan for turning on a specific TV program, yet the following minimum steps are involved:

1. Consult a TV listing for time and station.
2. Check the clock for the current time.
3. If it is time for the specific show, turn on the TV set.
4. Adjust the channel changer to the proper station.
5. Adjust the volume control.
6. Watch the show.

A plan for washing dishes (by hand) may further help to clarify the process:

1. Collect the dirty dishes.
2. Fill the dishpan with hot water.
3. Add some soap.
4. Place the dishes in the pan of hot, soapy water.
5. Wash the dishes.
6. Rinse the dishes.
7. Dry the dishes.

As ridiculous as the above examples may seem, they point out several facts. First, you do plan all the time. Second, these plans are concerned both with the individual activities that must take place and with the order or sequence of these activities. Since the computer executes statements (instructions) sequentially, it is absolutely essential that you set up these statements in the proper order to get the job done. A third point about the two plans is that you may disagree with the steps and their sequence. Obviously, the sequence of some steps may not be critical to the overall solution to the problem. For example, in washing dishes you may reverse steps 2 and 3 (filling the dishpan and adding soap) without changing the end result of the plan—clean dishes. On the other hand, placing step 7 (drying dishes) before step 4 (place dishes in water) is unreasonable and dooms your plan for washing dishes to failure.

In solving a simple payroll problem, the algorithm (or sequence of steps) would be as follows:

1. Enter the payroll data.
2. Calculate the gross pay.
3. Subtract the deductions to get the net pay.
4. Print the paycheck.

As simple and perhaps silly as this example sounds, it would *not* be correct to use the following sequence:

1. Subtract the deductions.
2. Print the paycheck (net pay).
3. Calculate the gross pay.
4. Enter the payroll data.

A program using the above sequence of statements would simply stop because the machine would not know from what to subtract the deductions. Absurd as the above example seems, many of you will write programs exactly like this because you have not thoroughly thought out the correct sequence of events. Others have not really grasped the meaning of the statement that the computer executes the instructions in *sequential* order and has no magical capability of rearranging the instructions into the correct order.

Where can you find further examples of plans like these? Very likely your house is full of detailed problem solutions. A recipe is a plan that details the input items, and, if followed exactly, should produce the output promised. Automotive manuals contain step-by-step procedures for simple to elaborate repair jobs on your car. So you have used and developed solutions to problems all your life, and now you are ready to apply this method to the programming of a computer.

Flowcharting—a design tool Most programmers eventually realize the need for some kind of design tool that will help them determine the best way to solve the problem. A written narrative of the job steps might be appropriate for some people, but most programmers rely on a visual design tool because it conveys the relationships between the parts of the program in a quick, easy-to-understand manner. Unfortunately, there is no one design method or tool that has been accepted by the majority of data-processing practitioners. Individual programmers and individual shops each have design methods they swear by; yet any method is appropriate if it does what it is supposed to do. Generally, any design tool is supposed to aid in the design process by showing the relationships of the parts of the solution and by serving as a form of documentation for the program.

One of the simplest and most common methods used is flowcharting. A flowchart is a graphic method of displaying a plan to solve a specific problem. A key point here is that the programmer should develop the flowchart *before* attempting to write the program instructions. Since a flowchart depicts the *logic,* or the order, of the instructions, it can be developed very quickly. It would seem foolish to spend a lot of time writing the detailed instructions in an entire program only to discover that your method was wrong. Thus, a few minutes devoted to flowcharting is usually time well spent.

From a practical standpoint, some problems to be solved on the computer are so simple that a flowchart is not necessary. In these cases the programmer can remember the sequence of steps without reference to diagrams. For more difficult problems, however, the programmer usually devises a rough flowchart to guide him or her through the complex part of the program. When actually writing the program statements, the programmer may find that the flowchart was faulty or lacked certain details. This is nothing to worry about since the critical point is that some thought had been given to the proper sequence of events.

A number of special symbols have been adopted for use in flowcharting, but only a few will be used in this text.

The oval is used to indicate the start or end of a program.

Start   or   End

The parallelogram indicates any type of input or output of data.

Read 4 data values

Print net pay

The rectangle depicts any type of calculation or general processing of data.

The diamond-shaped symbol is used whenever a decision is made or a test is performed.

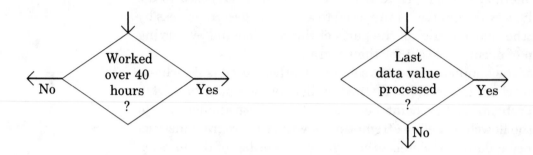

Note that arrows are used to further document the flow, or sequence, of events. Virtually all programs must, by necessity, follow the general logic shown below (Figure 1-5).

FIGURE 1-5

"Universal" Flowchart

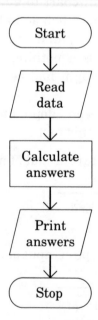

Although the flowchart shown in Figure 1-5 is correct, it is far too general to be of much value. Herein lies the problem: How much detail should you put into a flowchart? Part of the answer is that the flowchart should show all the *major* steps of your plan. On the other hand, your flowchart should not be so detailed that it becomes a duplicate of the program you intend to write. The following flow-charting example will help to illustrate these points.

Suppose that a school of engineering has far more applicants than it can handle. A computer program must be written that will print out a list of those people who will be admitted. In this case the acceptability of a student depends upon his or her high school grade-point average in which a 3.5 (B+) average is required. Note, too, that the program must handle this selection task over and over again until all the applicants have been processed.

At this point a good thing to consider is "How would I do it by hand?" For example, if you were a clerk in the school admissions office, how would you proceed if your boss said "Here is a stack of admission requests for the school of engineering. Find those that qualify with a B+ or better average and bring me a list of qualifiers when you get done"?

The first step is to analyze the problem, which at this stage probably would suggest three broad functions, or tasks, to be performed. One of the first things required with every report is a heading such as "List of qualifiers with a B+ or better average." That type of activity falls under the general category of *initialization*, or "getting ready," activities. While thinking about those beginning activities, you would also recognize comparable ending activities that might be as simple as a closing message such as "End of List." In between these two activities would be the main processing task. At this point a diagram of our analysis would look as follows:

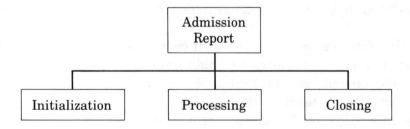

Now you are ready to do further analysis of the Initialization function to see if it should be broken down into smaller functions, or substeps. Apparently it is simple enough so we will leave it alone. The Processing activity contains several distinct functions that should be isolated. The input, or reading, function will have to take place before testing, and testing will determine whether or not printing will take place. We can block it out as follows:

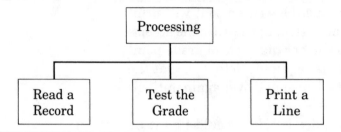

In narrative form the steps would be:

1. Read the admission request form (input function).
2. Check the grade-point average (testing function).
   If the average is 3.5 or higher, write the name on the list (output function).
   If the average is below 3.5, do not write the name on the list.
3. Repeat steps 1 and 2 until there are no more admission request forms to process.

Notice that (1) there is no way the form (or data) can be processed until it has been read and (2) you cannot determine who is qualified until the grade average is tested. Do not be deceived by thinking that you "just read the form" and write or don't write the name. The reading and testing are two very distinct steps. Unfortunately, you are so good at simple processes of this kind that the individual steps tend to blend into one.

An analysis of the Closing function would show that it contains only one step and needs no subdividing. Finally, we would have to realize that the Processing function (but *not* the Initialization or Closing function) would have to be repeated until all students have been processed. (The preceding discussion is the essence of top-down design—a topic that is covered in more depth in Chapter 2.) A flowchart of the solution to our admissions form problem is shown in Figure 1-6.

FIGURE 1-6

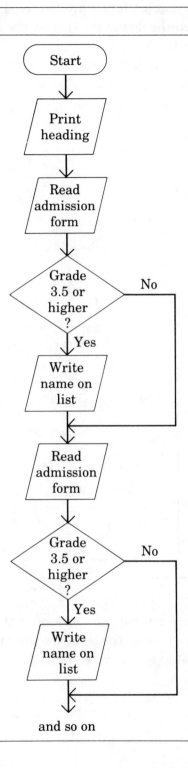

and so on

It is obvious from Figure 1-6 that the flowchart could get very long depending upon how many request forms are involved. Figure 1-7 illustrates how we can shorten the flowchart to show the *looping,* or repetitive nature, of the process.

FIGURE 1-7

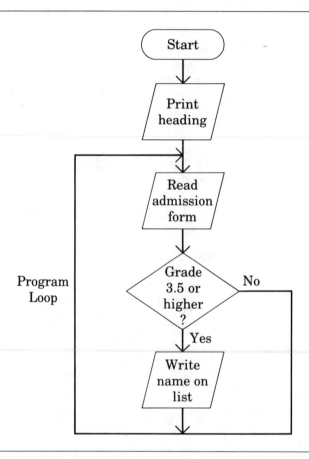

Although Figure 1-7 is far more concise and efficient, it still lacks one thing: there is no provision for ending the loop. We can take care of this problem by inserting a test to see if there are any more forms to read (Figure 1-8).

FIGURE 1-8

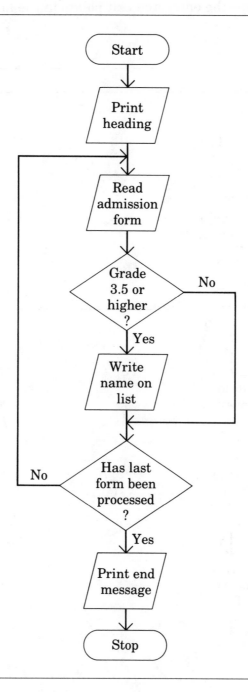

Figure 1-8 can still get us into difficulty since we have assumed there will always be at least one admission form to be read. This is a critical point that dramatically illustrates the very great difference between humans and computers. The human, upon recognizing that no admission forms are present, would simply do nothing. The computer does not work this way; it executes exactly the instructions contained in the program. Therefore, we must somehow account for this situation. An analysis of the problem would suggest that we move our test to the top of the flowchart, as shown in Figure 1-9. Note the use of the small circle to show the entry and exit points in the flow-chart.

FIGURE 1-9

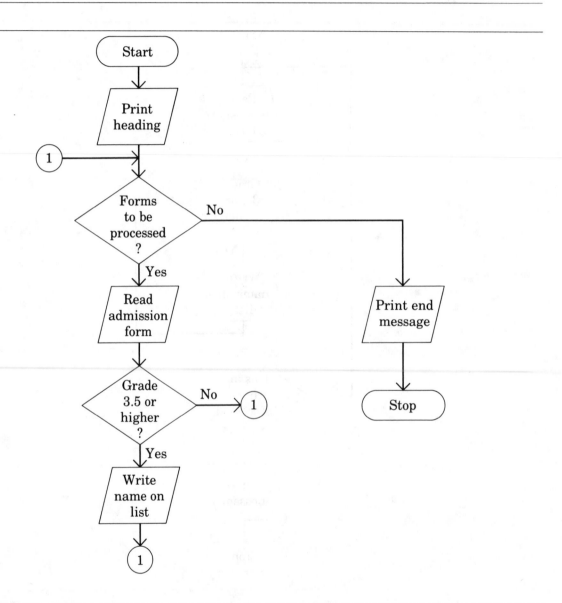

In the last few pages we presented a simple problem and, after some basic analysis, arrived at a method of solution. The solution involved the use of flowcharts, but flowcharts are not peculiar to data processing alone. As a matter of fact, for many clerking activities, forms or diagrams similar to the ones shown here are used to help new employees learn the specific operations on a new job.

Flowcharts will be shown throughout the text to help you understand the logic of a particular program. The symbols used have been fairly well standardized in the data processing industry, although some variations still exist. The main point is that the symbols act as a quick visual reference to the program logic. Once the flowchart is drawn, the next step is to write your COBOL program.

Trying the solution

In theory, every computer program works perfectly the first time. Real life, however, is very different from theory, and your program may not produce what you want. Even the use of an elaborate flowchart does not guarantee that your program is *logically* correct. Indeed, you may get some proper-looking answers that are entirely incorrect. The computer is incapable of correcting your errors in design logic since it only does what it is instructed to do. In programmer's terminology, you have a "bug" in your program, and it is up to you to remove the "bug" by reasoning to the point or points where the errors were made.

The three general error possibilities are that you have left out a needed instruction, that you have included an unnecessary instruction, or that you have all the proper instructions but in the wrong order. Later chapters show many examples of errors that are commonly made. Don't be afraid of errors since making them is a beautiful learning device. However, you can avoid the majority of errors and derive the same learning values by analyzing the problem thoroughly and designing a correct solution.

When an error occurs, you must go back to these two steps. You may not have analyzed the problem completely or, if your analysis was correct, you may have forgotten a step during the design of the computer solution.

The next chapter covers the design process in much greater detail, whereas the remaining chapters are devoted to the COBOL statements and how they work. Each chapter, however, contains information on how one solves problems on the computer because, ultimately, this is what programming is all about.

Problem-Solving Techniques

How do you solve a problem if you do not know where to start? Well, in theory you should never experience this sensation; you should always know where to start in your program design even though it may not be the best place.

The advice here is simple: Start someplace, anyplace—but start! Get something down on paper! It may be wrong and you may erase it, scratch it out, move it, and so on; but put down something. One possibility is to design the Initialization and Ending modules in great detail. For unknown reasons, just the act of designing, flowcharting, or coding *something—anything*—seems to get the vital "juices" flowing. You can study a problem forever and perhaps never know enough about it; but the design phase must begin sometime. As you try your design, questions you forgot to ask will emerge and the solution will become more and more apparent. The key point, however, is that you must make a start, even if it is wrong.

Another way of getting around this starting difficulty is shown by a statement a great many beginning programmers make (it seems to be prevalent in all languages). Their cry is "I don't know how to do this part!" The best answer to this is "Don't worry about what you don't know!" Instead, put down, design, or code what you *do* know, and things will start happening. Build upon similar instances in previous problems. These instances may not have been exactly the same, but surely they will suggest different approaches.

Self-Study: Questions and Answers

1. The problem-solving process sounds like something I have been doing all along. Why should it be any different when working on the computer?

   Answer

   You are exactly right. You have always used these three basic steps in the solution of a problem. The only difference now is that you are likely to be working in an area that is totally new to you, and the problems you encountered before will have to be analyzed in a little more detail and with greater precision. Remember to keep breaking the problem down into smaller and smaller parts until you are comfortable with them.

2. Why do I need a formal plan in order to solve a problem on the computer? So far everything seems very simple.

   Answer

   The beginning illustrations and problems used in most textbooks are, of necessity, very simple and you should not have any great difficulty with the concepts. Computer programs, however, can get exceedingly complex to the point that even the very best programmers would have to resort to some design tool in order to make any progress toward a solution. The time to learn this process is now while it is easy rather than later when it may be too late.

3. What good is a flowchart? Isn't a written plan just as good?

   Answer

   Written plans and flowcharts are very closely related. There is no question that the programmer needs some type of plan on which to prepare a program. However, flowcharts are extremely useful as they act as a visual extension to the steps of a written plan. Because a flowchart is a visual device, it is much easier to see and understand the relationships between the various parts of a program.

4. What do you mean by "debugging" a program?

   Answer

   Most programs contain errors, or "bugs"— even the so-called simple programs. The process of getting these errors out of your program is known as debugging and involves a logical thought process to determine where the error or errors might be.

Exercises

1. Revise the flowchart of the admissions problem (Figure 1-8) to consider the following circumstances.

    Two forms (input data) are required from each applicant to the school of engineering: a "proof of residency" card and the admissions form. If the student does not have the residency card, the admissions form is to be stamped with NOT ADMITTED and returned to the student. If the student has the card, then you are to proceed with the grade checking process. (Note: You may assume that a residency card will always be accompanied by an admissions form.)

2. Revise the flowchart in Figure 1-8 to consider the following. *1-6*

    Your employer requires that you prepare two lists: one for those of 3.5 grade point or higher and another for those between 3.0 and 3.49, since the people on the second list may be admitted if there are not enough people on the first list.

3. Draw the flowchart to determine your current checkbook balance. You may assume that your previous balance was correct and that all the checks were correctly recorded by the bank. Be sure to account for all checks written, deposits made, and special charges imposed by the bank. If the result of your calculations does not balance with the bank statement, you are to print the message ERROR IN CHECKSTUB CALCULATIONS and stop. If you do balance, you are to print the message BALANCES and stop.

4. Revise Problem 3 to process an unknown number of checkbook balancing applications.

5. Draw the flowchart for the six-month paycheck example discussed earlier in the text. Provide for a printout of the six-month total *and* the average monthly pay amount.

6. Write the problem solution to determine how much you will have to pay of a doctor's bill that recently arrived. Assume the medical insurance will cover 83% of the costs during the first year of coverage and 91% after the first year.

7. Write the problem solution and draw a flowchart for the following situations.
   a. Walking across a street at a corner where there are no signal lights or stop signs.
   b. Walking across a street at a corner where there are regular signal lights but no WALK sign.
   c. Walking across a street at a corner where the signal system also includes a WALK sign.

8. Grade-point averages are always important to students, so here is your chance to develop a solution to determine GPA on the computer. Assume your school gives letter grades of A, B, C, D, and F, where an A has a numerical value of 4.0, a B is 3.0, a C is 2.0, a D is 1.0, and an F is zero. Design the solution and draw the flowchart to calculate your grade-point average based on the number of courses taken. For example, if you had taken five courses, you would read in five grades and ultimately divide by five to get the grade-point average.

9. Revise Problem 8 to take into account the units granted in each course. Your GPA will now be calculated by dividing the number of units into the numerical grade value achieved. Design the solution and draw the flowchart as before. Note that an F grade generates no grade value, but it does count toward the number of units taken.

10. As a further refinement to the problem above, assume that the units attempted in F grade courses are not counted toward the total GPA.

Chapter 2

Top-Down Design and

Structured Programming

The previous chapter discussed the problem-solving process in which one of the major steps was designing a computer solution to a problem. Historically, programming has been considered something of an art form that reflected much of the individual style of the programmer. Each person had his or her own way of doing things, which worked reasonably well during the early years of electronic data processing. As computers became more complex and powerful, and as programming costs continued to soar during the late 1960s and early 1970s, business and industry could no longer afford the luxury of such methods. Because the design and coding had been done in an almost random manner, old programs became extremely difficult to maintain. They became, in fact, "maintenance nightmares." It became imperative that a disciplined, structured approach to program design and coding be found. This overall sense of discipline was provided by two interrelated ideas: top-down design and structured programming.

Professor E. W. Dijkstra laid the foundation for the new technique in 1966 in the article "Structured Programming." His ideas were incorporated in the so-called "New York Times project" in which an IBM team programmed an on-line retrieval system for the newspaper. Over 80,000 lines of coding were produced in just under two years—productivity nearly five times as great as the industry standards—and the coding was nearly free of errors. In contrast, unstructured programming had produced around 2000 lines of coding per year (using a high-level language such as COBOL or FORTRAN) with perhaps one error per 100 lines of code. Overall, it is estimated that individual output has gone up by at least 25%.

Although we often see productivity figures such as those quoted above, sheer volume of coded lines is not the main benefit of this new approach. Of greater importance is that the programs are more likely to be correct, are easier to follow and maintain, and are easier to debug if an error is found.

Top-down design

Using the top-down approach to program design, the programmer logically analyzes the problem by starting at the top with the most general function and carefully working down to the lowest-level function. As each function is identified, the process is carried on down to the lesser functions that are part of the major ones. Notice that this is a method of isolating the processing steps—that is, of determining *what* is to be done. The result is a hierarchy chart that breaks the overall job into a set of related tasks. The chart becomes a visual method of checking the *design* logic. A flowchart, on the other hand, diagrams the *program* logic and is prepared after the top-down chart has been completed.

In Chapter 1 we used this top-down approach (without really identifying it as such) on a simple clerk-processing problem. Now we will take the same approach and apply it to an everyday activity that involves more functions. The critical point is that a technique such as this can be applied to most non-computer tasks as well because it is a general problem-solving technique.

Let's assume that you want to do an oil change and tune-up job on your car. Our top-down chart will start with a single block at the top that will be our control function, or control module. (Later in the chapter you will see that this block will actually control the entire operation of the computer program.)

```
┌─────────────┐
│ Oil Change  │
│    and      │
│  Tune-up    │
└─────────────┘
```

The next step in our analysis of the problem is to determine some of the specific tasks, or functions, that will have to take place. Three functions immediately come to mind.

First, you have to prepare, or get ready, for the main job of oil change and tune-up. (This would involve buying the oil, oil filter, air filter, spark plugs, and assembling the required tools.) As mentioned earlier, this would be referred to as the Initialization (Get Ready) Module.

The opposite of the Initialization Module would be the Ending routine, or activities such as cleaning up, putting tools away, and so on. In between would be the Main Processing module that deals directly with the oil change and tune-up activities. At this point our top-down chart would look as follows:

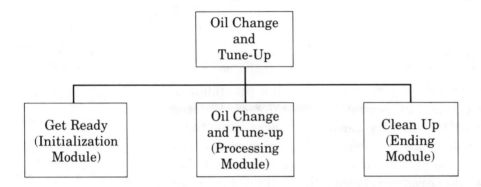

Obviously, our top-down chart is not complete because the Oil Change and Tune-up Module can logically be broken into smaller sub-tasks. One of the major advantages of top-down design is that the correctness of the design logic can be verified as the chart is being developed. Assuming that our logic is correct up to this point, we can now proceed to the next lower level. It appears that neither the Initialization nor the Ending modules will need further breakdown since each of these functions is quite simple. Now we can analyze the middle block and break it into smaller tasks. Although some of these sub-tasks might vary from car to car, we can identify such items as changing the oil and filter, changing the air filter, changing the spark plugs and distributor points, and adjusting the carburetor. Figure 2-1 shows our expanded top-down design chart.

At this point we can again pause to examine our design logic for its correctness. The questions we have to ask are: "Have we included all the tasks that are required under the Oil Change and Tune-up operation?" and "Have we performed these tasks in the proper sequence?"

The tasks, or modules, on the chart will be performed both from top to bottom and from left to right, so that at the second level we would first Get Ready, then process the main job (Oil Change and Tune-up), and then take care of the Cleanup activities. If we assume

---

FIGURE 2-1

Top-Down Design

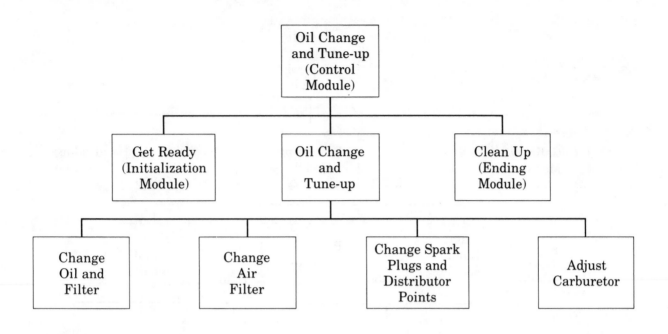

---

that our design is correct so far, then we must again analyze the blocks, or modules, to see if any need to be broken down. How detailed should the design chart be? There is no specific answer to the question, but a general answer would be that the design must be detailed enough so that no one can misunderstand what is taking place. In this case we may wish to break down two of the modules into another layer of sub-modules, as shown below.

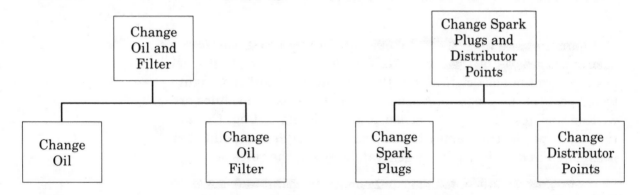

Now let's apply this same technique to a problem that can be solved on the computer. Figure 2-2 shows a top-down hierarchical design chart of a payroll operation. Note that the modules are lettered and numbered so that their position in the chart can be determined easily.

FIGURE 2-2

Top-Down Design Chart-Payroll Problem

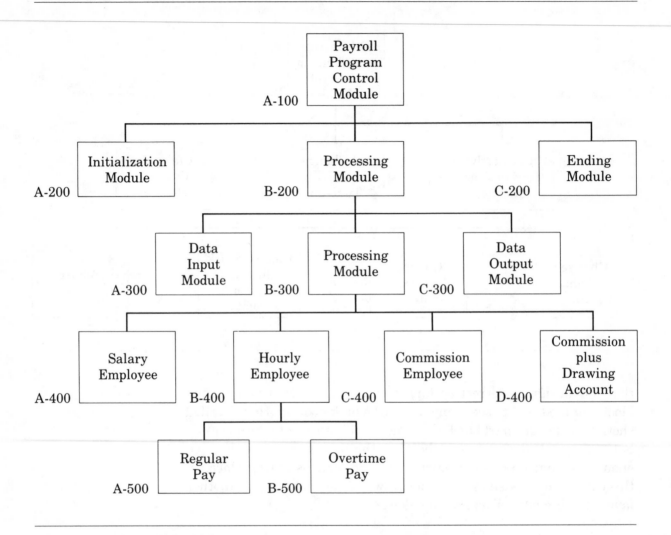

Coding for the highest-level modules is written first and tested before other parts of the structure. Obviously, these highest-level modules are the most critical, but they become the most thoroughly tested parts of the program. As successively lower-level modules are written and tested, they are added to the existing coding. Certain rigid and specific rules apply to the program modules—a point that is explored in detail shortly. In general, however, the rules are:

1. Each module must have only one entry point and one exit.
2. A module can never activate another module on its own level.
3. Individual modules should be as short as possible.

The use of top-down design and structured programming logic are at the root of modern programming concepts. The top-down approach is illustrated by the use of groups of program statements (or modules) to accomplish specific tasks at specific levels within the program. The most obvious of these is a *control module,* or paragraph, that is at the top of the design structure and directly or indirectly controls the actions of all other modules in the program.

The second part of the disciplined approach to programming is the use of what is known as structured programming.

Structured programming

As mentioned earlier, the basic idea of structured programming is to produce a program that is easy to read, easy to maintain, and easy to correct, or debug. By now you should have grasped the very important point that programming is not simply a matter of stringing together a series of instructions, or COBOL statements. Programming involves the application of logic (which is defined as the use of valid reasoning and correct inference), which means arranging the right statements in the proper order to achieve an exact, planned result.

The disciplined approach to programming introduces the idea that good programs can be developed using a limited number of logical programming structures. This idea is based on the mathematically developed structure theorem developed by C. Bohm and G. Jacopini in 1966, which states that a proper program can be coded using only three logical structures or patterns: linear sequence, selection structure, and the controlled loop structure.

Linear sequence structure

The linear sequence structure is nothing more than the sequential execution of one or more program statements. The flowchart form for this construct is the straight connection of processing steps.

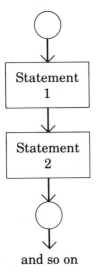

and so on

Although we have not yet discussed any specific COBOL statements, the following series of statements are very much self-explanatory. We are simply moving a series of fields from an input area to an output area and then writing a line of output on the printer. The statements will be executed sequentially—that is, one after another:

```
MOVE NAME-IN TO NAME-OUT.
MOVE ID-NBR-IN TO ID-NBR-OUT.
MOVE ADDRESS-IN TO ADDRESS-OUT.
MOVE BODY-LINE TO PRINT-LINE.
WRITE PRINT-LINE AFTER ADVANCING 2 LINES.
```

In flowchart form the above series would appear as shown in Figure 2-3.

FIGURE 2-3

Linear Sequence

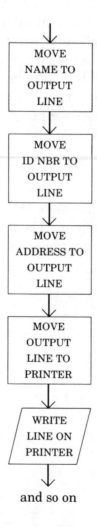

and so on

Selection structure (IFTHENELSE)

Every programming language has some statement that permits the programmer to perform logical (true-false) testing. The statement usually is very simple in its operation (as it is in COBOL), and is normally known as an IF statement. The actual statement will be discussed later, but a typical use of such a statement would be to test whether an employee has worked overtime. If the employee has worked in excess of 40 hours, we would want to follow one set of statements, whereas a different set of statements would be followed if no overtime were involved.

Although IF statements may be combined in complicated ways, their use in structured programming is severely limited. They are to be used in such a manner that there is only one entry point and one exit point from the module, as shown in the following diagram.

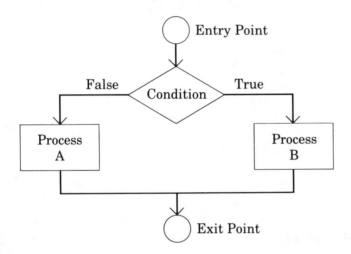

The following program segment again is self-explanatory and follows the selection structure format (which is also known as the IFTHENELSE structure). Note that both the true and the false conditions of the IF test end at the same statement (ADD PAY TO TOTAL-PAY) (Figure 2-4).

```
IF HOURS-WORKED IS GREATER THAN 40
    COMPUTE PAY = ((HRS-40 * 1.5 * RATE) + (RATE * 40))

ELSE
    COMPUTE PAY = RATE * HOURS.

ADD PAY TO TOTAL-PAY.
```

FIGURE 2-4

Selection Structure

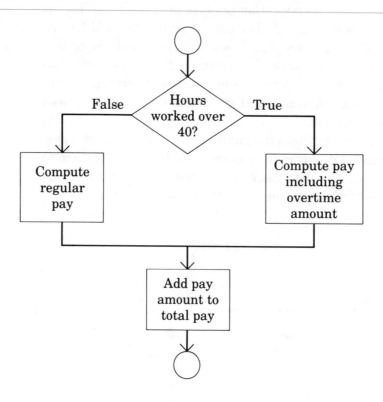

Controlled loop structure (DOWHILE)

In the controlled loop structure (also called the DOWHILE, or *iteration,* structure) a processing block is combined with a test of some type. The DOWHILE construct says "Do Process A as long as the test condition is false. When the test condition is true, exit from the loop."

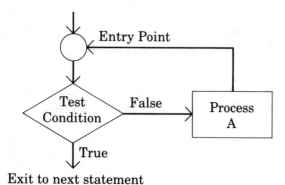

Note that with this structure, it is possible that Process A may never be executed at all. In either case, the structure has only one entry and one exit point from the module. In COBOL the DOWHILE structure is set up by means of a PERFORM UNTIL statement that says "PERFORM a certain process UNTIL a specific test has been met." Its most common use is in controlling a processing loop until there are no more input records to be processed. In the following example we assume that:

1. Process A (PAYROLL-CALCULATION) is a series of COBOL statements that read, calculate, and print payroll information.
2. The END-OF-INPUT-INDICATOR is a field that can be tested to see if we have reached the end of the input data.
3. The end-of-data condition will be signaled when the indicator has a value of 1.

```
PERFORM PAYROLL-CALCULATION
     UNTIL END-OF-INPUT-INDICATOR
     IS EQUAL TO 1.
```

Next statement

Figure 2-5 shows the controlled loop structure (DOWHILE) in a little more detail.

FIGURE 2-5

DOWHILE Structure

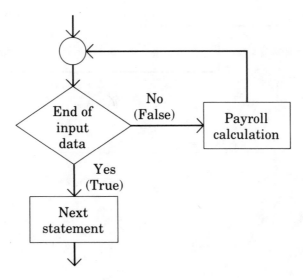

Now you know the three basic programming structures with which any problem can be programmed. There are some variations to the selection structure and the controlled loop structure, but they are not important now and will be discussed later.

Before leaving this section you should understand that these three structures can be put together like building blocks to solve whatever problem you have. It is up to you to use your logical problem-solving ability to decide on the correct structures for your program. Figure 2-6 shows that a linear sequence structure and a selection structure can be combined within a larger selection structure. Figure 2-7 illustrates a controlled loop structure within a selection structure.

FIGURE 2-6

Combined Structures

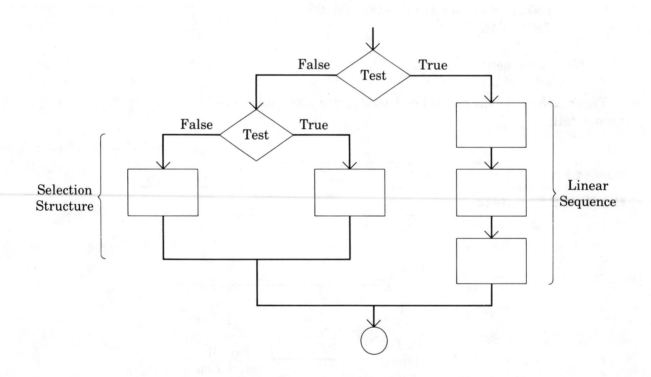

FIGURE 2-7

Combined Structures

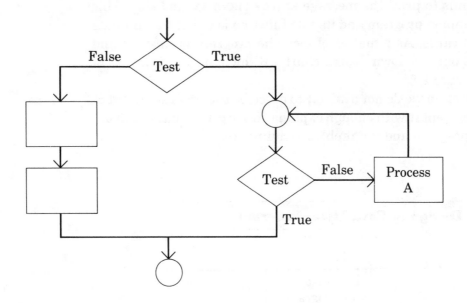

A sample COBOL program

In the previous section you learned some of the basic ideas of program discipline and structure. Now we take a look at a sample COBOL program so that you can get a better feel for how these concepts are put together. However, before seeing this program, you should be aware of the general makeup of a COBOL program.

Every COBOL program consists of four major parts called DIVISIONS. The first of these, the IDENTIFICATION DIVISION, is very short and serves to identify, or name, the program. The second part is known as the ENVIRONMENT DIVISION, and its most obvious function is to describe the physical environment in which your program will operate. The term "physical environment" refers to the various pieces of hardware that will be used, such as card readers, printers, tape drives, or disk drives.

Next, in the DATA DIVISION the programmer describes to the system the exact nature of the data elements that will be used in the program. Finally, the PROCEDURE DIVISION is the part in which you actually instruct the machine to perform the specific task of adding, moving, printing, and so on.

For our sample problem we have the following situation. A deck of punched cards will be our input data; each card will contain the name and address of a student attending our college. We are to write a program that will read-in a data card, print a line of output on the printer, and so on until all the cards are gone. When the end of the card deck (collectively known as a "file of data") has been reached, the program is to print the message END OF PROGRAM and stop. This is a very common program and its sole function is to list the contents of a deck of cards. As a matter of fact, the program is so short and simple that our top-down design chart will have only two layers of modules (Figure 2-8).

In this section we do not attempt to describe the program in exact detail, but present it with enough explanation to give you the "flavor" of a COBOL program and the problem-solving process.

FIGURE 2-8

Top-Down Design of Card Lister Program

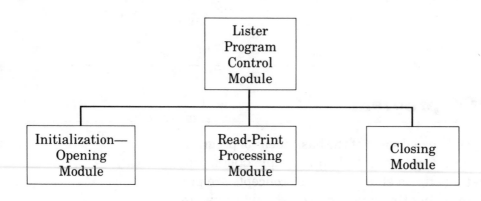

Now we have to give a little more thought to each of the modules. In designing the modules the programmer sometimes resorts to what is known as "pseudocode." Pseudocode is a short narrative form of English used to describe the control of flow and the function of the various modules. Note that at this point the programmer is not attempting to write the program, but merely to describe the functions that will have to be performed. For example, if we are working on an inventory program, we might describe the function of a particular module as shown below. Note that the key words are usually capitalized while the English description (pseudocode) is written in lower-case format.

```
READ inventory data record
     IF item purchased from us
          THEN subtract quantity from inventory
          PERFORM print routine 1
     ELSE
          add incoming inventory items to inventory on hand
          PERFORM print routine 2
```

The use of pseudocode is not restricted to top-down design or structured programming. It is a valuable programming technique that can be used at any time to help the programmer figure the best program logic. Viewed in this way, pseudocode is simply another design tool—sort of a narrative form of flowcharting. Let's apply this technique to our card lister program.

```
CARD LISTER
Open the files
Read a card record
PERFORM UNTIL there are no more card records
     Move card data to print line
     Write a line on the printer
     Read a card record
Close the files
STOP RUN
```

For our sample program we will adhere to our top-down design by having all operations controlled from a CONTROL-ROUTINE module at the top of the program. The steps in this one routine will, in turn, control the actions of several other modules, or paragraphs, within the program. If, at a later date, someone wanted to see exactly what our program is doing, he or she would only have to look at the Control Module to see which modules are being performed and the order of their performance. The Initialization and Closing Module tasks need be performed only once, but the Read-Print operation, however, must be performed repeatedly until the input card data has been exhausted.

The pseudocode just shown did a fairly good job of describing the program. Even without pseudocode, the "self-documenting" nature of COBOL is such that you should be able to look at the PROCEDURE DIVISION entries and determine what is happening in the program. Although the normal process would be to show a flowchart and then the actual program, the steps will be reversed here so that you can see the structure of a typical COBOL program. Remember that the whole purpose of the program is to list the contents of a deck of data cards (Figure 2-9).

FIGURE 2-9

Sample Program

```
                    IDENTIFICATION DIVISION.
                    PROGRAM-ID. LISTER.
 AUTHOR. ¥¥¥ name.  *

                    ENVIRONMENT DIVISION.
                    CONFIGURATION SECTION.
                    SOURCE-COMPUTER. IBM-360-F30.
                    OBJECT-COMPUTER. IBM-360-F30.
                    INPUT-OUTPUT SECTION.
                    FILE-CONTROL.
                        SELECT CARD-DATA
                            ASSIGN TO SYS007-UR-2540R-S.
                        SELECT PRINTFILE
                            ASSIGN TO SYS009-UR-1403-S.
                    *

                    DATA DIVISION.
                    FILE SECTION.
                    FD   CARD-DATA
                         LABEL RECORDS ARE OMITTED
                         DATA RECORD IS CARD-IN.
                    01   CARD-IN            PIC X(80).
                    FD   PRINTFILE
                         LABEL RECORDS ARE OMITTED
                         DATA RECORD IS LIST.
                    01   LIST.
                         03  FILLER         PIC X.
                         03  LIST-LINE      PIC X(120).
                    WORKING-STORAGE SECTION.
                    77   INDICATOR          PIC 9 VALUE ZERO.
                    *

                    PROCEDURE DIVISION.
                    CONTROL-ROUTINE.
                        PERFORM 010-OPENER.
                        PERFORM 020-READER UNTIL
                            INDICATOR = 1.
                        PERFORM 030-CLOSER.
                        STOP RUN.
                    010-OPENER.
                        OPEN INPUT CARD-DATA
                      IZ    OUTPUT PRINTFILE.
                        READ CARD-DATA
                            AT END MOVE 1 TO INDICATOR.
                    020-READER.
                        MOVE CARD-IN TO LIST-LINE.
                        WRITE LIST AFTER ADVANCING 2 LINES.
                        READ CARD-DATA
                            AT END MOVE 1 TO INDICATOR.
                    030-CLOSER.
                        MOVE 'END OF PROGRAM' TO LIST-LINE.
                        WRITE LIST AFTER ADVANCING 3 LINES.
                        CLOSE CARD-DATA, PRINTFILE.
```

As mentioned earlier, the IDENTIFICATION DIVISION is very short, and, in this case, the programmer has decided to name the program LISTER. Next, in the CONFIGURATION SECTION of the ENVIRONMENT DIVISION, the programmer identifies the computer on which the program will be run.

```
IDENTIFICATION DIVISION.
PROGRAM-ID. LISTER.
*
ENVIRONMENT DIVISION.
CONFIGURATION SECTION.
SOURCE-COMPUTER. IBM-360-F30.
OBJECT-COMPUTER. IBM-360-F30.
```

The INPUT-OUTPUT SECTION is the place where the system is first informed of the names of the data files the programmer will use (CARD-DATA and PRINTFILE) and the hardware devices through which they will pass (SYS007 and SYS009).

```
INPUT-OUTPUT SECTION.
FILE-CONTROL.
    SELECT CARD-DATA
        ASSIGN TO SYS007-UR-2540R-S.
    SELECT PRINTFILE
        ASSIGN TO SYS009-UR-1403-S.
```

The DATA DIVISION is appropriately named, since it is here that the programmer describes to the system the nature of the incoming and outgoing data elements. Note that each of the files named in the INPUT-OUTPUT SECTION of the ENVIRONMENT DIVISION is further described in the FILE SECTION of the DATA DIVISION. The incoming card record (80 columns) and the outgoing printer line (120 characters) are clearly shown.

```
DATA DIVISION.
FILE SECTION.
FD  CARD-DATA
    LABEL RECORDS ARE OMITTED
    DATA RECORD IS CARD-IN.
01  CARD-IN          PIC X(80).
FD  PRINTFILE
    LABEL RECORDS ARE OMITTED
    DATA RECORD IS LIST.
01  LIST.
    03  FILLER       PIC X.
    03  LIST-LINE    PIC X(120).
```

Earlier in the text the point was made that computer programs must have some mechanism by which the computer can detect the out-of-data condition. This will be accomplished by means of a field of data (INDICATOR) that is set up in the WORKING-STORAGE SECTION with a beginning value of zero. Later, when the system tries to READ and there are no more cards, a 1 will be moved to the INDICATOR field. This becomes a signal that tells the system to stop processing the Read-Print module and to go on to the Closing, or ending, module.

```
WORKING—STORAGE SECTION.
77  INDICATOR    PIC 9 VALUE ZERO.
```

The last part, the PROCEDURE DIVISION, is the easiest of all to understand, since it is here that the COBOL statements are the most English-like. As with most COBOL programs, the PROCEDURE DIVISION is broken into smaller parts called *paragraphs* (modules) at the discretion of the programmer. Typically, they are numbered and/or named (CONTROL-ROUTINE, 010-OPENER, etc.). The most important thing to notice is that the entire program is controlled from the first paragraph, or control module. The general steps in the program are listed below.

1. All modules are controlled from CONTROL-ROUTINE, including program termination, by means of the STOP RUN statement.
2. The first PERFORM statement causes the system to go out and execute the statements in the 010-OPENER paragraph and then automatically return to the next statement after the PERFORM. The first statement (OPEN) simply gets the data files ready for processing. Those of you with a sharp eye will note that the program contains two READ statements. The reason for the two READs will be discussed in detail later, but for now you can think of the first READ as a "priming" that is necessary to get the Read-Print processing started.

3. The PERFORM UNTIL statement causes the 020-READER paragraph to be executed until a specific condition is met—until INDICATOR is equal to 1. This process of repeating a section of code over and over is known as a loop, or program loop, and it is here that the power of the computer is most evident. Note that this is a *controlled* loop—controlled by the logic set up by the programmer. Specifically, this segment moves the contents of the card to the print area, prints a line, and then reads another card.

4. The third PERFORM causes the system to move a message (END OF PROGRAM) to the print area, print the message, and close the data files.

5. The automatic return to the CONTROL-ROUTINE stops the program (STOP RUN).

A flowchart of our structured lister program is shown in Figure 2-10. Note that each PERFORMed paragraph is shown in the flowchart of the CONTROL-ROUTINE and that, in turn, each of these paragraphs is individually flowcharted. This is indicated by the vertical lines within the rectangular processing symbol.

An important point to remember here is that a flowchart depicts the sequence of statements used in the PROCEDURE DIVISION. The other divisions, although of equal importance with the PROCEDURE DIVISION, exist to identify data and other elements of COBOL to the computer system. Since they are not concerned with the flow of logic, or the sequence of the programming steps, they do not appear as entries in the flowchart.

FIGURE 2-10

Structured Flowchart

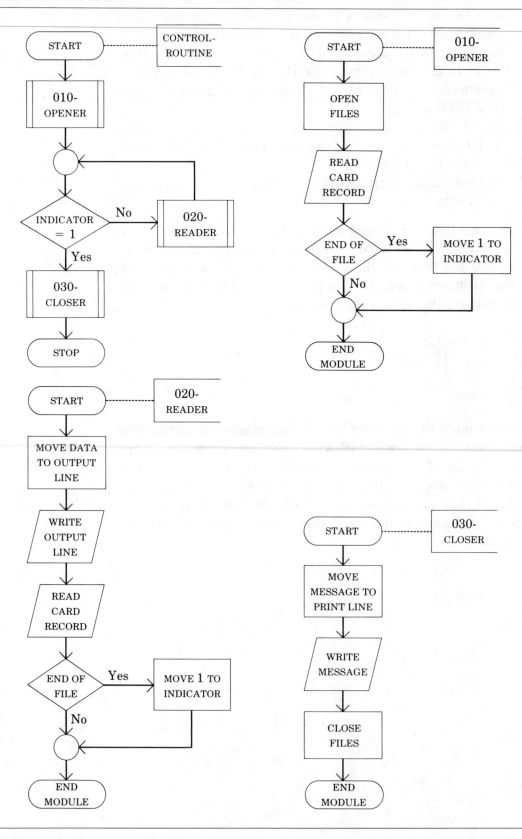

Warnier/Orr diagrams

The increased use of top-down design and structured programming concepts fueled the need for tools that would provide more and better information about logical program design. Today, many programming shops use Warnier/Orr diagrams because they can show logic at the system, program, or module level. In a beginning book such as this, the examples are simple and standard flowcharting techniques are more than adequate. However, some of you may be interested in Warnier/Orr diagrams, and a brief discussion about them is presented in the following pages. In addition, some of the more complex programs are diagrammed using both methods.

The diagrams are named after Jean-Dominique Warnier, who developed the system of logical design of programs. Ken Orr modified the work of Warnier to make it compatible with structured systems design and programming. These diagrams are hierarchical, but, unlike the hierarchy chart shown in Figure 2-8, Warnier/Orr diagrams proceed from left to right rather than top to bottom. Braces are used to show a process, and repetition of a process is indicated by a number, letter, or symbol within parentheses. Figure 2-11 compares traditional flowcharting with a Warnier/Orr diagram for the top levels of our card lister program. Note that the 010-OPENER, or initialization process, is performed only once, as is the 020-CLOSER routine. The 020-READER paragraph is performed until the INDICATOR field is equal to 1. So far the single Warnier/Orr diagram has taken the place of the top-down design structure in Figure 2-8 and the CONTROL-ROUTINE flow diagram in Figure 2-10.

One of the major advantages of Warnier/Orr diagrams is that they show the relationship of each module within the total program. As the reader progresses from left to right, the hierarchical nature of the modules is apparent and the relationship of one module to another is clearly shown. In addition, Warnier/Orr diagrams allow the programmer to show the three logical forms of structured programming that were presented in this chapter: sequence, selection (IFTHENELSE), and the controlled loop, or repetition structure.

FIGURE 2-11

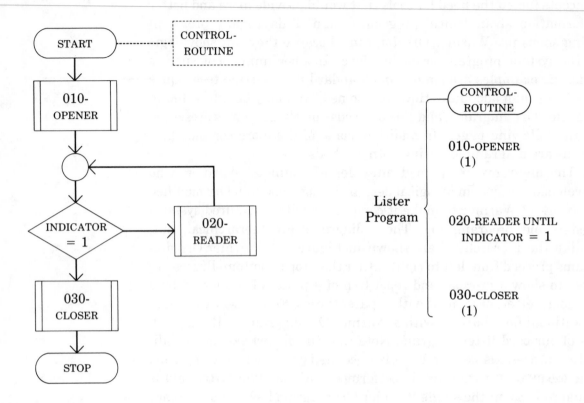

The sequential execution of program statements is shown by listing the operations from top to bottom within the process (as indicated by the braces). Earlier in the chapter you saw an example (Figure 2-4) of the selection structure in which one of two processes (regular pay or overtime pay) was executed depending upon a test. The two processes were mutually exclusive; that is, only one or the other could be executed. In Warnier/Orr format, this relationship is shown by a plus symbol within a circle: $\oplus$. Both the positive and negative sides of the test are shown with the negative indicated by a solid line drawn over the process.

```
HOURS—WORKED
     over 40        — — —   ⎰Compute
       (0,1)                ⎱pay including
                            ⎩overtime

            ⊕

HOURS—WORKED
     over 40        — — —   ⎰Compute
       (0,1)                ⎱regular pay
```

The numbers within parentheses indicate that the process is executed either zero or one time depending upon the test. Just as with any diagramming method, different shops interpret the diagramming rules in different ways. For example, some firms use an upward pointing arrow to represent the negative condition of a test. When that is done, our diagram will be as follows. In either case the word IF is not shown, since it is understood to be there whenever the ⊕ symbol is present.

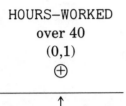

Figure 2-12 illustrates flowcharting versus Warnier/Orr diagramming of the selection structure.

FIGURE 2-12

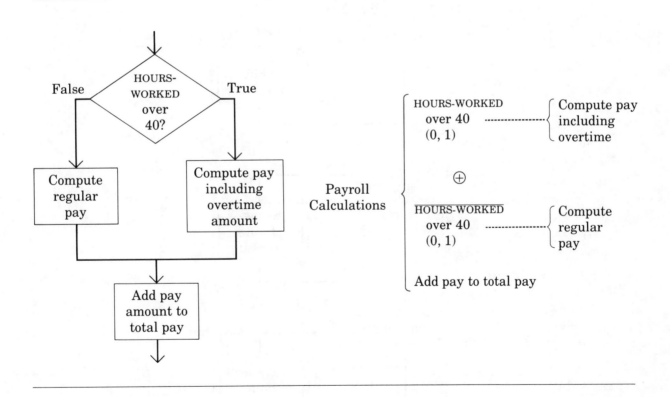

Multiple test conditions can be shown by repeated use of the ⊕ symbol. For example, suppose we wish to test a work-code field that will tell us whether an employee is a day-shift, swing-shift, or graveyard-shift worker.

$$\text{Process} \atop \text{WORK—CODE} \atop (0,1) \left\{ \begin{array}{l} \text{WORK—CODE} = 1 \quad - \ - \ - \left\{ \begin{array}{l} \text{Day-Shift} \\ \text{Processing} \end{array} \right. \\ \qquad\qquad \oplus \\ \text{WORK—CODE} = 2 \quad - \ - \ - \left\{ \begin{array}{l} \text{Swing-Shift} \\ \text{Processing} \end{array} \right. \\ \qquad\qquad \oplus \\ \text{WORK—CODE} = 3 \quad - \ - \ - \left\{ \begin{array}{l} \text{Graveyard-Shift} \\ \text{Processing} \end{array} \right. \\ \qquad\qquad \oplus \\ \underline{\qquad\qquad\qquad} \quad - \ - \ - \{\text{Skip} \end{array} \right.$$

In flowchart form this would be shown by three separate testing operations (Figure 2-13).

FIGURE 2-13

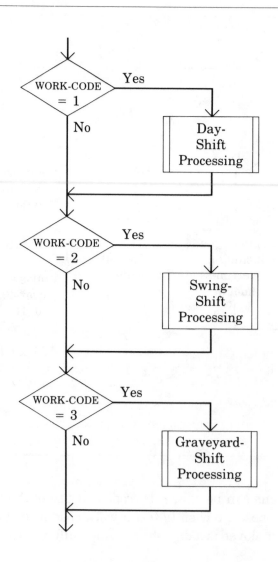

The plus symbol by itself—that is, not circled—can be used for several purposes, but in its simplest use means "and," or a concurrent condition. For example, we may want to perform a paragraph only if two conditions are true at the same time. A situation of this type might be worded as follows: "If the employee is a day-shift worker and has worked more than five years for the company, perform pay-raise routine."

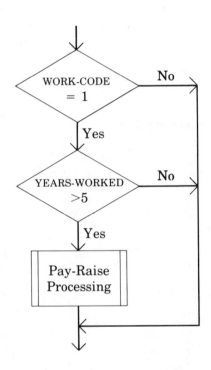

We can now get back to the Lister Program and diagram the actions of the 010-OPENER paragraph. The process starts by opening the files (once) and then goes into the READ statement, which has a conditional event associated with it (AT END MOVE 1 TO INDICATOR). The logic of the statement is that if the end of file (EOF) is detected, a 1 value is moved to INDICATOR and program control returns to the CONTROL-ROUTINE. If the end of file is not detected, control is returned to the CONTROL-ROUTINE without any intervening action.

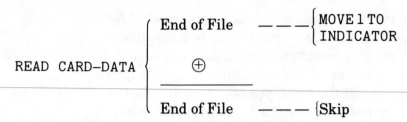

Note that the ⊕ symbol indicated two alternatives that are mutually exclusive; that is, only one or the other will be executed. Figure 2-14 contrasts the 010-OPEN module using flowcharting and a Warnier/Orr diagram. This illustration and the previous one point out another area of individual choice when diagramming. In one case the name of the paragraph, or module, appears in an enclosed symbol at the top of the braces.

Other shops require the paragraph, or module, name to appear in front of the braces.

010-OPENER

FIGURE 2-14

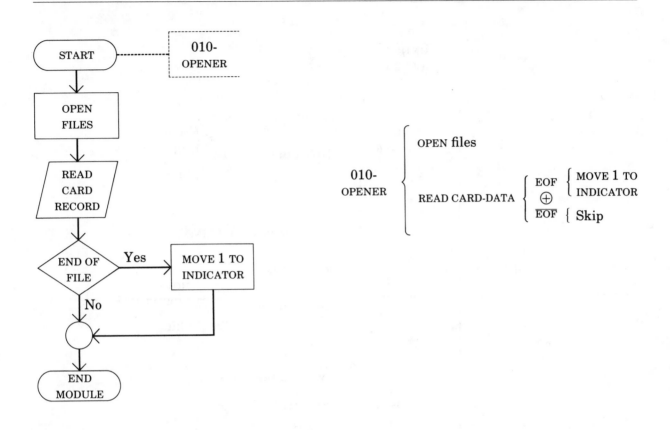

The complete Warnier/Orr diagram for our card lister program is shown in Figure 2-15. The program was so short that it contained only four paragraphs, but the Warnier/Orr diagram shows the hierarchial nature of the program structure. The CONTROL-ROUTINE paragraph was shown to the left of the others because it was at a higher level than the other three. The diagram also shows that the other paragraphs are at the *same* level yet subsidiary to the CONTROL-ROUTINE. If the 020-READER paragraph had contained a statement such as PERFORM 100-CALC-ROUTINE, it would have been shown within and to the right of the 020-READER diagram.

FIGURE 2-15

Sample Program Using a Warnier/Orr Diagram

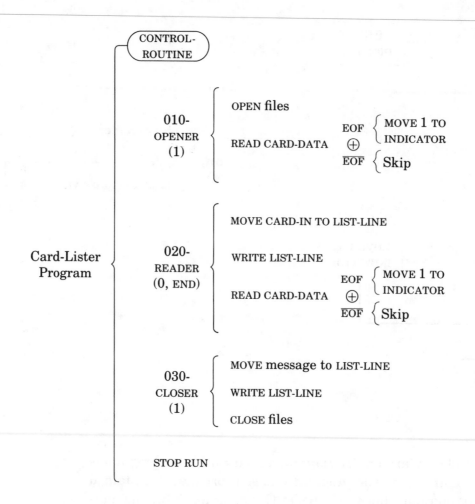

As just shown, Warnier/Orr diagrams can be used to represent a problem solution, but they also can be used to show the interrelationship of the problem solution and data elements, or to show the structure of data alone. These additional uses are outside the scope of the text, but obviously add to the versatility of the Warnier/Orr method.

Problem-Solving Techniques

You have been exposed to the ideas of program discipline, and the question is "How do you use this knowledge in designing the solution to a problem?" Well, there should be no difficulty in starting the top-down design process for any program because you know the first layer is a single control module box. The second layer is likely to be equally simple because just about every computer program will require an Initialization Module, a Processing Module, and an Ending Module. So, your first real area of concern in the problem-solving process will be at the third level, or layer.

At this beginning stage of COBOL most of the problems are likely to be very simple—so simple that no further breakdown of the Initialization and Ending modules will be required. We are then left with the Processing Module. How do you know whether or not to break it down into smaller modules? What is a module and how big should it be?

Although the scope of a module is hard to define exactly, the consensus is that the individual steps, or statements, within the module must be functionally related to each other. Thus a programming module that is described as doing the overtime payroll calculation task should do just that and nothing else. For example, one school of thought says that all input and output operations should be isolated from the calculating, or testing, functions. The advantage of the functional relationship between program modules is that they can be located, changed, and tested with a minimum of effort. As to exact size, the most commonly heard figure is that no module should be greater than 50 lines (one page) of code. If it is longer than this, the chances are very good that the module contains more than one function and should be broken down. Whatever its size, the module must be easily understood, easily coded, and easily tested.

Some of the modules you will encounter all the time have already been identified: Initialization, Ending, Data Input, Data Output, and General Processing. Some others might include modules for the output of error messages, utility routines to duplicate data from one storage medium to another, and input data validation routines. The problem-solving approach you must take here is to categorize the tasks you see during the analysis process. As you gain experience, the boundaries of the modules will become easier and easier to see. However, no matter how experienced you become, the basic rule is still the same: plan first, program later.

Self-Study: Questions and Answers

1. What do you mean by "program maintenance"?

   Answer
   In a classroom situation, such as that set up in this text, you are always writing new, short programs. In the "outside world," in a job situation, that is not the case. First, you are likely to write much, much longer programs—perhaps thousands of statements long. Second, it is very likely you will write few new programs. Instead, you will be making changes in existing programs. Recent estimates show that maintenance programming accounts for somewhere between 50% to 80% of the programs written.

   You can readily see why this is so as various changes in state and federal laws require changes in payroll calculations, welfare payments, unemployment compensations, tax deductions, and so on.

2. What difference does it make how the program is written as long as it works?

   Answer
   As indicated earlier in the chapter, each programmer traditionally did his or her "own thing" when it came to writing the program. The problem arises when the program needs to be changed. Programmers traditionally have moved easily from job to job, which means that the original programmer is unlikely to be around when the program needs to be revised. If the program was not written in a "style" you can understand, maintenance becomes difficult at best and impossible at worst.

   "Programs that work" often are concocted of patches of ill-conceived or tricky logic. In these cases it may be better to rewrite the whole program all over again rather than attempt to make corrections.

3. I'm not really sure that I understand what top-down and structured programming are all about.

   Answer
   Your comment is understandable as both ideas are relatively new and sometimes difficult to follow. In addition, as mentioned earlier, the problems you have encountered so far in the text are so short that there seems little need for the top-down approach.

   However, the main reason for including material on these topics is to make you understand that these methods will yield quicker and better results. In a job situation, particularly in the larger firms, the days of the programmer doing his or her "own thing" are numbered. Today, more and more firms are setting very precise rules as to how programs shall be designed and written, particularly in the COBOL language. Future versions of COBOL (and other popular languages) will have new statements to permit structured concepts.

4. Why is pseudocode such a good programming technique?

Answer
Pseudocode is extremely useful because it allows the programmer to write or show the logical processes of the program in a simple, English-like format. The programmer can think through the various program processes without being bound or held back by the actual statements used in a particular programming language.

   Also, pseudocode is very useful for those people who cannot grasp the visual logic presented in a flowchart. For these people, pseudocode is an alternative to flowcharting.

5. The text showed several programming structures, but it seems as though I may need other structures to do my programs.

Answer
It may seem that you need other programming structures to do your programs, but you will not. What we want is as few programming structures as possible and the uniform use of them. Therefore, it is a matter of you having to reassess your program logic. If you do so, you will find that these structures will work.

6. Does every COBOL program automatically require four separate divisions?

Answer
Yes, it does. There are no exceptions. Not only that, but the four divisions must always be in order: IDENTIFICATION, ENVIRONMENT, DATA, and PROCEDURE.

7. The PROCEDURE DIVISION looks easy, but it also looks like it takes a lot of work to get there. COBOL seems to be a "wordy" language.

Answer
Well, you are right again. However, the PROCEDURE DIVISION is easy *because* you have prepared everything so well in the previous divisions. Then, too, the "wordiness" of COBOL is what makes a program easy to understand.

   You should be aware that all the steps specified in the first three divisions *must* be done in every language. Whether you are aware of these steps in FORTRAN, RPG, and so forth, all the steps are there, although they may not be readily apparent.

Exercises

1. Using top-down design techniques, diagram the functional tasks required to change a tire on an automobile. Do the same thing for the preparation of a written report for a sociology class. Assume that this report will require extensive library research, interviews with local people, and correspondence with resource persons.

2. Expand the top-down design chart in Figure 2-2 to include the following conditions.
   a. The input data (module A-300) are to be checked for validity, and if faulty data are found, an error message is to be printed.
   b. The output data (module C-300) are also to be checked to see that they fall within a reasonable maximum amount. If they exceed this amount, an error message is to be printed.
   c. At the fourth level you are to provide for the pay calculations of employees on a salary plus a commission basis.
   d. Provide for the pay calculations of hourly paid employees who get a shift differential and also for those who require sick-pay calculations.

3. What is the advantage of using pseudocode during the program design process?

4. What are the objectives of a disciplined approach to programming?

5. Draw the selection structure (IFTHENELSE) for the inventory pseudocode example that was illustrated in the chapter.

6. Draw the controlled loop structure (DOWHILE) so that Process A, Process B, and Process C will be executed as long as the test condition is false.

7. Draw the flowchart for the following situation: As long as test A is true, Process B and either Process C (on the true condition of test B) or Process D (on the false condition of test B) will be executed.

8. Name the four COBOL divisions in order and explain briefly what each does.

9. Refer to the sample COBOL program (Figure 2-9) to answer the following questions.
   a. What was the name assigned to the incoming card data file?
   b. What was the name of the data record within the outgoing printer data file?
   c. What were the names of the PROCEDURE DIVISION paragraphs?
   d. What was the purpose of the PERFORM 020-READER UNTIL statement in the CONTROL-ROUTINE?
   e. What does OPEN statement do?
   f. In general terms, how does the program get out of the read-print loop?

10. In the sample program flowchart shown in Figure 2-10, there are three diamond-shaped decision symbols. Explain what this symbol means and how it works in the sample program.

11. What is the purpose of the INDICATOR field in the sample program?

12. What causes the sample program to end?

13. If your instructor allows you to do so, punch or enter the sample COBOL program as indicated in the text and run it so that you can see the output.

14. Try some of these other possibilities.
    a. Leave out the first priming read entirely. Run your program *with* data and see what happens. However, before running the program, flowchart exactly what you think will happen.
    b. Same as above, but now leave out the data cards entirely. Again, flowchart exactly what you think will happen.

Chapter 3

Getting Started in

COBOL

Technically speaking, a computer truly "understands" only one programming language—its own machine language. It is not the intent of this book to discuss machine language coding, but you should understand that writing programs at the machine level is very tedious. Rather than use words and names as you do in COBOL and most other languages, the programmer uses digits and letters to represent instructions and data locations. At this level, programming is extremely machine-dependent and not transferrable to another computer.

Since programming at this level is so difficult, time consuming, and expensive, a variety of high-level languages such as COBOL have been devised. Still, the problem exists that the computer really "understands" only machine language. We get around this problem by means of what is generally known as an *operating system*. An operating system is a very complex set of sophisticated programs provided by the manufacturer when the computer system is obtained.

Among these programs is one called the COBOL compiler, or translator. As I am sure you are aware by now, the compiler program translates your COBOL program into a machine language program. It is this machine language program that is then executed.

Compiling a COBOL program

The COBOL translator, or compiler, is stored on a magnetic disk and is brought in, or read into, memory as required. As indicated earlier, the operating system is comprised of many software programs of which the COBOL compiler is just a small part. Perhaps the single most important part of the operating system is a program generally called Supervisor, or Executive. This program normally is in memory all the time and has the task of determining which of the other software programs are needed at any given moment. In turn, Supervisor is controlled by the operator working at the system console device (typewriter). Figure 3-1 shows the relationship of the hardware and software elements of the system.

FIGURE 3-1

A Computer System Showing Hardware and Software

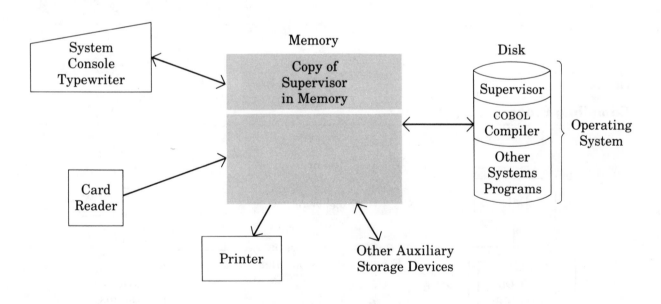

The steps that take place during the translation of a COBOL program are simple, but important for you to understand. The writer feels very strongly that the more you understand how the system operates, the fewer errors you will make and the more efficiently you will program. Figures 3-2a through 3-2d illustrate the major steps of the compiling process.

FIGURE 3-2a

Compiling Process: Step 1

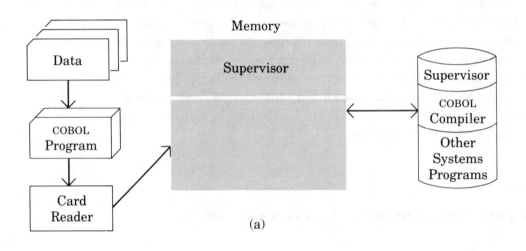

(a)

FIGURE 3-2b

Compiling Process: Step 2

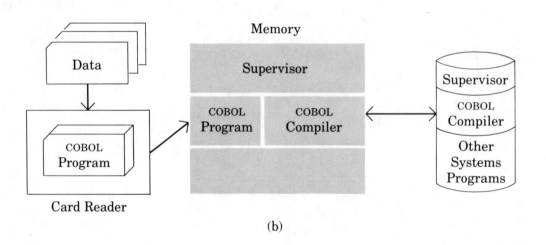

(b)

FIGURE 3-2c

Compiling Process: Step 3

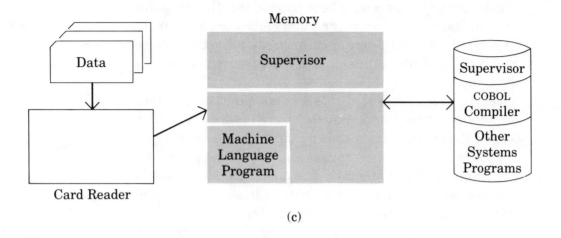

(c)

FIGURE 3-2d

Compiling Process: Step 4

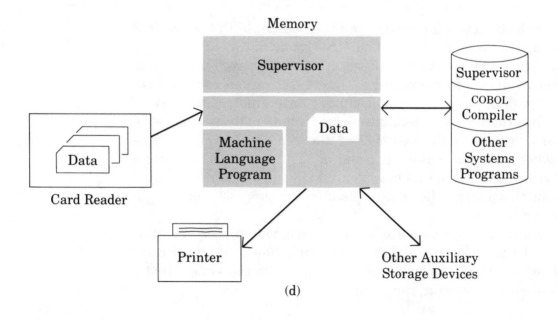

(d)

1. The COBOL program is punched into cards and placed in the card reader. The operator starts the process by executing the supervisor program, which reads your COBOL program into memory (Step 1). (*Note:*   This is the traditional way in which COBOL programs have been entered into the computer system. Many of the newer computers allow the program to be entered via a hard-copy or cathode ray tube (CRT) video terminal. Regardless, the action of the software is generally the same.)
2. Supervisor recognizes that it is a COBOL program and that the services of the COBOL translator are needed (Step 2). A copy of the COBOL translator is brought into memory.
3. The translator program changes your COBOL program into a machine language program. The memory area originally occupied by the COBOL compiler is no longer needed and reverts back to a general usage area (Step 3).
4. Your program (now in machine language form) is executed. Depending upon the nature of the problem you are solving, data may be brought in from cards, tape, or disk. Output may be to the printer or to any of the other output and/or auxiliary storage devices (Step 4).

Job control

Although the compiling process works as described in the previous section, there is no magic about how the system software knows what to do. The various actions of the system are "triggered" by means of special cards called *job control* cards inserted at various points in your program deck. Different manufacturers have different methods of providing these trigger mechanisms, but, traditionally, IBM has relied heavily on cards for this task. Indeed, the whole process of determining what control actions are to be initiated at what time has become so complex that specialists in job control language (JCL) are employed just for this purpose. Be sure to check for the proper JCL entries for your computer system.

Outlined below are some of the more common IBM disk operating system (DOS) JCL entries and their functions. Note that all the cards start with a slash symbol (/), which indicates to the system that a control card has been encountered.

// JOB - - -

This card, followed by other entries, as indicated by the three hyphens, tells the system that a new program, or job, is coming and names the program.

// OPTION LIST, ERRS, LOG, DUMP

The OPTION card informs the system of those software options you wish to have in effect for your program. Job control language may contain 50 or more such options, but the ones listed above are fairly typical.

LIST causes the system to list, or print, your COBOL program.

ERRS means that a list of the individual errors found during compilation of your program will be printed.

LOG gives a printout on the system console device showing that your program, or job, was initiated.

DUMP causes the system software to output, or print, a dump of memory if your program fails during execution. This printout may be of help in cases of program errors that are not readily apparent.

* Entries other than those shown above are permitted. Check your system for the exact format of the card.

// EXEC FCOBOL

The EXEC FCOBOL card causes the software to execute the COBOL compiler, which translates your program into machine language.

/*

The slash asterisk card indicates the end of a group of cards and may be used more than once within a program deck.

/&

The slash ampersand card indicates the end of that program, or job, and separates it from any jobs that might follow.

// EXEC LNKEDT

An explanation of the need for the EXEC LNKEDT card requires a further examination of the compiling process. The COBOL program that you write is known as a Source program and the machine language that is ultimately derived from it is known as an Object program. On most IBM computer systems, the output from the COBOL compiler is not a "ready to run" machine language program. Instead, the output is a series of smaller parts called modules. The Linkage Editor program then takes these modules and links them into an executable Object program.

// EXEC

This card now causes the system to execute your machine program.

To execute a typical COBOL program using card input and printer output, the following job deck makeup is required. Again, always check your machine to be sure of the exact entries that are required.

```
// JOB
// OPTION - - -
// EXEC FCOBOL
Source Deck        (Your COBOL program)
/*                 (To indicate the end of your Source program)
// EXEC LNKEDT
// EXEC
Data Deck          (If needed)
/*                 (To indicate the end of data)
/&                 (To indicate the end of the job)
```

A slightly different job control card arrangement is required for programs using magnetic disk or tape files.

COBOL and the structure of data

COBOL, a business-oriented language, was designed to handle a wide range of problems that are encountered in business activities. Although the language does have extensive data manipulation capabilities, it is not truly applicable to scientific programming tasks. At one time, each of the major computer manufacturers offered different versions of the language. Later, the American National Standards Institute (ANSI) adopted a standard version of COBOL so that programs written for one machine are, with a few changes, capable of being run on a different machine.

Another important point to remember about COBOL is that it was intended to resemble written English and to be self-documenting. This means that a newcomer to data processing should be able to pick up a COBOL program and generally understand the operations being performed. Because the language is so similar to English, the rules of punctuation and spelling are extremely important. The sooner you learn to adjust to these rules, the sooner you will eliminate many simple and annoying errors. Before learning the language itself, you should become acquainted with the nature and terminology of the data handled by the computer.

The smallest units of data with which COBOL can work are *characters*. Any of the digits, the alphabetic symbols (A, B, C, etc.), or the permissable special symbols such as the decimal point or the comma, are considered characters (Figure 3-3).

FIGURE 3-3

COBOL Characters

Digits 0 through 9
Letters A through Z
Special characters:

>   Blank or space
> +   Plus sign
> −   Minus sign or hyphen
> *   Check protection symbol, asterisk
> /   Slash
> =   Equal sign
> >   Inequality sign (greater than)
> <   Inequality sign (less than)
> $ Dollar sign
> ,   Comma
> .   Period or decimal point
> '   Quotation mark (also called an apostrophe; it is a 5-8 card punch.)
> (Left parenthesis
>)   Right parenthesis

Of the previous set, the following characters are used for words:

> 0 through 9
> A through Z
> - Hyphen

The following characters are used for punctuation:

> '   Quotation mark
> (Left parenthesis
>)   Right parenthesis
> ,   Comma
> .   Period

The following characters are used in arithmetic expressions:

> +   Addition
> −   Subtraction
> *   Multiplication
> /   Division
> **   Exponentiation

The following characters are used in relation tests:

> >   Greater than
> <   Less than
> =   Equal to

Characters are normally grouped together to form *fields* of data, such as a social security number field, rate of pay field, amount owed field, and so on. Fields are usually numeric (such as those indicated above) or alphabetic (customer name field), but COBOL also can work with fields that mix the two types of data (e.g., customer address field). Figure 3-4 shows the relationship of fields on a standard IBM card. At this point you should be aware that data can be recorded on a variety of storage media other than cards. Cards, however, are easy to visualize and, for this reason, will be used often throughout the book.

FIGURE 3-4

A Card Record Showing Individual Fields

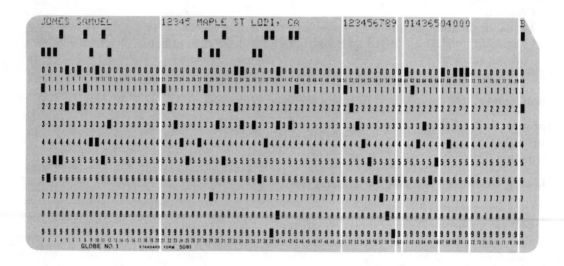

Individual data fields are usually grouped together in some meaningful way to form a *record* of data. The classic example of a record of data is the IBM card. The customary practice is to punch all the pertinent information on a single transaction into a single card, or record. Figure 3-4 also shows how a record is comprised of a number of related fields.

Finally, similar data records are grouped into *files* of data. For example, if we had one card record for each student enrolled in your school, the sum total of all these records would be a file of data. This file would have a name and would be just one of many files used by the school district in its normal course of work. The file would be given a name such as "student enrollment file" and used as required. Other typical files might be those of accounts receivable, accounts payable, inventory, payroll, and so forth. As Figure 3-5 shows, these files can be in several forms.

FIGURE 3-5

Data Files

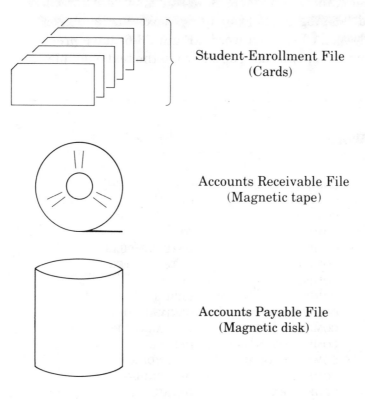

Student-Enrollment File
(Cards)

Accounts Receivable File
(Magnetic tape)

Accounts Payable File
(Magnetic disk)

COBOL: Rules of the game

Punctuation

Earlier, we mentioned the importance of punctuation in COBOL. The rules generally are the same as those you would follow in typing, such as always having a space after a period or spacing between two successive words. Another rule is that a space cannot appear directly after a left parenthesis symbol [( ] or before a right parenthesis [ )]. Commas may be inserted in COBOL statements to improve readability, but are not required elements of punctuation.

The critical point for you to understand about punctuation is that there is one major difference between English and COBOL punctuation: in English, a misplaced element of punctuation or a misspelled word may be noticed, but the message still gets through to the reader. In COBOL, a single error of this type is usually serious enough to cause your whole program to be canceled.

Words and names

The programmer assigns names to data fields by the rules of COBOL. Names are limited to a maximum of 30 characters made up of digits, alphabetic characters, and the hyphen. A word cannot start or end with a hyphen, and the programmer must take special care to avoid the use of reserved words. Reserved words (Figure 3-6) have preassigned meanings and can only be used as shown in the text examples.

FIGURE 3-6

COBOL Reserved Words

ACCEPT	CODE	C11
ACCESS	COLUMN	C12
ACTUAL	COM-REG	
ADD	COMMA	DATA
ADDRESS	COMP	DATE-COMPILED
ADVANCING	COMP-1	DATE-WRITTEN
AFTER	COMP-2	DE
ALL	COMP-3	DEBUG
ALPHABETIC	COMPUTATIONAL	DECIMAL-POINT
ALTER	COMPUTATIONAL-1	DECLARATIVES
ALTERNATE	COMPUTATIONAL-2	DELETE
AND	COMPUTATIONAL-3	DEPENDING
APPLY	COMPUTE	DESCENDING
ARE	CONFIGURATION	DETAIL
AREA	CONSOLE	DISP
AREAS	CONSTANT	DISPLAY
ASCENDING	CONTAINS	DISPLAY-ST
ASSIGN	CONTROLS	DISPLAY-n
AT	COPY	DIVIDE
AUTHOR	CORE-INDEX	DIVISION
	CORR	DOWN
BASIS	CORRESPONDING	
BEFORE	CSP	EJECT
BEGINNING	CURRENCY	ELSE
BLANK	CURRENT-DATE	END
BLOCK	CYL-INDEX	END-OF-PAGE
BY	CYL-OVERFLOW	ENDING
	C01	ENTER
CALL	C02	ENTRY
CANCEL	C03	ENVIRONMENT
CF	C04	EOP
CH	C05	EQUAL
CHANGED	C06	EQUALS
CHARACTERS	C07	ERROR
CLOCK-UNITS	C08	EVERY
CLOSE	C09	EXAMINE
COBOL	C10	EXCEEDS

EXHIBIT	LABEL	OUTPUT
EXIT	LABEL-RETURN	OV
EXTENDED-SEARCH	LAST	OVERFLOW
	LEADING	
FD	LEAVE	PAGE
FILE	LEFT	PAGE-COUNTER
FILE-CONTROL	LESS	PERFORM
FILE-LIMIT	LIBRARY	PF
FILE-LIMITS	LIMIT	PH
FILLER	LIMITS	PIC
FINAL	LINAGE	PICTURE
FIRST	LINAGE-COUNTER	PLUS
FOOTING	LINE	POSITION
FOR	LINE-COUNTER	POSITIONING
FROM	LINES	POSITIVE
	LINKAGE	PREPARED
GENERATE	LOCK	PRINT-SWITCH
GIVING	LOW-VALUE	PRIORITY
GO	LOW-VALUES	PROCEDURE
GOBACK	LOWER-BOUND	PROCEED
GREATER	LOWER-BOUNDS	PROCESS
GROUP		PROCESSING
	MASTER-INDEX	PROGRAM
HEADING	MEMORY	PROGRAM-ID
HIGH-VALUE	MODE	
HIGH-VALUES	MODULES	QUOTE
HOLD	MORE-LABELS	QUOTES
	MOVE	
I-O	MULTIPLE	RANDOM
I-O-CONTROL	MULTIPLY	RANGE
ID		RD
IDENTIFICATION	NAMED	READ
IF	NEGATIVE	READY
IN	NEXT	RECORD
INDEX	NO	RECORD-OVERFLOW
INDEX-n	NOMINAL	RECORDING
INDEXED	NOT	RECORDS
INDICATE	NOTE	REDEFINES
INITIATE	NSTD-REELS	REEL
INPUT	NUMBER	RELEASE
INPUT-OUTPUT	NUMERIC	REMAINDER
INSERT		REMARKS
INSTALLATION	OBJECT-COMPUTER	RENAMES
INTO	OBJECT-PROGRAM	REORG-CRITERIA
INVALID	OCCURS	REPLACING
IS	OF	REPORT
	OFF	REPORTING
JUST	OH	REPORTS
JUSTIFIED	OMITTED	REREAD
	ON	RERUN
KEY	OPEN	RESERVE
KEYS	OPTIONAL	RESET
	OR	RETURN
	OTHERWISE	RETURN-CODE

REVERSED	SYSLST	WHEN
REWIND	SYSOUT	WITH
REWRITE	SYSPCH	WORDS
RF	SYSPUNCH	WORKING-STORAGE
RH	S01	WRITE
RIGHT	S02	WRITE-ONLY
ROUNDED		WRITE-VERIFY
RUN	TALLY	
	TALLYING	ZERO
SA	TAPE	ZEROES
SAME	TERMINATE	ZEROS
SD	THAN	
SEARCH	THEN	
SECTION	THROUGH	
SECURITY	THRU	
SEEK	TIME-OF-DAY	
SEGMENT-LIMIT	TIMES	
SELECT	TO	
SELECTED	TOTALED	
SENTENCE	TOTALING	
SEQUENTIAL	TRACE	
SET	TRACK	
SIGN	TRACK-AREA	
SIZE	TRACK-LIMIT	
SKIP1	TRACKS	
SKIP2	TRANSFORM	
SKIP3	TYPE	
SORT		
SORT-CORE-SIZE	UNEQUAL	
SORT-FILE-SIZE	UNIT	
SORT-MODE-SIZE	UNTIL	
SORT-RETURN	UP	
SOURCE	UPON	
SOURCE-COMPUTER	UPPER-BOUND	
SPACE	UPPER-BOUNDS	
SPACES	UPSI-0	
SPECIAL-NAMES	UPSI-1	
STANDARD	UPSI-2	
START	UPSI-3	
STATUS	UPSI-4	
STOP	UPSI-5	
SUBTRACT	UPSI-6	
SUM	UPSI-7	
SUPERVISOR	USAGE	
SUPPRESS	USE	
SUSPEND	USING	
SYNC		
SYNCHRONIZED	VALUE	
SYSIN	VALUES	
SYSIPT	VARYING	

For example, suppose we wish to move a field of data called SS-NUMBER to another area called SS-NUMBER-PRINTER. (Both these names, by the way, are typical of names that a programmer chooses for the fields of data.) The COBOL statement to accomplish our move operation is

```
MOVE SS-NUMBER TO SS-NUMBER-PRINTER.
```

The words MOVE and TO are reserved words that are required in the MOVE operation, along with a period that terminates the statement. The self-documenting nature of this English-like statement tells you that the social security number is going to be moved from one location in memory to another. The use of the PRINTER with the second data field indicates that the value contained in this field will be output on a printing device. Also note that since blanks are not permitted in COBOL names, the hyphen is used to separate the parts of the word to make them more readable.

```
ADD TAX-AMOUNT-1, TAX-AMOUNT-2 TO TOTAL.
```

The second example illustrates the use of the reserved words ADD and TO and the use of the comma (which is not required). In this illustration the numeric values stored in the first two fields will be added to the value already in the field called TOTAL. Also note that the programmer chose names that were meaningful in relation to the problem being solved. It would be correct but very foolish for the programmer to use names such as shown below.

```
ADD APPLES, NUTS-AND-BOLTS TO ICE-CREAM.
```

Literals

Literals are actual values that are used in the program. Numeric literals may be up to 18 digits in length and may contain a sign and a decimal point.

Examples

```
ADD 1 TO COUNTER.
```

The numeric literal 1 will be added to the contents of the field called COUNTER.

```
DIVIDE AREA-AMOUNT BY 3.1415.
```

The value stored at AREA-AMOUNT will be divided by the literal 3.1415 (the value of pi).

Non-numeric literals may be used in a similar way. They may be up to 120 characters long and must be enclosed within quotation marks. (On most machines the single apostrophe is the quotation mark.)

Examples

```
MOVE 'COBOL IS NOT SO HARD' TO OUTPUT-AREA.
```

All characters, including blanks, count toward the maximum literal length of 120 characters.

```
DISPLAY 'MARCH 17, 1960' UPON CONSOLE.
```

Numeric characters enclosed within quotation marks are valid parts of non-numeric literals. This statement causes the message to be printed on the console typewriter.

Figurative constants

A figurative constant is a special type of literal to which a reserved name has been given. The two most commonly used figurative constants are ZERO (ZEROS, ZEROES) and SPACE (SPACES).

Examples

```
MOVE ZEROS TO COUNTER.
```

The correct number of zeros are moved to the field called COUNTER. (The computer system always knows the exact size and the nature of data fields because the fields have been defined earlier in your program.) The action of this statement is that the value previously in the COUNTER field is destroyed when zeros are moved in.

```
MOVE SPACES TO PRINTER-LINE.
```

Spaces are moved to the field called PRINTER-LINE.

The COBOL coding sheet

A special coding sheet is used for writing COBOL program statements. Each space on the coding sheet (Figure 3-7) corresponds to a column on a standard IBM card with each line having room for 80 characters. Some COBOL entries must begin at specific columns on the sheet, or card; but within these limitations the programmer may use a free-form approach to coding. When writing COBOL programs, the best approach is to have an example in front of you, such as shown in this text, or perhaps an old COBOL program. This will help to eliminate simple format errors.

Columns 1 through 6 (of the sheet and the card) are used for sequence numbering of your program statements, such as 000001, 000002, and so on. If your program is short, the work of numbering your cards is probably not worth the effort. For a long program, however, the punched sequence numbers allow you to reassemble a dropped deck quickly.

Card column 7 has two uses. An asterisk punched here will cause the system to treat the entire line as a comment. In the text you will see many examples of how the use of this feature can help to make your program more readable (Figure 3-7).

The second use of card column 7 is for the continuation of a non-numeric literal. A few paragraphs ago you saw that a non-numeric literal can be up to 120 characters long. Obviously, this is longer than one card and the way we indicate the continuation onto a second card is by means of a hyphen in card column 7 (Figure 3-7).

FIGURE 3-7

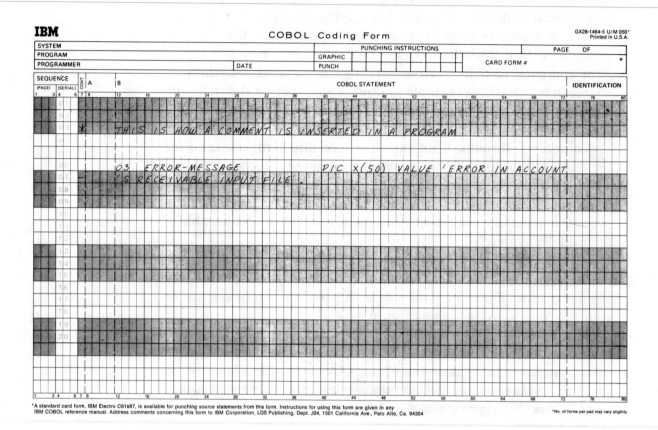

The actual statements in your COBOL program are written, or punched, in columns 8 through 72. Look closely at the book examples, since they illustrate just which entries must begin in area A (columns 8 through 11) and which must be within area B (columns 12 through 72). Although you can enter a COBOL statement up to and including card column 72, this often results in an awkward division of COBOL words. A better method is to break the statement between words and continue onto the next line.

Finally, columns 73 through 80 may be used to punch an identification code for the program. For practice or non-production programs, these columns would ordinarily be left blank.

Problem-Solving Techniques

The problem-solving techniques we need to consider here are not as directly related to the program as they are to your programming habits. First, the author feels very strongly that it is important for you to understand as much as possible about what goes on during the compiling of a COBOL program. The more thoroughly you understand the process, the greater will be your feeling for the language, which will result in fewer logic and coding errors.

Second, get to know the machine on which your COBOL programs are going to be run. Try to get a copy of that manufacturer's COBOL manual. If possible, try to see the machine. Look at the card reader or magnetic tape drive or disk drive so that you can visualize these devices when writing your programs. Later, the physical association with these pieces of hardware will not be so important, but identifying these devices seems to help beginning students.

Third, you can save yourself a lot of trouble by developing neat, precise work habits *now*. Print your COBOL statements with clear, bold marks and be extremely careful with punctuation and spelling, since the compiler is very intolerant of even the smallest error. Learn the rules of the game *now*.

Finally, the previous chapters indicated that every COBOL program contains four DIVISIONS, and that in almost every case you will have an Initialization, a Processing, and an Ending module. Since there is such a great likelihood that specific sections of one COBOL program are going to be very similar (or identical) to the same section in another COBOL program, it would be wise for you to code in a manner such that these sections can be used from one program to another. That, of course, is another reason for programming in modular form, since the modules are portable from one program to another. The suggestion, therefore, is for you to develop programming patterns and habits that will increase the use and portability of programming modules.

Self-Study: Questions and Answers

1. Translating a COBOL program into machine language must require a very complex translator or compiler program.

   Answer
   Compiler programs are extremely complex, particularly if you stop and think about what they have to do. During the translation process, for example, the compiler not only translates, but also checks for errors in format. Depending upon the computer system, the compiler may be able to detect up to several hundred different types of errors. If an error is detected, that particular entry cannot be translated correctly. This, in turn, can affect many other entries further along in your program. In some cases the software is sophisticated enough to detect a simple error, correct it, and print a warning message to you. Errors are discussed in more detail later on in the book.

2. What if I make a mistake in my job control cards?

   Answer
   Usually the system aborts or cancels your job by running out the rest of your cards. Check the job cards very carefully for two things: first, that each card is correct in itself, and second, that each job card is in the right place in the deck.

3. Is it really as important as you say to be so careful about spelling and punctuation in COBOL?

   Answer
   It certainly is, and, if you think about it for a minute, you can understand the reason. For example, if you make a mistake in an English composition, the reader usually can figure out what is incorrect and determine what you actually mean. The computer does not have this capability, which means that even a small error is very likely to result in termination of your program. Unfortunately, COBOL is not a very forgiving language.

4. If I do make a lot of simple errors, they should be easy to correct, shouldn't they?

   Answer
   Yes, these errors are simple to correct, but the problem is finding

them in your program. The computer system will print an error message for each mistake, but the messages themselves are not always very clear. The best plan is to learn the rules and format of COBOL right away and not make these types of errors.

5. The text discusses fields, records, and files that seem to be simple enough. What I want to know is whether this arrangement is always true or is it true just for COBOL.

Answer

The relationship of fields, records, and files is true for any language, not just COBOL. For that reason it is good that you understand it now and won't have to relearn it later when working with another language.

6. As I understand it, the programmer gives names to fields of data. Is that correct?

Answer

Generally, in all languages the programmer is able to assign names to fields of data. The rules for naming are very liberal in COBOL, which makes it easy to give meaningful names to the fields rather than use nonsense syllables. This point will become extremely important later when you have to refer back to a part of your program that was written earlier. It is very easy to forget what some of these field names stand for.

7. I looked at the reserved word list and there is no way I can learn all of those names.

Answer

Don't worry, you really won't have to learn all the reserved words. Most of them are required words you will be learning very quickly as you program in COBOL. Many of the rest are such that plain "horse sense" would tell you they might be on the list. A good idea is to read the list over from time to time just to become familiar with some of the words. Even so, you may still end up using a reserved word in an incorrect way. This should happen very infrequently and the problem is usually very easy to correct.

8. When moving figurative constants such as SPACES or ZEROS, how does the system "know" how many to move to the field?

Answer

The complete answer to your question will come later when the DATA DIVISION is discussed in detail. Right now, the main point to understand is that in just about any programming language the system somehow has to be informed of the size and type of every field. This is the major function of the DATA DIVISION.

Exercises

1. In reference to Figure 3-1, how can Supervisor be in memory and on disk at the same time?

2. Does Supervisor control the COBOL compiler, or is it the other way around?

3. Indicate which job control card performs each of the following functions.
   a. Executes your machine language program
   b. Indicates the beginning of a new program
   c. Executes the COBOL compiler
   d. Indicates the end of the job
   e. Executes the program that puts output modules into executable machine language form
   f. Indicates the end of your Source program

4. Explain in your own words the relationship between fields, records, and files.

5. Could a file ever contain just one record? Could a record consist of a single field? What is the minimum size of a field? What is the maximum size of a field?

6. How important are commas in COBOL statements?

7. Why are blanks not permitted in COBOL names?

8. Determine whether the following are correct or incorrect COBOL statements. If the statement is incorrect, change it so it is correct.
   a. MOVE NUMBER TO COUNTER.
   b. MOVE AMOUNT TO TOTAL
   c. MOVE SUZIE TO TOWN.
   d. ADD, GROSS, TO, TOTAL-AMOUNT.
   e. ADD REG-PAY.
   f. ADD REG-PAY TO OVERFLOW.
   g. ADD 123-ANSWER TO ANS-OUT.
   h. MORE INV-ITEM TO INV-ITEM-PR.
   i. MOVE SS NUMBER TO PRINT-FIELD-1.

9. Determine whether the following are correct or incorrect COBOL statements. If the statement is incorrect, change it so it is correct.
   a. ADD 7 TO AMOUNT.
   b. ADD −6.4 TO TOTAL.
   c. MOVE 'THE ANSWER IS TO OUTPUT-AREA.
   d. ADD 'AN ANSWER' TO TOTAL-1.
   e. DISPLAY 'ERROR #2' UPON CONSOLE
   f. MOVE 17 SPACES TO OUTPUT-AREA-3.
   g. ADD 16 TO 'GRAND-TOTAL'.
   h. MOVE ZEROS TO COUNTER.
   i. MOVE COUNTER TO ZEROS.

10. Define a figurative constant and give two examples of how they are used.

11. Identify or name each of the following.
    a. 456
    b. '456'
    c. 'END OF REPORT'
    d. 3,165
    e. '$365.14'
    f. −21.85
    g. ZERO
    h. 0
    i. 'ZERO'
    j. 'MARCH 17, 1960'

12. What are two purposes of card column (or coding sheet column) 7? Give an example of each use.

13. What is meant by the term "portability" in reference to programming modules? Give a brief example of how a portable module might be used.

Chapter 4

Setting Up the Program

If you had taken a good look at the sample program shown in Chapter 2 you might have noticed that a clear and simple relationship exists between the various DIVISIONS in COBOL. Actually, the first three divisions—IDENTIFICATION, ENVIRONMENT, and the DATA DIVISION—are there to prepare the computer system for the actual processing statements (such as ADD, READ, or WRITE) that will be used in the PROCEDURE DIVISION. Let's take a look at this "setting up," or preparation, process.

The identification division

Only two entries are required, and they both begin in card column 8. In the PROGRAM-ID entry the programmer tells the system the name by which the program is identified. On most systems the name may be up to 30 characters long, but only the first eight will be considered by the system. Also, the name cannot begin with a hyphen or contain blanks, but it may contain numeric values.

```
00001      IDENTIFICATION DIVISION.
00002      PROGRAM-ID. LISTER.
```

In the example, LISTER is the program name assigned by the programmer. Also note that the period is a required element of punctuation that is necessary in COBOL. Other entries may be used in the IDENTIFICATION DIVISION, but they are optional and will not be considered here.

The environment division

The entries in the ENVIRONMENT DIVISION are also simple and very logical. The division consists of two sections: the CONFIGURATION SECTION and the INPUT-OUTPUT SECTION. Our sample program was as follows:

```
00004      ENVIRONMENT DIVISION.
00005      CONFIGURATION SECTION.
00006      SOURCE-COMPUTER. IBM-360-F30.
00007      OBJECT-COMPUTER. IBM-360-F30.
```

The SOURCE-COMPUTER entry specifies the exact machine on which the source program will be compiled, and the OBJECT-COMPUTER entry indicates the machine on which the object program will be run. Normally, the two entries are identical, but it is possible to compile on one machine for execution on another.

The INPUT-OUTPUT SECTION entries are easy, but they do require a little more explanation.

```
00008      INPUT-OUTPUT SECTION.
00009      FILE-CONTROL.
00010          SELECT CARD-DATA
00011              ASSIGN TO SYS007-UR-2540R-S.
00012          SELECT PRINTFILE
00013              ASSIGN TO SYS009-UR-1403-S.
```

The SELECT entry does two things: First, it assigns a name to a file of data; second, it tells the system which device the file will be passing through. In the example, CARD-DATA is the name given by the programmer to the file of cards that will be passing through the card reader. The maximum size of the file name is 30 characters; it cannot contain any special characters or blanks, and on most systems must begin with a letter.

The second part of the SELECT entry ASSIGNS the file to a particular device. The example shows the IBM method of identifying a particular input/output (I/O) device, where:

SYS007 is the system number assigned to a specific I/O device (a card reader).

UR identifies it as a Unit Record piece of equipment. UR is used for card readers and printers as opposed to magnetic tape and disk devices, which have a different designation.

2540 is a specific model IBM card reader.

R indicates a Reading device (as opposed to P for a Punching device).

S indicates that the device will handle a Sequential file.

The SELECT PRINTFILE entry follows the same pattern, but, as you would expect, with a different SYS number and device number. On many computer systems the SELECT entries are simplified by using pre-assigned names for the commonly used devices such as the card reader, card punch, and printer. Then, your entry might look as follows:

```
SELECT CARD-DATA
     ASSIGN TO SYSTEM-INPUT
```

or

```
     ASSIGN TO SYSRDR
```

or

```
SELECT PRINTFILE
     ASSIGN TO SYSTEM-OUTPUT
```

or

```
     ASSIGN TO SYSLST
```

Up to this point our sample program looks as shown in Figure 4-1.

FIGURE 4-1

Sample Program

```
00001          IDENTIFICATION DIVISION.
00002          PROGRAM-ID. LISTER.
00003          *
00004          ENVIRONMENT DIVISION.
00005          CONFIGURATION SECTION.
00006          SOURCE-COMPUTER.  IBM-360-F30.
00007          OBJECT-COMPUTER.  IBM-360-F30.
00008          INPUT-OUTPUT SECTION.
00009          FILE-CONTROL.
00010              SELECT CARD-DATA
00011                  ASSIGN TO SYS007-UR-2540R-S.
00012              SELECT PRINTFILE
00013                  ASSIGN TO SYS009-UR-1403-S.
```

The DATA DIVISION

The DATA DIVISION is not hard, but, generally, it is the longest of the three preparatory divisions in COBOL. As explained earlier, the purpose of the division is to tell the system the specific details about the data that will be handled, or processed, in the PROCEDURE DIVISION.

You recall that in the ENVIRONMENT DIVISION you named the files of data you intended to use, such as CARD-DATA and PRINTFILE. At this point the system is expecting the programmer to provide a more detailed description of the file. This description begins with the FILE SECTION entry and continues with FD, which stands for "file description," and the name of the file that will be described.

```
00015          DATA DIVISION.
00016          FILE SECTION.
00017          FD   CARD-DATA
00018              LABEL RECORDS ARE OMITTED
00019              DATA RECORD IS CARD-IN.
00020          01   CARD-IN          PIC X(80).
00021          FD   PRINTFILE
00022              LABEL RECORDS ARE OMITTED
00023              DATA RECORD IS LIST.
00024          01   LIST.
00025              03  FILLER        PIC X.
00026              03  LIST-LINE     PIC X(120).
```

Immediately after the FD entry you will have a series of entries that further describe the file, the record, and the individual fields that are part of the record. All this, of course, goes back to the basic idea of a *file,* which is comprised of *records* made up of a series of *fields.* To be even more exact, the system *must* find an FD—file description entry—for *every* file named in a SELECT. Not only must there be a corresponding entry, but the SELECT file-name *must* exactly match the FD name, as Figure 4-2 indicates. Later in this chapter you will see what happens when this rule is violated. What is important now, however, is that you understand that a SELECT and FD entry are *always* tied together by the file name. The relationship is nothing more than that dictated by common sense: The SELECT entry only names the file; the FD entries will break the file down into its component parts.

FIGURE 4-2

Relationship of FILE-CONTROL and FILE SECTION

```
00009          FILE-CONTROL.
00010             SELECT CARD-DATA
00011                ASSIGN TO SYS007-UR-2540R-S.
00012             SELECT PRINTFILE
00013                ASSIGN TO SYS009-UR-1403-S.
00014          *
00015          DATA DIVISION.
00016          FILE SECTION.
00017          FD  CARD-DATA
00018             LABEL RECORDS ARE OMITTED
00019             DATA RECORD IS CARD-IN.
00020          01  CARD-IN          PIC X(80).
00021          FD  PRINTFILE
00022             LABEL RECORDS ARE OMITTED
00023             DATA RECORD IS LIST.
00024          01  LIST.
00025             03  FILLER         PIC X.
00026             03  LIST-LINE      PIC X(120).
```

As you can see from Figure 4-2, the file description contains several entries, some of which are dependent upon the particular computer you use. Some of the entries are required and some are optional but used nevertheless to provide good program documentation.

```
00017          FD  CARD-DATA
00018             LABEL RECORDS ARE OMITTED
00019             DATA RECORD IS CARD-IN.
00020          01  CARD-IN          PIC X(80).
```

The first entry after the FD indicates that LABEL RECORDS ARE OMITTED. This is a required entry and tells the system whether there is or is not a label associated with the file. Magnetic tape and disk storage devices do have labels (a series of magnetic spots, or bits, that indicate the name given to that particular file) that usually follow a standard format. (If we were using tape or disk, we would use the entry LABEL RECORDS ARE STANDARD.) However, card files and printer files do *not* have labels, and so our entry is correct in stating that LABEL RECORDS ARE OMITTED.

The next entry is one in which the programmer assigns a name to the series of incoming data records. Earlier, in the SELECT statement you named the entire *file of data*. Now you are naming the entire record (an 80-column card) of data. You must follow the rules of naming, and, in this case, the programmer has chosen the name CARD-IN. Note that the programmer could have chosen any name (except a reserved word) for the record, but could *not* have used CARD-DATA. CARD-DATA is the *file* name; CARD-IN is the *record* name. Also, note that the period is at the end of the *last* entry in the file description. Periods do *not* go at the end of each line in the FD entry.

Describing a record

As indicated above, you just finished assigning a name to a record. Immediately after this, the system must find an 01 entry beginning at card column 8. The 01 is required and is the programmer's way of telling the system that he or she is now ready to show how the record is broken into a series of fields. In our sample program the entry was extremely simple since the entire record (80 columns) was treated as a single field. In most cases, however, a record is comprised of many fields. Suppose our incoming data record was called STORE-DATA and looked as follows:

1 – 6	7 – 26	27 – 32	33 – 38	39 – 46	47 – 80
SLSM-NBR	SLSM-NAME	FILLER	MONTHLY-SALES	YTD-SALES	FILLER

We must start the record description with 01 since this number is reserved for a record as a whole. After this, the programmer has the chance to break the record into component fields. Following the diagram shown earlier, our complete record description entry is shown below.

```
01   STORE-DATA.
     03   SLSM-NBR            PIC 9(6).
     03   SLSM-NAME           PIC A(20).
     03   FILLER              PIC X(6).
     03   MONTHLY-SALES       PIC 9(4)V99.
     03   YTD-SALES           PIC 9(6)V99.
     03   FILLER              PIC X(34).
```

The 03 entries associated with each field named indicate that these fields are part of and subordinate to the whole record STORE-DATA. As a matter of fact, any number from 02 through 49 could have been used, but 02 or 03 is normally used for the next level of breakdown within a record.

The field names conform to the rules of naming and make some sort of sense so that a person reading the program could guess the contents of the field. The PIC clause (the full word PICTURE is also permissible) entries are usually lined up as an aid to detecting misspellings and other common key entry errors. The 9 entry indicates to the system that the field is numeric and is six digits long. Any of the entries in this area may be written with or without parentheses. For example, PIC 9(6) and PIC 999999 are equally correct. The second field is alphabetic, as designated by the letter A, and is 20 characters long.

The next entry describes a six-column blank field, or a field that may be punched but is not going to be used by the programmer. The reserved word FILLER is generally used for this purpose although the programmer could make up names for unused fields. The X indicates that the field could contain any type of character—numeric, alphabetic, or mixed alphanumeric.

The monthly sales field is obviously numeric and contains dollars and cents information. Decimal points are seldom punched into cards (it slows the data entry process), but the system must be informed of the location of the unpunched decimal point. This is done by means of the V character inserted in the PIC entry. PIC 9(4)V99 says that the numeric field is a total of six card columns wide and has two places to the right of the assumed, or implied, decimal point. The following field follows the same pattern except that it is eight digits long. The last entry simply accounts for the blank or unused portion of the card out to the 80th column.

A second example will illustrate another aspect of the breakdown of fields within a record. In this case, let's assume our card record is called DATE-RECORD and that the first six columns contain the date in the following form: month (two digits), day (two digits), and year (two digits). We could correctly describe the record as shown below.

```
01    DATE-RECORD.
      03    DATE-INFO   PIC 9(6).
      03    FILLER      PIC X(74).
```

In this case the DATE-INFO field is six digits long and can be handled only as a six-digit field. Thus, the PROCEDURE DIVISION statement

```
MOVE DATE-INFO TO DATE-AREA.
```

moves the entire six digits. With this arrangement there is no problem in handling the entire field, but it is not possible for the programmer to get to the two middle digits that represent the day information.

If the programmer had any idea that it might be necessary to process the sub-parts of the DATE-INFO field, he or she should have broken the field down further. One method is shown below.

```
01    DATE-RECORD.
      03    DATE-INFO.
            05    MONTH      PIC   99.
            05    DAY        PIC   99.
            05    YEAR       PIC   99.
      03    FILLER           PIC   X(74).
```

Now the programmer has the best of all possibilities. The PROCEDURE DIVISION statement

```
      MOVE DAY TO DAY-DATA.
```

moves only those two digits, while the statement

```
      MOVE DATE-INFO TO DATE-AREA.
```

moves the six digits that were subordinate to DATE-INFO. The system "understands" that DATE-INFO is comprised of lesser fields because of the numbering system. The 05 entries indicate a breakdown of the 03 entry. Also, note that the breakdown stops when the 03 is encountered again.

DATE-INFO is known as a *group* item because it is further broken down. A PIC entry *cannot* be used on a group item. MONTH, DAY, and YEAR are called *elementary* items because they are not broken down any further. A PIC entry *must* be used with every elementary item.

Describing a printer record

After this bit of a diversion into the description of records within a field, we should again look at the file entries in our sample program. As you would expect, we have a similar series of entries for our PRINT-FILE. Label records are omitted and the data record is called LIST. Subordinate to the record LIST is a very simple breakdown consisting of two entries. The first entry is typical on most printers in that a single position must be set aside for use by the system for controlling the spacing of the printer (single, double, triple spacing, etc.). This topic is discussed more fully in a later chapter. The second entry describes the width of a fairly standard print line of 120 characters.

Once more, it is important for you to realize the logical sequence of naming and describing the file, the record, and the fields, as shown for the CARD-DATA file in Figure 4-3. Naturally, the same process applies to the PRINTFILE entry.

FIGURE 4-3

Relationship of File Name and Record Name

```
00001              IDENTIFICATION DIVISION.
00002              PROGRAM-ID. LISTER.
00003         *
00004          ENVIRONMENT DIVISION.
00005          CONFIGURATION SECTION.
00006          SOURCE-COMPUTER. IBM-360-F30.
00007          OBJECT-COMPUTER. IBM-360-F30.
00008          INPUT-OUTPUT SECTION.
00009          FILE-CONTROL.
00010              SELECT CARD-DATA
00011                  ASSIGN TO SYS007-UR-2540R-S.
00012              SELECT PRINTFILE
00013                  ASSIGN TO SYS009-UR-1403-S.
00014         *
00015          DATA DIVISION.
00016          FILE SECTION.
00017          FD  CARD-DATA
00018              LABEL RECORDS ARE OMITTED
00019              DATA RECORD IS CARD-IN.
00020          01  CARD-IN          PIC X(80).
00021          FD  PRINTFILE
00022              LABEL RECORDS ARE OMITTED
00023              DATA RECORD IS LIST.
00024          01  LIST.
00025              03  FILLER       PIC X.
00026              03  LIST-LINE    PIC X(120).
```

Common errors

In this section you will see some of the common errors that are made in the first three divisions. All the errors are simple ones, but notice the messages generated by the computer. Remember that your computer system may come up with error messages different from the ones shown, but the messages are fairly representative of those found on any system.

Each message refers to a card or line number so that you can find it quickly. In addition, the message is usually preceded by a number so that further information concerning the message could be looked up in a technical manual. The letter at the end of the message number indicates the severity of the error.

w, or Warning, level errors are provided for the programmer's interest, but normally will have no effect on the compilation or execution of the program. C, or Conditional, level errors may affect the execution of the program, but are not severe enough to stop compilation of the program. E for Execution level errors are serious enough to prevent execution, and compiling continues only in an effort to identify further errors. (Different systems may use different letters, such as S for Severe, F for Fatal, or D for Disaster level errors.)

The first error results when the SELECT file name in line 12 (PRINT-FILE) does not agree with the FD name (PRINTFILE) in line 21 (Figure 4-4). The error is so serious (E level) that the program is terminated after compilation. The problem is easily corrected by repunching one of the cards so that the names agree. Note that the error is indicated as line 23 because this is the end of the FD three-line entry.

FIGURE 4-4

Sample Program—Error One

```
00001              IDENTIFICATION DIVISION.
00002              PROGRAM-ID. LISTER.
00003         *
00004              ENVIRONMENT DIVISION.
00005              CONFIGURATION SECTION.
00006              SOURCE-COMPUTER. IBM-360-F30.
00007              OBJECT-COMPUTER. IBM-360-F30.
00008              INPUT-OUTPUT SECTION.
00009              FILE-CONTROL.
00010                  SELECT CARD-DATA
00011                      ASSIGN TO SYS007-UR-2540R-S.
00012                  SELECT PRINT-FILE
00013                      ASSIGN TO SYS009-UR-1403-S.
00014         *
00015              DATA DIVISION.
00016              FILE SECTION.
00017              FD  CARD-DATA
00018                  LABEL RECORDS ARE OMITTED
00019                  DATA RECORD IS CARD-IN.
00020              01  CARD-IN          PIC X(80).
00021              FD  PRINTFILE
00022                  LABEL RECORDS ARE OMITTED
00023                  DATA RECORD IS LIST.
00024              01  LIST.
00025                  03  FILLER       PIC X.
00026                  03  LIST-LINE    PIC X(120).

CARD    ERROR MESSAGE
23      ILA1056I-E    FILE-NAME NOT DEFINED IN A SELECT.
                      DESCRIPTION IGNORED.
```

The next error is very simple: misspelling the word ENVIRONMENT in the DIVISION entry. Although it generates an E level error just as the other mistake did, the error has deeper consequences. As Figure 4-5 shows, the system ignores *all* ENVIRONMENT DIVISION entries even though they are correct. Accordingly, the next entry it considers is for the DATA DIVISION, but the COBOL compiler is still expecting to find the ENVIRONMENT DIVISION line. Also, since the entire ENVIRONMENT DIVISION entries were ignored, the system is not aware of the file assignments for CARD-DATA and PRINTFILE.

FIGURE 4-5

Sample Program—Error Two

```
00001          IDENTIFICATION DIVISION.
00002          PROGRAM-ID. LISTER.
00003          *
00004          ENVIROMENT DIVISION.
00005          CONFIGURATION SECTION.
00006          SOURCE-COMPUTER. IBM-360-F30.
00007          OBJECT-COMPUTER. IBM-360-F30.
00008          INPUT-OUTPUT SECTION.
00009          FILE-CONTROL.
00010              SELECT CARD-DATA
00011                  ASSIGN TO SYS007-UR-2540R-S.
00012              SELECT PRINTFILE
00013                  ASSIGN TO SYS009-UR-1403-S.
00014          *
00015          DATA DIVISION.
00016          FILE SECTION.
00017          FD  CARD-DATA
00018              LABEL RECORDS ARE OMITTED
00019              DATA RECORD IS CARD-IN.
00020          01  CARD-IN          PIC X(80).
00021          FD  PRINTFILE
00022              LABEL RECORDS ARE OMITTED
00023              DATA RECORD IS LIST.
00024          01  LIST.
00025              03  FILLER       PIC X.
00026              03  LIST-LINE    PIC X(120).
```

```
CARD    ERROR MESSAGE

4       ILA1087I-W    ' ENVIROMENT ' SHOULD NOT BEGIN IN AREA A.
15      ILA1026I-W    FOUND DATA . EXPECTING ENVIRONMENT. ALL ENV.
                          DIV. STATEMENTS IGNORED.
19      ILA1056I-E    FILE-NAME NOT DEFINED IN A SELECT. DESCRIPTION
                          IGNORED.
23      ILA1056I-E    FILE-NAME NOT DEFINED IN A SELECT. DESCRIPTION
                          IGNORED.
```

The third error illustrates yet another keypunching mistake. In this case the programmer has struck the letter "O" instead of the numeric zero in line 11. Errors of this type are hard to detect, so be careful with zero and the letter "O" (Figure 4-6).

FIGURE 4-6

Sample Program—Error Three

```
00001                    IDENTIFICATION DIVISION.
00002                    PROGRAM-ID. LISTER.
00003           *
00004                    ENVIRONMENT DIVISION.
00005                    CONFIGURATION SECTION.
00006                    SOURCE-COMPUTER. IBM-360-F30.
00007                    OBJECT-COMPUTER. IBM-360-F30.
00008                    INPUT-OUTPUT SECTION.
00009                    FILE-CONTROL.
00010                        SELECT CARD-DATA
00011                            ASSIGN TO SYSOO7-UR-2540R-S.
00012                        SELECT PRINTFILE
00013                            ASSIGN TO SYS009-UR-1403-S.
00014           *
00015                    DATA DIVISION.
00016                    FILE SECTION.
00017                    FD   CARD-DATA
00018                         LABEL RECORDS ARE OMITTED
00019                         DATA RECORD IS CARD-IN.
00020                    01   CARD-IN           PIC X(80).
00021                    FD   PRINTFILE
00022                         LABEL RECORDS ARE OMITTED
00023                         DATA RECORD IS LIST.
00024                    01   LIST.
00025                         03   FILLER       PIC X.
00026                         03   LIST-LINE    PIC X(120).
```

```
CARD    ERROR MESSAGE

11      ILA1132I-E      INVALID SYSTEM-NAME. SKIPPING TO NEXT CLAUSE.
19      ILA1056I-E      FILE-NAME NOT DEFINED IN A SELECT. DESCRIPTION
                            IGNORED.
```

The fourth, and last, of the common errors in this section involves placing a period in the wrong place. Remember that the period in an FD entry goes at the end of the last line. Usually this will be the line DATA RECORD IS _____ . An incorrectly placed period or an additional period will cause a severe error, as Figure 4-7 shows.

FIGURE 4-7

Sample Program—Error Four

```
00001                    IDENTIFICATION DIVISION.
00002                    PROGRAM-ID. LISTER.
00003           *
00004                    ENVIRONMENT DIVISION.
00005                    CONFIGURATION SECTION.
00006                    SOURCE-COMPUTER. IBM-360-F30.
00007                    OBJECT-COMPUTER. IBM-360-F30.
00008                    INPUT-OUTPUT SECTION.
00009                    FILE-CONTROL.
00010                        SELECT CARD-DATA
00011                            ASSIGN TO SYS007-UR-2540R-S.
00012                        SELECT PRINTFILE
00013                            ASSIGN TO SYS009-UR-1403-S.
00014           *
00015                    DATA DIVISION.
00016                    FILE SECTION.
00017                    FD  CARD-DATA.
00018                        LABEL RECORDS ARE OMITTED.
00019                        DATA RECORD IS CARD-IN.
00020           01  CARD-IN            PIC X(80).
```

CARD   ERROR MESSAGE

10   ILA2133I-C   LABEL RECORDS CLAUSE INVALID OR MISSING.
                          OMITTED ASSUMED.
18   ILA1004I-E   INVALID WORD LABEL . SKIPPING TO NEXT
                          RECOGNIZABLE WORD.

Problem-Solving Techniques

For most beginners the IDENTIFICATION and ENVIRONMENT divisions cause no difficulty at all. The data files that will be used by your program have been indicated, or in some way described, in a statement of the problem that was given to you by the instructor. Even if you think you understand the problem, a good technique at this point is to draw yourself a quick, simple diagram of the files that will be used. The diagram doesn't have to be a work of art—it is just for you to get a better visual picture of what is happening. As shown below, label the diagram with the file names to reinforce the idea even further.

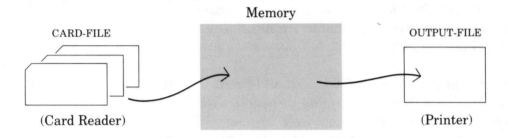

Now, on to the DATA DIVISION, which is an entirely different matter. It starts out easily enough since you know that for each file appearing in a SELECT entry in the ENVIRONMENT DIVISION you must have an FD entry in the DATA DIVISION. The first entries are standard, but the big question is "How far should I break down the fields within the record?" Of course, there is no set answer to that question, other than "It depends".

The degree of breakdown of fields in the DATA DIVISION depends upon the use you expect to make of these fields in the PROCEDURE DIVISION. If you think you will have to work with subfields (such as MONTH, DAY, and YEAR) within a field, then break it down now. If you are not sure, then don't break it down. After all, you can always go back to the DATA DIVISION later and make the changes necessitated by your statements in the PROCEDURE DIVISION.

Self-Study: Questions and Answers

1. Explain again the difference between the SOURCE-COMPUTER and OBJECT-COMPUTER entries. I don't see the need for both entries.

   Answer
   If you recall, the COBOL program you write is called a Source program. It is translated by the COBOL Compiler, and the output from the compiler software is known as an Object program. It is this Object program that actually gets run, or executed, on the computer. Perhaps well over 99% of the time you will compile your program on the same computer (Source computer) on which it is executed (Object computer). In these cases the two entries in the CONFIGURATION will be the same. On those rare occasions when the compiling and executing computer are not the same, COBOL provides for this possibility.

2. I understand that the purpose of a SELECT statement is to give a name to a file of data that will be going through a specific input/output device. However, it seems that every example I have ever seen shows names like CARD-FILE, PRINTFILE, TAPE-FILE, and so on. Do I have to use the FILE in the name?

   Answer
   No, you don't have to use the word FILE at all in the file name. However, since it actually is a file, it is good practice to do so because it makes it easier for you and anyone who reads your program to understand that it is a *file* and nothing else.

3. Several times in the chapter you stressed the relationship between files, records, and fields. It seems simple enough, but is it really that important?

   Answer
   It sure is! As the section on common errors showed, one simple mistake in this area gets compounded because of the file-record-field relationship. Unfortunately, this seems to be an area of some confusion, or at least an area in which students make many errors.

The real problem is not so much one of making errors. Usually, the errors are few and easily corrected. The difficulty is that a single error may generate perhaps as many as ten error messages. For many students—particularly those who don't understand the file-record-field relationship—the multiple error messages are extremely discouraging.

4. Do the FD entries in the FILE SECTION have to be in the same order as the SELECT statements?

Answer

No, they don't, but every SELECT must have an FD entry. Still, it is good practice to do the FD entries in the same order as the SELECT entries so that they are easy to find and so that you don't forget any of them.

5. Could you explain a little more about a file label. Why isn't there a label on card or print files?

Answer

In a beginning text we can't go thoroughly into labels, but perhaps a few comments will relieve your mind on the question. Card and printer files do not have labels simply because there is no room or place for them. On disk and tape, however, an area is set aside for label data. When the programmer creates a file, he or she gives the file a name, such as "Inventory Data," and this is written magnetically on the recording surface. Later, when a program tries to access a particular file, the label is checked by the system to be sure that the correct reel or disk was mounted on the I/O device. If the label does not match, the job is automatically canceled.

6. In describing a file, how do I know how far to break down the fields within the record?

Answer

First, remember that the programmer *always* knows the makeup of the fields within a record. By "makeup" we mean the order within the record, the size, and type of each field. After this, the answer to your question is that you learn with experience. If you have analyzed thoroughly what will be required in the PROCEDURE DIVISION, you will know just how far to break down the fields. If you have not done a good job of analysis, you will get into the PROCEDURE DIVISION and find that you cannot do what you want because of the lack of a thorough breakdown. Actually, this isn't as bad as it sounds, since all you have to do is go back to the DATA DIVISION and make some new entries.

7. Since a field described as X can contain any type of character, why can't I just use PIC X for every field?

   Answer

   Technically you could do so, but don't—it is a bad habit to get into. The problem is that a field with a picture of X cannot be worked upon arithmetically. So the general rule is that, unless you have an extraordinary reason for not doing so, you make all numeric fields PIC 9. This would be true even for numeric fields (such as an ID number) that are not going to be processed arithmetically. By identifying them as PIC 9, there is no doubt to anyone else that the field is numeric.

Exercises

1. Define or explain each of the following terms or phrases.
   a. File name
   b. Record name
   c. Field name
   d. SOURCE-COMPUTER
   e. OBJECT-COMPUTER
   f. The function of the SELECT entry
   g. The function of the ASSIGN entry
   h. FILLER
   i. PICTURE, or PIC
   j. Reserved word

2. Indicate whether the following entries are correct or incorrect. If the statement is incorrect, change it so it is correct.
   a. IDENTIFICATION DIVISION
   b. PROGRAM-ID. NBR ONE.
   c. PROGRAM ID. LISTER.
   d. CONFIGURATION SECTION.
   e. ENVIROMENT DIVISION
   f. FD OUTPUT-FILE
      LABEL RECORDS ARE OMITTED
      DATA RECORD IS OUTPUT-LINE.

3. The following problems involve a SELECT entry. You are to write the appropriate DATA DIVISION entries through DATA RECORD IS for each SELECT.
   a. SELECT CARD-FILE ASSIGN TO SYS-INPUT.
   b. SELECT PRINTER ASSIGN TO SYSLST.

4. The following problems involve the FD entries as shown. Write the appropriate SELECT entry.
   a. Printer output on system device 003, which is a 1403 printer.

```
FD   PRINTED-DATA
     LABEL RECORDS ARE OMITTED
     DATA RECORD IS PR-DATA.
```

b. Card input on system device 011, which is a 1442 card reader.

```
FD   INPUT-FILE
     LABEL RECORDS ARE OMITTED
     DATA RECORD IS STANDARD-CARD.
```

c. Printer output on system device SYSPRINT.

```
FD   OUTPUT-FILE-DATA
     LABEL RECORDS ARE OMITTED
     DATA RECORD IS INVENTORY-RECORD.
```

5. In the next exercise you are to write the record description based on the following information: Record name is Inventory-data. Fields are as follows.

Card Column	Field Description
1–10	Part number
11–15	Blank
16–30	Part name
31–35	Bin number
36–40	Shelf number
41–79	Blank
80	One character code field

6. Write the record description based on the following information: Record name is Employee-record. Fields are as follows.

Card Column	Field Description
1–20	Blank
21–29	Social security number
30–50	Name
51–70	Address
71–72	Numeric pay code
73–80	Blank

7. Modify Exercise 6 so that the social security number is broken down into its component parts. Each of these fields must be at the elementary level, but also create a social security number field so that the whole field can be moved by a single instruction.

8. Explain the difference between an assumed (or implied) decimal point and a real decimal point.

9. Write the PICTURE entry for the following numeric values.
   a. 3645
   b. 0039
   c. 156.93
   d. 0001.75
   e. 00.01
   f. .456
   g. .00059

10. Define or explain each of the following terms or phrases. If necessary, use examples or diagrams in your answers.
    a. FD
    b. 01
    c. Group item
    d. Elementary item
    e. LABEL RECORDS ARE OMITTED
    f. LABEL RECORDS ARE STANDARD
    g. 02–49

11. Write the *complete* FD and record description based on the following information: file name is CARD-FILE; record name is ACCOUNT-CARD. Fields are as follows and decimal points are *not* punched in the card.

Card Column	Field Description
1–7	Account number
9–13	Location code (all numeric)
14–19	Retail price (dollar and cents figure)
21–30	Blank
30–35	Cost price (dollar and cents figure)
36–45	Item description
46–50	Salesperson code (mixed numeric and alphabetic)
51–55	Credit code—numeric
56–80	Blank

Chapter 5

The PROCEDURE DIVISION—

Part I

The PROCEDURE DIVISION usually is the most interesting part of a COBOL program because it is here that the programmer finally gets the chance to direct the computer to perform specific operations such as adding, subtracting, and so on. However, the ease or difficulty of programming in the PROCEDURE DIVISION is, to a great extent, dependent upon how well you have laid out the files, records, and fields you will be using.

By now you should be thoroughly familiar with the individual statements in the first three divisions of our sample program, but let's see the whole COBOL program, including the PROCEDURE DIVISION (Figure 5-1).

FIGURE 5-1

Sample Program

```
      IDENTIFICATION DIVISION.
      PROGRAM-ID. LISTER.
*
      ENVIRONMENT DIVISION.
      CONFIGURATION SECTION.
      SOURCE-COMPUTER. IBM-360-F30.
      OBJECT-COMPUTER. IBM-360-F30.
      INPUT-OUTPUT SECTION.
      FILE-CONTROL.
          SELECT CARD-DATA
              ASSIGN TO SYS007-UR-2540R-S.
          SELECT PRINTFILE
              ASSIGN TO SYS009-UR-1403-S.
*
      DATA DIVISION.
      FILE SECTION.
      FD   CARD-DATA
           LABEL RECORDS ARE OMITTED
           DATA RECORD IS CARD-IN.
      01   CARD-IN            PIC X(80).
      FD   PRINTFILE
           LABEL RECORDS ARE OMITTED
           DATA RECORD IS LIST.
      01   LIST.
           03   FILLER        PIC X.
           03   LIST-LINE     PIC X(120).
      WORKING-STORAGE SECTION.
      77   INDICATOR          PIC 9 VALUE ZERO.
*
      PROCEDURE DIVISION.
      CONTROL-ROUTINE.
          PERFORM 010-OPENER.
          PERFORM 020-READER UNTIL
              INDICATOR = 1.
          PERFORM 030-CLOSER.
          STOP RUN.
      010-OPENER.
          OPEN INPUT CARD-DATA
              OUTPUT PRINTFILE.
          READ CARD-DATA
              AT END MOVE 1 TO INDICATOR.
      020-READER.
          MOVE CARD-IN TO LIST-LINE.
          WRITE LIST AFTER ADVANCING 2 LINES.
          READ CARD-DATA
              AT END MOVE 1 TO INDICATOR.
      030-CLOSER.
          MOVE 'END OF PROGRAM' TO LIST-LINE.
          WRITE LIST AFTER ADVANCING 3 LINES.
          CLOSE CARD-DATA, PRINTFILE.
```

Paragraph headers

COBOL was designed to closely resemble the English language, and, as a result, many of the terms are taken from English grammar. The individual instructions are called *statements* and a series of logically related statements are headed by *paragraph headers*. In the sample program, CONTROL-ROUTINE, 010-OPENER, 020-READER, and 030-CLOSER are paragraph headers. They follow the rules of naming that have been discussed before, and are created by the programmer as needed.

The first paragraph header is our control module, which was discussed in the top-down section presented earlier in the text. Complete control of the program occurs from this paragraph.

The second header (010-OPENER) is there because the programmer wanted to show, set aside, or document the fact that he or she was doing some opening, or "housekeeping," activities prior to getting into the main part of the program.

The third header (020-READER) not only separates one part of the program from another, but also provides a point for the programmer to branch to later on. A quick look at all the statements within the PROCEDURE DIVISION shows that this paragraph is the heart of the program. It is here that we move the contents of the card to the output line, print it, and read another card. Since this is a task that we wish to repeat over and over, we use the UNTIL version of the PERFORM statement to control the looping process, which executes that paragraph over and over until there are no more data cards.

The last header (030-CLOSER) establishes the ending paragraph, which will be executed when the READ statement recognizes that the last valid data card has been processed.

By now you are probably wondering why the headers are numbered. They don't have to be numbered at all, but it is good programming practice to do so since you can waste a great amount of time trying to find a particular paragraph header in a long program. If they are numbered in some logical way, the task is much easier. Remember, however, that the number is part of the paragraph name.

The time has come to get down to the specifics of the individual COBOL statements in our sample program. You will find that most of these statements are easy to learn and remember.

Program statements

In general, COBOL statements can be grouped into a few broad categories: input/output, data movement, arithmetic, sequence control, and miscellaneous. Our sample program used seven statements that are basic to almost every program. In describing and explaining these statements, we will follow the rules concerning format.

1. Uppercase words, such as OPEN, READ, WRITE, and so on, are reserved words. If underlined, they are required when the entry is used.
2. Lowercase words, such as *file name,* are words, or terms, chosen by the programmer.
3. Brackets [ ] enclose entries that are optional.
4. Braces { } are used to indicate that a choice is to be made between two or more clauses.
5. Ellipses . . . indicate repetition of an entry.

For example, the first statement that will be discussed is OPEN, which has the following format:

$$\text{OPEN} \quad \left\{ \begin{array}{l} \underline{\text{INPUT}} \\ \underline{\text{OUTPUT}} \end{array} \right\} \text{file-name-1} \ldots$$

The format indicates that the word OPEN is required and that the programmer must make a choice between the words INPUT and OUTPUT followed by a programmer-supplied file name. The ellipses indicate that the process in braces may be repeated.

The OPEN and CLOSE statements

Both the OPEN and CLOSE statements are very simple as far as the programmer is concerned, but are very complex in their internal operations. The OPEN statement causes the system software to get the file ready for processing and has the following format:

$$\text{OPEN} \quad \left\{ \begin{array}{l} \underline{\text{INPUT}} \\ \underline{\text{OUTPUT}} \end{array} \right\} \text{file-name-1} \ldots$$

In our sample program the statement is written as:

```
OPEN INPUT CARD-DATA OUTPUT PRINTFILE.
```

Commas may be inserted in COBOL statements if you feel they are needed, but they have no effect on the statement.

Example:

```
OPEN INPUT CARD-DATA, OUTPUT PRINTFILE.
```

Multiple OPEN statements are also permissible although it is generally more efficient to use a single OPEN statement.

Example:

```
OPEN INPUT CARD-DATA.
OPEN OUTPUT PRINTFILE.
```

The CLOSE statement performs the reverse function in that it closes files that have been previously OPENed. It differs from the OPEN statement in that you *must not* indicate whether the file is INPUT or OUTPUT; CLOSE followed by the file name(s) is sufficient.

Example:

```
CLOSE CARD-DATA PRINTFILE.
```

The following is incorrect:

Example:

```
CLOSE INPUT CARD-DATA OUTPUT PRINTFILE.
```

Also, as with OPEN statements, multiple CLOSE statements may be used.

The READ statement

For sequential files such as cards, the READ statement brings the next available record into memory. (For nonsequential files the operation is a little different and will not be considered here.) To be more specific, the data record is brought into the memory area you set aside in the DATA DIVISION when you said DATA RECORD is CARD-IN. It is from this input area that you are able to manipulate the various fields by means of statements such as ADD, SUBTRACT, MOVE, and so forth. Figure 5-2 shows a schematic of this basic form of the READ statement.

FIGURE 5-2

Schematic: READ Operation

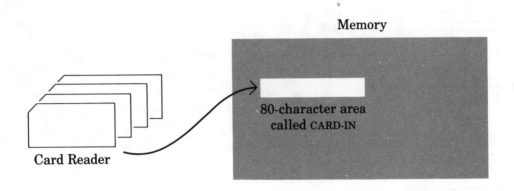

When a card is read in, the *whole* card enters memory, not just those fields you want to work with. In our sample program we have no need for breaking the record into fields, so the whole record is treated as a single field. On the other hand, if we had a card record such as that shown in Chapter 4, the only difference would be that the record would be divided into a series of fields, as shown in Figure 5-3.

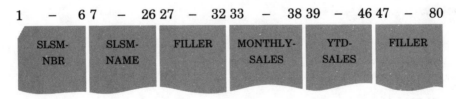

```
01   STORE-DATA.
     03   SLSM-NBR            PIC 9(6).
     03   SLSM-NAME           PIC A(20).
     03   FILLER              PIC X(6).
     03   MONTHLY-SALES       PIC 9(4)V99.
     03   YTD-SALES           PIC 9(6)V99.
     03   FILLER              PIC X(34).
```

FIGURE 5-3

Read-in Area Showing Fields within the Record

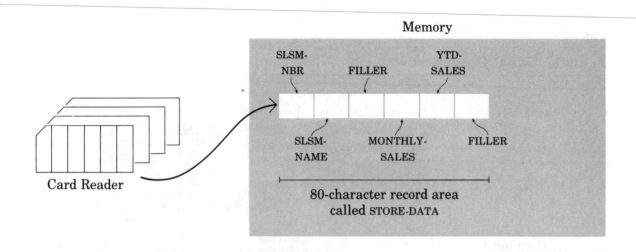

The READ statement, when used with sequential files, requires the words AT END followed by one or more COBOL statements. The basic format of the statement is shown below.

<u>READ</u> file-name AT <u>END</u> statement(s)

The AT END clause is necessary because the system must know what to do after the last data card has passed through the card reader. The system detects this "last card" condition because of the /* job control card that was inserted immediately after the last data card, as shown below.

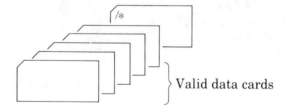

In effect, the AT END situation is triggered when your program executes the READ statement once too often. In this case the system detects the /* card and activates the AT END portion of the statement. Actually, the COBOL software is looking for the /* card *every* time the READ statement is executed, but will find it only after the last card has been processed.

In the sample program the AT END entry is followed by a single statement—MOVE. Technically, the AT END may be followed by any number of COBOL statements—not just one, and not always MOVE. For example, the following sequence of statements is correct. (Note that the period appears at the end of the series of statements you want executed.)

```
READ CARD-DATA
    AT END
            MOVE 'END OF DATA' TO LIST-LINE
            WRITE LIST AFTER ADVANCING 2 LINES.
```

The MOVE statement

The MOVE might very well be the most used statement in COBOL. As with most COBOL statements, it is simple but does a lot of work for the programmer. Generally, it makes a *copy* of a data field and moves this copy to another location. Wherever this copy arrives, it destroys the old value that was in the receiving area. Note that the sending field data remains the same.

The simplest form of the MOVE statement uses a figurative constant. The statement

```
MOVE SPACES TO LIST
```

causes the correct number of spaces to be moved into the area called LIST. In the sample program we used the statement

```
MOVE CARD-IN TO LIST-LINE.
```

In this case the contents of the card input area (80 characters) are moved into the area called LIST-LINE (120 characters), as shown below.

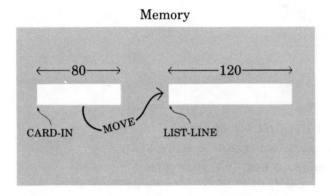

Memory

Both fields were defined as PIC X, and when one PIC X field is moved into another, the move goes from left to right and the remaining characters on the right (if any) are cleared to spaces.

Examples

```
MOVE FIELD-A TO FIELD-B.
```

		Before	After
1.	FIELD-A PIC X(8)	15 R ST.	15 R ST.
	FIELD-B PIC X(8)	ABCDEFGH	15 R ST.

Both fields are the same size and the incoming data replaces the old data in FIELD-B.

		Before	After
2.	FIELD-A PIC X(8)	15 R ST.	15 R ST.
	FIELD-B PIC X(10)	ABCDEFGHIJ	15 R ST. BB

The receiving field is larger and the extra positions on the right are automatically filled with blanks.

		Before	After
3.	FIELD-A PIC X(8)	15 R ST.	15 R ST.
	FIELD-B PIC X(6)	ABCDEF	15 R S

The receiving field is too small and the first six characters are moved in from left to right. The right most two characters are lost (truncated) and the compiler produces an error message during compilation.

In the sample program we showed another way of moving non-numeric data to a field: by means of a literal. The statement

```
MOVE 'END OF PROGRAM' TO LIST-LINE
```

moves the actual characters END OF PROGRAM from left to right into the 120-character LIST-LINE area. The extra positions on the right are automatically filled with blanks.

When numeric fields are moved, the action is a little different since the system automatically aligns the data on the decimal point.

Examples

MOVE NUMBER—A TO NUMBER—B.

		Before	After
1.	NUMBER-A PIC 999V99	123$_\wedge$45	123$_\wedge$45
	NUMBER-B PIC 999V99	777$_\wedge$77	123$_\wedge$45

Both fields are of the same size, and the numeric values are aligned on the assumed (V) decimal point.

		Before	After
2.	NUMBER-A PIC 999V99	123$_\wedge$45	123$_\wedge$45
	NUMBER-B PIC 9999V999	7777$_\wedge$777	0123$_\wedge$450

The receiving field is larger on both sides of the decimal point, and the system automatically inserts zeros at both ends.

		Before	After
3.	NUMBER-A PIC 999V99	123$_\wedge$45	123$_\wedge$45
	NUMBER-B PIC 99V9	77$_\wedge$7	23$_\wedge$4

The receiving field is smaller on both sides of the decimal point and a digit is lost at both ends. On most systems the software will produce an error message during compilation.

A variety of other MOVE options are possible and are covered in later chapters.

The WRITE statement

The purpose of the WRITE statement is to send a data record to an output device such as a printer, card punch, tape, or disk. For the printer, the most common form is

```
WRITE record name
    {BEFORE}  ADVANCING integer LINES.
    {AFTER }
```

Note that the READ statement reads a *file name* while the WRITE statement writes a *record name*. In our sample program we moved the CARD-IN record to LIST-LINE and then wrote the *record* with the following statement:

```
WRITE LIST
     AFTER ADVANCING 2 LINES.
```

The following is *incorrect* since it does not use the record name:

```
WRITE LIST-LINE
     AFTER ADVANCING 2 LINES.
```

Earlier in the text we said that the programmer normally sets aside one character just before the beginning of the print line for system use. (Not all systems work this way, so check your machine to be sure.) The operation is quite simple and logical. The system looks at the number of lines you wish to advance (such as two lines in this case) and generates a single character that is inserted into the one position area located just before the print line. Then, when this line of 121 characters (1 + 120) is sent to the printer, the printer "knows" how many lines to advance.

Please note that if you fail to set aside room for this extra character, the system will take it anyway. Therefore, if your printout seems to be missing the first character, the chances are very good that you forgot about the one character printer requirement. ANS 74 COBOL permits the use of both LINE (singular) and LINES (plural), but older COBOL versions use only the plural form LINES. On these systems you must always use LINES even when spacing only a single line. The correct COBOL format then becomes

```
WRITE LIST AFTER ADVANCING 1 LINES.
```

Check your system concerning this requirement.

The PERFORM and PERFORM UNTIL statements

The PERFORM statement has many variations, or options, that may be strung together to provide a very versatile statement. The simple form of PERFORM is

```
PERFORM paragraph-name.
```

Example

```
PERFORM 010-OPENER-ROUTINE.
ADD 1 TO COUNTER-A.
```

Upon encountering the PERFORM statement, the system goes to the 010-OPENER-ROUTINE paragraph in your program, executes the statements in that paragraph, and *automatically returns* to the next statement in sequence after PERFORM.

All variations of the PERFORM statement follow this same pattern of branching out to the paragraph, executing the paragraph, and returning. In flowcharting this statement it is customary to provide some indication that an entire module, or routine, paragraph was PERFORMed.

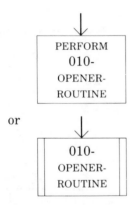

In the second example the vertical lines indicated that this is a PERFORMed paragraph. This arrangement also means that the processing steps in the 010-OPENER-ROUTINE will have to be flowcharted separately, as shown below.

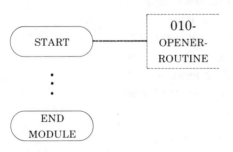

The second form of the PERFORM statement—PERFORM UNTIL—allows us to use the controlled loop structure discussed earlier in Chapter 2.

> PERFORM paragraph-name
>   UNTIL test condition

This is how the controlled loop structure was shown in flowchart form earlier in the chapter.

The flowchart of the DOWHILE or controlled loop structure exactly fits the action of the PERFORM UNTIL statement.

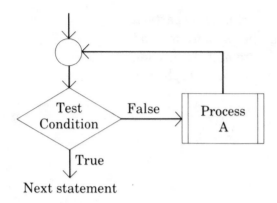

Example

```
PERFORM READ-LOOP-MODULE
    UNTIL END-INDICATOR = 1.
```

When the system reaches the PERFORM UNTIL statement, it checks the condition *first* (as shown by the flowchart). This is a critical point because the result of the test determines whether or not READ-LOOP-MODULE will be executed. If the result of the test is false—that is, the END-INDICATOR field is *not* equal to 1—the module will be PERFORMed. If END-INDICATOR *is* equal to 1, the paragraph is *not* PERFORMed and the system will go to the next statement in sequence.

Now let's get back to a very critical idea we skimmed over in Chapter 2. At that time we presented the same sample program you just saw in Figure 5-1 and we noted that the program contained two READ statements: one in the 010-OPENER paragraph and one at the end of the 020-READER paragraph. On the surface it appears foolish to have the first READ at all. Why not make things easier and simply omit the first READ and then move the *second* read up to the top of the 020-READER paragraph, as shown below?

```
010-OPENER.
    OPEN ————
020-READER.
    READ ————
        AT END MOVE 1 TO INDICATOR.
    MOVE ———— .
    WRITE ———— .
```

This approach will work for a while, but then we run into a problem because of the way in which the PERFORM UNTIL statement works. Quite correctly the system will PERFORM the 020-READER paragraph until INDICATOR = 1. For example, on the first card the condition of the INDICATOR field will be tested before the system goes back to again execute the 020-READER paragraph. But what happens *after* the last card has been processed? The sequence of events is as follows—pay particular attention to steps four, five, and six:

1. The last valid data card is read.
2. The data are moved to the output area.
3. A line of data is written.
4. The system checks the INDICATOR field to see if it contains a value of 1. Since it does not, the 020-READER paragraph will be PERFORMED again.
5. The system now reads in the end-of-file card (/*), which activates the AT END portion of the READ statement and moves a 1 to INDICATOR.
6. The problem is that the system can't get back to the PERFORM UNTIL to do this testing until *it comes to the end of the 020-READER paragraph*. Thus, even though the value of the INDICATOR is changed to 1 right away, the MOVE and WRITE statements in the remainder of that paragraph will be executed and invalid data will be moved and printed.

The solution to the problem is to put the READ statement at the *end* of the paragraph so that the INDICATOR can be tested as soon as that statement is completed. In order to make this plan work, we must have an *extra* READ statement that is executed *before* going into the 020-READER paragraph loop. Note that this statement is placed in the 010-OPENER paragraph to act as the "priming" sort of device so that the 020-READER paragraph can use the sequence MOVE-WRITE-READ.

The STOP statement

The STOP statement terminates the execution of your program and normally transfers control to the system software. The format for most machines is as indicated below.

    STOP RUN.

Structured programming and the GO TO statement

The GO TO statement is an unconditional branch statement that is used to transfer control to another point in the program. The format of the statement is very simple.

    GO TO paragraph header.

Note that you cannot branch to a data area nor can you branch directly to a program statement. Instead, you must branch to the paragraph that contains the statement or statements you wish to execute. In recent years this COBOL statement has fallen into disrepute, although virtually every programming language has GO TO or a closely related statement. With the advent of top-down design and structured programming techniques, the use of GO TO has been nearly eliminated. The problem of the past use of GO TO was that programmers were under no obligation to thoroughly plan the program logic. Instead, if they came to a dead-end situation, they could simply insert a GO TO and, in effect, apply patches to a poorly planned program. These programs became a thicket of GO TO statements that were nightmares to maintain.

A top-down, structured program on the other hand can be followed from beginning to end by reference to a control module that develops the program structure in an orderly fashion. With this approach the programmer does not have to make a conscious effort to eliminate GO TOS. They simply aren't there because the regular logic structures are sufficient.

As nice as all this sounds, you should be aware that not all programmers and managers are in total agreement as to exactly what constitutes a structured program. In general they all agree that a "good" program is correct, readable, and easily maintained. To some, this means, among other things, *no* GO TO statements. Other managers, however, take a more liberal view and permit the use of GO TO statements in those places where they think their use makes for more clear and simple code. Generally this means limited use of GO TO in conjunction with the THRU variation of the PERFORM UNTIL statement. In all of this discussion, remember that the key point is to produce clear, understandable COBOL code.

Many data processing professionals feel that the READ-MOVE-WRITE sequence is more logical and natural than the "priming" READ followed by the MOVE-WRITE-READ sequence. Therefore, they are willing to permit the limited use of the GO TO statement to overcome the problem of how to skip over a series of program statements once the AT END situation is detected. In their method the "priming" READ is eliminated entirely because of the combined action of a PERFORM THRU and a "downward" GO TO statement.

PERFORM THRU and the EXIT statement

The simple version of the PERFORM THRU statement is as follows.

<u>PERFORM</u> paragraph name <u>THRU</u> paragraph name.

Example

```
PERFORM 050-READ-ROUTINE
    THRU 090-PRINT-ROUTINE.
```

In this example the system performs (executes) all the paragraphs beginning with 050-READ-ROUTINE down through 090-PRINT-ROUTINE. Any paragraphs within the range of the two named paragraphs are executed.

The UNTIL option simply adds a test to the operation by specifying that paragraphs A through B will be executed repeatedly until a particular test is met.

Example

```
PERFORM 050-READ-ROUTINE
    THRU 090-PRINT-ROUTINE
    UNTIL INDICATOR = 1.
```

The major drawback to the THRU version of PERFORM is that the whole operation—that is, the success of the whole program—is dependent upon the paragraphs being in the right place. For structured purists this is not tolerable in that individual paragraphs, or modules, should be able to be located anywhere in the program.

The non-purist gets around this problem by stipulating that PER-FORM THRU can only be used with another programming statement—EXIT. The EXIT statement consists of just the single word—EXIT—and it must appear in a paragraph by itself. No other statement may appear in a paragraph that contains EXIT. Furthermore, managers who allow these coding variations generally permit only *downward* GO TO statements. We can now put all three of these ideas together (PERFORM THRU, EXIT, downward GO TO) to reconstruct our sample program that appeared in Chapter 2.

```
    77  INDICATOR            PIC 9 VALUE ZERO.
  *
    PROCEDURE DIVISION.
    CONTROL-ROUTINE.
        PERFORM 010-OPENER.
        PERFORM 020-READER
            THRU 020-EXIT
            UNTIL INDICATOR = 1.
        PERFORM 030-CLOSER.
        STOP RUN.
    010-OPENER.
        OPEN INPUT CARD-DATA
            OUTPUT PRINTFILE.
    020-READER.
        READ CARD-DATA
            AT END MOVE 1 TO INDICATOR
                    GO TO 020-EXIT.
        MOVE CARD-IN TO LIST-LINE.
        WRITE LIST AFTER ADVANCING 2 LINES.
    020-EXIT. EXIT.
    030-CLOSER.
        _____ .
        _____ .
```

Note what is happening in our revised program.

1. The control is still retained in the CONTROL-ROUTINE.
2. The 010-OPENER paragraph does *not* contain a "priming" READ statement.
3. The second PERFORM statement has been changed to PER-FORM THRU UNTIL, which means that any and all paragraphs from 020-READER through 020-EXIT will be executed repeatedly until the INDICATOR is equal to 1.
4. The 020-READER paragraph now contains a READ-MOVE-WRITE sequence plus a GO TO 020-EXIT statement that is executed when the AT END situation is detected.

5. When AT END is detected, the GO TO statement proceeds to the 020-EXIT paragraph, which contains the single statement EXIT. Control is then returned back to the PERFORM THRU UNTIL statement. The value of INDICATOR will be tested and, since it does equal 1, control passes to the next statement in sequence.

Those shops that permit this type of programming usually follow very explicit rules to prevent uncontrolled use of these statements. Normally, the EXIT paragraph must appear immediately after the PERFORMed paragraph—that is, with no intervening paragraphs. Also, the GO TO must only be downward and always to the exit paragraph.

When GO TO is permitted, there is a temptation to simply replace the GO TO statement with a PERFORM as follows:

```
020-READER.
    READ _____
        AT END PERFORM 030-CLOSER.
    MOVE _____ .
    WRITE _____ .
030-CLOSER.

    _____ .
```

This will work in the sense that it will get us out of the 020-READER loop. However, it destroys the top-down design idea in which we want all program control to be in the top of the program. It also "frustrates" the PERFORM UNTIL statement we set up earlier by branching out of the PERFORM without allowing it to test a condition.

Another temptation when making the transition from unstructured to structured programming is that of simply replacing a GO TO with PERFORM. A typical unstructured loop looks as follows:

```
020-READER.
    READ _____
        AT END _____ .
    MOVE _____ .
    WRITE _____ .
    GO TO 020-READER.
```

If we replace the last GO TO with another PERFORM (PERFORM 020-READER) we are, in effect, PERFORMing ourselves. This is known as a "recursive" technique and is not permitted since it can lead to serious programming difficulties.

The case structure and GO TO DEPENDING

Although most true structured programmers do not permit the use of the GO TO statement, there is one situation in which its use makes programming easier to code and understand. This GO TO variation is found in many languages and is known by a variety of names, but the action of the statement is generally the same. In COBOL it is called the GO TO DEPENDING statement and is really a conditional branch instruction. It has the following format:

```
GO TO procedure-name-1
      procedure-name-2
          .
          .
          .
      procedure-name-n
      DEPENDING ON identifier.
```

Example

```
GO TO DAY-SHIFT-ROUTINE
      SWING-SHIFT-ROUTINE
      GRAVE-SHIFT-ROUTINE
          DEPENDING ON JOB-CODE.
```

In the example the system will branch to one of the three routines depending upon the value of the JOB-CODE field. If JOB-CODE contains a 1, the branch is to DAY-SHIFT-ROUTINE; if it contains a 2, the branch is to SWING-SHIFT-ROUTINE, and so on. If the value of the identifier goes beyond 3 (which is the maximum number of branch points in the example), the statement is ignored and the system goes to the next statement in sequence.

The so-called case structure derives its name from wanting to branch to many different points depending upon the case being considered currently. It is flowcharted as follows:

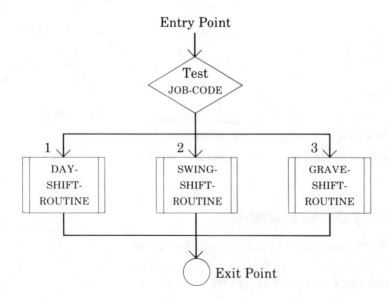

Coding of the structure very likely will involve both forms of the GO TO and the EXIT statements. Remember that in shops that normally use top-down, structured programming, often this is the *only* permitted use of GO TO.

```
PROCEDURE DIVISION
    .
    .
    .
    PERFORM A300-PAY-CALC
        THRU A300-PAY-CALC-EXIT.
        .
        .
        .
A300-PAY-CALC.
    GO TO DAY-SHIFT-ROUTINE
        SWING-SHIFT-ROUTINE
        GRAVE-SHIFT-ROUTINE
            DEPENDING ON JOB-CODE.
JOB-CODE-ERROR-ROUTINE.
    _____

    GO TO A300-PAY-CALC-EXIT.
DAY-SHIFT-ROUTINE

    _____
    _____ }   Statements to calculate day-pay
    _____

    GO TO A300-PAY-CALC-EXIT.
SWING-SHIFT-ROUTINE

    _____
    _____ }   Statements to calculate swing-shift pay
    _____

    GO TO A300-PAY-CALC-EXIT.
GRAVE-SHIFT-ROUTINE.

    _____
    _____ }   Statements to calculate graveyard-shift pay
    _____

    GO TO A300-PAY-CALC-EXIT.
A300-PAY-CALC-EXIT.
    EXIT.
```

Common errors

At this point you should have a good understanding of the function of each line in the sample program. We add to that understanding by presenting more common errors and analyzing the diagnostic messages that the system generates.

The first error discussed in Chapter 4 was a very simple one: We SELECTed PRINT-FILE and then used PRINTFILE (without a hyphen) in the file description. Figure 4-4 showed that an error message was generated in the DATA DIVISION indicating that the SELECT file name and the FD file name did not agree. Although the single error message shown in that illustration was correct, it was only one of several that the software printed. The additional messages (as shown in Figures 5-4a and 5-4b) came in the PROCEDURE DIVISION whenever the programmer tried to use or make reference to PRINTFILE.

FIGURE 5-4a

Common Errors: "PRINTFILE"

```
      IDENTIFICATION DIVISION.
      PROGRAM-ID. LISTER.
*
      ENVIRONMENT DIVISION.
      CONFIGURATION SECTION.
      SOURCE-COMPUTER. IBM-360-F30.
      OBJECT-COMPUTER. IBM-360-F30.
      INPUT-OUTPUT SECTION.
      FILE-CONTROL.
          SELECT CARD-DATA
              ASSIGN TO SYS007-UR-2540R-S.
          SELECT PRINT-FILE
              ASSIGN TO SYS009-UR-1403-S.
*
      DATA DIVISION.
      FILE SECTION.
      FD   CARD-DATA
          LABEL RECORDS ARE OMITTED
          DATA RECORD IS CARD-IN.
      01   CARD-IN          PIC X(80).
      FD   PRINTFILE
          LABEL RECORDS ARE OMITTED
          DATA RECORD IS LIST.
      01   LIST.
          03   FILLER       PIC X.
          03   LIST-LINE    PIC X(120).
      WORKING-STORAGE SECTION.
      77   INDICATOR        PIC 9 VALUE ZERO.
*
```

```
PROCEDURE DIVISION.
CONTROL-ROUTINE.
    PERFORM 010-OPENER.
    PERFORM 020-READER UNTIL
        INDICATOR = 1.
    PERFORM 030-CLOSER.
    STOP RUN.
010-OPENER.
    OPEN INPUT CARD-DATA
        OUTPUT PRINTFILE.
    READ CARD-DATA
        AT END MOVE 1 TO INDICATOR.
020-READER.
    MOVE CARD-IN TO LIST-LINE.
    WRITE LIST AFTER ADVANCING 2 LINES.
    READ CARD-DATA
        AT END MOVE 1 TO INDICATOR.
030-CLOSER.
    MOVE 'END OF PROGRAM' TO LIST-LINE.
    WRITE LIST AFTER ADVANCING 3 LINES.
    CLOSE CARD-DATA, PRINTFILE.
```

FIGURE 5-4b

Error Listing

CARD	ERROR MESSAGE	
23	ILA1056I-E	FILE-NAME NOT DEFINED IN A SELECT. DESCRIPTION IGNORED.
38	ILA3001I-E	PRINTFILE NOT DEFINED. DELETING TILL LEGAL ELEMENT FOUND.
41	ILA4072I-W	EXIT FROM PERFORMED PROCEDURE ASSUMED BEFORE PROCEDURE-NAME.
44	ILA4050I-E	SYNTAX REQUIRES RECORD-NAME. FOUND DNM=1-155. STATEMENT DISCARDED.
46	ILA4072I-W	EXIT FROM PERFORMED PROCEDURE ASSUMED BEFORE PROCEDURE-NAME.
49	ILA4050I-E	SYNTAX REQUIRES RECORD-NAME . FOUND DNM=1-155. STATEMENT DISCARDED.
50	ILA3001I-E	PRINTFILE NOT DEFINED. DELETING TILL LEGAL ELEMENT FOUND.

Don't let the number of errors bother you! They are all entirely logical and easily corrected. The first message said "FILE-NAME NOT DEFINED IN A SELECT. DESCRIPTION IGNORED." Since the description was ignored, it means that any reference in the program to that file will generate an error. The messages for cards 38 and 50 have to do with the OPEN and CLOSE statements for the PRINT-FILE. Obviously, a non-existent file cannot be opened or closed. Lines 44 and 49 refer to the two WRITE statements that try to make use of the PRINT-FILE. The record name for the PRINT-FILE (LIST) does not exist since the file description was ignored. Note that even though the DATA DIVISION entries concerning LIST are correct, the system has deleted everything to do with the file. This again shows the close relationship between the SELECT and FD entries even though they are in two different COBOL divisions.

The second error example (Figure 5-5a) is another repeat of an error shown earlier. This time Figure 5-5b shows the full listing of errors that were caused by misspelling the word ENVIRONMENT. As with the previous error example, the key term is found in the message for card or line number 15, where it says that all ENVIRONMENT DIVISION statements are ignored. The end result is that this single spelling error generates a total of 14 diagnostic messages.

FIGURE 5-5a

Program Error: "ENVIROMENT"

```
      IDENTIFICATION DIVISION.
      PROGRAM-ID. LISTER.
*
      ENVIROMENT DIVISION.
      CONFIGURATION SECTION.
      SOURCE-COMPUTER. IBM-360-F30.
      OBJECT-COMPUTER. IBM-360-F30.
      INPUT-OUTPUT SECTION.
      FILE-CONTROL.
          SELECT CARD-DATA
              ASSIGN TO SYS007-UR-2540R-S.
          SELECT PRINTFILE
              ASSIGN TO SYS009-UR-1403-S.
*
```

```
DATA DIVISION.
FILE SECTION.
FD  CARD-DATA
    LABEL RECORDS ARE OMITTED
    DATA RECORD IS CARD-IN.
01  CARD-IN           PIC X(80).
FD  PRINTFILE
    LABEL RECORDS ARE OMITTED
    DATA RECORD IS LIST.
01  LIST.
    03  FILLER        PIC X.
    03  LIST-LINE     PIC X(120).
WORKING-STORAGE SECTION.
77  INDICATOR         PIC 9 VALUE ZERO.
*
PROCEDURE DIVISION.
CONTROL-ROUTINE.
    PERFORM 010-OPENER.
    PERFORM 020-READER UNTIL
        INDICATOR = 1.
    PERFORM 030-CLOSER.
    STOP RUN.
010-OPENER.
    OPEN INPUT CARD-DATA
        OUTPUT PRINTFILE.
    READ CARD-DATA
        AT END MOVE 1 TO INDICATOR.
020-READER.
    MOVE CARD-IN TO LIST-LINE.
    WRITE LIST AFTER ADVANCING 2 LINES.
    READ CARD-DATA
        AT END MOVE 1 TO INDICATOR.
030-CLOSER.
    MOVE 'END OF PROGRAM' TO LIST-LINE.
    WRITE LIST AFTER ADVANCING 3 LINES.
    CLOSE CARD-DATA, PRINTFILE.
```

FIGURE 5-5b

Error Listing

CARD	ERROR MESSAGE	
4	ILA1087I–W	' ENVIROMENT ' SHOULD NOT BEGIN IN AREA A.
15	ILA1026I–W	FOUND DATA . EXPECTING ENVIRONMENT. ALL ENV. DIV. STATEMENTS IGNORED.
19	ILA1056I–E	FILE–NAME NOT DEFINED IN A SELECT. DESCRIPTION IGNORED.
23	ILA1056I–E	FILE–NAME NOT DEFINED IN A SELECT. DESCRIPTION IGNORED.
38	ILA3001I–E	CARD–DATA NOT DEFINED. DELETING TILL LEGAL ELEMENT FOUND.
38	ILA3001I–E	PRINTFILE NOT DEFINED. DELETING TILL LEGAL ELEMENT FOUND.
38	ILA4002I–E	OPEN STATEMENT INCOMPLETE. STATEMENT DISCARDED.
40	ILA3001I–E	CARD–DATA NOT DEFINED. STATEMENT DISCARDED.
44	ILA4050I–E	SYNTAX REQUIRES RECORD–NAME. FOUND DNM=1–122 . STATEMENT DISCARDED.
45	ILA3001I–E	CARD–DATA NOT DEFINED. STATEMENT DISCARDED.
49	ILA4050I–E	SYNTAX REQUIRES RECORD–NAME . FOUND DNM=1–122 . STATEMENT DISCARDED.
50	ILA3001I–E	CARD–DATA NOT DEFINED. DELETING TILL LEGAL ELEMENT FOUND.
50	ILA3001I–E	PRINTFILE NOT DEFINED.
50	ILA4002I–E	CLOSE STATEMENT INCOMPLETE. STATEMENT DISCARDED.

About this time some of you will be tempted to leave off the AT END portion of the first READ statement on the reasoning that it is unnecessary. First of all, you can't because AT END is required for all sequential files. Second, think about what it does for you. Remember our sequence.

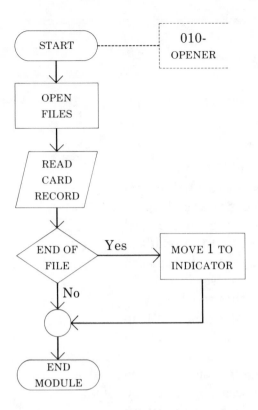

Suppose you forget to place any data cards in the program deck. Notice what happens when the 010-OPENER paragraph is PERFORMed.

1. The files are opened.
2. A card is read by the READ statement.
3. Since this card is not a valid data card, the AT END part of the READ statement is executed—1 is moved to the INDICATOR field.
4. The system automatically branches back to the statement immediately after the PERFORM.
5. The system encounters PERFORM UNTIL, but remember how the statement works: The test condition is evaluated *first*. Since the INDICATOR field *is* already equal to 1, the 020-READER paragraph is *not executed at all* and control passes down to the next statement in sequence.
6. The 020-CLOSER paragraph is executed and the system returns to the STOP-RUN statement to end the program.

Problem-Solving Techniques

When designing the solution to a problem you should be on the look-out for those functions, or tasks, that will have to be executed repeatedly. In other words, look for places in which you can use the looping capability of the computer. All too often beginning programmers fail to look for these loops during the analysis phase, and the result is that their program ends up being a series of lines of code that are copied over and over. Although we have not yet discussed the main COBOL testing statement—IF—it should be obvious that the UNTIL version of PERFORM is a test that allows you to control a program loop very effectively. The only real limitation to it is your ability to see when and how it can be used.

A second point to consider here is the error messages such as those shown in the COMMON ERRORS section. On some occasions you may have a great many error messages; just looking at the error listing will be incredibly frustrating. You will have thought that you did a good job of analysis and design, and a careful job of coding and entering the program. But don't panic! Don't drop the course! *Do* remember the nature of COBOL errors such as those shown earlier. Each "real" error is very likely to generate three or four error messages so that the correction of a few errors will clean up the program considerably. Unless you are under severe CPU time constraints, correct those errors that are obvious to you and then recompile the program.

Self-Study: Questions and Answers

1. Do you always have to have paragraph headers in a COBOL program?

   Answer
   Technically, I suppose you could write a COBOL program that does not have headers at all. However, this would be extremely rare, particularly for a lengthy program. Remember that paragraph headers serve two purposes: as a place to branch to and as a divider between the logical parts of your program. A paragraph can consist of as few as one statement or as many statements as you wish, but a more practical limit would be about 30 entries.

   While we are discussing headers, you are reminded to number them and, as far as possible, pick meaningful names. Whatever numbering or naming scheme you use, be sure it is simple, logical, and easy to use.

2. How can the OPEN and CLOSE statements be so complex internally when they are so simple to use?

   Answer
   You are right about the fact that both statements are very simple. Internally, however, they are very complex in that they trigger a series of software operations involving the control of input/output operations for the files you have chosen. The COBOL programmer is most fortunate that he or she does not have to write all the instructions generated by the OPEN or CLOSE. For card and printer files the operations are fairly simple, but for tape and disk operations the process is far more complex.

3. I understand how the READ statement works, but do I always have to include AT END? What if I don't want to use AT END?

   Answer
   The first part of the answer is yes—you must use AT END whenever you are reading sequential files. For nonsequential files COBOL has a slightly different clause that takes the place of AT END. As to the second part of the question, there are times when the programmer may wish to do away with the AT END portion of the statement, but, unfortunately, it must be included.

4. When reading in data, it seems to be a waste of time to have to account for all the positions in the record, especially since I may wish to use only a few fields. Is there any way around this?

   Answer

   No, there isn't. The rule is that you must account for all the positions in a record. This is particularly true with magnetic storage media such as tape and disk. For cards, you can "bend" the rule slightly by accounting for all the fields up to and including the last one you are going to use. It is still good practice to account for all 80 positions.

5. The MOVE statement seems so simple that nobody could get into trouble using it. Is that correct?

   Answer

   You're right that it is hard to get into trouble using MOVE, but don't be deceived by it. As you will see in later chapters, some very interesting actions can take place with MOVE and some of its variations. For now, the only problem might be in trying to move numeric data to an alphabetic field, and vice versa.

6. In discussing the MOVE statement, you said that the software generates an error message when the receiving field is too small. Won't that error stop the execution of the program?

   Answer

   Good question. The answer generally is no because the error usually is at the warning or conditional level. If you stop to think about it, there may be some occasions when the programmer deliberately wants to truncate part of a field during a MOVE operation. The nice part about the low-level message is that the programmer is warned, but execution can proceed.

7. With the WRITE statement must I always use either BEFORE or AFTER ADVANCING?

   Answer

   No, unlike the AT END portion of the READ statement, the WRITE statement may be written without the ADVANCING portion. The format is

        WRITE record name.

   However, there is a problem you should know about. Another rule says that "if you once use the ADVANCING option with a particular file, you must always use ADVANCING with that file." Since writing on the printer almost always involves some type of vertical spacing, the WRITE statement was shown this way.

Exercises

1. Indicate whether the following entries are correct or incorrect. If the statement is incorrect, change it so that it is correct.
   a. PERFORM OPEN.
   b. PROCEDURE-DIVISION
   c. READER-120-PARAGRAPH.
   d. From the sample program would it be correct to say "READ CARD-IN"?
   e. From the sample program would it be correct to say "WRITE PRINTFILE"?
   f. OPEN CARD-DATA
   g. CLOSE OUTPUT PRINTFILE.
   h. WRITE LIST AFTER ADVANCING 1 LINES.

2. Look at the following series of statements that are variations on the sample program. If you see anything wrong, make the appropriate correction.
   a. MOVE SPACES TO FILLER.
      WRITE LIST AFTER ADVANCING 2 LINES.
   b. READ CARD-DATA
          AT END
              MOVE 'END OF REPORT' TO LIST-LINE
              WRITE LIST AFTER ADVANCING 2 LINES.
   c. WRITE LIST AFTER ADVANCING 2 LINES.
      MOVE 'END OF REPORT' TO LIST-LINE.
      WRITE LIST-LINE.
   d. MOVE SPACES TO LIST-LINE.
      WRITE LIST AFTER ADVANCING 3 LINES.
   e. MOVE 'INVENTORY REPORT' TO LIST-LINE.
      WRITE LIST-LINE BEFORE ADVANCING 3 LINES.

3. Modify the sample program as follows: Change the file names, record names, and field names throughout the program. Use names of your own choice, but make sure they are appropriate to the problem.

4. Change the paragraph header names in the sample program and make whatever other changes in the program statements that this would require.

5. If the sample program had contained the statement

   ```
   MOVE SPACES TO LIST
   ```

   in the 010-OPENER paragraph, would that statement be necessary? Explain your answer in detail and use diagrams if necessary to illustrate the action of the machine.

6. Indicate the outcome of the following MOVE statements. The caret ($\wedge$) indicates the position of the assumed decimal point.

		Sending Field	Receiving Field
a.	MOVE AMT-1 TO AMT-2.	$4\,5\,6\,7_\wedge$	
b.	MOVE AMT-3 TO AMT-4.	$4\,5_\wedge5\,0$	
c.	MOVE AMT-5 TO AMT-6.	$1\,2\,3_\wedge0$	
d.	MOVE AMT-7 TO AMT-8.	$_\wedge1\,2\,3\,4$	
e.	MOVE ZEROS TO TOTAL.		
f.	MOVE SPACES TO TOTAL.		

7. Indicate the outcome of the following MOVE statements.

		Sending Field	Receiving Field
a.	MOVE ALPHA-1 TO ALPHA-2.	A B C	
b.	MOVE ALPHA-3 TO ALPHA-4.	A B C D E	
c.	MOVE ALPHA-5 TO ALPHA-6.	A B C D	
d.	MOVE SPACES TO ALPHA-7.		

8. Explain in detail the action of the PERFORM UNTIL statement. If necessary use diagrams in your explanation.

9. Can you PERFORM a single statement? Explain.

10. How can PERFORMed paragraphs be recognized in a flowchart? Can a PERFORMed module contain all three of the programming structures discussed so far?

11. Using the regular PERFORM statement, code the statements that will execute READ-LOOP two times.

12. Using PERFORM UNTIL, code the statement that will execute PRO-GRAM-LOOP until the following occur:
    a. B is greater than A
    b. C is not equal to D
    c. AMOUNT is less than TEST-AMT
    d. COUNTER is equal to 50

13. Address label problem. You have an unknown number of data cards containing information on subscribers to a magazine we publish. The card format is as follows.

Card Column	Field Description
1–20	Customer name
21–40	Street Address
41–60	City, state, ZIP code
61–66	Expiration date
67–80	Blank

Write a program that prints mailing labels in the following format:

    Name
    Street address
    City, State   ZIP   Expiration date

14. As a refinement to the previous problem, you are to print two mailing labels for each subscriber. Use the following format.

    Name   Name
    Street Address   Street Address
    City, State ZIP City, State ZIP
    Expiration Date Expiration Date

Chapter 6

Handling Data

Chapter 5 introduced you to the basic COBOL statements that are needed in virtually every program. Obviously, there is more to it than could be shown in the sample program. In this chapter you will see more ways in which data can be created, changed, and handled.

The WORKING-STORAGE SECTION

A second—and optional—part of the DATA DIVISION, called the WORKING-STORAGE SECTION, is usually present in most COBOL programs. Our sample program was so short that we had only one entry in WORKING-STORAGE.

WORKING-STORAGE is exactly what the term indicates. As opposed to the FILE SECTION where you set aside room for incoming and outgoing records, the WORKING-STORAGE SECTION is the place where you can set aside either fields or records according to your needs in the problem. For example, one of the most common uses of WORKING-STOR-AGE is to set aside total areas—that is, fields in which you wish to total certain values. The following example shows how we would create two total areas (TOTAL-1 and TOTAL-2) for use in the program:

```
WORKING-STORAGE SECTION.
01  TOTAL-AREAS.
    03   TOTAL-1        PIC 9(5).
    03   TOTAL-2        PIC 9(4)V99.
```

Although the above entry is correct, it usually leads to serious trouble in a program. The problem is that no one would attempt to add total values in a field without first knowing that it contains zeros. In the above example the only assumption the programmer can make is that the two fields contain garbage. The easiest way to solve the problem is to use the VALUE clause, which allows you to put specific values into fields as shown below:

```
WORKING-STORAGE SECTION.
01   TOTAL-AREAS.
     03   TOTAL-1        PIC 9(5)      VALUE ZEROS.
     03   TOTAL-2        PIC 9(4)V99 VALUE ZEROS.
```

The values you create do not always have to be zero, as the next example shows in creating the value for pi. Note that the PIC clause must correspond exactly to the size of the value created.

```
WORKING-STORAGE SECTION.
01   TOTAL-AREAS.
     03   TOTAL-1        PIC 9(5)      VALUE ZEROS.
     03   TOTAL-2        PIC 9(4)V99   VALUE ZEROS.
     03   PI             PIC 9V9999    VALUE 3.1415.
```

The above values could have been created in another way by means of what are known as level 77 entries. Level 77 is a special level number reserved for creating individual fields that are not part of a record.

```
WORKING-STORAGE SECTION.
77   TOTAL-1        PIC 9(5)      VALUE ZEROS.
77   TOTAL-2        PIC 9(4)V99   VALUE ZEROS.
77   PI             PIC 9V9999    VALUE 3.1415.
```

If both level 77's and 01's are used in the WORKING-STORAGE SECTION, *all* level 77's must come before 01 level entries.

The VALUE clause may be used to create whatever values you wish—not just numerics. WORKING-STORAGE is commonly used to create heading and ending lines for output on the printer. We can now modify our sample program to have output that looks as follows:

```
                        Card Listing
        _____
        _____
        _____
        _____
        _____

        End of Report
```

In setting up the heading line, we will have to account for all the printing positions across the page (120 in this case). To center it on the page, we will have to create 54 spaces (120 minus 12 divided by 2) on both sides of the message.

```
WORKING-STORAGE SECTION.
01   HEAD-LINE.
     03   FILLER          PIC X.
     03   FILLER          PIC X(54) VALUE SPACES.
     03   FILLER          PIC X(12)
                          VALUE 'CARD LISTING'.
     03   FILLER          PIC X(54) VALUE SPACES.
```

By now, you must realize that, since COBOL is a business-oriented language, output from your programs normally will involve printed material such as reports to management, pay checks, inventory listings, and the like. Almost always these reports are going to have at least three general kinds of output lines: heading lines at the top of the report, a main body line for the center of the report, and ending lines for totals, and so forth.

The easy way to handle all of these different output lines is to set up each one in WORKING-STORAGE. Printer output, of course, *has* to come from the record area established for the print file. Here, all we do is set up a record large enough for printer output with the following:

```
FD   PRINTFILE
     LABEL RECORDS ARE OMITTED
     DATA RECORD IS PRINT-LINE.
01   PRINT-LINE       PIC X(121).
```

The next step is to set up the individual lines in WORKING-STORAGE for exactly the same length—121 characters. Then, when you are ready to print, you MOVE the particular heading, body, or ending line to the PRINT-LINE and then WRITE PRINT-LINE. This method makes for a very clean, simple way of handling multiple types of output lines. Figure 6-1 shows, in skeletal form, how this would look in your program.

FIGURE 6-1

Skeletal Program Showing the Three Types of Lines

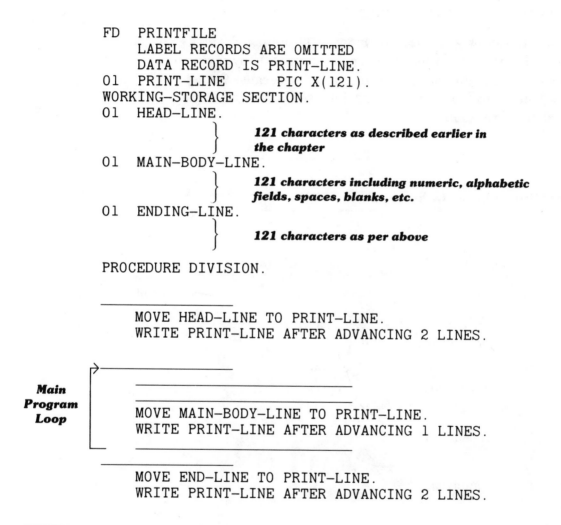

```
FD   PRINTFILE
     LABEL RECORDS ARE OMITTED
     DATA RECORD IS PRINT-LINE.
01   PRINT-LINE      PIC X(121).
WORKING-STORAGE SECTION.
01   HEAD-LINE.
```
          } *121 characters as described earlier in the chapter*
```
01   MAIN-BODY-LINE.
```
          } *121 characters including numeric, alphabetic fields, spaces, blanks, etc.*
```
01   ENDING-LINE.
```
          } *121 characters as per above*

```
PROCEDURE DIVISION.
```

```
     MOVE HEAD-LINE TO PRINT-LINE.
     WRITE PRINT-LINE AFTER ADVANCING 2 LINES.
```

Main Program Loop
```
     MOVE MAIN-BODY-LINE TO PRINT-LINE.
     WRITE PRINT-LINE AFTER ADVANCING 1 LINES.
```

```
     MOVE END-LINE TO PRINT-LINE.
     WRITE PRINT-LINE AFTER ADVANCING 2 LINES.
```

As Figure 6-2 illustrates, all the lines are of the same length and are moved to the PRINT-LINE when required. Again, notice that the only place from which you can print is PRINT-LINE. It is <u>incorrect</u> to say

```
     WRITE HEAD-LINE etc.
```

However, you can cut down the number of statements by using the FROM option of the WRITE statement. The statement

```
WRITE PRINT-LINE FROM ENDING-LINE
     AFTER ADVANCING 2 LINES.
```

is exactly equivalent to the following statements:

```
MOVE ENDING-LINE TO PRINT-LINE.
WRITE PRINT-LINE
     AFTER ADVANCING 2 LINES.
```

As you can see, the FROM option is a combination of MOVE and WRITE.

Also notice that there is no need to clear the PRINT-LINE (by saying MOVE SPACES TO PRINT-LINE) prior to printing each line because the act of moving a line from WORKING-STORAGE into PRINT-LINE destroys whatever was in there before.

FIGURE 6-2

Schematic: Output Lines in Storage

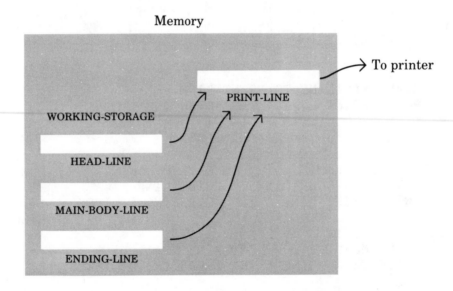

COBOL has the equivalent option for the READ statement. Called the INTO option, it is a combination of READ and MOVE and allows you to read in a record and move it to WORKING-STORAGE with a single statement. Using a card record as an example, we can set up an 80-character card input area the same as we did the sample program.

```
FD  CARD-DATA
    LABEL RECORDS ARE OMITTED
    DATA RECORD IS CARD-IN.
01  CARD-IN      PIC X(80).
```

Assuming that the card record contains various fields that we wish to access, we could set up the following in WORKING-STORAGE.

```
WORKING-STORAGE SECTION.
01  CARD-RECORD.
    03   FIELD-1 _____ .
    03   FIELD-2 _____ .
    03   FIELD-3 _____ .

             etc.
```

To get the card read in and moved into the CARD-RECORD area, we can say

```
READ CARD-DATA INTO CARD-RECORD
    AT END _____ .
```

This statement is exactly the equivalent of

```
READ CARD-DATA
    AT END _____ .
MOVE CARD-IN TO CARD-RECORD.
```

Printer control—SPECIAL-NAMES

Until now you have had only one way of controlling the action of the printer: by using BEFORE or AFTER ADVANCING so many lines. The maximum number of lines you can advance with a single WRITE statement is 99, which certainly gives you a lot of room for choice. However, there is a way of providing more control over the printer if you desire to do so.

On IBM computers an additional entry in the ENVIRONMENT DIVI-
SION called SPECIAL-NAMES allows you to assign a name to the first
printing line on the top of a new page. The reserved word C01 (Cee
zero one) identifies the top line and is used as shown below:

```
OBJECT-COMPUTER.
SPECIAL-NAMES. CØ1 IS TOP-OF-PAGE.

PROCEDURE DIVISION.

    WRITE PRINT-LINE FROM HEADING-LINE
        AFTER ADVANCING TOP-OF-PAGE.
```

Of course, there is no "magic" in the name TOP-OF-PAGE, and any
name that is not a reserved word can be used. This is an easy and
efficient way to get your heading lines positioned at the top of a new
page. With ANS 74 COBOL the process is even easier. Use of the
reserved word PAGE causes the system to skip to the top of a new
page; the SPECIAL-NAMES entry is not required. The statement

```
    WRITE PRINT-LINE FROM HEADING-LINE
        AFTER ADVANCING PAGE.
```

achieves the same result as the previous example.

Editing

Since COBOL is a business-oriented language, it has the capability of
providing for very precisely arranged printer output for items such
as checks, customer invoices, management reports, and the like. The
general term used to describe output that contains characters such
as dollar signs, commas, debit and credit symbols, decimal points, and
so on is that of *editing*. Editing is not hard, but it does involve special
edit fields in your output line.

In an earlier example we read in a card record and simply moved
the fields to the output line without any regard for editing. In actual
practice, however, editing is the more common situation; that is, most
fields are edited. Let's set up an example to see how editing works.
Suppose we have a card file containing information on magazine sub-
scriptions (Figure 6-3).

FIGURE 6-3

Subscription Input Card Record

1 – 20	21 – 40	41 – 45	46 – 49	50 – 55	56 – 58	59 – 60	61 – 80
CUSTOMER NAME	ADDRESS	ORIGINAL BALANCE	MONTHLY BILL	ENDING DATE OF SUBSCRIPTION	CODE FIELD ONE	CODE FIELD TWO	FILLER
		XXX•YY	XX YY	MMDDYY	XXX	XX	

In this case all we want to do is read in the data and print a listing of subscribers. So, no data manipulation is involved, but we will want to edit the output. Output is to be as shown in Figure 6-4. Pseudocode specifications for the program are shown below.

Pseudocode Specification: SUBSCRIPTION LIST PROGRAM

```
CONTROL-ROUTINE
     PERFORM 010-OPENER
     PERFORM 020-READER UNTIL indicator = 1
     PERFORM 020-CLOSER
     STOP RUN

010-OPENER
     Open files
     Write heading line
     Read card record: at end move 1 to indicator

020-READER
     Move (edit) card fields to output area
     Write main report line
     Read card record: at end move 1 to indicator

030-CLOSER
     Move end message to output area
     Write end message
     Close files
```

FIGURE 6-4

Printer Spacing Chart

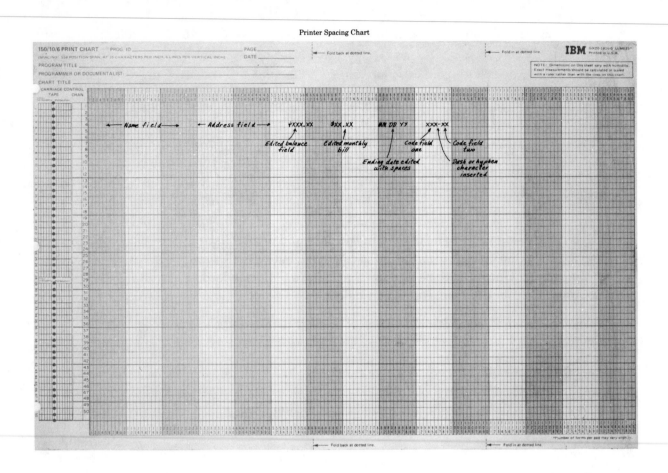

Our card input format is straightforward except for the code field, which we will break into two parts. Later in the problem you will see why this is necessary.

```
01   CARD-IN.
     03   NAME                    PIC A(20).
     03   ADDRESS-IN              PIC X(20).
     03   ORIG-BALANCE            PIC 999V99.
     03   MO-BILL                 PIC 99V99.
     03   ENDING-DATE             PIC 9(6).
     03   CODE-1                  PIC 999.
     03   CODE-2                  PIC 99.
     03   FILLER                  PIC X(20).
```

The standard output line is as discussed before, but we will need to set up a heading line and a main body line in WORKING-STORAGE. There will be quite a few entries in the heading-line record in order

to space the material across the page. The main-body-line record will
follow the same pattern, but will contain edit fields.

```
01   MAIN-LINE.
     03   FILLER                    PIC X.
     03   FILLER                    PIC X(5) VALUE SPACES.
     03   NAME-OUT                  PIC X(20).
     03   FILLER                    PIC X(5) VALUE SPACES.
     03   ADDRESS-OUT               PIC X(20).
     03   FILLER                    PIC X(5) VALUE SPACES.
     03   BALANCE-OUT               PIC $999.99.
     03   FILLER                    PIC X(5) VALUE SPACES.
     03   MONTHLY-OUT               PIC $99.99.
     03   FILLER                    PIC X(8) VALUE SPACES.
     03   END-DATE-OUT              PIC 99B99B99.
     03   FILLER                    PIC X(5) VALUE SPACES.
     03   CODE-1-OUT                PIC 999.
     03   FILLER                    PIC X VALUE '-'.
     03   CODE-2-OUT                PIC 99.
     03   FILLER                    PIC X(19) VALUE SPACES.
```

Note that, in setting up the relationship between the heading-line
characters and the body of the report, a printer spacing chart is an
indispensable tool. In the PROCEDURE DIVISION, editing takes place
simply by moving a field into the field containing the edit characters.
Thus, the statement

MOVE ORIG-BALANCE TO BALANCE-OUT

will cause the ORIGINAL-BALANCE field to be edited into the format
$XXX.XX. The 010-OPENER paragraph is shown below. Note how it
makes use of the WRITE FROM and the ADVANCING TOP-OF-PAGE formats.

```
010-OPENER.
     OPEN INPUT CARD-DATA
         OUTPUT PRINTFILE.
     WRITE OUTPUT-LINE FROM HEADING-LINE
         AFTER ADVANCING TOP-OF-PAGE.
     READ CARD-DATA
         AT END MOVE 1 TO INDICATOR.
```

The heart of the move, print, read loop looks as follows:

```
020-READER.
    MOVE NAME TO NAME-OUT.
    MOVE ADDRESS-IN TO ADDRESS-OUT.
    MOVE ORIG-BALANCE TO BALANCE-OUT.
    MOVE MO-BILL TO MONTHLY-OUT.
    MOVE ENDING-DATE TO END-DATE-OUT.
    MOVE CODE-1 TO CODE-1-OUT.
    MOVE CODE-2 TO CODE-2-OUT.
    WRITE OUTPUT-LINE FROM MAIN-LINE
        AFTER ADVANCING 2 LINES.
    READ CARD-DATA
        AT END MOVE 1 TO INDICATOR.
```

The CODE field presents some problems to us in that COBOL does not have the capability of inserting hyphens. Therefore, we will have to do our own editing by breaking up the field and creating a hyphen at the proper place. The MOVE statements are the same as usual.

```
MOVE CODE-1 TO CODE-1-OUT.
MOVE CODE-2 TO CODE-2-OUT.
```

Figure 6-5 shows the entire program and the resulting output. Figure 6-6 illustrates the action as it takes place inside memory.

FIGURE 6-5

Subscription Program and Output

```
IDENTIFICATION DIVISION.
PROGRAM-ID. SUBSCR.
*
ENVIRONMENT DIVISION.
CONFIGURATION SECTION.
SOURCE-COMPUTER. IBM-360-F30.
OBJECT-COMPUTER. IBM-360-F30.
SPECIAL-NAMES.
    C01 IS TOP-OF-PAGE.
INPUT-OUTPUT SECTION.
FILE-CONTROL.
    SELECT PRINTFILE
        ASSIGN TO SYS009-UR-1403-S.
    SELECT CARD-DATA
        ASSIGN TO SYS007-UR-2540R-S.
*
```

```
DATA DIVISION.
FILE SECTION.
FD   PRINTFILE
     LABEL RECORDS ARE OMITTED
     DATA RECORD IS OUTPUT-LINE.
01   OUTPUT-LINE                    PIC X(121).
FD   CARD-DATA
     LABEL RECORDS ARE OMITTED
     DATA RECORD IS CARD-IN.
01   CARD-IN.
     03   NAME                      PIC A(20).
     03   ADDRESS-IN                PIC X(20).
     03   ORIG-BALANCE              PIC 999V99.
     03   MO-BILL                   PIC 99V99.
     03   ENDING-DATE               PIC 9(6).
     03   CODE-1                    PIC 999.
     03   CODE-2                    PIC 99.
     03   FILLER                    PIC X(20).
WORKING-STORAGE SECTION.
77   INDICATOR                      PIC 9 VALUE ZERO.
01   MAIN-LINE.
     03   FILLER                    PIC X.
     03   FILLER                    PIC X(5) VALUE SPACES.
     03   NAME-OUT                  PIC X(20).
     03   FILLER                    PIC X(5) VALUE SPACES.
     03   ADDRESS-OUT               PIC X(20).
     03   FILLER                    PIC X(5) VALUE SPACES.
     03   BALANCE-OUT               PIC $999.99.
     03   FILLER                    PIC X(5) VALUE SPACES.
     03   MONTHLY-OUT               PIC $99.99.
     03   FILLER                    PIC X(8) VALUE SPACES.
     03   END-DATE-OUT              PIC 99B99B99.
     03   FILLER                    PIC X(5) VALUE SPACES.
     03   CODE-1-OUT                PIC 999.
     03   FILLER                    PIC X VALUE '-'.
     03   CODE-2-OUT                PIC 99.
     03   FILLER                    PIC X(19) VALUE SPACES.
01   HEADING-LINE.
     03   FILLER                    PIC X.
     03   FILLER                    PIC X(13) VALUE SPACES.
     03   FILLER                    PIC X(4) VALUE 'NAME'.
     03   FILLER                    PIC X(19) VALUE SPACES.
     03   FILLER                    PIC X(7) VALUE 'ADDRESS'.
     03   FILLER                    PIC X(12) VALUE SPACES.
     03   FILLER                    PIC X(7) VALUE 'BALANCE'.
     03   FILLER                    PIC X(5) VALUE SPACES.
     03   FILLER                    PIC X(7) VALUE 'MONTHLY'.
     03   FILLER                    PIC X(5) VALUE SPACES.
     03   FILLER                    PIC X(11) VALUE 'ENDING DATE'.
     03   FILLER                    PIC X(5) VALUE SPACES.
     03   FILLER                    PIC X(4) VALUE 'CODE'.
     03   FILLER                    PIC X(36) VALUE SPACES.
*
```

```
PROCEDURE DIVISION.
CONTROL-ROUTINE.
    PERFORM 010-OPENER.
    PERFORM 020-READER
        UNTIL INDICATOR = 1.
    PERFORM 030-CLOSER.
    STOP RUN.
010-OPENER.
    OPEN INPUT CARD-DATA
        OUTPUT PRINTFILE.
    WRITE OUTPUT-LINE FROM HEADING-LINE
        AFTER ADVANCING TOP-OF-PAGE.
    READ CARD-DATA
        AT END MOVE 1 TO INDICATOR.
020-READER.
    MOVE NAME TO NAME-OUT.
    MOVE ADDRESS-IN TO ADDRESS-OUT.
    MOVE ORIG-BALANCE TO BALANCE-OUT.
    MOVE MO-BILL TO MONTHLY-OUT.
    MOVE ENDING-DATE TO END-DATE-OUT.
    MOVE CODE-1 TO CODE-1-OUT.
    MOVE CODE-2 TO CODE-2-OUT.
    WRITE OUTPUT-LINE FROM MAIN-LINE
        AFTER ADVANCING 2 LINES.
    READ CARD-DATA
        AT END MOVE 1 TO INDICATOR.
030-CLOSER.
    MOVE 'END OF PROGRAM' TO OUTPUT-LINE.
    WRITE OUTPUT-LINE
        AFTER ADVANCING 3 LINES.
    CLOSE CARD-DATA, PRINTFILE.
```

NAME	ADDRESS	BALANCE	MONTHLY	ENDING DATE	CODE
JONES, EDWIN	456 19TH ST LODI, CA	$043.76	$04.50	12 31 82	004-53
SMITH, SHIRLEY	PO BOX 48 SACTO,CA	$019.59	$05.00	06 15 82	009-00
NEWTON, JOHN	RT 15 RENO, NEV	$107.16	$24.00	08 30 84	038-62
CARDOZA, RAUL	1004 ELM ST S F, CA	$000.00	$09.50	05 30 82	014-00
FONG, ROBERT	274 FIR DR BRYTE, CA	$051.91	$08.00	02 28 83	112-53

END OF PROGRAM

FIGURE 6-6

Subscription Program

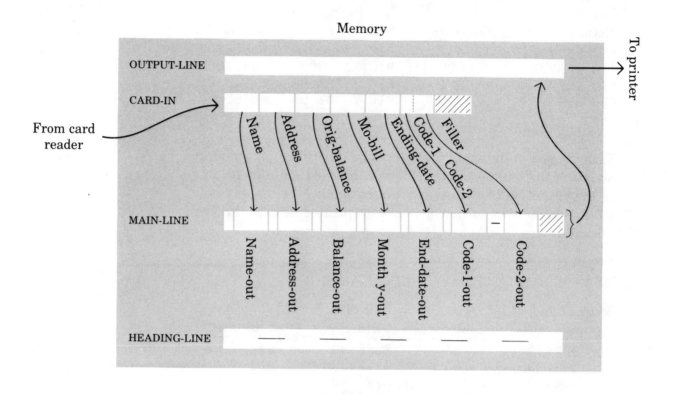

The following charts show some of the more common editing capabilities of COBOL:

NUMERIC DATA—DECIMAL POINT

Source Field Picture	Contents	Edit Field Picture	Result
PIC 999V99	12345	PIC 999.99	123.45
PIC 999V99	05678	PIC 999.99	056.78

NUMERIC DATA—DOLLAR SIGN AND COMMAS

PIC 999V99	12345	PIC $999.99	$123.45
PIC 9999V99	684021	PIC $9,999.99	$6,840.21
PIC 9999V99	039550	PIC $9,999.99	$0,395.50

In two of the above examples the left-most, or insignificant, zero digit was printed. This is technically correct, but usually is not acceptable for reports. The Z edit character allows you to suppress leading zeros as far as you want. Normal practice is to suppress up to the decimal point, but not beyond it. The small "b" (blank) in the following examples shows the suppression of leading zeros.

Source Field Picture	Contents	Edit Field Picture	Result
PIC 999V99	12345	PIC ZZZ.99	123.45
PIC 999V99	05678	PIC ZZZ.99	b56.78
PIC 9999V99	684021	PIC Z,ZZZ.99	6,840.21
PIC 9999V99	039550	PIC Z,ZZZ.99	bb395.50

Earlier you saw the use of the dollar sign ($) printed immediately to the left of the left-most digit. If the source field contains leading zeros, the output will not look very professional. A better way is to "float" the dollar sign so that it is always printed next to the first significant digit.

NUMERIC DATA—FLOATING DOLLAR SIGN

Source Field Picture	Contents	Edit Field Picture	Results
PIC 999V99	49763	$$$$.99	$497.63
PIC 999V99	09763	$$$$.99	b$97.63
PIC 999V99	00763	$$$$.99	bb$7.63
PIC 9999V99	157875	$$,$$$.99	$1,578.75
PIC 9999V99	057875	$$,$$$.99	b$578.75
PIC 9999V99	157875	$,$$$.99	—

An error condition will result when there is an insufficient number of dollar signs to accommodate all the digits in the output field.

The last example is incorrect because in a floating dollar sign editing operation there must always be one dollar sign more than the number of digits to the left of the decimal point.

Although most numbers you will encounter are positive, negative numbers can arise in two ways. One, of course, is as the result of arithmetic calculations. The second source is from negative values that come in from the input file. In the case of card data, negative values are indicated by an 11-row punch over the right-most digit of the field. This is known as an "overpunch" and is generally shown by means of a short line or bar in the appropriate position.

Incoming Data Record

4595	2700̄	⌐	"Overpunch" (11 punch in card) to indicate a negative value
Monthly Payment	Credit Amount		

According to everything you have learned so far, each of the two fields would be set up as PIC 99V99. Although the PICTURE entry of 99V99 is technically correct for positive numbers, it is not correct for fields whose contents could become negative. In the example shown above, the Credit Amount field would actually contain a *positive* 27 dollars. In order for the machine to handle negative values correctly, the programmer must insert an S before the 9's in the PICTURE entry: PIC S99V99. So the general rule is that for any numeric field whose contents might become negative, the programmer must insert the S. Many data processing shops avoid the worry of which fields may become negative and which won't by requiring that all numeric fields be set up with an S. Our incoming card fields would be set up as follows.

```
03   MONTHLY-PAYMENT                    PIC S99V99.
03   CREDIT-AMT                         PIC S99V99.
```

When editing numeric fields to show whether the values are positive or negative, the programmer has several choices in addition to the dollar sign, commas, and decimal point. The choice of symbols includes the plus sign (+) or the minus sign (−) before or after the field and the debit or credit symbols (DB or CR) after the field. Note the following examples.

NUMERIC DATA—POSITIVE OR NEGATIVE VALUES

Source Field Picture	Contents	Edit Field Picture	Result
PIC S99V99	2145	PIC +99.99	+21.45
PIC S99V99	2145	PIC +99.99	−21.45
PIC S99V99	4619	PIC −99.99	b46.19
PIC S99V99	4619	PIC −99.99	−46.19

Note that the plus sign edit character places either a plus *or* minus in the result field. However, the minus sign edit character places only the minus sign for a negative field.

PIC S999V99	38124	PIC $999.99+	$381.24+
PIC S999V99	38124	PIC $999.99+	$381.24−
PIC S999V99	97350	PIC $999.99−	$973.50b
PIC S999V99	97350	PIC $999.99−	$973.50−
PIC S999V99	48812	PIC ZZZ.99CR	488.12bb
PIC S999V99	48812	PIC ZZZ.99CR	488.12CR
PIC S999V99	09688	PIC ZZZ.99DB	b96.88bb
PIC S999V99	09688	PIC ZZZ.99DB	b96.88DB

One additional editing operation was present in the subscription listing shown in Figure 6-4. The six-digit ending date field was edited to make the date more readable by inserting blanks between the month, day, and year values. In the examples shown below, the capital B indicates the position of blanks imbedded in the result field.

Source Field Picture	Contents	Edit Field Picture	Result
PIC 9(6)	123182	PIC 99B99B99	12 31 82

Data formats—usage

One of the major advantages of COBOL is that it can handle data that are in a variety of formats. For example, the data entering from a card, whether numeric, alphabetic, or alphanumeric, are said to be in DISPLAY format. On most computers (particularly IBM machines) this means that each character occupies one position of memory. Our previous example,

```
03   MONTHLY-PAYMENT            PIC S99V99.
03   CREDIT-AMT                 PIC S99V99.
```

is correct because the system *assumes* DISPLAY format unless told otherwise. The following is correct but unnecessary:

```
03   MONTHLY-PAYMENT            PIC S99V99
        USAGE IS DISPLAY.
03   CREDIT-AMT                 PIC S99V99
        USAGE IS DISPLAY.
```

As a matter of fact, the words USAGE and IS are optional, so

```
03   MONTHLY-PAYMENT     PIC S99V99   DISPLAY.
```

is correct, but still the word DISPLAY is not necessary.

So, card data will not cause you any difficulty nor will data fields that are going to the printer. They also must be in DISPLAY format. The difficulty comes when you want to manipulate fields arithmetically. Suppose you set up a field for use as a counter. The WORKING-STORAGE entry

```
01   MISC-FIELDS.
     03   ITEM-COUNTER     PIC 99 VALUE ZERO.
```

establishes the field *in* DISPLAY *format* because you did not specify otherwise. Later in your program it is very likely that you will want to add to it by means of the statement

```
ADD 1 TO ITEM-COUNTER.
```

The statement is correct, and addition will take place exactly as indicated. However, the general rule is that the computer *cannot* do any arithmetic on a field that is in DISPLAY format. What happens is that the system itself must first change the field (or fields) into another format. The arithmetic is done on these new fields, and afterwards the ITEM-COUNTER is changed back to DISPLAY format.

For the beginning programmer there is a great temptation to say "If the machine does all the work, why tell me about it?" The reason is that this method is grossly inefficient in terms of machine time. With the effort of a few extra entries on your part, arithmetic operations can take place much more rapidly and efficiently. All you have to do is change the field into a format that makes this possible. There are two general formats that allow this: COMPUTATIONAL and COM-PUTATIONAL-3.

The entry USAGE IS COMPUTATIONAL applied to a field means that the system creates the field in binary format (the details of which will not be covered in this text). The second possibility—USAGE IS COMPU-TATIONAL-3—is used with IBM machines and indicates that the field is packed format. Arithmetic performed on fields in either of these formats is far more efficient than a DISPLAY field. Going back to our original example, your program would be more efficient using the following:

```
01   MISC-FIELDS.
     03   ITEM-COUNTER          PIC 99
          VALUE ZERO USAGE COMPUTATIONAL.
```

As you already know, the words USAGE and IS may be omitted. In addition, COMPUTATIONAL may be shortened to COMP and COMPUTA-TIONAL-3 shortened to COMP-3. (*Note:* On IBM machines you may use either COMP or COMP-3. One of these formats may be more efficient than the other depending upon the circumstance. Check your particular machine manual for details on this matter.) Again, note that you are not obligated to set up fields in these formats since the machine will do so automatically when the arithmetic is performed. A good programmer, however, will do so.

You saw how a field can be created in the proper format by means of the USAGE entry. Another common occurrence is that you have incoming card data fields you know must be worked on arithmetically. These fields automatically are in DISPLAY format and *must* be read in that way. To change these fields to another format, all you have to do is MOVE the values to another field that is in COMP (or COMP-3) format. Suppose we have payroll data as shown below:

In WORKING-STORAGE we could set up the following fields:

```
WORKING-STORAGE SECTION.
01  WORK-FIELDS.
    03  HRS-PACKED              PIC 99 COMP-3.
    03  RATE-PACKED             PIC 99V99 COMP-3.
```

The statements

```
MOVE HRS-IN TO HRS-PACKED.
MOVE RATE-IN TO RATE-PACKED.
```

will move the values in the incoming data fields to the packed format areas where conversion will take place. Again, this is far more efficient than making the system do the work on its own.

Duplicate names and move corresponding

The general practice in COBOL is to give each field a unique and meaningful name. In addition, it is helpful to identify the source of the field by attaching some identifier to the name, such as ID-NBR-CARD (for a card input field), TOTAL-SALES-WS (for a WORKING-STORAGE entry), and so on. At the beginning level of programming, duplicate names normally are not used even though they are permissible in COBOL. The reason for this, of course, is that beginning programs seldom are long enough to cause any problem in the naming of fields. If duplicate names are used, the programmer must *qualify* them by indicating the record to which they belong. Note the following example of data fields within the input and output records.

```
01  CARD-RECORD.
    03  ID-NBR                  PIC 9(5).
    03  NAME                    PIC X(20).
    03  PHONE-NBR               PIC 9(7).
    03  ADDRESS                 PIC X(30).
    03  FILLER                  PIC X(18).
WORKING-STORAGE SECTION.
01  MAIN-REPORT-LINE.
    03  FILLER                  PIC X(16)    VALUE SPACES.
    03  NAME                    PIC X(20).
    03  FILLER                  PIC X(10)    VALUE SPACES.
    03  ADDRESS                 PIC X(30).
    03  FILLER                  PIC X(10)    VALUE SPACES.
    03  ID-NBR                  PIC 9(5).
    03  FILLER                  PIC X(30)    VALUE SPACES.
```

Moving the three card fields to the appropriate report line fields would involve three separate MOVE statements *with qualifiers*.

```
MOVE NAME OF CARD-RECORD TO
    NAME OF MAIN-REPORT-LINE.
MOVE ADDRESS OF CARD-RECORD TO
    ADDRESS OF MAIN-REPORT-LINE.
MOVE ID-NBR OF CARD-RECORD TO
    ID-NBR OF MAIN-REPORT-LINE.
```

The use of the qualifiers as shown above provides good documentation, but requires a lot of extra coding. MOVE CORRESPONDING, however, can simplify the whole process as the next example shows.

```
MOVE CORRESPONDING CARD-RECORD TO
    MAIN-REPORT-LINE.
```

The result of this statement is that the ID-NBR, NAME, and ADDRESS fields within the CARD-RECORD are moved to the corresponding fields in the MAIN-REPORT-LINE record. Some special rules must be followed when using MOVE CORRESPONDING.

1. The references must be to group items, as shown in the example.
2. All data items with corresponding names are moved and FILLER fields are ignored.
3. As the example shows, the corresponding fields in the two records do not have to be in the same order for the move to take place.
4. Technically, the fields do not have to be equal in size, although the normal practice is to have fields of the same size. If, in our example, ID-NBR in MAIN-REPORT-LINE had a PICTURE of 9(3), truncation of the left-most digits would occur.

Group moves in COBOL

Group move operations are tempting but tricky in COBOL. The rule is that data in group moves are treated alphanumerically, and that the move takes place without regard to the individual fields that are part of the group. Note the following example:

```
03   CUSTOMER-RECORD.
     05   CUST-NBR-IN              PIC 9(05).
     05   CUST-NAME-IN             PIC X(30).
     05   CUST-ADDRESS-IN          PIC X(25).
     .
     .
     .
WORKING-STORAGE SECTION.
     .
     .
     .
03   CUSTOMER-RECORD-WS.
     05   CUST-NBR-WS              PIC 9(05).
     05   CUST-NAME-WS             PIC X(30).
     05   CUST-ADDRESS-WS          PIC X(25).
```

The statement

```
MOVE CUSTOMER-RECORD TO CUSTOMER-RECORD-WS.
```

will move the correct data because the length of each group is exactly the same—60 characters. The fact that the fields are mixed—that is, both 9s and xs—makes no difference. If the CUSTOMER-RECORD-WS fields were in a different order or were of different lengths, the proper values would not get into the various fields. Setting up the WORKING-STORAGE fields in the following manner will result in an *incorrect* group move even though the total lengths of the fields are the same as before.

```
03   CUSTOMER-RECORD-WS.
     05   CUST-ADDRESS-WS        PIC X(25).
     05   CUST-NBR-WS            PIC 9(05).
     05   CUST-NAME-WS           PIC X(30).
```

One other example should be mentioned here concerning group moves and the use of the figurative constant ZEROS. As shown in many examples so far, you are very likely to have various indicators, counters, totals, and so on to set to zero in WORKING-STORAGE. Normally you would include the VALUE ZEROS entry for each of the fields because you wish to be certain of the field contents. Everything is fine so far, but suppose you use these fields in computations and then wish to reset them to zero before going on to the next part of your program. Instead of writing individual MOVE ZEROS statements, you may be tempted to try a group MOVE. Let's assume we have the following fields in WORKING-STORAGE:

```
03   MISC-FIELDS.
     05   INDICATOR    PIC 9         VALUE ZEROS.
     05   COUNTER      PIC 99        VALUE ZEROS.
     05   TOTAL-1      PIC 999V99    VALUE ZEROS.
```

The group move statement

```
MOVE ZEROS TO MISC-FIELDS.
```

will work *only because* each of these fields is in DISPLAY format. Since, by definition, alphanumeric MOVES move data (zeros in this case) in DISPLAY format, there is no problem; "correct" zeros are moved. If any of the above fields were in COMP or COMP-3 format, "correct" zeros would not get moved. Then, either incorrect answers would result or the program would abort when the programmer tried to do arithmetic on these fields.

Current date

The reserved word list for most computer systems includes the name CURRENT-DATE. This term is most frequently used with IBM machines, but virtually every COBOL compiler has a field that contains today's date. (Check the manual on your machine for the exact name of the date field.) Usually the field is eight characters long and contains the date in the form MM/DD/YY, where MM represents the month, DD is the day, and YY is the year.

This is a pre-defined field that you *cannot* define in your program. However, you may use it by moving the field to an appropriate area in an output line.

```
WORKING-STORAGE SECTION.
.
.
.

01   HEADING-LINE.
     03
     03
     .
     .
     .
     03   DATE-AREA              PIC X(8).
     .
     .
PROCEDURE DIVISION.
     .
     .
     .
     MOVE CURRENT-DATE TO DATE-AREA.
```

Common errors

One very common error in COBOL involves the misuse of the first space of the printing line. Remember that the system requires this first space for carriage control—a topic introduced in Chapter 5. A variation on the sample program shown in Figure 6-5 illustrates what happens when the rules of printer control are violated. At the end of the subscription program we moved 'END OF PROGRAM' to the OUTPUT-LINE. The space before the first letter was there to allow room for the carriage control character in the OUTPUT-LINE, as shown below.

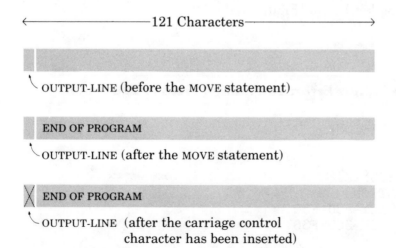

←——————————121 Characters——————————→

OUTPUT-LINE (before the MOVE statement)

END OF PROGRAM

OUTPUT-LINE (after the MOVE statement)

END OF PROGRAM

OUTPUT-LINE (after the carriage control
              character has been inserted)

If we were to move 'END OF PROGRAM' (i.e., without the leading space), the first character—the E—would be destroyed when the carriage control character is moved in. Figure 6-7 shows the pertinent parts of the program and the resulting output.

FIGURE 6-7

Error in Printer Output

```
FD   PRINTFILE
     LABEL RECORDS ARE OMITTED
     DATA RECORD IS OUTPUT-LINE.
01   OUTPUT-LINE                    PIC X(121).

030-CLOSER.
     MOVE 'END OF PROGRAM' TO OUTPUT-LINE.
     WRITE OUTPUT-LINE
          AFTER ADVANCING 3 LINES.
     CLOSE CARD-DATA, PRINTFILE.
```

NAME	ADDRESS	BALANCE	MONTHLY	ENDING DATE	CODE
JONES, EDWIN	456 19TH ST LODI, CA	$043.76	$04.50	12 31 82	004-53
SMITH, SHIRLEY	PO BOX 48 SACTO, CA	$019.59	$05.00	06 15 82	009-00
NEWTON, JOHN	RT 15 RENO, NEV	$107.16	$24.00	08 30 84	038-62
CARDOZA, RAUL	1004 ELM ST S F, CA	$000.00	$09.50	05 30 82	014-00
FONG, ROBERT	274 FIR DR BRYTE, CA	$051.91	$08.00	02 28 83	112-53

```
ND OF PROGRAM
```

The second error example illustrates what happens when an edit field is too small for the incoming data. In this case, the BALANCE-OUT field (PIC $99.99) is not large enough to accept all the incoming data values from BALANCE (PIC 999V99). Compare the output with that shown in Figure 6-5 and you will notice that the left-most digit has been eliminated. Also note that the software detected the error, but indicated it only as a warning level error (Figure 6-8).

FIGURE 6-8

Subscription Report with Editing Error: The Editing Field Is Too Small.

```
     IDENTIFICATION DIVISION.
     PROGRAM-ID. SUBSCR.
*
     ENVIRONMENT DIVISION.
     CONFIGURATION SECTION.
     SOURCE-COMPUTER. IBM-360-F30.
     OBJECT-COMPUTER. IBM-360-F30.
     SPECIAL-NAMES.
          C01 IS TOP-OF-PAGE.
     INPUT-OUTPUT SECTION.
     FILE-CONTROL.
          SELECT PRINTFILE
               ASSIGN TO SYS009-UR-1403-S.
          SELECT CARD-DATA
               ASSIGN TO SYS007-UR-2540R-S.
*
```

```
DATA DIVISION.
FILE SECTION.
FD  PRINTFILE
    LABEL RECORDS ARE OMITTED
    DATA RECORD IS OUTPUT-LINE.
01  OUTPUT-LINE                          PIC X(121).
FD  CARD-DATA
    LABEL RECORDS ARE OMITTED
    DATA RECORD IS CARD-IN.
01  CARD-IN.
    03  NAME                             PIC A(20).
    03  ADDRESS-IN                       PIC X(20).
    03  ORIG-BALANCE                     PIC 999V99.
    03  MO-BILL                          PIC 99V99.
    03  ENDING-DATE                      PIC 9(6).
    03  CODE-1                           PIC 999.
    03  CODE-2                           PIC 99.
    03  FILLER                           PIC X(20).
WORKING-STORAGE SECTION.
77  INDICATOR                            PIC 9 VALUE ZERO.
01  MAIN-LINE.
    03  FILLER                           PIC X.
    03  FILLER                           PIC X(5) VALUE SPACES.
    03  NAME-OUT                         PIC X(20).
    03  FILLER                           PIC X(5) VALUE SPACES.
    03  ADDRESS-OUT                      PIC X(20).
    03  FILLER                           PIC X(5) VALUE SPACES.
    03  BALANCE-OUT                      PIC $99.99.
    03  FILLER                           PIC X(6) VALUE SPACES.
    03  MONTHLY-OUT                      PIC $99.99.
    03  FILLER                           PIC X(8) VALUE SPACES.
    03  END-DATE-OUT                     PIC 99B99B99.
    03  FILLER                           PIC X(5) VALUE SPACES.
    03  CODE-1-OUT                       PIC 999.
    03  FILLER                           PIC X VALUE '-'.
    03  CODE-2-OUT                       PIC 99.
    03  FILLER                           PIC X(19) VALUE SPACES.

01  HEADING-LINE.
    03  FILLER                           PIC X.
    03  FILLER                           PIC X(13) VALUE SPACES.
    03  FILLER                           PIC X(4) VALUE 'NAME'.
    03  FILLER                           PIC X(19) VALUE SPACES.
    03  FILLER                           PIC X(7) VALUE 'ADDRESS'.
    03  FILLER                           PIC X(12) VALUE SPACES.
    03  FILLER                           PIC X(7) VALUE 'BALANCE'.
    03  FILLER                           PIC X(5) VALUE SPACES.
    03  FILLER                           PIC X(7) VALUE 'MONTHLY'.
    03  FILLER                           PIC X(5) VALUE SPACES.
    03  FILLER                           PIC X(11) VALUE 'ENDING DATE'.
    03  FILLER                           PIC X(5) VALUE SPACES.
    03  FILLER                           PIC X(4) VALUE 'CODE'.
    03  FILLER                           PIC X(36) VALUE SPACES.
*
```

```
PROCEDURE DIVISION.
CONTROL-ROUTINE.
    PERFORM 010-OPENER.
    PERFORM 020-READER
        UNTIL INDICATOR = 1.
    PERFORM 030-CLOSER.
    STOP RUN.
010-OPENER.
    OPEN INPUT CARD-DATA
        OUTPUT PRINTFILE.
    WRITE OUTPUT-LINE FROM HEADING-LINE
        AFTER ADVANCING TOP-OF-PAGE.
    READ CARD-DATA
        AT END MOVE 1 TO INDICATOR.
020-READER.
    MOVE NAME TO NAME-OUT.
    MOVE ADDRESS-IN TO ADDRESS-OUT.
    MOVE ORIG-BALANCE TO BALANCE-OUT.
    MOVE MO-BILL TO MONTHLY-OUT.
    MOVE ENDING-DATE TO END-DATE-OUT.
    MOVE CODE-1 TO CODE-1-OUT.
    MOVE CODE-2 TO CODE-2-OUT.
    WRITE OUTPUT-LINE FROM MAIN-LINE
        AFTER ADVANCING 2 LINES.
    READ CARD-DATA
        AT END MOVE 1 TO INDICATOR.
030-CLOSER.
    MOVE 'END OF PROGRAM' TO OUTPUT-LINE.
    WRITE OUTPUT-LINE
        AFTER ADVANCING 3 LINES.
    CLOSE CARD-DATA, PRINTFILE.
```

```
CARD     ERROR MESSAGE
80       ILA5011I-W     HIGH ORDER TRUNCATION MIGHT OCCUR.
```

NAME	ADDRESS	BALANCE	MONTHLY	ENDING DATE	CODE
JONES, EDWIN	456 19TH ST LODI, CA	$43.76	$04.50	12 31 82	004-53
SMITH, SHIRLEY	PO BOX 48 SACTO,CA	$19.59	$05.00	06 15 82	009-00
NEWTON, JOHN	RT 15 RENO, NEV	$07.16	$24.00	08 30 84	038-62
CARDOZA, RAUL	1004 ELM ST S F, CA	$00.00	$09.50	05 30 82	014-00
FONG, ROBERT	274 FIR DR BRYTE, CA	$51.91	$08.00	02 28 83	112-53

END OF PROGRAM

↑
Digit truncated

Problem-Solving Techniques

Some beginning COBOL programmers seem to have difficulty understanding the use of or need for the WORKING-STORAGE section. Although this section appears at the end of the DATA DIVISION, you should be thinking of it early in the design phase of the problem-solving process. WORKING-STORAGE is exactly what it says it is: a storage area for fields you will be working with in the program. Using it is much like packing a suitcase for a trip: You take those items you think you will need. In COBOL, as in packing a suitcase, the decision is yours. If you think you will need a working area during PROCEDURE DIVISION operations, then set up whatever is required.

The most common usages of WORKING-STORAGE were shown in the chapter examples: total areas, indicators, and various heading and ending lines. Constant values such as pi (3.1415), which might be used in mathematical applications, pay rate increases, and so forth, are commonly set up here. So, during the coding stage, set up those fields you know you are going to need. Later, when coding the PROCEDURE DIVISION entries, you may find that you have need for another WORKING-STORAGE field, but it should be no problem to add it as required. The general rule is that unless you intend to MOVE (GIVING) into a WORKING-STORAGE field, it should contain an initial value established by the VALUE entry.

Self-Study: Questions and Answers

1. Why are there two parts to the DATA DIVISION? It seems as though all the entries could go in the FILE SECTION so that WORKING-STORAGE wouldn't be needed.

   Answer
   The two parts of the DATA DIVISION serve two different functions, and there are slightly different rules concerning the entries in each part. The FILE SECTION identifies the files named in the SELECT entries made earlier. The WORKING-STORAGE SECTION, on the other hand, is the place where you create fields and records that are not directly part of the files you are using.

   In addition to the obvious difference between the two sections, there is a difference in philosophy between them. In WORKING-STORAGE you not only create fields, but also have the capability of placing actual values into specific areas. In the FILE SECTION (with one exception) you cannot use the VALUE clause. All you can do is identify the nature, size, and sequence for the data fields. So, both sections are necessary.

2. Do I always have to use the VALUE entry with fields that I create in the WORKING-STORAGE SECTION?

   Answer
   No, you do not. There would be nothing gained by assigning a specific value to a field into which you are going to move some data. The move, of course, would destroy the old contents of the field anyway.

   Also, you are not obligated to say VALUE ZEROS even for fields such as TOTAL-1 or TOTAL-2, as shown in the chapter example. Rather than use the VALUE entry at that point, you could use the MOVE ZEROS statement in the PROCEDURE DIVISION to accomplish the same result. However, this is not nearly as efficient as using VALUE. Perhaps even more important is that it is very easy to forget the MOVE ZEROS when actually writing the PROCEDURE DIVISION statements.

3. Do most COBOL programs have multiple types of output lines? All those different lines make the WORKING-STORAGE SECTION quite long.

   Answer
   Unfortunately, "fancy" output for reports, checks, bills, and so on is the nature of COBOL, and the normal way of things is that you will have several types of output lines in most programs. You are right, COBOL is a wordy language.

4. Is C01 always used for the top printing line on a new page?

   Answer
   No, although it is common to a great many machines, including most IBM computers. Check your computer to be sure.

5. Editing seems simple although there are a great many possibilities from which to choose. Does all editing take place when you move a numeric field to an edit field?

   Answer
   As far as the programmer is concerned, editing is very simple although the system is doing an enormous amount of work you don't see. Editing is accomplished by means of the MOVE statement or by the GIVING option with arithmetic statements—a topic not yet discussed. Certain specific computers may not accept all the possible combinations of editing that were shown, but usually it is easy to work around these problems. The most common editing features such as zero suppression, dollar signs, decimal points, and commas are well standardized.

6. Must all incoming card data and outgoing printer data be in DISPLAY format? Why can't it be COMPUTATIONAL or COMPUTATIONAL-3?

   Answer
   Both COMPUTATIONAL (binary) and COMPUTATIONAL-3 (packed) imply a format of something other than one character per memory position. Standard card format can only be DISPLAY because we can punch only one character per card column, and, of course, the same is true for the printer—it can print only one character per print position. With magnetic storage, such as memory, disk, and tape, other combinations are possible so that COMP and COMP-3 are permitted.

   Remember that you are not required to set up fields in anything other than DISPLAY format (in the examples used so far), but you can make the computer operations far more efficient by using COMP or COMP-3 when appropriate.

Exercises

1. What is the purpose of the WORKING-STORAGE SECTION? How does it differ from the FILE SECTION of the DATA DIVISION?

2. Although there is one exception we have not covered yet, the general rule is that the VALUE clause cannot be used in the FILE SECTION. Why is this? What is the logic behind this rule?

3. The text showed several examples in which a HEADING-LINE was set up in the WORKING-STORAGE SECTION (Figure 6-5). Each of the individual fields that made up the record called HEADING-LINE were FILLERS. Why weren't these fields given names? Explain.

4. Diagram the action of the WRITE FROM statement. Contrast this with a diagram of the READ INTO statement.

5. In Figure 6-5 there is an incoming CARD-IN record containing the six-digit field ENDING-DATE. Make the necessary changes in the DATA DIVISION so that the field is subdivided into month, day, and year during input. Also change the necessary MAIN-LINE fields so that the ENDING-DATE is printed with a space between each of the subfields *without* using the blank (B) edit character.

6. Here is a thought question: Suppose the ENDING-DATE field comes in as PIC 9(6). Without using any edit features of COBOL, how could you isolate (and print) just the middle two digits (the day figure) of this six-digit field?

7. In the WORKING-STORAGE SECTION of the Subscription Program (Figure 6-5), the INDICATOR field was established with an initial value of zero by means of the VALUE entry. What would have happened if the VALUE part of the entry had been omitted? What would have happened if the entry had been written as PIC 9 VALUE 5?

8. Another thought question. Every time we have used an indicator with PERFORM UNTIL, it has been set up as a numeric field. Could we have used an A or an X field instead? AT END could we have moved something other than a numeric character?

9. Write the WORKING-STORAGE entries for the following fields where arithmetic manipulations are going to be performed.
   a. A three-position total area called NO-OF-SALES; display format.
   b. A five-position total area called COUNTER-1; display format.
   c. A seven-position total area for the storage of dollar and cents data; packed format.
   d. A six-position total area for the storage of dollar and cents data; binary format.
   e. An eight-position total area for the storage of dollar and cents data; display format.
   f. A six-position dollar and cents area in packed format into which a data value will be moved.
   g. A four-position numeric area in binary format into which a data value will be moved.

10. Write the WORKING-STORAGE entries for the following fields.
    a. A field called KONSTANT that contains the value 763.714.
    b. A field called FUDGE-AMT that contains the value 21.65 in binary format.
    c. A field called ONE-AMT that contains the value 9 in packed format.
    d. A three-digit field that contains the value 6 in binary format.
    e. An alphanumeric field containing the message BAD CARD DATA.
    f. An alphanumeric field containing the current month, day, and year.
    g. A 30-character alphabetic field containing your name.

11. Write the WORKING-STORAGE entries for the following output (printer) records. Provide one extra position for carriage control.
    a. 120-character line containing the heading INCOME STATEMENT centered on the page.
    b. 132-character line containing the heading FOR THE YEAR 1983 indented 30 spaces from the left margin.
    c. Same as above, but indented 30 spaces from the right margin.

12. Write the WORKING-STORAGE entries for the following edited fields.
    a. Source field PIC 999V99: Output field to suppress leading zeros up to the decimal point and to include the decimal point.
    b. Same as above, but to have a floating dollar sign up to the decimal point.
    c. Source field PIC 9999V99: Output field to contain a decimal and a comma and to suppress leading zeros up to the decimal point.
    d. Same as above, but float the dollar sign up to the decimal point.

e. Source field PIC S999V99: Output field to suppress leading zeros up to the decimal point and to include the decimal point and the CR symbol in case the field is negative.

f. Same as above, except to provide for the printing of a trailing + or − sign in case the field is negative.

g. Source field PIC S99999V99.: Output field is to contain a fixed dollar sign, a comma, and a decimal point, no zero suppression, and is to provide for the printing of a DB symbol in case the field is negative.

h. Source field PIC 9(9), which contains a social security number: Output is to break the number into its component parts (three digits, two digits, and four digits) by inserting a blank in the appropriate location.

13. Write complete output lines according to the following formats. You may assume that the printer line is 120 characters plus one position for carriage control. Space the fields appropriately across the page.

a.

TOTALS	EDIT-1	EDIT-2
	$XXX.XX	$X,XXX.XX

   (fixed dollar sign; no zero suppression)

b. Same as above with floating $.

c.   XXX RECORDS WERE PROCESSED
   (provide for zero suppression up to but not including the last digit)

d.   GROSS PAY IS $XXXX.XX. NET PAY IS $XXX.XX
   (provide for a floating dollar sign up to the decimal point)

e.   SUBSCRIPTION EXPIRES ON XX XX XX. RENEW NOW.
   (provide for blanks in the date field)

14. Data file A in the appendix section of the text contains data that can be used for a variety of programs. Assume that the data are available in card form with each record having the following format for this problem:

Card Columns	Field Description
1–9	Social security number
10–29	Employee name
30–34	Filler
35–36	Number of dependents
37–40	Insurance deduction amount in the format xx $_\wedge$ xx
41–45	Credit union deduction amount in the format xxx $_\wedge$ xx
46–50	Other deductions in the format xxx $_\wedge$ xx
51–80	Filler

Write a program to produce the output according to the following requirements.
1. Advance the printer to the top of a new page before printing any output.
2. The output is to be spaced appropriately across the page.
3. The social security number field is to be output with the format XXX-XX-XXXX.
4. Provide for zero suppression completely through the dependents field.
5. The insurance and credit union amount fields are to be edited with a floating dollar sign and the decimal point.
6. The other deductions amount field is to be edited with a fixed dollar sign, zero suppression to the left of the decimal point, and the decimal point.

```
                        EMPLOYEE LIST


NAME    SS-NUMBER    DEPENDENTS   INSURANCE   CREDIT UNION   OTHER DEDUCTIONS
_____  XXX-XX-XXXX      XX        $XX.XX       $XXX.XX          $XXX.XX
```

Chapter 7

The Procedure Division—

Part II

COBOL offers the programmer a variety of statements that permit manipulating and testing the contents of data fields. Before getting to the actual statements (which, by the way, are quite easy to learn and use), we had better take care of a subject that normally comes up about now. Beginning students constantly ask "How do I know the size of the results of arithmetic computations?"

The size of data fields

Obviously, you always know the size of incoming data fields, such as name, address, social security number, and so on. Knowing that, the answer to the question asked above is really very simple. With one possible exception, you *always* know the size of the answers because the answers are generated the same way they are in real life.

First, let's take care of the one occasion when you have to think about the matter. For example, if you were adding a two-digit field into a total area each time through a loop, you certainly would not make the total field only two digits long. But how long should it be? The most logical solution is that you inquire into the matter. Perhaps the operation was done manually before, and the size of the answer can be estimated very closely. Another possibility is to get a close guess as to the number of times the loop will be executed. Then, by assuming that each two-digit field will contain the maximum value of 99, you can easily determine the required size of the total field.

With the exception of the above case, you always know the size of the results. A three-digit field subtracted from a three-digit field *always* gives a three-digit answer even though the left-most digit may be zero. The rules for multiplication and division are the same as they are in regular arithmetic. In multiplication, the product, or answer size, is always equal to the sum of the lengths of the fields being multiplied, even though there may be leading zeros on the left.

Examples

A large five-digit number multiplied by a large two-digit number.

```
   987.50      PIC   999V99
        95      PIC   99
  ─────────
  4937 50
  8887 50
  ─────────
 93812.50      PIC   9(5)V99.
```

A medium value five-digit number multiplied by a medium value two-digit number.

```
   407.25      PIC   999V99
        50      PIC   99
  ─────────
  000 00
  2036 25
  ─────────
 20362.50      PIC   9(5)V99
```

A small value five-digit number multiplied by a small value two-digit number.

```
   123.50      PIC   999V99
        15      PIC   99
  ─────────
  617 50
  123 50
  ─────────
 01852.50      PIC   9(5)V99
```

Note that the product contains a nonsignificant zero on the left. Normally, when multiplying by hand we would not show this zero. However, it is actually there and the computer system must account for *all* positions in the field since there is no way of knowing in advance the actual values that will be processed.

Division follows the same rules where the remainder is always the size of the divisor and the quotient is always the size of the dividend.

$$\text{DIVISOR} \overline{)\,\text{DIVIDEND}}^{\text{QUOTIENT}}$$

Examples

A one-digit number divided into a three-digit number.

```
                085       PIC 999
  PIC 9      3 256        PIC 999
                24
                16
                15
                 1        PIC 9
```

A two-digit number divided into a five-digit number.

```
               007.08     PIC   999V99
  PIC 99   15 106.28      PIC   999V99
              105
                1 28
                1 20
                  08      PIC   99
```

Calculating in COBOL

Four arithmetic statements (ADD, SUBTRACT, MULTIPLY, and DIVIDE) plus the versatile COMPUTE statement allow the programmer a wide range of choices when he or she performs calculations. Two operations—ROUNDED and ON SIZE ERROR—may also be used with each of the arithmetic statements. All the fields are automatically aligned on the decimal point during computations. Only the more common forms of the statements will be illustrated here.

The ADD statement

The easiest form of the ADD statement is

$$\text{\underline{ADD}} \quad \begin{Bmatrix} \text{identifier-1} \\ \text{literal-1} \end{Bmatrix} \cdots \begin{Bmatrix} \text{identifier-2} \\ \text{literal-2} \end{Bmatrix} \cdots \text{\underline{TO}} \text{ identifier n}$$

where the term "identifier" refers to a field that is an elementary numeric item.

Examples

    ADD 1 TO COUNTER-B.

The contents of COUNTER-B are increased by one. The programmer would have set up the COUNTER-B field somewhere in the DATA DIVISION prior to the execution of this statement.

03 ∧ 5		04 ∧ 5
COUNTER-B		COUNTER-B
before		after

    ADD REG-PAY TO TOTAL-PAY.

The contents of REG-PAY remain unchanged in this operation.

098 ∧ 50		0000 ∧ 00
REG-PAY		TOTAL-PAY
before		before
098 ∧ 50		0098 ∧ 50
REG-PAY		TOTAL-PAY
after		after

Multiple fields and/or literals can be added in one ADD statement as the next examples illustrate.

Examples

    ADD REG-PAY OVER-TIME-PAY TO TOTAL-PAY.

The values contained in REG-PAY and OVER-TIME-PAY are unchanged. TOTAL-PAY is increased by the sum of the values in the first two fields. The system performs this operation by adding the values stored in REG-PAY and OVER-TIME-PAY in a special system work area. This amount is then added to TOTAL-PAY.

098 ∧ 50	030 ∧ 00	0000 ∧ 00
REG–PAY before	OVER–TIME–PAY before	TOTAL–PAY before

098 ∧ 50	030 ∧ 00	0128 ∧ 50
REG–PAY after	OVER–TIME–PAY after	TOTAL/PAY after

    ADD 15.00, REG-PAY, OVER-TIME-PAY TO TOTAL-PAY.

Same as above except that we have now included a literal value. Commas are shown in this example to illustrate that they may be used to provide better readability but are not required.

A second version of the ADD statement allows the result of the computation to be transferred to another field by means of the GIVING option. In addition, either or both of the options ROUNDED or ON SIZE ERROR may be used.

$$\text{ADD} \left\{ \begin{array}{l} \text{identifier-1} \\ \text{literal-1} \end{array} \right\} \cdots \left\{ \begin{array}{l} \text{identifier-2} \\ \text{literal-2} \end{array} \right\} \begin{array}{l} \text{GIVING identifier-n} \\ \text{ROUNDED ON SIZE ERROR} \\ \text{imperative statement.} \end{array}$$

Note that TO and GIVING are *not* permitted in the same ADD statement. The identifier following GIVING may be a field containing numeric edit characters.

Examples

```
ADD FIELD-A FIELD-B GIVING GRAND-TOTAL.
```

The contents of FIELD-A and FIELD-B are unchanged. The contents of GRAND-TOTAL are destroyed and replaced by the sum of the values in FIELD-A and FIELD-B. As before, the summing operation is performed in the system work area.

15 ∧ 00	21 ∧ 55	956 ∧ 88
FIELD-A before	FIELD-B before	GRAND-TOTAL before

15 ∧ 00	21 ∧ 55	036 ∧ 55
FIELD-A after	FIELD-B after	GRAND-TOTAL after

```
ADD 5.00, FIELD-A, FIELD-B GIVING GRAND-TOTAL.
```

The format is the same as the first example, except that a literal has been included along with optional commas.

```
ADD OLD-BAL SALES GIVING NEW-AMT ON SIZE ERROR PERFORM ERROR-
    ROUTINE.
```

The calculation part of the ADD statement is the same as before, but the SIZE ERROR option indicates what is to be done if a SIZE ERROR is encountered. This situation arises when the result of the addition is too large to fit into the NEW-AMT field. If the SIZE ERROR option were omitted, truncation—that is, loss of digits from the field—could result and the system would continue on to the next statement in sequence.

21 ∧ 25	40 ∧ 00	95 ∧ 72
OLD-BAL before	SALES before	NEW-AMT before
and after	and after	61 ∧ 25 NEW-AMT after

In the situation above there is no size error even though the total field (NEW-AMT) is really too small for the purpose. The second situation shows how a SIZE ERROR condition arises.

86 ∧ 00		40 ∧ 00		95 ∧ 72
OLD—BAL		SALES		NEW—AMT
before		before		before
and after		and after		

26 ∧ 00

NEW—AMT
after

The inadequate size of the NEW-AMT field will be detected when the system recognizes that the 1 digit to the left cannot fit in. The system then branches (GO TO) to ERROR-ROUTINE, which probably prints a message to the operator. Without SIZE ERROR the situation would go undetected and the 1 would be lost (truncated).

The ROUNDED option may be used with any of the COBOL arithmetic statements, as can SIZE ERROR. In working with pay calculations, you know that the ultimate result must be a dollar and cents figure. Because of the intricacies of many pay rate calculations, the intermediate steps may contain more than two digits to the right of the decimal point. When these values are finally moved (GIVING) to the final pay field, you will want to round the cents amount. If the third digit to the right of the decimal point is 5 or greater, you should round up to the next cent in the second digit position. The ROUNDED option does this by rounding into the size of the receiving field.

Examples

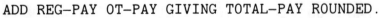

```
ADD REG-PAY OT-PAY GIVING TOTAL-PAY ROUNDED.
```

098 ∧ 755		030 ∧ 100		8765 ∧ 43
REG—PAY		OT—PAY		TOTAL—PAY
before		before		before
and after		and after		and after

0128 ∧ 86

```
098.755
030.100
```
128.855   rounded to .86 because the third digit is 5 or greater.

Without the ROUNDED, the answer would have been truncated to 0128.85.

```
ADD REG-PAY OT-PAY GIVING
    TOTAL-PAY ROUNDED ON SIZE ERROR PERFORM ERROR-ROUTINE.
```

The second example illustrates the use of both options in the same statement. In the previous example there was no size error, but suppose the TOTAL-PAY field had a picture of 99V99. The system could round as above, but the size error would occur because the left-most digit could not fit into the receiving field.

The SUBTRACT statement

The SUBTRACT statement follows the same general pattern as ADD in that you may use GIVING, ON SIZE ERROR, and ROUNDED when appropriate. The basic format is

$$\underline{\text{SUBTRACT}} \left\{ \begin{array}{l} \text{identifier-1} \\ \text{literal-1} \end{array} \right\} \cdots \left\{ \begin{array}{l} \text{identifier-2} \\ \text{literal-2} \end{array} \right\} \cdots \underline{\text{FROM}} \text{ identifier n.}$$

Example

```
SUBTRACT AMOUNT FROM TOTAL.
```

The value in AMOUNT is unchanged but the value of TOTAL is reduced by the value that was in AMOUNT.

143
AMOUNT
before
and after

568
TOTAL
before

425
TOTAL
after

Note: In an earlier part of the book you saw that the PICTURE entry must contain an S in order for the system to store a negative result. Observe the following examples using the same SUBTRACT statement.

AMOUNT	TOTAL			RESULT
Value 143	original value 568	PIC	999	+425
Value 850	original value 300	PIC	999	+550
Value 850	original value 300	PIC	S999	−550

Example

```
SUBTRACT 9.75 STATE-TAX FROM GROSS.
```

As before, the system sums 9.75 with the value of STATE-TAX in a system work area and subtracts this from GROSS. STATE-TAX remains unchanged. Commas may be used, but are not required.

The second version of the SUBTRACT statement makes use of the various options.

Examples

```
SUBTRACT AMOUNT FROM TOTAL GIVING NEW-TOTAL.
```

In this case the original values of AMOUNT and TOTAL remain unchanged, but the result of the subtraction is moved into NEW-TOTAL. The subtract calculation is done in a work area on copies of the values in AMOUNT and TOTAL.

143	568	987
AMOUNT	TOTAL	NEW-TOTAL
before	before	before
and after	and after	

		425
		NEW-TOTAL
		after

```
SUBTRACT DISCOUNT FROM BILL GIVING INV-AMT ROUNDED.
```

The result of the subtraction is moved and rounded to the size of the receiving field (INV-AMT).

04 ∧ 376		517 ∧ 000		349 ∧ 75
DISCOUNT		BILL		INV-AMT
before		before		before

				512 ∧ 62
and after		and after		

The answer was ROUNDED into INV-AMT, but was not rounded up since 4.376 from 517.000 equals 512.₿24. The last place was not large enough to round up to 63¢.

The MULTIPLY statement

Unlike ADD and SUBTRACT, where you can add or subtract multiple fields with a single statement, you may only multiply two values at a time. The first format is

$$\text{MULTIPLY} \left\{ \begin{array}{l} \text{identifier-1} \\ \text{literal-1} \end{array} \right\} \text{BY identifier-2.}$$

Examples

```
MULTIPLY HOURS BY RATE.
```

The value in HOURS remains unchanged and the answer (product) replaces the original value stored in RATE.

```
MULTIPLY 10 BY BASE-RATE.
```

As in the first example, the answer replaces the previous value of BASE-RATE.

The following example is incorrect because a literal cannot be used in place of identifier-2.

```
MULTIPLY BASE-RATE BY 10.
```

The original version of MULTIPLY (MULTIPLY HOURS BY RATE) was correct, but it presents some problems if you recall our original rule that the size of the answer is equal to the sum of the sizes of the fields being multiplied. According to that rule, the answer could never fit identifier-2. For example, if HOURS had a PICTURE of 99 and RATE a PICTURE of 9V99, the product would be 999V99, which cannot be stored in the RATE field. One solution is to move RATE (PIC 9V99) to a larger field (RATE-RESULT PIC 999V99) so that we know there are two leading zeros on the left. Then we multiply HOURS BY RATE-RESULT and know that an answer of the correct size will be stored. A much easier solution is to use the GIVING option.

$$\underline{\text{MULTIPLY}} \left\{ \begin{array}{l} \text{identifier-1} \\ \text{literal-1} \end{array} \right\} \underline{\text{BY}} \left\{ \begin{array}{l} \text{identifier-2} \\ \sout{\text{literal-2}} \end{array} \right\} \begin{array}{l} \underline{\text{GIVING}} \text{ identifier-2} \\ \underline{\text{ROUNDED}} \text{ ON } \underline{\text{SIZE ERROR}} \\ \text{imperative statement.} \end{array}$$

Examples

```
MULTIPLY HOURS BY RATE GIVING GROSS.
```

The values of HOURS and RATE are unchanged as the multiplication is done in the system work area and moved into GROSS.

40	06 ∧ 50	1853 ∧ 72
HOURS	RATE	GROSS
before	before	before
and after	and after	

0260 ∧ 00
GROSS
after

```
MULTIPLY  ORIG-BILL  BY  DISCOUNT-RATE  GIVING
DISCOUNT-ROUNDED. ROUNDED
```

The values stored in ORIG-BILL and DISCOUNT-RATE are unchanged. The result of the calculation is moved into DISCOUNT-ROUNDED and rounding takes place if necessary.

245 ∧ 75	∧ 025	00 ∧ 00
ORIG-BILL	DISCOUNT-RATE	DISCOUNT-ROUNDED
before	before	before
and after	and after	

06 ∧ 14
DISCOUNT-ROUNDED
after

```
MULTIPLY ORIG-BILL BY DISCOUNT-RATE GIVING DISCOUNT-ROUNDED
    ON SIZE-ERROR PERFORM DISC-ERROR.
```

The operation is the same as above except that an error routine is entered if a size error is detected. An abnormally large discount might generate an answer larger than the DISCOUNT-ROUNDED field.

The DIVIDE statement

DIVIDE follows the same general pattern as MULTIPLY in that you can only work with two values. The simple form is shown below, but the most useful version uses GIVING.

$$\underline{\text{DIVIDE}} \left\{ \begin{array}{l} \text{identifier-1} \\ \text{literal-1} \end{array} \right\} \left\{ \underline{\text{INTO}}\ \text{identifier-2.} \right.$$

Examples

```
DIVIDE NBR-OF-SCORES INTO TOTAL-POINTS.
```

The value of NBR-OF-SCORES remains unchanged and the answer (quotient) replaces the original value of TOTAL POINTS.

```
DIVIDE 12 INTO YEARLY-SALES.
```

The action is the same as the first example except that a literal was used instead of an identifier (data field). Note that a literal cannot be used in place of the second field.

The most useful version of the DIVIDE statement allows you to use GIVING and either INTO or BY plus ROUNDED and ON SIZE ERROR.

$$\underline{\text{DIVIDE}} \left\{ \begin{array}{l} \text{identifier-1} \\ \text{literal-1} \end{array} \right\} \left\{ \begin{array}{l} \underline{\text{INTO}} \\ \underline{\text{BY}} \end{array} \right\} \left\{ \begin{array}{l} \text{identifier-2} \\ \text{literal-2} \end{array} \right\}$$

<u>GIVING</u> identifier-3
<u>ROUNDED</u> ON <u>SIZE ERROR</u>
imperative statement.

Examples

```
DIVIDE ITEMS-SOLD INTO DOLLAR-VALUE GIVING AVG-VALUE.
```

The values stored at ITEMS-SOLD and DOLLAR-VALUE are used as indicated in the computation, but remain unchanged. The answer replaces the initial value stored in AVG-VALUE.

23	963 ∧ 85	587 ∧ 68
ITEMS-SOLD	DOLLAR-VALUE	AVG-VALUE
before	before	before
and after	and after	041 ∧ 90

```
DIVIDE DOLLAR-VALUE BY ITEMS-SOLD GIVING AVG-VALUE.
```

The BY version of this DIVIDE statement is exactly equivalent to the first example.

```
DIVIDE ITEMS-SOLD INTO DOLLAR-VALUE GIVING AVG-VALUE ROUNDED.
```

If the ROUNDED version is used, the answer moved into AVG-VALUE will be 041.91 because the third place after the decimal is a 6 and will round the zero-digit up to a 1. Note that although DIVIDE INTO without GIVING is permitted, the DIVIDE BY statement *must* contain the GIVING entry.

The COMPUTE statement

The last of the arithmetic statements is the composite statement COMPUTE, which allows you to do any of the previous arithmetic operations as specified by ADD, SUBTRACT, MULTIPLY, or DIVIDE plus exponentiation (raising to a power). The general form is

```
COMPUTE identifier-1 ROUNDED
        = arithmetic expression ON SIZE ERROR.
```

The arithmetic operators used with COMPUTE are:

- ** Exponentiation (raising to a power)
- * Multiplication
- / Division
- + Addition
- − Subtraction

When the arithmetic expression is calculated, the system follows a set pattern known as the "order of arithmetic operations." The order is:

1. All expressions in parentheses are evaluated first.
2. Exponentiation is performed next.
3. Multiplication and division are of the same rank and performed from left to right.
4. Addition and subtraction are of the same rank and performed from left to right.

The values stored in the fields used in the arithmetic expression are unchanged by the COMPUTE statement and the answer is moved to identifier-1. Each arithmetic operator must be preceded and followed by at least one space. The programmer must be aware of the order of operations in order to be certain that the desired arithmetic operation is carried out. Note the following examples.

Arithmetic Operation	COBOL COMPUTE Statement
TOTAL = AMT1 + AMT2	COMPUTE TOTAL = AMT1 + AMT2
$X = \dfrac{A+B}{C}$	COMPUTE X = (A + B) / C
	The parentheses are required in order to have the system calculate $\dfrac{A+B}{C}$. If the parentheses are omitted, COMPUTE X = A + B / C, the system will divide B by C and then add A to the result.
$X = \dfrac{A+B}{B-C}$	COMPUTE X = (A + B) / (B - C)
Rounding	COMPUTE X ROUNDED = (A + B) / (B - C)
Net pay rounded	COMPUTE NET-PAY ROUNDED = HOURS * RATE - DEDUCTIONS.

Assuming that we have come to this part of the program knowing that the hours worked figure is greater than 40, we can compute NET-PAY (with time and a half pay for hours in excess of 40) by the following COMPUTE statement:

```
COMPUTE NET-PAY
    = ((HOURS - 40) * (1.5 * RATE) + (40 * RATE)) - DEDUCTIONS.
```

Testing in COBOL

Like all programming languages, COBOL has the ability to compare the values stored in data fields and to take different paths through the program depending upon the result of the test. The IF statement is used to test in a variety of ways depending upon the needs of the programmer. In the following discussion you will see that it is a statement not only simple to understand, but easy to use.

The IF statement

The IF statement is used to perform three general types of tests: relational tests, sign tests, and class tests.

Relational tests   Relational tests are performed on fields to determine the equality or inequality of various fields. The permissible operations are outlined below.

IS EQUAL TO

IS NOT EQUAL TO

IS GREATER THAN

IS NOT GREATER THAN

IS LESS THAN

IS NOT LESS THAN

The programmer has the option of writing out the relationship as shown above or of using the operational signs: = (equal), < (less than), > (greater than), NOT = (not equal), NOT < (not less than), and NOT > (not greater than).

The simplest form of a relational test is shown below.

IF test-condition statement-1.

Examples

```
IF AMOUNT IS EQUAL TO TEST-DATA MOVE 'PROPER VALUE' TO
    OUTPUT-LINE.
ADD 1 TO COUNTER-A.
```

A relational test is performed on the values stored at AMOUNT and TEST-DATA to see if they are equal. If the two values are equal, the message 'PROPER VALUE' is moved to OUTPUT-LINE and the next statement in sequence is executed. If the result of the test is false, the

MOVE statement is ignored and the next statement in sequence is executed. A flowchart of the operation is shown below.

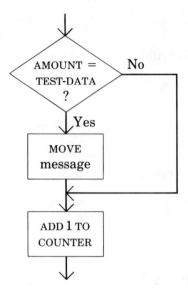

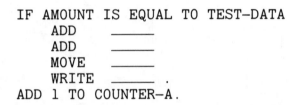

```
IF AMOUNT IS EQUAL TO TEST—DATA
       ADD      _____
       ADD      _____
       MOVE     _____
       WRITE    _____  .
ADD 1 TO COUNTER—A.
```

The second example is the same as the first except that multiple statements are executed when the test is true. Note that all the statements down to the period will be executed. As before, the last ADD statement will be processed whether the test is true or false because it follows the period that ends the IF statement.

The most common version of the IF statement involves the use of the word ELSE and has the following format.

IF test condition statement-1
    ELSE statement-2

Examples

IF test condition

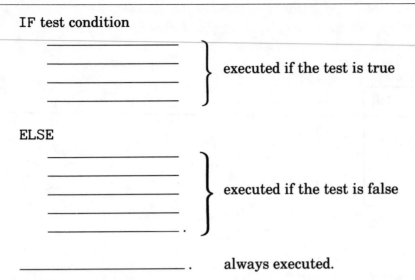

ELSE

A general flowchart of this form of the IF statement is shown below.

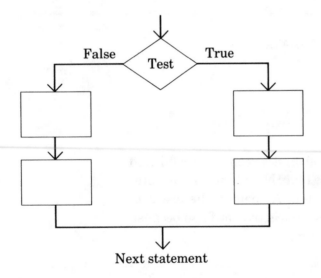

```
IF COUNTER IS LESS THAN 10
    MOVE FIELD-A TO FIELD-A-ED
    MOVE FIELD-B TO FIELD-B-ED
ELSE
    SUBTRACT AMOUNT FROM INPUT-VALUE.
ADD 1 TO COUNTER.
```

The test is performed on the value in COUNTER, and as a result of the test the system executes either the two MOVE statements (if the test is true) or the SUBTRACT statement (if the test is false). In either case the ADD statement is always executed.

So far the examples have shown the testing of numeric fields such as AMOUNT or COUNTER. It is also possible to test non-numeric fields such as NAME. The action of the IF statement is exactly the same except that the comparison is done on the basis of the collating sequence of the characters that are being compared. Every permissible character in COBOL has a unique internal code and the order or relationship of these items is known as a collating sequence. Generally, the numeric values are at the top of the order, next come the alphabetic characters (z is the highest), and then the special characters. Therefore, it is perfectly correct to write IF statements as follows.

Examples

```
IF NAME IS EQUAL TO 'JONES' _____ .

IF NAME-1 IS GREATER THAN NAME-2 _____ .

IF MIXED-FIELD-1 IS NOT EQUAL TO MIXED-FIELD-2 _____ .
```

The latter example shows that fields with a picture of X may also be compared but they both must have the same USAGE format.

Sign tests   The sign test is a very simple form of the IF statement that allows the programmer to determine whether a field is positive, negative, or zero.

$$\underline{\text{IF}} \quad \left\{ \begin{array}{l} \text{identifier} \\ \text{arithmetic expression} \end{array} \right\} \quad \text{IS } [\underline{\text{NOT}}] \quad \left\{ \begin{array}{l} \underline{\text{POSITIVE}} \\ \underline{\text{NEGATIVE}} \\ \underline{\text{ZERO}} \end{array} \right\}$$

Examples

```
IF BALANCE IS POSITIVE _____ .

IF TOTAL IS NOT ZERO    _____ .

IF NBR-OF-ITEMS IS ZERO _____ .

IF A + B - C IS NEGATIVE _____ .
```

One common use of the sign test involves the testing of a divisor field just before a DIVIDE statement. In a particular situation it may be permissible for the divisor to be either positive or negative, but, of course, division by zero is not a permissible arithmetic operation.

Class tests   The third general type of test is known as a class test in which the programmer may test to see if a field is or is not alphabetic or numeric. The general rule is that a numeric test may be performed only on a field that has a numeric picture. In the test, the alphabetic characters are the letters A through Z and the space.

$$\text{IF identifier IS [\underline{NOT}]}\begin{Bmatrix}\underline{\text{ALPHABETIC}}\\\underline{\text{NUMERIC}}\end{Bmatrix}$$

Examples

```
IF INPUT-AMT IS NOT NUMERIC _____ .
```

```
IF NAME IS ALPHABETIC _____ .
```

(*Note:*   The following example is *incorrect* assuming that the field NAME was set up with an A PICTURE entry.)

```
IF NAME IS NUMERIC
```

The proper test would be:

```
IF NAME IS NOT ALPHABETIC
```

Compound conditions

The programmer may see the need for tests with compound conditions involving AND and OR. Generally, the beginning programmer should avoid compound testing in favor of multiple simple tests. If the word AND is used, then both expressions must be true.

```
IF TEMP IS GREATER THAN 75 AND TEMP IS LESS THAN 90
    PERFORM NORMAL-ROUTINE.
```

Two points in the above example are important to note. First, the subject of the comparison must be restated each time. (*Note:*   Most systems require the subject to be restated. Check your system to be sure.) Second, both conditions must be met for the system to PERFORM NORMAL-ROUTINE.

If OR is used, it means either or both.

```
IF TEST-GRADE-AVG IS GREATER THAN 92 OR TERM-PAPER-GRADE
    IS EQUAL TO 'A' MOVE 'A' TO TERM-GRADE.
```

In the above example an 'A' will be moved if either or both conditions are true. There are many other combinations of compound conditions in COBOL, but they are beyond the scope of this text.

Condition name test

One additional type of test, known as the condition name test, is really a variation of a test explained earlier. It involves relational testing, but provides a slightly different format that is far more readable, thus providing better program documentation. Suppose we have a payroll operation in which hourly paid workers get an extra amount of pay for working the less desirable shifts such as the swing shift or graveyard shift. We will read in the employee data record from a card and immediately test a CODE-FIELD to see which shift the employee works (assume that Day Shift = 1, Swing Shift = 2, and Grave Shift is coded as a 3). Depending upon the value in the CODE-FIELD we will want to branch to various places in the program. Figure 7-1 shows, in skeletal form, the COBOL coding that is required.

FIGURE 7-1

Relational Tests

```
FD   CARD-FILE
     _____
     _____
     _____

01   CARD-PAY-RECORD
     _____
     _____
     _____

     03   CODE-FIELD   PIC 9.
     .
     .
     .
PROCEDURE DIVISION
     IF CODE-FIELD IS EQUAL TO 1
         PERFORM DAY-SHIFT-ROUTINE.
     IF CODE-FIELD IS EQUAL TO 2
         PERFORM SWING-SHIFT-ROUTINE.
     IF CODE-FIELD IS EQUAL TO 3
         PERFORM GRAVE-SHIFT-ROUTINE.
```

The coding is very straightforward and should cause no problems. However, we can modify it to use a condition name test instead. So far the rule has been that the VALUE entry is not permitted in the FILE SECTION. Condition names, also known as level 88 entries, are an exception to this rule. Figure 7-2 shows a revised version of the sample program using level 88 entries—conditional names.

The level 88 entries are "saying" that if CODE-FIELD has a value of 1, you want to be able to refer to it by the name DAY-SHIFT. If it has a value of 2, to be able to refer to it by the name SWING-SHIFT, and so on. Also note that you really don't save any coding in your program, but that level 88 entries make the program more readable.

FIGURE 7-2

Condition Name Tests

```
      FD  CARD-FILE
          _____
          _____
          _____


      01  CARD-PAY-RECORD
          _____
          _____
          _____
          _____

          03  CODE-FIELD  PIC 9.
              88  DAY-SHIFT VALUE 1.
              88  SWING-SHIFT VALUE 2.
              88  GRAVE-SHIFT VALUE 3.
          .
          .
          .

      PROCEDURE DIVISION.
          .
          .
          .

          IF DAY-SHIFT
            PERFORM DAY-SHIFT-ROUTINE.
          IF SWING-SHIFT
            PERFORM SWING-SHIFT-ROUTINE.
          IF GRAVE-SHIFT
            PERFORM GRAVE-SHIFT-ROUTINE.
          .
          .
          .
```

Special input-output operations

Two additional COBOL input-output statements need to be mentioned here briefly. Both the input statement ACCEPT and the output statement DISPLAY should be used sparingly in the program. In a class situation you may not be able to use ACCEPT at all, but the DISPLAY statement may be very useful to you. Let's take a look at these new statements.

The ACCEPT statement

The ACCEPT statement allows the entry of a small amount of data from the system console or from the logical input device (such as the card reader).

$$\underline{\text{ACCEPT}} \text{ identifier } \underline{\text{FROM}} \begin{Bmatrix} \underline{\text{CONSOLE}} \\ \text{mnemonic name} \end{Bmatrix}$$

Examples

```
ACCEPT COUNTER-MAX FROM CONSOLE.
```

The operator or person tending the system console can now enter a value that will be stored in COUNTER-MAX, a field which you have defined previously in the WORKING-STORAGE SECTION.

```
ACCEPT ID-NUMBER FROM INPUT-DEVICE.
```

The action is the same as before except that the system would have to know which device you mean. This is established by an entry in SPECIAL-NAMES.

```
SPECIAL-NAMES.
    SYS-RDR IS INPUT-DEVICE.
```

The DISPLAY statement

Generally, the DISPLAY statement is used to output a small amount of information on the console or on the system output device. The format for DISPLAY is

$$\underline{\text{DISPLAY}} \begin{Bmatrix} \text{identifier-1} \\ \text{literal-1} \end{Bmatrix} \dots \begin{Bmatrix} \text{identifier-n} \\ \text{literal-n} \end{Bmatrix} \underline{\text{UPON}} \begin{Bmatrix} \underline{\text{CONSOLE}} \\ \text{mnemonic name} \end{Bmatrix}$$

Any fields that are DISPLAYed must be in DISPLAY format (just as if they were going out to the printer device).

Examples

```
DISPLAY 'ERROR IN SEQUENCE' UPON CONSOLE.
```

The message ERROR IN SEQUENCE will be printed on the system console device.

```
DISPLAY COUNTER-T UPON CONSOLE.
```

The value stored in the field COUNTER-T will be printed upon the CONSOLE.

```
DISPLAY 'COUNTER TOTAL IS ' COUNTER-T UPON CONSOLE.
```

Same as above except that a mixture of literal and field data is printed.

```
DISPLAY 'END OF LOOP' UPON LPR.
```

The message END OF LOOP is displayed on the device identified as LPR in the SPECIAL-NAMES area.

```
SPECIAL-NAMES.
    SYSTEMS-OUTPUT IS LPR.
```

One of the most common uses of the DISPLAY statement is to help debug a program. Sometimes in complex programs involving many loops it is difficult to tell exactly where the program failed. DISPLAY statements can be inserted to print short messages that help trace the path of the program up to the point of failure. Then, when the program is corrected, the DISPLAY statements are removed.

Common errors

Most of the statements presented in this chapter are easy to use and generally don't cause much of a problem for the programmer. However, some errors do seem to occur more often than others and are worth mentioning here.

The first error involves the use of the ADD statement in making sure that total areas are cleared to zero before attempting to do any arithmetic. This error was discussed at some length in Chapter 6. The second error concerning ADD is the format of the statement itself. Remember, the rule is that you cannot have both TO and GIVING in the same ADD statement. The following is *incorrect*.

```
ADD A TO B GIVING C.
```

The severity of the diagnostic error message that the system gives to you depends upon the quality of the software. On some systems the level of the error is severe enough to prevent execution of your program. On other systems, the software will delete the TO, print a low-level warning message, and permit the execution of the program.

A second error that is extremely common concerns arithmetic operations on fields that contain edit characters. Such operations are simply not permitted. Note the following examples.

```
AMOUNT   PIC   S999V99.
```

This is an arithmetic field—that is, one that can be manipulated arithmetically.

```
AMOUNT-ED        PIC    999.99.
TOTAL            PIC   $999.99.
BALANCE-OUT      PIC   Z,ZZZ.99.
PAY-AMT          PIC   $$$.99.
```

All of the above are edit fields and *cannot* be worked on arithmetically. Observe that it is not a question of how many edit characters are contained in a field. If the field contains *any* edit characters, it cannot be manipulated arithmetically.

The programmer may MOVE into or give into (GIVING) or COMPUTE *into* the above fields, but cannot work on them with arithmetic statements. The statement

```
COMPUTE AMOUNT-ED  =  _____  .
```

is correct as long as the fields used in the calculations (that is, to the right of the equal sign) are proper arithmetic fields. In the COMPUTE statement, the answer is calculated and then MOVEd to AMOUNT-ED.

The last of the errors that applies to statements presented in this chapter concerns the ELSE version of the IF statement. You recall that the form of the statement is as follows:

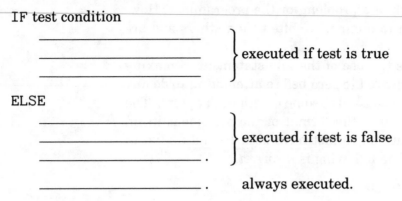

IF test condition

_____
_____ } executed if test is true
_____

ELSE

_____
_____ } executed if test is false
_____ .

_____ .   always executed.

One very common error involves the misplacement of the ending period. Note the following example:

```
IF COUNTER IS EQUAL TO TEST-VALUE
    MOVE MSSG-1 TO MSSG-AREA
    WRITE OUTPUT-LINE FROM MESSG-REC
        AFTER ADVANCING 2 LINES
ELSE
    MOVE VALUE-A TO VALUE-A-PACK
    COMPUTE ANS = (VALUE-A - B + C) / D.
READ _____ .
```

A flowchart of this operation is shown below.

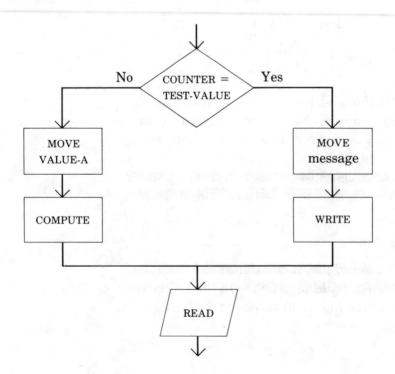

If the period that ends the IF-ELSE operation is misplaced at the end of the second MOVE statement,

```
IF   _____
      MOVE _____
      WRITE _____
ELSE
      MOVE _____ .
      COMPUTE  ANS = (VALUE-A - B + C) / D.
      READ _____ .
```

then the logic of the operation is changed considerably as the following flowchart shows. Now the COMPUTE statement is executed *every* time—not on just the false condition of the IF test.

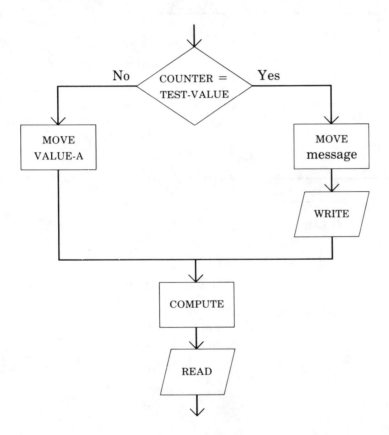

Another situation that can cause a problem occurs in using READ within the IF-ELSE statement. Suppose we change our original example to include READ:

```
IF   _____
      READ INPUT-FILE
            AT END
      MOVE _____
      WRITE _____
ELSE
      MOVE _____
      COMPUTE _____ .
      READ _____ .
```

In this example the MOVE and WRITE statements are executed when AT END is triggered by the end-of-file condition. The flowchart will look as follows.

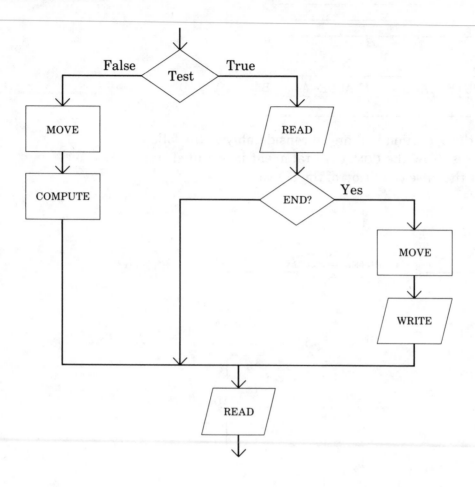

Problem-Solving Techniques

Generally, programmers are elated when their program runs to a natural conclusion—that is, without what is known as an "abend," which stands for "abnormal ending." But even a program that ends normally is not necessarily correct. You might very well end with beautifully printed pages of garbage. But whether your program abends or whether it outputs incorrect answers, the result is still the same in that it is your responsibility to make it work properly. How do you find your errors?

In the case of an abnormal ending, the system will print some type of error message indicating the point in your program at which the error occurred. That message, plus any printed output lines, will give you a good clue where to look. In the author's experience with beginning COBOL students, the single most common abend is found on an ADD statement. As mentioned in the text, the ADD statement itself is seldom in error. In at least 90% of the cases the error is in adding into a total area that was not initialized at the beginning of the program. Obviously, errors of this type will decrease as you become more familiar with the way COBOL works.

The second situation in which the program reaches a natural conclusion but generates incorrect answers is a little more difficult to correct. What should you look for? The best answer is to tell you to look for patterns in the output. Are the errors repeated exactly? If so, how many times before a change occurs? Are the answers off by the same amount for each record? Is the error amount cumulative from record to record? Does the error occur on only one part of the IF condition?

If you can't find an obvious pattern, look at the input data. Are they correct? Are your input specifications correct? Are your output specifications correct? Under what condition does the error happen?

Suppose you try everything you can and the errors are still not apparent? Your alternatives are becoming fewer, and one of these involves desk checking the program line by line. By "desk checking" we mean that you "play" computer and try to figure out statement by statement exactly what the computer did (not what it *should have done*) in each case. Then, if that fails, seek outside help and, if no one can find the problem, you may have to reanalyze, redesign, and rewrite the program. A crucial point here: It is *your* responsibility to produce a program that will solve the problem.

Self-Study: Questions and Answers

1. Does it make any difference if I use multiple arithmetic statements such as ADD, SUBTRACT, and so on to solve a formula? Or should I use COMPUTE instead?

   Answer
   Technically it makes no difference at all. The main thing is to solve the problem in the correct manner. There is some feeling that the use of COMPUTE in arithmetic operations is more "natural" than are the specific operations of ADD, SUBTRACT, MULTIPLY, and DIVIDE.

2. When I do use the COMPUTE statement, do all the fields have to be of the same USAGE format—such as all DISPLAY—or all COMPUTA-TIONAL-3?

   Answer
   No, the fields used in any arithmetic operation can be of a mixture of USAGE formats. However, as discussed in the previous chapter, the system must convert those fields that are in DISPLAY format to a format usable in arithmetic operations. You can provide for greater machine efficiency by doing these conversions yourself prior to executing the specific arithmetic operation of COMPUTE, ADD, and so on.

3. Regarding the IF statement. Am I correct in saying the relational test simply compares two values to determine their arithmetic relationship?

   Answer
   You are exactly right. The relational test is a very simple comparison. For example, in the statement

   ```
   IF HOURS-WORKED IS GREATER THAN TEST-AMT
   ```

   the test is concerned solely with whether the value in the HOURS-WORKED field is greater than the value stored in the TEST-AMT field. Neither the system nor the programmer is concerned with *how much* the first field is greater than the second. The test is just as true if the comparison is 40.1 vs 40.0 as it is if the test is 40.1 vs 65.9. Also remember that neither of the values is changed during the operation of the comparison.

4. How complex can the test be in an IF statement?

   Answer
   The test may be as complex as you wish and may involve any combination of literals and data fields, but the result of the test is simply "true" or "false."

5. Why do you say to be careful using a compound condition in an IF statement?

   Answer
   Compound IF statements can present problems for the programmer unless they have been thought out thoroughly. It is easy to get into a situation where you think you know what is happening but the machine is doing something entirely different. I suggest they be avoided unless you feel they are absolutely necessary. A good rule to follow is "if you can flowchart it—use it."

Exercises

1. Indicate whether the following examples are correct or incorrect. If the statement is incorrect, make the necessary changes.
   a. ADD 1 TO TOTAL.
   b. ADD TOTAL TO 16.
   c. ADD 1 TO COUNT GIVING COUNT-A.
   d. ADD TAX-1 TAX-2 TAX-3 TAX-4 TO TOTAL-TAX.
   e. ADD TAX-1 TAX-2 TAX-3 GIVING TOTAL-TAX.
   f. ADD SALES-AMT AND TAX-AMOUNT GIVING TOTAL-AMT.
   g. ADD BAL-DUE, OLD-BAL GIVING NEW-BAL ROUNDED.
   h. ADD BAL-DUE ROUNDED TO OLD-BAL ROUNDED.
   i. ADD DISCOUNT TO OLD-DISC ROUNDED ON SIZE ERROR GO TO ERROR-MODULE.
   j. ADD $5.00 TO TOTAL.
   k. ADD 1 FIELD-A 17 TO NEW-RATE.

2. Indicate whether the following examples are correct or incorrect. If the statement is incorrect, make the necessary changes.
   a. SUBTRACT DISCOUNT FROM GROSS-SALES.
   b. SUBTRACT 1 FROM COUNT.
   c. SUBTRACT COUNT FROM 1.
   d. SUBTRACT 1 FROM COUNT GIVING TOTAL-COUNT.
   e. SUBTRACT FIELD-A FIELD-B GIVING ANSWER.
   f. SUBTRACT TAX-AMT FROM GROSS-PAY GIVING NEW-PAY ROUNDED.
   g. SUBTRACT TAX-AMT ROUNDED FROM GROSS-PAY.
   h. SUBTRACT FIRST-ANS FROM 15.75 GIVING BALANCE-DUE ROUNDED. ON SIZE ERROR GO TO SIZE-ERROR-ROUTINE.
   i. SUBTRACT LINES FROM TOTAL-LINES.
   j. SUBTRACT ROUNDED DISCOUNT FROM BOOK-RATE.

3. Indicate whether the following examples are correct or incorrect. If the statement is incorrect, make the necessary changes.
   a. MULTIPLY .05 BY BASE-RATE.
   b. MULTIPLY BASE-RATE BY .05.
   c. MULTIPLY INTERMEDIATE-AMT BY CHANGE-RATE GIVING NEW-AMT.
   d. MULTIPLY FIELD-A, FIELD-B BY NEW GIVING TOTAL-NEW.
   e. MULTIPLY GRADE BY POINTS GIVING GRADE-POINTS ON SIZE ERROR WRITE OUTPUT-LINE FROM ERROR-1.
   f. DIVIDE UNITS INTO POINTS GIVING GPA.
   g. DIVIDE POINTS BY UNITS GIVING GPA.

   h. DIVIDE 12 INTO YRLY-TOTAL ROUNDED GIVING MO-TOTAL ROUNDED.

   i. DIVIDE YEARLY-TOTAL BY 12 GIVING MO-TOTAL ROUNDED.

   j. DIVIDE 150 BY 13 GIVING ANS ROUNDED.

4. Write the COMPUTE statement that would be used to solve the following equations.

   a. $X = \dfrac{A+B}{C}$

   b. $X = \dfrac{A}{C} + B$

   c. $X = A^2 + B^3$

   d. $X = 6AB + 4RQG$

   e. $X = \dfrac{6AB}{4QG}$

   f. Same as above, but round the answer.

   g. $X = \dfrac{A + A^2 + (A^3 - 15)}{T}$

   h. Same as Exercise 4a, but round the answer and go to an error message routine in case of a size error.

   i. Add 1 to the counter R.

5. Indicate the size of the following result or answer fields.

   a. PIC 99V99 multiplied by 99V99 gives a product size of _____ .

   b. PIC 999V99 multiplied by V999 gives a product size of _____ .

   c. PIC 999V99 divided by 999 gives a quotient of _____ and a remainder of _____ digits.

   d. PIC V9999 divided by 9V9 gives a quotient of _____ and a remainder of _____ digits.

6. Write the COBOL statements to perform the following tests.

   a. Branch to ROUTINE-1 if A-FIELD is not equal to zero.

   b. If A-FIELD is greater than LIMIT, you are to add 1 to COUNTER-A, otherwise you are to subtract CONSTANT from COUNTER-B.

   c. If NAME-FIELD (PICTURE A) contains any numeric characters, you are to display the message "NAME-FIELD NOT ALPHABETIC" upon the console and ADD 1 TO COUNT-B; otherwise you are to go on to the next statement, which is ADD 1 TO COUNT-C.

   d. If AMT-OF-PAY contains any non-numeric characters, you are to display the message 'DATA OF WRONG TYPE'; otherwise you are to move BODY-LINE to OUTPUT-LINE and write it after advancing three lines. No matter what the result of the test is, you are to execute the statement that multiplies the contents of SUB-TOTAL by RATE to get a rounded answer in ANSWER-1.

7. Write the IF statement(s) that correspond to the following flow-charts.

a.

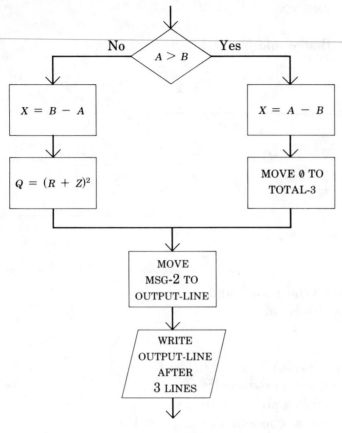

b.

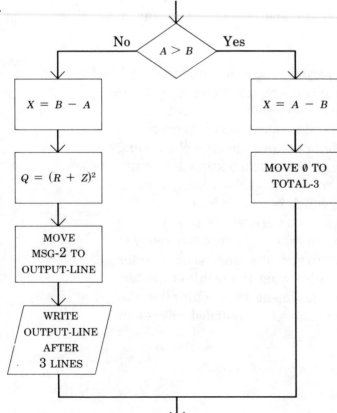

c. *Note:* This next example was not shown in the text, but you should be able to reason through it. It involves an IF statement within an IF statement.

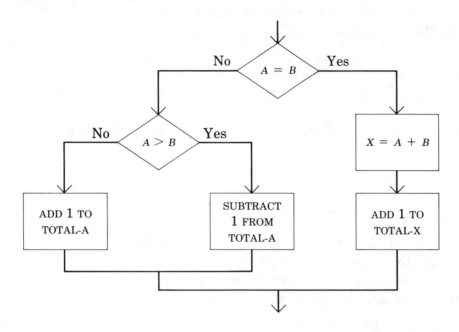

8. This problem uses Data File A (card file) (see the appendix) to produce a payroll report.

Card Columns	Field Description
1–9	Social security number
10–29	Name
30	Filler
31–34	Rate of pay in the format xx ∧ xx
35–36	Filler
37–40	Insurance deduction amount in the format xx ∧ xx
41–45	Credit union deduction in the format xxx ∧ xx
46–50	Other deductions in the format xxx ∧ xx
51–52	Hours worked
53–80	Filler

Specific output requirements are listed below and shown in the attached diagram.

a. Calculate Gross Pay by multiplying the hours field (card columns 51 and 52) by rate of pay (card columns 31–34 with a format of xx ∧ xx).

b. Provide for a floating dollar sign and decimal point for all dollar and cents fields.

c. Keep a running total of the Gross Pay, Total Deductions, and Net Pay fields so that totals can be printed at the end of the program.

d. Begin the output at the top of a new page and space it appropriately across the printer line.

```
                         PAYROLL REPORT

NAME     SS-NUMBER    GROSS PAY   TOTAL DEDUCTIONS   NET PAY

_____   XXX-XX-XXXX  XXXX.XX          XXX.XX        XXXX.XX




     TOTALS                    _____        _____           _____
```

9. Modify the previous program (output format is the same) to print output lines only for those employees who have three or more dependents (the Dependents field is in card columns 35 and 36). Also, after printing your total line, print the following:

```
TOTAL RECORDS IN FILE XXX
EMPLOYEES WITH 3 OR MORE DEPENDENTS XXX
```

10. Using Card Data File A, you are to perform an input editing operation in which you check a field to see if it contains the proper characters. The record format is:

Card Column	Field Description
1–9	Social security number
10–29	Name
30–52	Filler
53–55	Work area field consisting of a two-digit section number and single alphabetic character for the work department
56–80	Filler

Write a program that checks the work area field to see that the first two characters are numeric and the last character is alphabetic. If the data fail either test, write a line on the printer as follows. (*Note:* You will be writing a line only for those records that contain an error.)

```
                    INPUT EDIT RUN
     NAME  SOCIAL SECURITY NUMBER  WORK AREA CODE
       .             .                  .
       .             .                  .
       .             .                  .

     TOTAL NUMBER OF ERRORS
```

11. Modify the previous problem to provide the following output.

```
                 INPUT EDIT RUN
        RECORD NUMBER   NAME   WORK AREA CODE
              X         _____      _____
              X         _____      _____
        TOTAL NUMBER OF ERRORS
```

12. Modify Exercise 13 in Chapter 5 (mailing labels) so that the program prints six labels for each subscriber. Control the loop by means of a PERFORM UNTIL and a counter.

Chapter 8

Magnetic Tape Processing

So far in the text all incoming data records have been in the form of
IBM cards. Traditionally, card files have been used with beginning
programming students because cards are easy to visualize and relate
to. Now you are ready to work with another type of storage medium—
magnetic tape. Obviously it differs from cards, but these differences
really shouldn't cause you any trouble.

Introduction to magnetic tape

Magnetic tape is made of plastic that is $\frac{1}{2}$ inch wide, and is coated on
one side with an easily magnetized material such as iron oxide. Reels
containing up to 2400 feet of tape are mounted on *tape drives,* which
perform the tasks of reading from or writing onto the tape storage
media. The tape transport mechanism (Figure 8-1) physically moves
the tape past a read/write head assembly where reading or writing
takes place. Just as with cards, you *read* from tape *into* memory and

write from memory *onto* tape. Reading from tape is nondestructive in the sense that the data on tape are still there and can be read repeatedly. Writing onto tape is destructive since the data that originally were on that area of tape are destroyed by the new material being written.

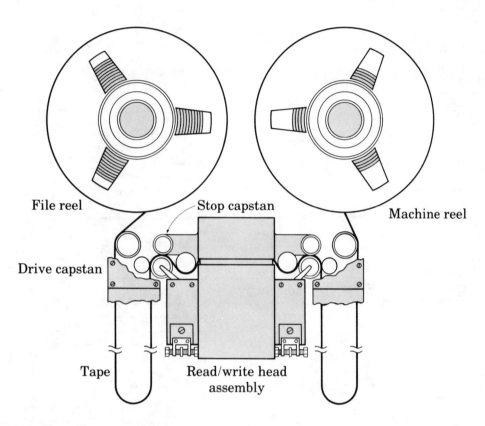

File reel   Stop capstan   Machine reel

Drive capstan

Tape   Read/write head assembly

FIGURE 8-1. *Tape Transport Mechanism*

The data on tape are in the form of a column of tiny magnetic spots, or "bits" (binary digits), written by the electrically activated read/write head. Most modern computers use 9-channel tape, which is another way of saying that each character on tape is comprised of some combination of one to nine spots. Older computers often used a different coding structure that recorded the data in terms of seven marks and was known as 7-channel tape (Figure 8-2).

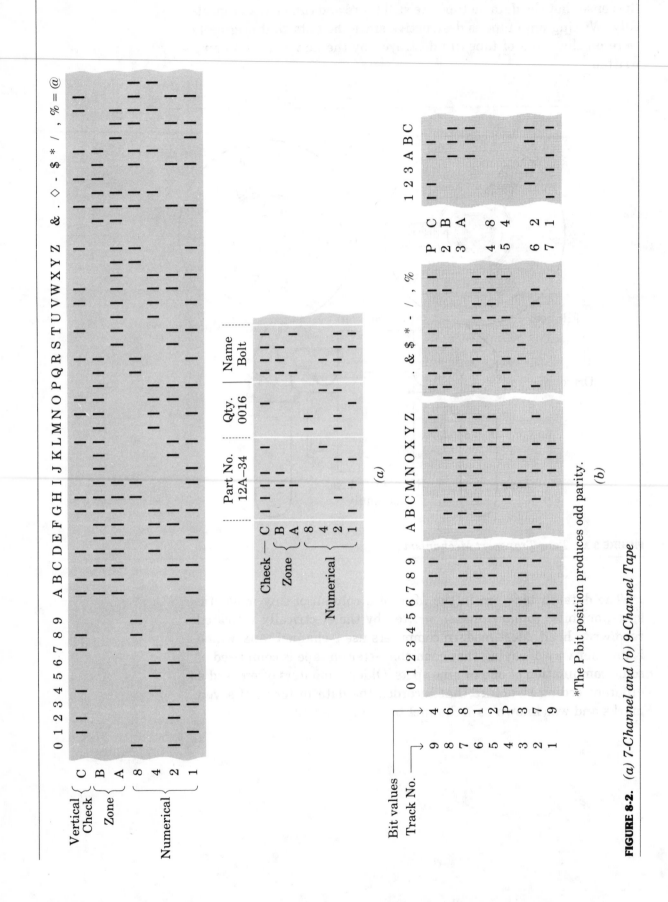

FIGURE 8-2. *(a) 7-Channel and (b) 9-Channel Tape*

*The P bit position produces odd parity.

Creating a tape file: Data records

To illustrate the use of tape data files suppose we have a file of 5000 80-column card records that contains information on employees in our organization. Each card contains the following fields:

1 – 30	31 – 60	61 – 69	70 – 77	78 – 80
Employee name	Address	Social Security Number (9 digits)	Telephone number XXX-XXXX	Work code (3 digits)

The programming manager has decided that the card file data are to be copied onto tape since it will be easier and more efficient to process them in this form later on.

The logic of our card-to-tape program is a very simple program loop that is almost identical to the Lister program discussed in previous chapters.

```
        SELECT CARD-DATA ASSIGN TO _____ .
        SELECT TAPEFILE  ASSIGN TO _____ .
        .
        .
        .
    FD  TAPEFILE
        LABEL RECORDS ARE STANDARD
        DATA RECORD IS TAPE-RECORD.
        .
        .
        .
    PROCEDURE DIVISION
    CONTROL-MODULE
        PERFORM 010-OPENER
        PERFORM 020-READ-AND-WRITE
            UNTIL CARD-EOF IS EQUAL TO 1.
            .
            .
            .
    010-OPENER
        OPEN INPUT CARD-DATA OUTPUT TAPEFILE
        READ CARD-DATA
            AT END MOVE 1 TO CARD-EOF.
    020-READ-AND-WRITE.
        MOVE card fields to tape record area
        WRITE TAPE-RECORD
        READ CARD-DATA
            AT END MOVE 1 TO CARD-EOF.
```

Let's see what changes will have to be made in our program to take care of this job.

1. The SELECT entry for our tape file is much the same as any SELECT, except that we will use UT to indicate that the magnetic tape unit is a utility device instead of a unit record (UR) piece of equipment. The "s" again shows that tape is a sequential access device.

2. Our file description for TAPEFILE is as you would expect, except for the entry that LABEL RECORDS ARE STANDARD rather than OMITTED. Magnetic storage devices such as tape and disk require this form of the LABEL RECORDS entry for a reason discussed a little bit later.

3. The PROCEDURE DIVISION entries are the same as before and follow the regular top-down, structured format. We did not bother to open a printer file, so the ending message TAPE FILE WRITING IS COMPLETE is DISPLAYed rather than written (Figure 8-3).

FIGURE 8-3

Writing on Magnetic Tape

```
     IDENTIFICATION DIVISION.
     PROGRAM-ID. LISTER.
*
     ENVIRONMENT DIVISION.
     CONFIGURATION SECTION.
     SOURCE-COMPUTER. IBM-360-F30.
     OBJECT-COMPUTER. IBM-360-F30.
     INPUT-OUTPUT SECTION.
     FILE-CONTROL.
         SELECT CARD-DATA
             ASSIGN TO SYS007-UR-2540R-S.
         SELECT TAPEFILE
             ASSIGN TO SYS010-UT-2400-S.
*
```

```
DATA DIVISION.
FILE SECTION.
FD  CARD-DATA
    LABEL RECORDS ARE OMITTED
    DATA RECORD IS CARD-IN.
01  CARD-IN.
    03  E-NAME                      PIC X(30).
    03  E-ADDRESS                   PIC X(30).
    03  SS-NBR                      PIC 9(9).
    03  PHONE                       PIC X(8).
    03  W-CODE                      PIC 9(3).
FD  TAPEFILE
    LABEL RECORDS ARE STANDARD
    DATA RECORD IS EMPLOYEE-DATA.
01  EMPLOYEE-DATA.
    03  E-NAME-T                    PIC X(30).
    03  E-ADDRESS-T                 PIC X(30).
    03  SS-NBR-T                    PIC 9(9).
    03  PHONE-T                     PIC X(8).
    03  W-CODE-T                    PIC 9(3).
WORKING-STORAGE SECTION.
77  INDICATOR                       PIC 9 VALUE ZERO.
*
PROCEDURE DIVISION.
CONTROL-ROUTINE.
    PERFORM 010-OPENER.
    PERFORM 020-READER UNTIL
        INDICATOR = 1.
    PERFORM 030-CLOSER.
    STOP RUN.
010-OPENER.
    OPEN INPUT CARD-DATA
        OUTPUT TAPEFILE.
    READ CARD-DATA
        AT END MOVE 1 TO INDICATOR.
020-READER.
    MOVE CARD-IN TO EMPLOYEE-DATA.
    WRITE EMPLOYEE-DATA.
    READ CARD-DATA
        AT END MOVE 1 TO INDICATOR.
030-CLOSER.
    DISPLAY   'TAPE FILE WRITING IS COMPLETE'.
    CLOSE CARD-DATA, TAPEFILE.
```

The action of our card-to-tape program is quite simple. A card record is read in and that record of data is then written onto tape in the form of columns of tiny magnetic marks, or spots, you saw earlier. Schematically, each record on tape is the same as the original card record from which the tape data were taken.

Card Record

Employee name	Address	Social Security Number	Telephone number	Work code

Tape Record

Employee name	Address	Social Security Number	Telephone number	Work code

There is, however, one way in which tape records physically differ from card records. At the conclusion of every tape WRITE operation, the computer system automatically skips a small portion of tape (usually about $\frac{1}{2}$ inch), which is known as the inter-record gap (IRG). This is something over which the programmer has no control since the system requires this gap in order to physically handle the tape as it moves through the tape read-write mechanism. A gap, then, will appear between each tape record.

...ecord	Gap	Record	Gap	Record	Gap	Record	Gap	Record

When the tape spool is mounted on the tape drive, about 15 feet at the beginning is used as "leader" to thread through the winding system. The actual recording area of tape is recognized by the tape drive because it senses a small, light-reflecting silver patch positioned just after the leader area. The physical end of the tape is marked in a similar way so that reading or writing does not progress beyond the usable area.

Each WRITE instruction advances the tape until we write the last record on the tape file. The system does not "know" that this is the last record; but when the file is CLOSEd, the system writes a special configuration of bits that indicate that this is the end of the file (EOF). Later, when a program reads the tape file, the EOF configuration triggers the AT END portion of the sequential file READ statement.

Recording density and blocked records

Although the above diagram is correct in that it does represent the layout of tape records, it is grossly out of perspective because it does not consider one of the features of magnetic storage media—*recording density*. By recording density we mean the closeness with which the columns of magnetic spots are written onto magnetic tape. Some fairly typical recording densities are 800 and 1600 characters per inch (often called bpi for "bytes" per inch in reference to the storage terminology used on most IBM machines). This means, for example, that at 800 characters per inch (cpi) an 80-column card record would take up $\frac{1}{10}$ of an inch and at 1600 cpi the record would occupy only $\frac{1}{20}$ of an inch. When you think back to the fact that the inter-record gap is approximately $\frac{1}{2}$ inch, it means that tape is mostly gaps, as the following illustration indicates.

1600 cpi Recording Density
80-Character Data Record

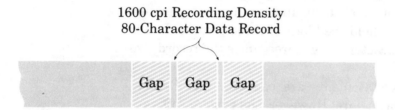

Obviously, this means that we are not using tape efficiently, but the problem is easily avoided by *blocking* the tape records. The term "blocking" means we will group a series of records together into a block *before* writing the data onto tape. If we had a *blocking factor* of 3 (that is, three records per block), a *schematic* layout (not actual size) of our tape data would look as follows:

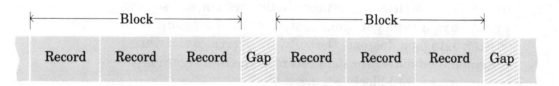

It is possible to block hundreds of records together in a block with the main limiting factor being the amount of memory available in the computer system. Blocking is extremely simple to do in COBOL. In fact, it is so simple that all it requires is a single change to the program shown in Figure 8-3. In the File Description entry for TAPEFILE we did the following:

```
FD  TAPEFILE
    LABEL RECORDS ARE STANDARD
    DATA RECORD IS EMPLOYEE-DATA.
```

To get the system to write the records in blocked format we insert the line

```
BLOCK CONTAINS 3 RECORDS
```

so that FD entry now reads

```
FD  TAPEFILE
    LABEL RECORDS ARE STANDARD
    BLOCK CONTAINS 3 RECORDS
    DATA RECORD IS EMPLOYEE-DATA.
```

which triggers into the COBOL software system to cause the tape records to be written in blocked format. However, there is *no* change in the PROCEDURE DIVISION statements nor is there any change in the program logic!

Even though the system software does all the work for you, you should understand exactly what is happening. When the system "sees" the BLOCK CONTAINS entry, it sets up an area in memory (called a buffer area) large enough to hold the block of three records. In our example the buffer is 240 characters long (three times the record size of 80).

The PROCEDURE DIVISION statements are based on the Read-a-record, Write-a-record logic as before. However, the system software overrides this logic to take care of your blocking requirements by doing the following:

1. The first card is read into the CARD-IN area as you would expect.
2. The card data are moved to the tape record area (EMPLOYEE-DATA) (Figure 8-4a).
3. The system encounters the tape WRITE statement, but the record is *not* written onto tape. If the system did so, we would have a tape gap immediately after the record was written onto tape. Instead, the software overrides the WRITE statement and moves the data record to the first record area in the three-record block (Figure 8-4b).
4. The program (using structured logic) reads another card and branches back through the looping process. The second card record is *not* written onto tape, but is moved into the second record area of the three-record block.
5. The buffer area, of course, will be filled after the third card record is moved in. Then, and only then, are the contents of the buffer area (block) written onto tape. Again, note that your program logic (as shown in your PROCEDURE DIVISION statements) is done as if the data records are unblocked (Figure 8-4c).

FIGURE 8-4

Buffer Action—Blocked Tape Records

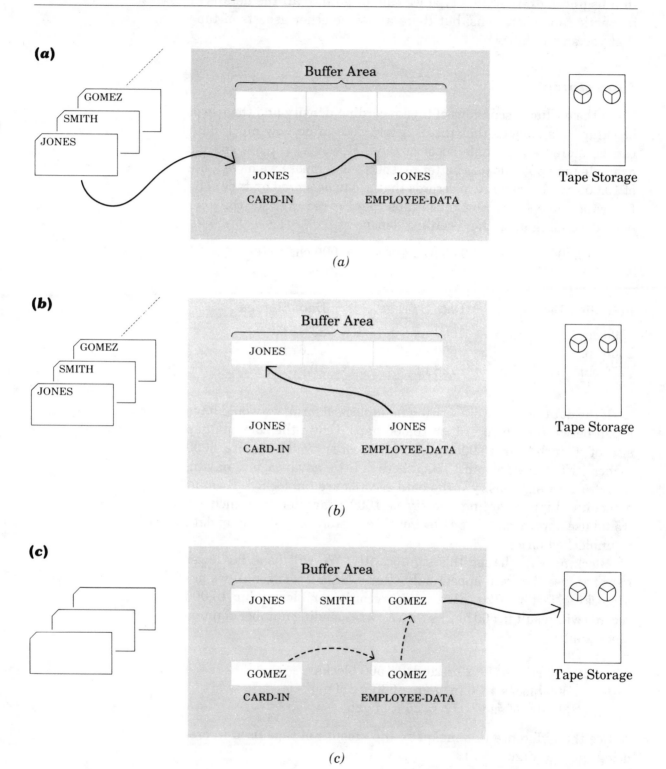

(a)

(b)

(c)

Working with magnetic tape

In a beginning text of this type we cannot go into all the details of magnetic tape operations; but there are some other aspects of tape that you should know.

Tape storage

From the earlier discussions of tape recording density and the use of blocking it is obvious that these factors determine how much data can be stored on a single spool of tape. However, a more specific example may put this into better perspective. Suppose we have a file of 10,000 80-character card records that are to be stored on tape. The following table shows how much tape space is required for the *data only,* depending upon the recording density:

10,000 records × 80 characters = 800,000 characters

Recording Density	Data Storage	Data Storage
800 cpi	1000 in.	83.3 ft
1600 cpi	500 in.	41.67 ft
6250 cpi	128 in.	10.67 ft

If the data records were written in unblocked form, we would have a gap between each record, or 10,000 gaps. Using the common gap size of .6 inch, our 10,000 unblocked records would require 6000 inches, or 500 feet, of gaps! Thus there is little advantage to having a high recording density if the data records are unblocked. Even at a medium-high recording density of 1600 characters per inch we would use approximately 541 feet of tape to store only 41 feet of data in unblocked form.

Blocking will change this significantly: We will have far fewer gaps because they will appear only after a *block* is written. If we use a blocking factor of 20—that is, 20 records per block—our 10,000 records will result in 500 blocks with a corresponding number of inter-block gaps:

10,000 records ÷ 20 records = 500 blocks
500 blocks × .6 in. gap = 300 in. of gap
300 in. of gap ÷ 12 = 25 ft of gap

Notice the difference this makes in the amount of tape used in creating the file (Figure 8-5).

FIGURE 8-5

Magnetic Tape Storage

10,000 80-Character Records—Unblocked

Recording Density	Data Storage (ft)	Gaps— Unblocked Data (ft)	Total
800	83.3	500	583.3
1600	41.67	500	541.67
6250	10.67	500	510.67

10,000 80-Character Records—Blocked 20

800	83.3	25	108.3
1600	41.67	25	66.67
6250	10.67	25	35.67

Of course, there are limitations to how large tape blocks may be. One obvious limitation is the size of available memory, but there are other points to be considered as well. Since the CPU and I/O devices are more or less matched to each other, there is an optimum size of data blocks. This size can be calculated by consulting formulas in the appropriate operations manual, and, in general, the closer you are to this size, the more efficient your tape operations (Figure 8-5).

In Chapter 6 we briefly discussed various formats that data can take in COBOL. With incoming or outgoing card data you had no choice since the data had to be in DISPLAY format. With magnetic storage media, however, we are not limited to DISPLAY format. We may wish to store numeric fields in packed (COMP-3) format to gain additional space savings and to save time converting from one format to another.

For example, our SS-NBR field coming in from the card in DISPLAY format could be changed to packed format before being written to tape simply by moving it to a COMP-3 field. Before, we had a group MOVE operation, which was correct because all the sending and receiving fields were of the same length and usage. If we wish to make SS-NBR-T a packed field, we will have to move the various fields separately. Note the following example of the move of the social security number to a packed field:

```
01   CARD-IN.
     03   SS-NBR          PIC 9(9).

01   EMPLOYEE-DATA.
     03   SS-NBR-T        PIC 9(9) COMP-3.

MOVE   SS-NBR TO SS-NBR-T.
```

The result of the MOVE will be that the incoming card value will be changed into packed format. This field along with the other data fields in the record will be written onto tape. Note what happens when the numeric data are packed. Essentially the machine places two numeric values into one position of memory. Most IBM machines have a memory configuration that makes this packing possible and that results in a great savings in the amount of memory used. The storage savings is not an exact "1 for 2" relationship as the sign of the field (positive or negative) takes up the right-most half of the right-most storage position (byte).

| S | 4 | S | 8 | S | 5 | S | 3 | S | 7 | S | 4 | S | 6 | S | 1 | S | 9 |

SS-NBR   PIC 9(9)   *(Social Security Number in memory in unpacked format, where S indicates the sign of the field)*

SS-NBR-T   PIC 9(9) COMP-3.   *(contents unknown)*

The MOVE operation takes place as follows.

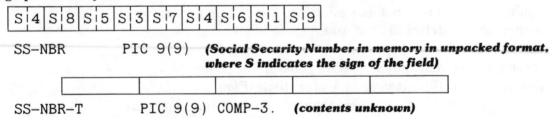

 *(sign)*

A few points worth noting:

1. The programmer does *not* establish the SS-NBR-T field as PIC 9(5). Instead, the "machine" calculates that a 9(9) packed field will actually occupy only five positions (or bytes) of memory.
2. The sign of the field is automatically placed in the right-most half of the right-most position.
3. If the sending field contained an even number of digits, the system would fill in a zero at the left to "pad" out the field.

Transfer rate

Tape blocking also has an important effect upon transfer rate, which is the rate at which tape data are read into memory. Common transfer rates range from 60,000 to 100,000 or more characters per second. Our example of 10,000 80-character records (800,000 characters) would take 10 seconds to read using a tape system with a transfer rate of 80,000 characters per second. This 10-second figure, however, is misleading since this rate pertains to *data* only.

When the system encounters a gap, it stops and then has to start again to read the next portion of data. If we assume a stop-start gap time of eight one-thousandths of a second, we can easily calculate the effect that gaps have upon the time it takes to read tape data into memory. If our 10,000-record file is unblocked, the 10,000 gaps will require 80 seconds.

$$10{,}000 \text{ gaps} \times .008 \text{ sec per gap} = 80 \text{ sec}$$

Total read time will then be 90 seconds—10 for the data and 80 for the gaps. If the data are blocked 20, we will now require only 4 seconds for the passage through the gaps.

$$500 \text{ gaps} \times .008 \text{ sec per gap} = 4 \text{ sec}$$

Total read time will now be 14 seconds.

Tape identification and protection

When we created a tape file earlier in this chapter we used the entry

    LABEL RECORDS ARE STANDARD

in the file description area. We are now at the point where we need to discuss tape labels and how they are created. When we use the term "label" we are referring to an *internal* label, or name, that is given to the file at the time it is created. This label is in the form of magnetic spots (the same format as data), and is common to any magnetic storage medium such as tape or disk. Obviously, card files and printer files are not magnetic and, therefore, cannot have labels. For those files, we say LABEL RECORDS ARE OMITTED. (Of course, any file can have an *external* label if you write on the deck with a marking pen or attach a printed label.)

With tape or disk, the entry LABEL RECORDS ARE STANDARD says that the name given to this file is in a standard format as specified by the system software. This label (again, remember it is in the form of magnetic spots) appears at the beginning of the tape and identifies that file from all other files. When a file is created (such as we did earlier in the chapter), the programmer gives the file a name and the system writes this name in a standard format on the beginning of the tape.

The name, or label, that will be associated with that tape is made known to the system in one of two general ways. On most IBM computer systems there is a control card, or control entry of some sort, that specifically indicates the name you wish to use. A control card entry used on some of the older IBM machines shows this very clearly. Remember that in our sample program we said

```
SELECT TAPEFILE
     ASSIGN TO SYS010-UT-2400-S.
```

A control card is then used to tell the system the name, or label, that you wish to assign to the file.

```
TLBL SYS010,'EMPLOYEE-DATA-FILE'
```

On some systems the tape label information is communicated to the system by an entry in the file description part of the program.

```
FD  TAPEFILE
    LABEL RECORDS ARE STANDARD
    VALUE OF ID IS 'EMPLOYEE-DATA-FILE'
    DATA RECORD IS EMPLOYEE-DATA.
```

Anyone wanting to use the file (that is, read from it) must know the label, or name, that was originally assigned to the file. This is a routine form of protection to make sure you are reading from the correct file. For example, when you specify that you wish to use (read from) the 'EMPLOYEE-DATA-FILE', the system *first* checks the label to see that the correct file has been mounted on the tape drive. If the tape spool with the exact matching label is not found, the system will automatically cancel, or abort, the program.

A second form of protection for tape files exists in the form of a plastic ring on the tape spool itself. The ring must be on the spool in order for writing to take place. In order to prevent accidental writing over or destruction of a file, we will pull out the plastic ring. Now the tape cannot be written on and an attempt to do so will again cancel the program. The general rule is "no ring, no write."

Common errors

There aren't really too many errors you can make with tape, but at least one error can be somewhat difficult to detect and correct. Let's take the easy errors first.

You recall that each file created has a label assigned to it in some way—most likely through job control cards or entries. This label is a very precise name and there is no "give" or room for error when the system attempts to match up the names. For example, if the label associated with the file is STUDENT-DATA ("student hyphen data"), do not expect the system to recognize that this is the file you mean when requesting STUDENT DATA ("student blank data"). As far as the computer system is concerned, these two names are as different as it is possible for two names to be. If a tape with the label STUDENT-DATA has been mounted on the drive, the OPEN statement (which causes the system to check the actual label against the requested label) will generate an error message indicating that the correct file cannot be found. At this point your program will be terminated.

A second type of error is one common to any file, but which seems to be made most frequently with tape. By simple logic, you can only use a file that has been OPENed, and you cannot CLOSE a file unless it has been OPENed. Any combination of errors in this area will result in the cancellation of your program.

So much for the easy errors. Now we run into a more subtle one. This error holds true whether the data are blocked or unblocked, but let's suppose we are reading a tape file containing data records that have a blocking factor of 5 (that is, five records make up a block). Suppose a record consists of the following fields:

Name	20 characters
Address	20 characters
Sales amount	7 digits (dollars and cents)
Sales area	6 digits

Our FD entry would look as follows (note the use of an *optional* line—RECORD CONTAINS—for documentation purposes):

```
FD  TAPE-FILE
    LABEL RECORDS ARE STANDARD
    RECORD CONTAINS 53 CHARACTERS
    BLOCK CONTAINS 5 RECORDS
    DATA RECORD IS TAPE-RECORD.
01  TAPE-RECORD.
    03 NAME-T        PIC X(20).
    03 ADDRESS-T     PIC X(20).
    03 SALES-AMT     PIC 9(5)V99.
    03 SALES-AREA    PIC 9(6).
```

The system goes through a series of very logical steps.

1. It "sees" the BLOCK CONTAINS entry, which triggers into the software that will set up the buffer area for the incoming *block* of data.
2. The system counts up the number of characters (or bytes) in the incoming record based upon the USAGE of the individual fields. Since all the fields are in DISPLAY format, the count comes to 53.

3. The actual count made by the system is compared to the count supplied by the programmer, and the two are the same.
4. A buffer area of 265 bytes, or positions, is set up to accept the incoming blocked data from tape. The PROCEDURE DIVISION statement

```
READ TAPE-FILE
    AT END
```

will be executed properly.

Now, let's make two changes. Suppose that both numeric fields were written onto tape in packed format (COMP-3) and that the programmer does not indicate this to the system in the file description entry. The correct entry for the two fields would be as follows:

```
03   SALES-AMT     PIC 9(5)V99 COMP-3.
03   SALES-AREA    PIC 9(6) COMP-3.
```

The SALES-AMT field will only take up four bytes, or memory positions, in packed format (remember: half a position for the sign and then two digits per position from there on). The SALES-AREA field will also take up four bytes (half a position, or byte, for the sign and two digits per position from there on). We are left, however, with half a position unused at the left and this will automatically be filled in with a zero.

0	X X	X X	X	S

If you forget to "say" COMP-3 for these fields, the system will calculate a record size of 53 characters and set up the buffer as before. Actually, the buffer area (265 characters) is *too large* for the incoming block because the correct record size is 20 + 20 + 4 + 4 positions for a total of 48 bytes, or positions. Even though the buffer area is too large, it is still not correct and is just as wrong as if you had made it too small. Normally, the system will abort, or cancel, the program as soon as reading is attempted. The error message varies from machine to machine, but generally indicates that this buffer or transient area is not of the proper size.

Problem-Solving Techniques

Let's continue our discussion from the previous chapter about what to do when your program won't work. Recall that what the whole thing may boil down to is the laborious task of desk checking—that is, playing computer with your program statements. Obviously, you should not have to do this with every statement—only those in the module(s) you suspect of causing the problem. Application of appropriate "horse sense" logic will have allowed you to narrow down the area of search. If you still cannot find the error, this is a good time to insert DISPLAY statements at strategic points in the module(s). You can display the contents of counter, input fields, result fields, and so on both before and after the suspected programming takes place.

If this fails, you may have to break a complex statement into more simple parts. For example, a COMPUTE statement that *should* be working but is suspect may be replaced with a series of very simple COM-PUTEs or simple ADD, SUBTRACT, and so forth. And that brings out the second major point of this section: One old-fashioned rule of programming is the rule of KIS—Keep It Simple.

The author believes very firmly that programs should be written simply. Furthermore, this rule holds true for both beginning and experienced programmers. Problems that are programmed simply are a lot easier to follow, debug, and maintain. A good rule to follow in this matter is: If you can flowchart it (the construction), use it; if not, don't use it. This rule is particularly applicable to compound/complex IF statements. Be careful, since they may not be doing what you think they should be doing.

Self-Study: Questions and Answers

1. I keep hearing a lot about magnetic disk storage. How does it differ from magnetic tape?

   Answer
   Disk storage is not the topic of this chapter, but a general answer may help. Both disk and tape are magnetic storage media and the same general methods are used for the reading and writing of data on these media. Tape, however, differs greatly from magnetic disk in one very important aspect: method of access, or the way by which we locate the data stored on the magnetic media. With tape, the data can only be accessed in a sequential manner. By this we mean that to locate (or READ) a specific data record you must start at the beginning and read through the data record by record (or block by block) until you find the desired material. This is precisely what we mean when we say "sequential" access. Disk, on the other hand, is said to be a direct-access device, or medium, because we can go almost directly to the location of the data record we want. The difference between the two methods of access does not mean that disk storage is better than tape. It is simply a matter of having two types of storage media available for different uses on the computer system.

2. I see the space-saving advantage of blocking tape data, but are there any other advantages?

   Answer
   Perhaps you forgot about the increased transfer rate of data from tape to memory when data are blocked. Remember that each gap forces the tape drive to come to a complete stop and then start up again. The time (and space) saved by blocking may not seem significant, but when you begin to consider some large files of many *millions* of records, the savings can become tremendously important.

3. It hardly seems possible that the BLOCK CONTAINS entry can have such a large effect on my program.

   Answer
   From reading the chapter you now have an idea of the power of that very simple entry. The important thing to remember is that it is not "magic" since the software that you trigger into is extremely sophisticated. In general, this software does two things. First, it sets up the memory buffer area for the incoming or outgoing data block. Second, it allows you to write your tape program in such a way that you do not have to consider where the data are blocked or unblocked.

4. When a tape file is created, how or what causes the system to write the label onto tape?

   Answer
   Earlier in the chapter you saw that executing the CLOSE statement caused the system to write the end of file (EOF) material on the tape. You also read that execution of the OPEN statement caused the system to check the actual tape label against the label requested in the program. When a file is created, the OPEN statement takes the label information from the source (job control card, etc.) and writes this (plus some other information) on the beginning of the tape. As indicated throughout the text, OPEN and CLOSE are very powerful COBOL statements.

Exercises

1. Define or explain the following terms as they relate to magnetic tape.
   a. End of file
   b. Label (internal)
   c. Reflective marker
   d. Inter-record gap
   e. Inter-block gap
   f. Blocked records
   g. Tape transfer rate
   h. Tape protection (from accidental writing)
   i. Recording density
   j. Transfer rate

2. How does the BLOCK CONTAINS entry affect the logic used by the programmer in the PROCEDURE DIVISION? Explain in detail.

3. Why is the AT END part of the READ statement required when you read from magnetic tape?

4. What "triggers" the AT END part of the tape READ statement? Explain in detail.

5. Modify the program shown in Figure 9-3 as follows:
   a. The numeric fields being written onto tape are to be in packed format.
   b. The blocking factor is to be seven records per block.
   c. Include the proper RECORD CONTAINS clause.

6. What is wrong with the following entries that are being written onto tape?
   a. 03 NAME-T PIC X(30) COMP-3
   b. 03 FILLER PIC X(5) COMP-3
   c. 03 ADDRESS PIC X(30) COMP-3

7. Assume you are working with tape that has a recording density of 6250 characters and a gap size of .5 inch. How much tape space will the following files take?
   a. 100,000 80-byte records blocked 5
   b. 65,000 35-byte records blocked 25
   c. 65,000 35-byte records that are unblocked
   d. 50,000 70-byte records blocked 2
   e. 50,000 70-byte records blocked 10

8. Using the figures from Exercise 7, calculate the storage required if the recording density was 1600 characters per inch.

9. Assume a tape transfer rate of 100,000 characters per second and a gap stop/start time of $\frac{1}{10}$ of a second. Use this information to calculate the transfer times for Exercises 7a, 7b, 7d, and 7e.

10. Indicate how many bytes, or memory positions, the following packed fields will require. Diagram your answer if necessary.
    a. YTD-PAY PIC 9(6)V99 COMP-3
    b. COUNTER-1 PIC 9 COMP-3
    c. COUNTER-2 PIC 99 COMP-3
    d. COUNTER-3 PIC 999 COMP-3
    e. GRAND-TOTAL PIC 9(9)V99

11. Revise the program you wrote in Chapter 7 Exercise 8 on the basis that the incoming data are from a tape file with the data records blocked 4 (Data File A). In addition, assume that the tape label is PAY-DATA and that the following numeric fields are in packed format: social security number, rate of pay, insurance deductions, credit union deductions, and other deductions.

12. In this exercise you will make use of Data File B (see the appendix), which contains sales data information blocked 5. The file label name is SALES-DATA. The record format is as follows:

Field	Characters	Type
Sales territory	3	Numeric
ID number	5	Numeric
Salesperson's name	20	Alphabetic
Year to date sales	7	Numeric, packed format, dollars and cents
Year to date sales returns	6	Numeric, packed format, dollars and cents

The sales manager is concerned about sales in territories 103 and 107. Punch two cards as shown below.

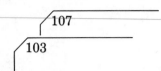

Write a program that will do the following:
a. Read in the sales territory number from a card.
b. Read sequentially through the file and print a line of output for each salesperson in the matching sales territory as shown in the diagram below. Note that the ID number is to be separated into two parts by a dash. Net YTD sales is calculated by subtracting YTD returns from YTD sales.
c. You are to keep a running total of the net YTD sales and print this at the end of the listing for that particular department. All numeric fields are to be appropriately edited.
d. In order to go through the tape file a second time to search for the next territory number, you will have to close the tape file and open it again. This program is not particularly efficient, but should convince you of the sequential nature of magnetic tape storage.
e. There is a possibility that a salesperson can have returns that exceed sales in the case of return items that were sold in a previous year. Your program is to account for this situation and print a credit symbol (CR) immediately after the year-to-date net sales figure.

```
          NAME         ID#     YTD SALES    YTD RETURNS    YTD NET SALES

Jones, Fred   20-136    _____        _____          _____
_____   _____     _____        _____          _____
_____   _____     _____        _____          _____

TOTAL NET YTD SALES—TERRITORY 003

Smith, Sam    50-904    _____        _____          _____
_____   _____     _____        _____          _____
_____   _____     _____        _____          _____

TOTAL NET YTD SALES—TERRITORY 107

PROGRAMMED BY
```

Chapter 9

Manipulating Data Files

The previous chapter covered the nature of magnetic tape activities and emphasized the point that tape is a sequential storage medium. In this chapter we will take a closer look at tape and some of the typical operations that are performed when working with sequential files. Recall that Figure 8-3 showed a program that created a tape file on SYS010. The data records originated from cards and consisted of Employee Name, Address, Social Security Number, Telephone Number, and Work Code fields. Figure 9-1 is a program that lists the contents of the file by printing the Social Security Number, Name, and Telephone Number fields. Figure 9-2 shows the output.

FIGURE 9-1

Tape Listing: TAPE-DATA File

```
 1          IDENTIFICATION DIVISION.
 2          PROGRAM-ID. TAPELIST.
 3      *
 4          ENVIRONMENT DIVISION.
 5          CONFIGURATION SECTION.
 6          SOURCE-COMPUTER. IBM-360-F30.
 7          OBJECT-COMPUTER. IBM-360-F30.
 8          SPECIAL-NAMES. C01 IS TOP-OF-PAGE.
 9          INPUT-OUTPUT SECTION.
10          FILE-CONTROL.
11              SELECT PRINTFILE
12                  ASSIGN TO SYS009-UR-1403-S.
13              SELECT TAPEFILE
14                  ASSIGN TO SYS010-UT-2400-S.
15      *
16          DATA DIVISION.
17          FILE SECTION.
18          FD  PRINTFILE
19              LABEL RECORDS ARE OMITTED
20              DATA RECORD IS PRINT-LINE.
21          01  PRINT-LINE                  PIC X(121).
22          FD  TAPEFILE
23              LABEL RECORDS ARE STANDARD
24              DATA RECORD IS EMPLOYEE-DATA.
25          01  EMPLOYEE-DATA.
26              03  E-NAME-T                PIC X(30).
27              03  E-ADDRESS-T             PIC X(30).
28              03  SS-NBR-T                PIC 9(9).
29              03  PHONE-T                 PIC X(8).
30              03  W-CODE-T                PIC 9(3).
31          WORKING-STORAGE SECTION.
32          77  INDICATOR                   PIC 9 VALUE ZERO.
33          01  PRINT-RECORD.
34              03  FILLER                  PIC X.
35              03  FILLER                  PIC X(15) VALUE SPACES.
36              03  SS-NBR-T                PIC 999B99B9999.
37              03  FILLER                  PIC X(5) VALUE SPACES.
38              03  E-NAME-T                PIC X(30).
39              03  FILLER                  PIC X(5) VALUE SPACES.
40              03  PHONE-T                 PIC X(8).
41              03  FILLER                  PIC X(46) VALUE SPACES.
42      *
```

```
43              PROCEDURE DIVISION.
44              CONTROL-ROUTINE.
45                  PERFORM 010-OPENER.
46                  PERFORM 020-READER UNTIL
47                      INDICATOR = 1.
48                  PERFORM 030-CLOSER.
49                  STOP RUN.
50              010-OPENER.
51                  OPEN INPUT TAPEFILE
52                      OUTPUT PRINTFILE.
53                  MOVE SPACES TO PRINT-LINE.
54                  WRITE PRINT-LINE
55                      AFTER ADVANCING TOP-OF-PAGE.
56                  READ TAPEFILE
57                      AT END MOVE 1 TO INDICATOR.
58              020-READER.
59                  MOVE CORRESPONDING EMPLOYEE-DATA TO PRINT-RECORD.
60                  WRITE PRINT-LINE FROM PRINT-RECORD
61                      AFTER ADVANCING 2 LINES.
62                  READ TAPEFILE
63                      AT END MOVE 1 TO INDICATOR.
64              030-CLOSER.
65                  CLOSE PRINTFILE TAPEFILE.
```

FIGURE 9-2

Program Output

123 45 6789	JONES, JOHN	555-5555
314 80 3800	LEE, SALLY	566-7777
438 31 6914	SMITH, SUE	556-0140
500 30 5432	ROBERTS, SAM	556-9188
777 68 5948	GONZALES, ED	555-3817
900 39 6542	JOHNSON, ROBERT	566-4444

Several points are worth noting about the program. The original tape-write program wrote the data using unblocked records; we must retrieve it the same way. The MOVE CORRESPONDING statement moved like-named fields from the tape input record (EMPLOYEE-DATA) to the output record (PRINT-RECORD) with a single statement. With MOVE CORRESPONDING, it is the receiving area fields that determine which fields will be moved. Finally, note that the tape records are in ascending order according to Social Security Number because this was the order of the card deck from which the data records originated.

Updating a tape file

Updating is the general term applied to file maintenance activities that cover any of the three logical possibilities outlined below.

1. Making changes to records in the file (matching)
2. Deleting records from the file (matching)
3. Adding records to the file (merging)

It is possible to do all three actions at the same time, that is, within the same program; but we will show each of these operations separately.

Updating tape records (matching)

Perhaps the simplest operation performed on tape files is that of updating, or making changes to, existing records. The output from our tape-lister program was shown in Figure 9-2 and it indicated the contents of the file before updating. Let's assume that some of the data records in the file are no longer correct and they must be updated to reflect the following changes:

> Employee Sue Smith has married and is now known as SUE BERTOLI.
>
> Employee Sam Roberts has changed his telephone number to 583-0014.

We will start by punching into cards the complete *revised* employee record for each of these employees. We could have entered just those fields that have changed, but in this case we will enter a complete, new record of data for the employee.

What we want to do, of course, is to read-in a card record and make the appropriate changes on the master tape file. The first problem that arises is that we want to be sure we update the correct record on the tape file. We will make certain that we get the proper record by matching the Social Security Number of the incoming card record with the Social Security Number on the tape record. The most efficient way to program this type of operation is to have both files in ascending order according to the key field (SS-NBR). This is easy to do since we have only two cards in the card file; but sequencing would be the normal practice no matter how large the files.

The existing tape file is normally called the Master File since it contains master, or relatively unchanging, data. The file containing the changes (the card file in this case) would be known as the Detail or Transaction File and would contain data that probably will be used only once.

The next difficulty is that you really don't update the existing Master File; that is, you do not make changes directly on it. Instead, you update by creating a New Master File that contains the "good" or unchanged records from the Old Master File plus the changes that we entered from the Transaction, or Detail, File. As described so far, our operation will involve three files:

1. The incoming Detail File (cards)
2. The incoming Master File (tape)
3. The outgoing New Master File (tape)

To this we will add a printer file on which we will list the contents of the revised file, or New Master File. Schematically, the operation will be as shown in Figure 9-3.

FIGURE 9-3

File Update

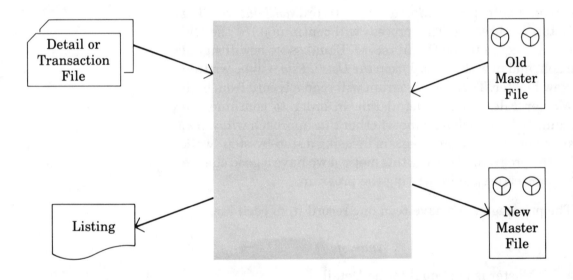

The logic of our file update program is dependent upon both files being in ascending order according to Social Security Number—an assumption we make in this case. In a real life situation you might have to run a sequence check of the file records prior to executing the update program. This could be done either in a separate program or as part of the file update program itself. As indicated before, we will assume that both the card and tape file are in ascending order.

We can use this knowledge of the order of the records in the file to determine our program logic. Obviously, we will have to read from both files, but we cannot assume that a reading of records from both files will automatically result in finding equal or matching records.

A simple diagram is a handy way to approach the logic of matching file records.

Let's assume that the two files contain the following records as identified by these single-digit key fields:

Detail File (card file): ③ ⑤ Card EOF Marker

Old Master File (tape file): ① ② ③ ④ ⑤ ⑥ Tape EOF Marker

We will start by reading a record from each file (two separate READ statements) and then compare the Social Security Numbers. There are several different approaches that could be used, but let's try this one. (Again, remember that both files are in ascending order according to Social Security Number.) If the SS-NBR field from the Old Master File is not equal to the SS-NBR field from the card file (Detail, or Transaction, File), then we can simply write the Old Master record onto the New Master File. A look at our simplified diagram tells you that, in the example above, there could never be an equal (or matching) condition for Old Master record #1.

Since we have not yet found the match for Detail record #3, we will now read another Old Master tape record *without* reading another Detail card record. This process will continue until the Old Master record is equal to the Detail record. Equal SS-NBRs will signal this condition, and now the record *from the Detail File* will be written onto the New Master. Then, the program will read a record from both the Old Master File and the Detail File in order to continue the process again. To help us determine whether this approach will work, we can expand on the previous diagram by using a step-by-step "walk through" of the program. By using this method we have a good chance of spotting logic errors before writing the program.

Step 1   The priming READs have read one record from each file.

M	D	*Analysis*
1	3	Master is not equal to the Detail.
		The New Master is written from the Old Master File.
		An Old Master record is read.

Step 2

M	D	*Analysis*
2	3	Same as Step 1.

Step 3

M	D
3	3

Analysis

Master is equal to the Detail.

The New Master is written from the Detail File.

Both an Old Master and a Detail record are read.

Step 4

M	D
4	5

Analysis

Same as Step 1.

Step 5

M	D
5	5

Analysis

Same as Step 3.

The program logic is fine to this point, but we have not considered the AT END condition when reading sequential files (card and tape). When we reach the end of the Detail (card) File, we cannot just stop the program since there may be more records on the Old Master File that have to be written onto the New Master tape. At first glance it would seem that we can just continue with the 015-UPDATE module because all succeeding Old Master records will be unequal (larger) to the last Detail record. This is true, but we will get into trouble with the IF statement in that paragraph. It will attempt to compare the Master SS-NBR with a nonexisting Detail SS-NBR. In essence, the system will try to compare against garbage, and the program will be terminated.

To get around this problem we will get out of the 015-UPDATE module by means of the end of file indicator (CARD-SWITCH) that controls the PERFORM for the 015-UPDATE module. Upon exiting from that PERFORM, we will enter into another PERFORM that will control another module that duplicates the remaining Old Master records onto the New Master File.

```
PERFORM 015-UPDATE
    UNTIL CARD-SWITCH = 1.
PERFORM 025-DUP-OLD-MASTER
    UNTIL OLD-MSTR-SWITCH = 1.
```

Our analysis for the rest of the items will now change.

Step 6

Analysis

M	D
6	EOF

Exit from 015-UPDATE module to 025-DUP-OLD-MASTER module.

Write New Master from Old Master Read Old Master.

Step 7

Analysis

M	D
EOF	EOF

Exit from 25-DUP-OLD-MASTER module.

Pseudocode specifications are shown below, and Figures 9-4*a* and 9-4*b*, 9-5, and 9-6 show the structured flowchart, Warnier/Orr diagram, program, and printer listing.

Pseudocode Specifications: TAPE UPDATE

```
CONTROL-ROUTINE
    PERFORM 010-OPENER
    PERFORM 015-UPDATE UNTIL card switch = 1
    PERFORM 030-DUP-OLD-MASTER UNTIL master switch
        = 1
    PERFORM 035-END-ROUTINE
    STOP RUN


010-OPENER
    Open the files
    Write heading line
    Read a card record at end move 1 to card switch
    Read old master tape file at end move 1 to master switch


015-UPDATE
    IF    social security number old master equals social
            security number card
            Move card fields to new master tape record
            Write new master tape record
            Move card fields to print area
            Write a report line on the printer
            Read a card record at end move 1 to card switch
            Read old master tape file at end move 1 to master
                switch
    ELSE
            PERFORM 030-DUP-OLD-MASTER
    ENDIF


030-DUP-OLD-MASTER
    Move old master fields to new master
    Write new master tape record
    Move old master fields to print area
    Write a report line on the printer
    Read old master tape file at end move 1 to master switch


035-END-ROUTINE
    Close files
```

FIGURE 9-4a

File Change Flowchart

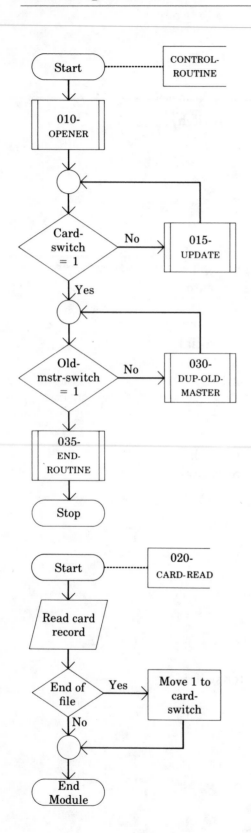

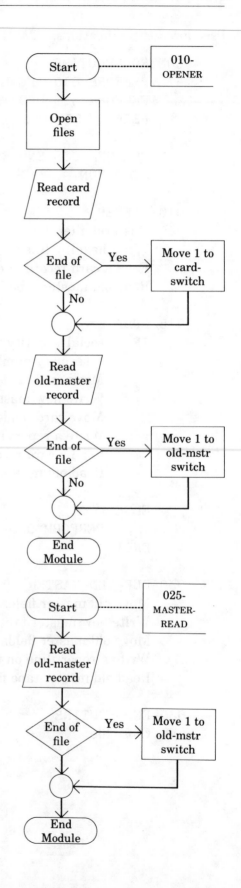

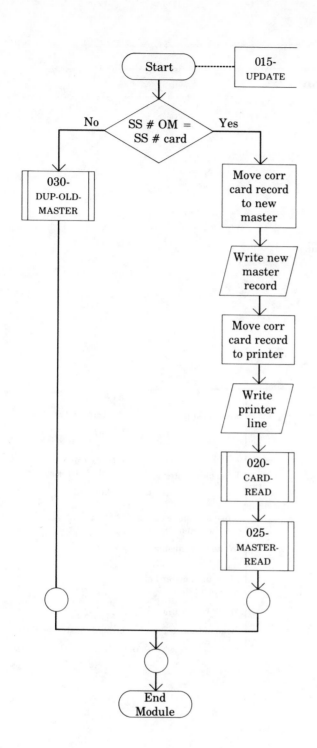

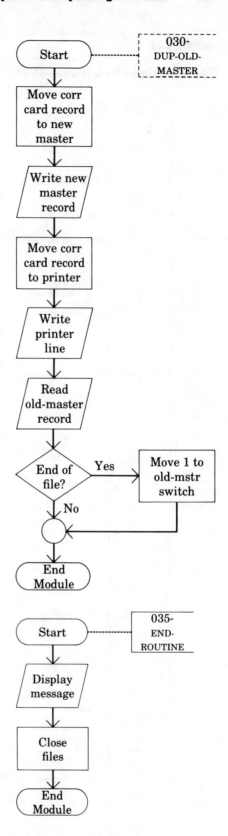

FIGURE 9-4b

Tape Update Program—Warnier/Orr Diagram

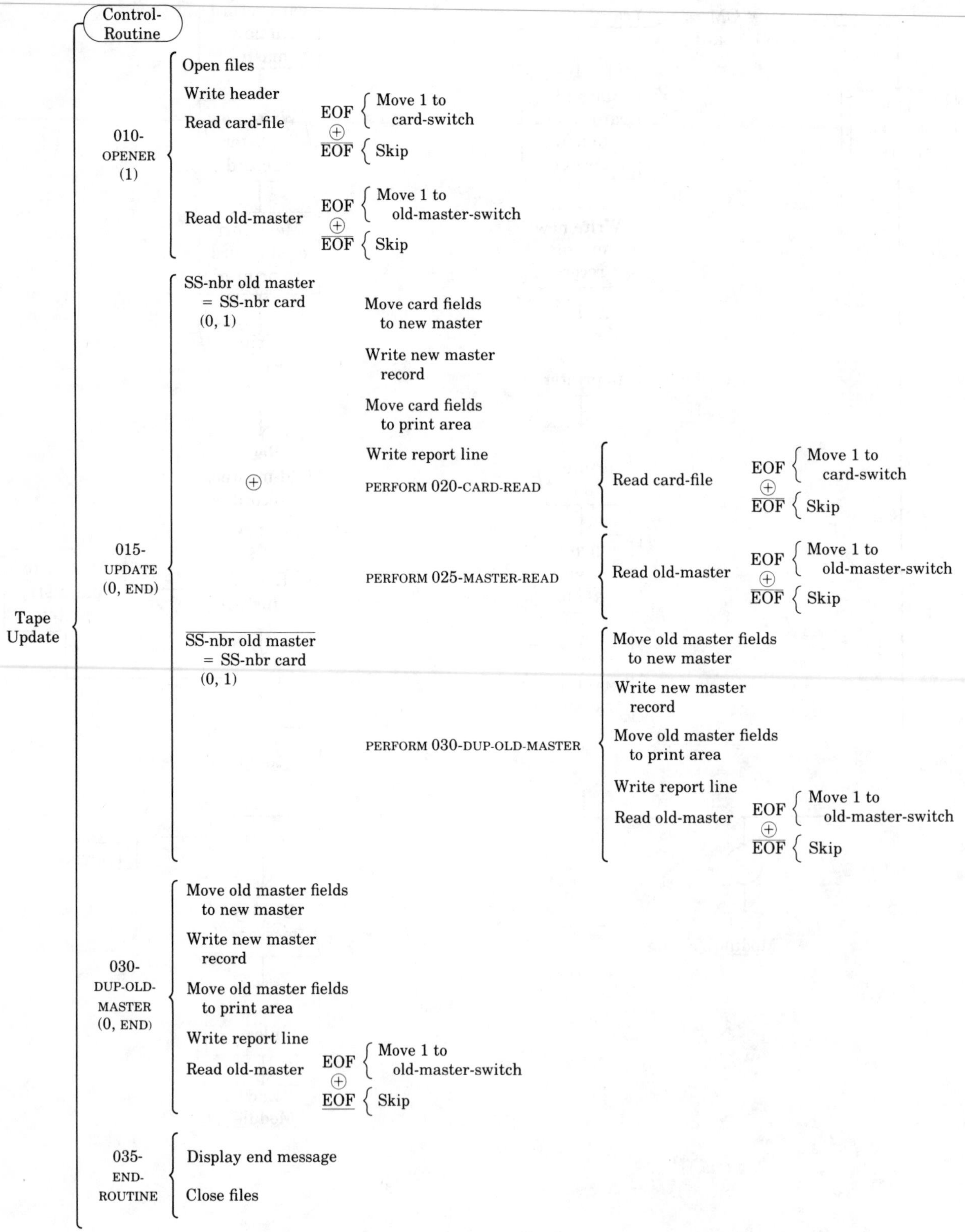

Tape Update

Control-Routine

010-OPENER (1)
- Open files
- Write header
- Read card-file
  - EOF { Move 1 to card-switch
  - ⊕
  - EOF { Skip
- Read old-master
  - EOF { Move 1 to old-master-switch
  - ⊕
  - EOF { Skip

015-UPDATE (0, END)
- SS-nbr old master = SS-nbr card (0, 1)
  - Move card fields to new master
  - Write new master record
  - Move card fields to print area
  - Write report line
  - PERFORM 020-CARD-READ
    - Read card-file
      - EOF { Move 1 to card-switch
      - ⊕
      - EOF { Skip
  - PERFORM 025-MASTER-READ
    - Read old-master
      - EOF { Move 1 to old-master-switch
      - ⊕
      - EOF { Skip
  - ⊕
- SS-nbr old master = SS-nbr card (0, 1)
  - Move old master fields to new master
  - PERFORM 030-DUP-OLD-MASTER
    - Write new master record
    - Move old master fields to print area
    - Write report line
    - Read old-master
      - EOF { Move 1 to old-master-switch
      - ⊕
      - EOF { Skip

030-DUP-OLD-MASTER (0, END)
- Move old master fields to new master
- Write new master record
- Move old master fields to print area
- Write report line
- Read old-master
  - EOF { Move 1 to old-master-switch
  - ⊕
  - EOF { Skip

035-END-ROUTINE
- Display end message
- Close files

FIGURE 9-5

File-Change Program

```
                IBM DOS AMERICAN NATIONAL STANDARD COBOL

     IDENTIFICATION DIVISION.
     PROGRAM-ID. UPDATE1.
*

     ENVIRONMENT DIVISION.
     CONFIGURATION SECTION.
     SOURCE-COMPUTER. IBM-360-F30.
     OBJECT-COMPUTER. IBM-360-F30.
     INPUT-OUTPUT SECTION.
     FILE-CONTROL.
         SELECT CARD-FILE
             ASSIGN TO SYS007-UR-2540R-S.
         SELECT OLD-MASTER
             ASSIGN TO SYS010-UT-2400-S.
         SELECT NEW-MASTER
             ASSIGN TO SYS011-UT-2400-S.
         SELECT PRINT-FILE
             ASSIGN TO SYS009-UR-1403-S.
*
```

```
DATA DIVISION.
FILE SECTION.
FD   CARD-FILE
     LABEL RECORDS ARE OMITTED
     DATA RECORD IS CARD-IN.
01   CARD-IN.
     03   E-NAME                         PIC X(30).
     03   E-ADDRESS                      PIC X(30).
     03   SS-NBR                         PIC 9(9).
     03   PHONE                          PIC X(8).
     03   W-CODE                         PIC 9(3).
FD   OLD-MASTER
     LABEL RECORDS ARE STANDARD
     DATA RECORD IS EMPLOYEE-DATA-OM.
01   EMPLOYEE-DATA-OM.
     03   E-NAME                         PIC X(30).
     03   E-ADDRESS                      PIC X(30).
     03   SS-NBR                         PIC 9(9).
     03   PHONE                          PIC X(8).
     03   W-CODE                         PIC 9(3).
FD   NEW-MASTER
     LABEL RECORDS ARE STANDARD
     DATA RECORD IS EMPLOYEE-DATA-NM.
01   EMPLOYEE-DATA-NM.
     03   E-NAME                         PIC X(30).
     03   E-ADDRESS                      PIC X(30).
     03   SS-NBR                         PIC 9(9).
     03   PHONE                          PIC X(8).
     03   W-CODE                         PIC 9(3).
FD   PRINT-FILE
     LABEL RECORDS ARE OMITTED
     DATA RECORD IS PRINT-LINE.
01   PRINT-LINE                          PIC X(121).
WORKING-STORAGE SECTION.
77   CARD-SWITCH                         PIC 9 VALUE ZERO.
77   OLD-MSTR-SWITCH                     PIC 9 VALUE ZERO.
01   PRINT-RECORD.
     03   FILLER                         PIC X.
     03   FILLER                         PIC X(10) VALUE SPACES.
     03   SS-NBR                         PIC 999B99B9999.
     03   FILLER                         PIC X(5) VALUE SPACES.
     03   E-NAME                         PIC X(30).
     03   FILLER                         PIC X(5) VALUE SPACES.
     03   PHONE                          PIC X(8).
     03   FILLER                         PIC X(46) VALUE SPACES.
01   HEAD1.
     03   FILLER                         PIC X.
     03   FILLER                         PIC X(15) VALUE SPACES.
     03   FILLER                         PIC X(12)
                                             VALUE 'REVISED FILE'.
     03   FILLER                         PIC X(93) VALUE SPACES.
*
```

```
PROCEDURE DIVISION.
CONTROL-ROUTINE.
    PERFORM 010-OPENER.
    PERFORM 015-UPDATE
        UNTIL CARD-SWITCH = 1.
    PERFORM 030-DUP-OLD-MASTER
        UNTIL OLD-MSTR-SWITCH = 1.
    PERFORM 035-END-ROUTINE.
    STOP RUN.
010-OPENER.
    OPEN INPUT CARD-FILE OLD-MASTER
        OUTPUT NEW-MASTER PRINT-FILE.
    WRITE PRINT-LINE FROM HEAD1
        AFTER ADVANCING 2 LINES.
    READ CARD-FILE
        AT END MOVE 1 TO CARD-SWITCH.
    READ OLD-MASTER
        AT END MOVE 1 TO OLD-MSTR-SWITCH.
015-UPDATE.
    IF SS-NBR OF EMPLOYEE-DATA-OM IS EQUAL TO
        SS-NBR OF CARD-IN
        MOVE CORRESPONDING CARD-IN
            TO EMPLOYEE-DATA-NM
        WRITE EMPLOYEE-DATA-NM
        MOVE CORRESPONDING CARD-IN
            TO PRINT-RECORD
        WRITE PRINT-LINE FROM PRINT-RECORD
            AFTER ADVANCING 2 LINES
        PERFORM 020-CARD-READ
        PERFORM 025-MASTER-READ
    ELSE
        PERFORM 030-DUP-OLD-MASTER.
020-CARD-READ.
    READ CARD-FILE
        AT END MOVE 1 TO CARD-SWITCH.
025-MASTER-READ.
    READ OLD-MASTER
        AT END MOVE 1 TO OLD-MSTR-SWITCH.
030-DUP-OLD-MASTER.
    MOVE CORRESPONDING EMPLOYEE-DATA-OM
        TO EMPLOYEE-DATA-NM.
    WRITE EMPLOYEE-DATA-NM.
    MOVE CORRESPONDING EMPLOYEE-DATA-OM
        TO PRINT-RECORD.
    WRITE PRINT-LINE FROM PRINT-RECORD
        AFTER ADVANCING 2 LINES.
    READ OLD-MASTER
        AT END MOVE 1 TO OLD-MSTR-SWITCH.
035-END-ROUTINE.
    DISPLAY '           END OF JOB'.
    CLOSE CARD-FILE OLD-MASTER
        NEW-MASTER PRINT-FILE.
```

FIGURE 9-6

New Master Showing Changed Fields

REVISED FILE

123 45 6789	JONES, JOHN	555–5555
314 80 3800	BERTOLI, SALLY	566–7777
438 31 6914	SMITH, SUE	556–0140
500 30 5432	ROBERTS, SAM	583–0014
777 68 5948	GONZALES, ED	555–3817
900 39 6542	JOHNSON, ROBERT	566–4444

END OF JOB

Deleting records from file (matching)

The second major task involved in updating a tape file is that of deleting records. For example, our master employee data file contains a record on each employee who works for the company. Of course, some of these people quit or retire and therefore must be deleted from the Master File.

For our example we will use the same data we had before. If you recall, the file consisted of six employees, as shown below:

123 45 6789	JONES, JOHN	555–5555
314 80 3800	LEE, SALLY	566–7777
438 31 6914	SMITH, SUE	556–0140
500 30 5432	ROBERTS, SAM	556–9188
777 68 5948	GONZALES, ED	555–3817
900 39 6542	JOHNSON, ROBERT	566–4444

We will use the same files we did in the first example except that now our incoming card file will contain the records indicating those employees who are to be deleted from the file. Again, our program logic will be based on the knowledge that both files are in ascending order. In our example, employees Sally Lee and Sam Roberts are to be deleted from the file. The process is generally the same as before: We must create a new master tape file by copying onto it the records of those employees who are being retained.

Again, a simple diagram will help to decide what logic to use.

   Detail File (card file): ② ④

   Old Master File (tape file): ① ② ③ ④ ⑤

The priming READs will start us off by reading in one record from each file. An IF statement in the 020-UPDATE module will test for the equality of the two SS-NBR fields. If they are not equal, the record from the Old Master File will be written to the New Master File and another Old Master record will be read.

This process continues until an equal condition is encountered in the case of record ② in the diagram. At this point we will *not* write the Old Master record to the New Master. Instead, the record will be moved to the printer and entered on a Deletion Report. A flowchart of the 015-UPDATE module is shown in Figure 9-7 while Figures 9-8 and 9-9 show the PROCEDURE DIVISION and the program output.

FIGURE 9-7

File Deletion Flowchart

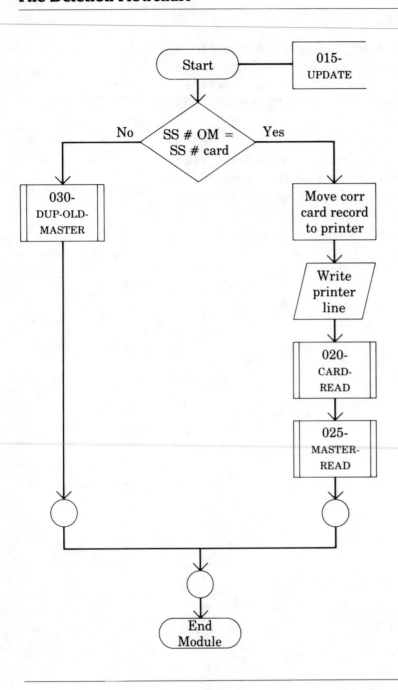

FIGURE 9-8

File Deletion Program

```
PROCEDURE DIVISION.
CONTROL-ROUTINE.
    PERFORM 010-OPENER.
    PERFORM 015-UPDATE
        UNTIL CARD-SWITCH = 1.
    PERFORM 030-DUP-OLD-MASTER
        UNTIL OLD-MSTR-SWITCH = 1.
    PERFORM 035-END-ROUTINE.
    STOP RUN.
010-OPENER.
    OPEN INPUT CARD-FILE OLD-MASTER
        OUTPUT NEW-MASTER PRINT-FILE.
    WRITE PRINT-LINE FROM HEAD1
        AFTER ADVANCING 2 LINES.
    READ CARD-FILE
        AT END MOVE 1 TO CARD-SWITCH.
    READ OLD-MASTER
        AT END MOVE 1 TO OLD-MSTR-SWITCH.
015-UPDATE.
    IF SS-NBR OF EMPLOYEE-DATA-OM IS EQUAL TO
        SS-NBR OF CARD-IN
        MOVE CORRESPONDING CARD-IN
            TO PRINT-RECORD
        WRITE PRINT-LINE FROM PRINT-RECORD
            AFTER ADVANCING 2 LINES
        PERFORM 020-CARD-READ
        PERFORM 025-MASTER-READ
    ELSE
        PERFORM 030-DUP-OLD-MASTER.
020-CARD-READ.
    READ CARD-FILE
        AT END MOVE 1 TO CARD-SWITCH.
025-MASTER-READ.
    READ OLD-MASTER
        AT END MOVE 1 TO OLD-MSTR-SWITCH.
030-DUP-OLD-MASTER.
    MOVE CORRESPONDING EMPLOYEE-DATA-OM
        TO EMPLOYEE-DATA-NM.
    WRITE EMPLOYEE-DATA-NM.
    READ OLD-MASTER
        AT END MOVE 1 TO OLD-MSTR-SWITCH.
035-END-ROUTINE.
    DISPLAY '            END OF JOB'.
    CLOSE CARD-FILE OLD-MASTER
        NEW-MASTER PRINT-FILE.
```

FIGURE 9-9

Deletion List

```
                        DELETED RECORDS

     314 80 3800      LEE, SALLY                          566-7777

     500 30 5432      ROBERTS, SAM                        556-9188
     END OF JOB
```

Adding records to a file (merging)

The third possibility when updating a file is that of making additions by interspersing the records of one file with the records of another file. In programming terminology this is known as merging. Once more we will go back to our original master employee file and create a New Master File that contains the following additions:

```
     248-39-9618    ADDISON, CHARLES    551-8890
     883-11-1529    MASON, NANCY        556-6346
```

Basically, our program will be the same as those used previously, but with one significant difference. The simplified diagram to help us decide on what logic to use is illustrated below.

Detail File (card file): ② ⑤

Old Master File (tape file): ① ③ ④ ⑥

As opposed to the two previous examples, we cannot test for equality because we no longer have a matching situation. The test will be to see whether the ss-nbr of the Old Master is less than the Detail File. If it is, an entry is made to the New Master File from the Old Master File and another Old Master record is read. If the Old Master record is *not* less than the Detail record, the New Master File is written from the Detail File and the merged record is entered into the new file listing. As before, a step-by-step analysis will help to visualize the operation.

Step 1   The priming READs have read one record from each file.

M	D
1	2

Analysis

Master is less than the Detail.

The New Master File is written from the Old Master File.

An Old Master record is read.

Step 2

M	D
3	2

Analysis

Master is *not* less than the Detail.

The New Master File is written from the Detail File.

A Detail record is read.

Step 3

M	D
3	5

Analysis

Same as Step 1.

Step 4

M	D
4	5

Analysis

Same as Step 1.

Step 5

M	D	*Analysis*
6	5	Master is *not* less than the Detail.

The New Master File is written from the Detail File.

The end of file condition is detected in the Detail File.

Step 6

M	D	*Analysis*
6	EOF	Exit from 015-UPDATE module.

Write New Master from Old Master.

Read Old Master.

Step 7

M	D	*Analysis*
EOF	EOF	Exit from 025-DUP-OLD-MASTER module.

Pseudocode specifications are shown on the next page, and Figures 9-10 and 9-11 show the PROCEDURE DIVISION entries and the program output.

Pseudocode Specifications: MERGING

```
CONTROL-ROUTINE
    PERFORM 010-OPENER
    PERFORM 015-UPDATE UNTIL card switch = ON
    PERFORM 025-DUP-OLD-MASTER UNTIL old master
      switch = ON
    PERFORM 030-END-ROUTINE
    STOP RUN


010-OPENER
    Open files
    Write heading line
    Read a card record at end move ON to card switch
    Read old master tape file at end move ON to old master
    switch


015-UPDATE
    IF social security number master less than social secu-
      rity number card
        Move old master fields to new master tape record
        Write new master tape record
        Move old master fields to print area
        Write a report line on the printer
        Read old master tape file at end move ON to old mas-
        ter switch
    ELSE
        Move card fields to new master tape record
        Write new master tape record
        Move card fields to print area
        Write a report line on the printer
        Read a card record at end move ON to card switch
    ENDIF


025-DUP-OLD-MASTER
    Move old master fields to new master tape record
    Write new master tape record
    Move old master fields to print area
    Write a report line on the printer
    Read old master tape file at end move ON to old master
      switch


030-END-ROUTINE
    Close files
```

FIGURE 9-10

File Merging Program

```
PROCEDURE DIVISION.
CONTROL-ROUTINE.
    PERFORM 010-OPENER.
    PERFORM 015-UPDATE
        UNTIL CARD-SWITCH = 'ON'.
    PERFORM 025-DUP-OLD-MASTER
        UNTIL OLD-MSTR-SWITCH = 'ON'.
    PERFORM 030-END-ROUTINE.
    STOP RUN.
010-OPENER.
    OPEN INPUT CARD-FILE OLD-MASTER
        OUTPUT NEW-MASTER PRINT-FILE.
    WRITE PRINT-LINE FROM HEAD1
        AFTER ADVANCING 2 LINES.
    READ CARD-FILE
        AT END MOVE 'ON' TO CARD-SWITCH.
    READ OLD-MASTER
        AT END MOVE 'ON' TO OLD-MSTR-SWITCH.
015-UPDATE.
    IF SS-NBR OF EMPLOYEE-DATA-OM IS LESS THAN
        SS-NBR OF CARD-IN
        MOVE CORRESPONDING EMPLOYEE-DATA-OM
            TO EMPLOYEE-DATA-NM
        WRITE EMPLOYEE-DATA-NM
        MOVE CORRESPONDING EMPLOYEE-DATA-OM
            TO PRINT-RECORD
        WRITE PRINT-LINE FROM PRINT-RECORD
            AFTER ADVANCING 2 LINES
        READ OLD-MASTER
            AT END MOVE 'ON' TO OLD-MSTR-SWITCH
    ELSE
        MOVE CORRESPONDING CARD-IN
            TO EMPLOYEE-DATA-NM
        WRITE EMPLOYEE-DATA-NM
        MOVE CORRESPONDING CARD-IN
            TO PRINT-RECORD
        WRITE PRINT-LINE FROM PRINT-RECORD
            AFTER ADVANCING 2 LINES
        READ CARD-FILE
            AT END MOVE 'ON' TO CARD-SWITCH.
025-DUP-OLD-MASTER.
        MOVE CORRESPONDING EMPLOYEE-DATA-OM
            TO EMPLOYEE-DATA-NM.
        WRITE EMPLOYEE-DATA-NM.
        MOVE CORRESPONDING EMPLOYEE-DATA-OM
            TO PRINT-RECORD.
        WRITE PRINT-LINE FROM PRINT-RECORD
            AFTER ADVANCING 2 LINES.
        READ OLD-MASTER
            AT END MOVE 'ON' TO OLD-MSTR-SWITCH.
030-END-ROUTINE.
    CLOSE CARD-FILE OLD-MASTER
        NEW-MASTER PRINT-FILE.
```

FIGURE 9-11

Merged File

REVISED FILE

123 45 6789	JONES, JOHN	555-5555
248 39 9618	ADDISON, CHARLES	551-8890
314 80 3800	LEE, SALLY	566-7777
438 31 6914	SMITH, SUE	556-0140
500 30 5432	ROBERTS, SAM	556-9188
777 68 5948	GONZALES, ED	555-3817
883 11 1529	MASON, NANCY	556-6346
900 39 6542	JOHNSON, ROBERT	566-4444

Common errors

Perhaps the single most common error associated with file updating is that of the programmer not considering all the logic alternatives that arise between two or more files. The chapter presented a few conditions, but there is no way that a text can cover all the combinations involving multiple files. Experience with students has shown that one common error involves the last record of a file. Frequently students will read the last record but not process it; that is, the record does not get written to either the Master File or to the printer. A similar fault occurs when the last record is recorded or printed twice rather than once.

Other variations on this theme involve the skipping (reading a record but not processing it) of a record immediately after a particular combination of steps. And, it can occur with both the Detail File and the Master File. Another source of error involves duplicate or multiple records in either or both the Detail File and Master File. The solution to all these error conditions is thorough program design that takes into account all the possible variations of logic. The design phase can be helped immensely by drawing the simple diagrams shown in this chapter. The trick is not to make the examples too long or cumbersome—just long enough to cover the situation so that you can see the logic that will be required.

Problem-Solving Techniques

Those of you who have been giving some serious thought to the previous examples have probably come up with some "flaws," or conditions under which the programs will not work properly. You would be quite right, of course, because the programs illustrated only a simplified approach to file updating. Let's take a look at some of these additional problem areas.

Perhaps the single most critical point is that both files are supposed to be in ascending order. In our sample program we made this assumption, and in a job situation you may be assured by someone that the file is in the proper order and that sequence checking is not necessary. Even so, it would be wise for you to include the statements to check the sequence of the records in *both* files (or however many files you are using) before writing the New Master File.

Notice what can happen if a file is not in the proper sequence during the merge operation we had in the last section.

Detail File: ③ ② ⑦

Master File: ① ④ ⑤ ⑥ ⑧

The comparison between records ① and ③ proceeds correctly. Record ① is written to the New Master and another Old Master record is read. Now the comparison is between ④ of the Old Master and ③ of the Detail File, and since ④ is not less than ③, record ③ is written (correctly) to the New Master and another record is read from the Detail File. So far, the New Master looks as follows:

①   ③

The next comparison is between ④ and ②, and, since the Old Master is again not less than ②, record ② is written to the New Master File. The end result of not checking the sequence is a New Master File that looks as follows:

① ③ ② ④ ⑤ ⑥ ⑦ ⑧

Another problem that arises concerns an unmentioned assumption made in the first two examples that involved the matching of Social Security Numbers. In both those examples we assumed that there *would be* a match of the records from the Detail File with records on the Old Master File. One possibility is that if our Detail File were not in sequence, we could by-pass the matching record on the Master

File so that a match could never be accomplished. Another variation on this problem results when both files *are* in the correct order but the Social Security Number of a Detail record is incorrect or mispunched. A well-written program would take these and other possibilities into account.

In a way, the third example (merging) is almost the reverse of the first and second examples. In those cases you *wanted* matching numbers; in the third example you do *not* want a match of Social Security Numbers since this would indicate an error condition. To confuse things a bit further, it is also possible to have a situation where duplicate numbers are permissible and *both* must be written to the new file. In that case a decision will have to be made as to which duplicate entry has precedence.

Some problems, particularly those using multiple detail files, require both matching and merging. For example, a series of Daily Transaction files are likely to require that data records be matched and then merged into a combined Weekly Transaction file. Appropriately, this is known as a match-merge operation.

Your program should take into account the variations outlined above and provide for the output of error messages where needed.

Finally, you must be aware that many different approaches to program logic (other than those shown in the sample programs) may be used. File manipulation is not limited to any set number of incoming or outgoing files. The only practical limit is the complexity of the problem and the system hardware itself. The easiest way to take care of all these complex situations is to do what we did in the chapter—use a simple diagram to show the file conditions you will encounter. If the conditions seem too complex, diagram each condition separately and then combine them.

Self-Study: Questions and Answers

1. The chapter examples showed how a single Detail File was processed against a Master File to produce a new or updated master. Can multiple Detail files be used?

   Answer
   Yes, you certainly can use multiple Detail files in an updating situation. For example, you might have four Weekly Detail files and they must be merged into a single Monthly Detail File before the main processing program can be run. In effect, you are creating a consolidated Detail File rather than a Master File, but the logic process is still the same.

2. Just how important is it to draw those Master-Detail File diagrams you showed throughout the text?

   Answer
   Extremely important. As a matter of fact, it is difficult to over-emphasize their importance. They are an adjunct, or helpmate, to flowcharting and top-down design techniques. Unless you feel entirely comfortable with all the possible combinations that could arise, you should prepare simple diagrams such as those shown. Really, they take very little time and make program planning much easier.

3. Throughout the chapter you make a great distinction between Master and Detail files. Is there really that much difference?

   Answer
   Yes there is, and it is important you understand the difference between the two. A note of caution here: Don't treat Master files lightly. Files of this type contain exactly what the term indicates— master data. As opposed to Detail files, Master files are likely to be used by many programs. Detail files, on the other hand, may only be used once. Master files are so important that a common practice is to have a duplicate stored nearby (but not in the same place) in case the original gets destroyed.

Exercises

1. Define or explain each of the following:
   a. Detail File
   b. Transaction File
   c. Master File
   d. Old Master File
   e. New Master File

2. Draw Master-Detail File diagrams to represent the following *matching* situations in which there are no duplicate key fields.
   a. A file matching situation in which one Detail record is out of sequence. Assume there is one Detail File and one Master File.
   b. A file matching situation in which there are two Detail files and one Master File. All records are in sequential order.
   c. A file matching situation in which one record from the Master File and one record from the Detail File are out of sequence.
   d. Revise 2b above so that records from one of the Detail files is out of order.

3. Let's assume that you have decided on the matching logic you wish to use in a program. Explain what will happen if the *first* record in the Detail File is the one that is out of sequence. Then, explain what will happen if the *last* record in the Detail File is out of sequence.

4. Draw Master-Detail File diagrams to represent the following *merging* situations. Assume that there cannot be any matching key values.
   a. A file *merging* situation in which both the Master File and single Detail File are in the correct order.
   b. A file *merging* situation in which the Master File is correct but the Detail File is out of sequence.
   c. A file *merging* situation involving two Detail files and a single Master File. All files are in sequential order.

5. A file *match-merging* situation involves two Detail files that will be merged into a single combined Detail File. Both files are in sequential order and duplicate Detail keys are permitted. Draw the diagram.

6. Modify the PROCEDURE DIVISION logic in the first sample program in the text to include sequence checking of the Detail File. If an error is found, a message is to be printed on the system console device.

7. Modify Exercise 6 to provide sequence checking of both the Master and Detail files.

8. Modify the PROCEDURE DIVISION logic in the second sample program to include sequence checking of both files and the output of error messages when needed.

9. The data for this problem will be a master payroll tape (Data File A) with the file name PAY-DATA. Tape labels are standard and each block contains five records; each record contains 55 characters, as shown below.

Field	Length	Example
Social security number	9	Numeric, DISPLAY
Employee name	20	Alphabetic
Filler	1	———
Rate of pay	4	Numeric, dollar and cents, packed format
Number of dependents	2	Numeric, DISPLAY
Insurance deduction	4	Numeric, packed format
Credit Union deduction	5	Numeric, packed format
Other deductions	5	Numeric, packed format
Filler	5	———

In order to calculate payroll information, you will need to know the actual number of hours each employee has worked this week. This information is to be punched into cards having the following format:

Field	Length	Example
Employee SS Number	9	431265972
Hours worked	2	41

Data

05012539540
06044391638
19045630140
23096577742
24686461508
30416529840
35021410141
55543861940

Note: The tape records and card records are *not* in the same order. Both files are in ascending order by Social Security Number, but not all employees work each week. Therefore, before processing any data, it will be necessary to make sure that the card record and the tape record match. Write a program to do the following:

a. Using the data from both files, calculate Gross Pay, Total Deductions, and Net Pay for each employee.

b. The deductions for Group Insurance, United Crusade, and the Credit Union are given in the Master Payroll record. The deduction amount for Income Tax, however, will have to be calculated. Our company uses the following rule:

1. If the employee has three or fewer dependents, a flat 20% of the Gross Pay figure is deducted.

2. If the employee has more than three dependents, 18% is used as the deduction rate.

c. All employees working in excess of 40 hours per week are paid on a time-and-a-half basis.

d. Output fields are to be appropriately spaced on a print line and *edited* according to the following format:

Name	SS Nbr	Gross Pay	Inc Tax	Insurance	Credit Union	Other	Total Ded	Net Pay
		Total					Total	Total

Note: The deductions for each employee are totaled and made part of the output line. In addition, the Grand Totals of the Gross Pay, Total Deductions, and Net Pay amounts are to be printed at the end of the program to provide accounting controls.

e. There is a possibility that there is no match for an *input card* record. This will be detected by your program logic. Be sure you plan for this and print an appropriate error message whenever this occurs.

f. When finished, print out PROGRAMMED BY and your name.

g. *Note:* Output data will not exceed one page.

Chapter 10

Control Breaks

Most of the programs you have seen so far have involved only final or grand totals that were printed after the individual records were processed. Some types of reports, however, require that subtotals be printed in the body of the report, and this action is triggered by what is known as a control break. For example, suppose you have been asked to prepare a sales report using data from a card file that has the following format:

Sales Department	Card columns	6 and 7	PIC 99
Sales Amount	Card columns	10 – 14	PIC 999V99

The actual card data and control breaks based on the department number are shown in Figure 10-1. Note that a control break can occur even if the group contains only a single record (as in the case of departments 03 and 09). When a break is detected we will print what is known as a *minor total*, which is the total of the sales in that particular department. Of crucial importance to all the examples in this chapter is the necessity either that the data records be sorted in a predetermined sequence or that all the same department numbers are grouped together. The output that will be generated is shown in Figure 10-2.

FIGURE 10-1

Data Cards Showing Minor Control Breaks

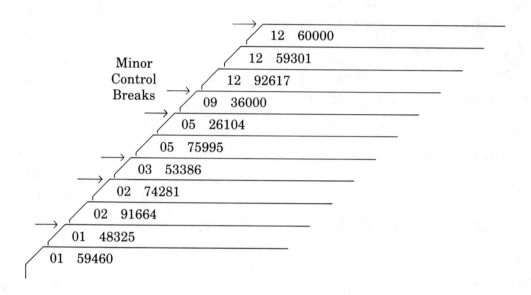

FIGURE 10-2

Output Showing Control Breaks and a Final Total

DEPARTMENT	SALES AMOUNT
01	$594.60
01	$483.25
MINOR TOTAL	$1077.85
02	$916.64
02	$742.81
MINOR TOTAL	$1659.45
03	$533.86
MINOR TOTAL	$533.86
05	$759.95
05	$261.04
MINOR TOTAL	$1020.99
09	$360.00
MINOR TOTAL	$360.00
12	$926.17
12	$593.01
12	$600.00
MINOR TOTAL	$2119.18
FINAL TOTAL	$6771.33

Control logic—Minor totals

The strategy to be used in control break programs is one of comparing the department number of the *previous* record against the department number of the *current* card record. To do this means that we will have to set up a field (OLD-DEPT-NBR) in working storage specifically for this purpose. As usual, we will use a LAST-CARD-INDICATOR field (often called a flag or switch) plus fields in which to accumulate the minor and final totals.

```
WORKING-STORAGE SECTION.
01  MISC-FIELDS.
      03   LAST-CARD-INDICATOR        PIC X(03) VALUE 'OFF'.
      03   OLD-DEPT-NBR               PIC 9(02).
      03   MINOR-TOTAL                PIC 9(05)V99 VALUE ZERO.
      03   GRAND-TOTAL                PIC 9(06)V99 VALUE ZERO.
```

As indicated earlier, our strategy is straightforward: Simply compare the current and previous department number values to see whether a minor break routine that will print the department subtotal should be executed. There is one "catch" in the plan and that concerns the first card: Against what are we to compare it? The incoming card record will place the department number in the field called DEPARTMENT; but if we try to compare it against OLD-DEPT-NBR, our program will come to an abnormal end (abend) because the OLD-DEPT-NBR field contains garbage. Even if we had said VALUE ZERO for this field, we would not be improving the situation because the comparison would be 00 against 01 and that *would* trigger a minor break process. The solution lies in the A100-OPENER paragraph. Here we execute our regular priming READ and move the department number from the first card to the OLD-DEPT-NBR field in WORKING-STORAGE. Our comparison in the main processing module A200-MAIN-PROCESSING for this first card will always result in an equal condition, but this is all right at this point since we do not want to trigger the minor break routine. From then on, however, we *do* want to trigger the break routine whenever an unequal department comparison is detected. Pseudocode specifications follow, and the flowchart for the A100-OPENER part of the program is shown in Figure 10-3.

Pseudocode Specifications: MINOR BREAK

```
CONTROL-MODULE
    PERFORM A100-OPENER
    PERFORM A200-MAIN-PROCESSING UNTIL end of file
       indicator = ON
    PERFORM B100-MINOR-BREAK-ROUTINE
    PERFORM A300-CLOSER
    STOP RUN


A100-OPENER
    Open the files
    Write a heading line
    Read a card record at end move ON to end of file indicator
    Move card department number to storage
```

```
A200-MAIN-PROCESSING
     IF card department number is not = storage department
       number
         PERFORM B100-MINOR-BREAK-ROUTINE
     ENDIF
     Move card department number to storage
     Add to minor total
     Move card fields to print area
     Write a report line on the printer
     Read a card record at end move ON to end of file indicator

B100-MINOR-BREAK-ROUTINE
     Move minor total to print area
     Add minor total to grand total
     Clear minor total area
     Write a minor total line on the printer

A300-CLOSER
     Move grand total to print area
     Write a grand total line on the printer
     Close the files
```

FIGURE 10-3

Program Flowchart Opening Operations

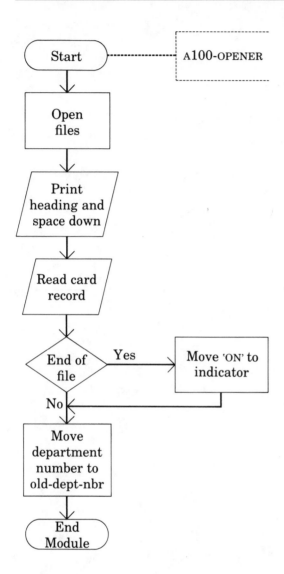

The logic in the main processing module follows the normal process-write-read pattern with one exception. The MOVE DEPARTMENT TO OLD-DEPT-NBR statement in the A100-OPENER paragraph took care of the department number comparison problem for the first card. However, every time a regular record is processed, the current department number must be moved to WORKING-STORAGE in preparation for the comparison that will take place when the *next* record is processed. This arrangement results in the department number from the first card being moved to OLD-DEPT-NBR *twice,* but it is a small price to pay for setting up the logic for the rest of the comparisons (Figure 10-4).

FIGURE 10-4

Program Flowchart Main Processing

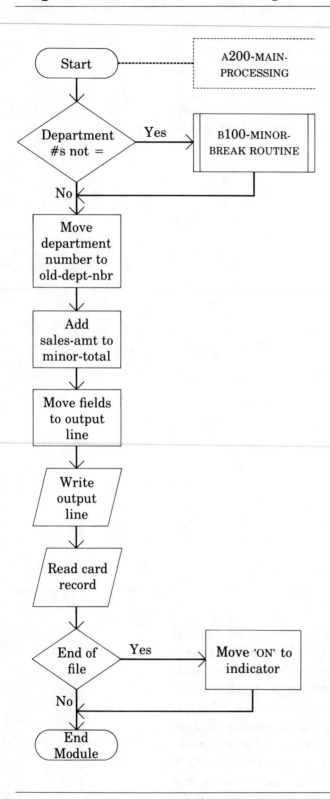

The minor break routine, triggered by the unequal department number comparison, will move the minor total to the print line. Then, since we wish to accumulate a final total, the MINOR-TOTAL value will be added to the GRAND-TOTAL field. This act of continuing totals on to a higher level total is known as "rolling a total." Immediately after rolling the total we will clear the MINOR-TOTAL field in preparation for summing the values from the group of entries in the next department. The final point to notice is that after the B100-MINOR-BREAK-ROUTINE is PERFORMED, control returns to the MOVE statement in the A200-MAIN-PROCESSING module. This point is critical because if we do not return there, the first record of each new group would not get processed (Figure 10-5). Figure 10-6 shows the complete program.

FIGURE 10-5

Program Flowchart Minor Break Routine

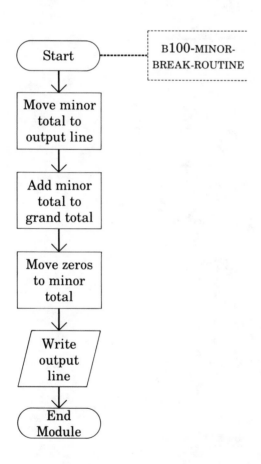

FIGURE 10-6

Minor Level Control Break

```
        IDENTIFICATION DIVISION.
        PROGRAM-ID. BREAK1.
        ********************************************
        *                                          *
        *   THIS PROGRAM PROVIDES FOR A DETAIL     *
        *   PRINTED REPORT WITH A MINOR TOTAL      *
        *   WHENEVER A CHANGE IN DEPARTMENT        *
        *   NUMBER IS ENCOUNTERED.  A FINAL        *
        *   OR GRAND TOTAL IS ALSO PRINTED.        *
        *                                          *
        ********************************************
        ENVIRONMENT DIVISION.
        CONFIGURATION SECTION.
        SOURCE-COMPUTER. IBM-360-F30.
        OBJECT-COMPUTER. IBM-360-F30.
        SPECIAL-NAMES.
            C01 IS TOP-OF-PAGE.
        INPUT-OUTPUT SECTION.
        FILE-CONTROL.
            SELECT CARD-FILE
                ASSIGN TO SYS007-UR-2540R-S.
            SELECT PRINT-FILE
                ASSIGN TO SYS009-UR-1403-S.
```

```
DATA DIVISION.
FILE SECTION.
FD   CARD-FILE
     LABEL RECORDS ARE OMITTED
     DATA RECORD IS CARD-REC.
01   CARD-REC                      PIC X(80).
FD   PRINT-FILE
     LABEL RECORDS ARE OMITTED
     DATA RECORD IS PRINT-LINE.
01   PRINT-LINE                    PIC X(121).
WORKING-STORAGE SECTION.
01   MISC-FIELDS.
     03   LAST-CARD-INDICATOR      PIC X(03) VALUE 'OFF'.
     03   OLD-DEPT-NBR             PIC 9(02).
     03   MINOR-TOTAL              PIC 9(05)V99 VALUE ZERO.
     03   GRAND-TOTAL              PIC 9(06)V99 VALUE ZERO.
01   CARD-REC-WS.
     03   FILLER                   PIC X(05).
     03   DEPARTMENT               PIC 9(02).
     03   FILLER                   PIC X(02).
     03   SALES-AMT                PIC 999V99.
     03   FILLER                   PIC X(66).
01   HEAD-LINE.
     03   FILLER                   PIC X.
     03   FILLER                   PIC X(31) VALUE SPACES.
     03   FILLER                   PIC X(10) VALUE 'DEPARTMENT'.
     03   FILLER                   PIC X(10) VALUE SPACES.
     03   FILLER                   PIC X(12) VALUE 'SALES AMOUNT'.
     03   FILLER                   PIC X(57) VALUE SPACES.
01   REPORT-LINE.
     03   FILLER                   PIC X.
     03   FILLER                   PIC X(35) VALUE SPACES.
     03   DEPARTMENT-PR            PIC 9(02).
     03   FILLER                   PIC X(17) VALUE SPACES.
     03   SALES-AMT-PR             PIC $$$$.99.
     03   FILLER                   PIC X(59) VALUE SPACES.
01   MINOR-TOTAL-LINE.
     03   FILLER                   PIC X.
     03   FILLER                   PIC X(10) VALUE SPACES.
     03   FILLER                   PIC X(11) VALUE 'MINOR TOTAL'.
     03   FILLER                   PIC X(31) VALUE SPACES.
     03   MINOR-TOTAL-PR           PIC $(6).99.
     03   FILLER                   PIC X(59) VALUE SPACES.
01   GRAND-TOTAL-LINE.
     03   FILLER                   PIC X.
     03   FILLER                   PIC X(10) VALUE SPACES.
     03   FILLER                   PIC X(11) VALUE 'FINAL TOTAL'.
     03   FILLER                   PIC X(30) VALUE SPACES.
     03   GRAND-TOTAL-PR           PIC $(7).99.
     03   FILLER                   PIC X(59) VALUE SPACES.
```

```
        PROCEDURE DIVISION.
        CONTROL-MODULE.
            PERFORM A100-OPENER.
            PERFORM A200-MAIN-PROCESSING
                UNTIL LAST-CARD-INDICATOR IS EQUAL TO ' ON'.
            PERFORM B100-MINOR-BREAK-ROUTINE.
            PERFORM A300-CLOSER.
            STOP RUN.
        A100-OPENER.
            OPEN INPUT CARD-FILE OUTPUT PRINT-FILE.
            WRITE PRINT-LINE FROM HEAD-LINE
                AFTER ADVANCING TOP-OF-PAGE.
            MOVE SPACES TO PRINT-LINE.
            WRITE PRINT-LINE AFTER ADVANCING 2 LINES.
            READ CARD-FILE INTO CARD-REC-WS
                AT END MOVE ' ON' TO LAST-CARD-INDICATOR.
            MOVE DEPARTMENT TO OLD-DEPT-NBR.
        A200-MAIN-PROCESSING.
            IF DEPARTMENT IS NOT EQUAL TO OLD-DEPT-NBR
                PERFORM B100-MINOR-BREAK-ROUTINE.
            MOVE DEPARTMENT TO OLD-DEPT-NBR.
            ADD SALES-AMT TO MINOR-TOTAL.
            MOVE DEPARTMENT TO DEPARTMENT-PR.
            MOVE SALES-AMT TO SALES-AMT-PR.
            WRITE PRINT-LINE FROM REPORT-LINE
                AFTER ADVANCING 1 LINES.
            READ CARD-FILE INTO CARD-REC-WS
                AT END MOVE ' ON' TO LAST-CARD-INDICATOR.
        B100-MINOR-BREAK-ROUTINE.
            MOVE MINOR-TOTAL TO MINOR-TOTAL-PR.
            ADD MINOR-TOTAL TO GRAND-TOTAL.
            MOVE ZEROS TO MINOR-TOTAL.
            WRITE PRINT-LINE FROM MINOR-TOTAL-LINE
                AFTER ADVANCING 2 LINES.
            MOVE SPACES TO PRINT-LINE.
            WRITE PRINT-LINE AFTER ADVANCING 2 LINES.
        A300-CLOSER.
            MOVE GRAND-TOTAL TO GRAND-TOTAL-PR.
            WRITE PRINT-LINE FROM GRAND-TOTAL-LINE
                AFTER ADVANCING 3 LINES.
            CLOSE CARD-FILE PRINT-FILE.
```

Control logic—Intermediate totals

In the previous program we used the change in department numbers
to activate the printing of minor totals. A report may have several
levels of totals, and our next example illustrates how you can deal
with both a minor and an intermediate level break. We will start by
revising the incoming card data to include a sales territory number

in card columns 1 through 3. As before, the success or failure of the program rests on the fact that the data deck is sorted into groups by department number *within* the territory number. Our strategy will be much the same as before except that now a change in territory number will trigger the printing of *both* a minor and an intermediate total. Whenever a minor total is detected, the department total will be printed and rolled into an intermediate total field. Whenever an intermediate break is detected, a minor total will be printed and followed by an intermediate total. The data and output are shown in Figures 10-7 and 10-8. Note that a single asterisk is printed next to the minor total value and two asterisks next to each intermediate total. A pattern of this type is commonly used in business so that various levels of totals can be recognized quickly.

FIGURE 10-7

Data Cards Showing Intermediate Control Breaks

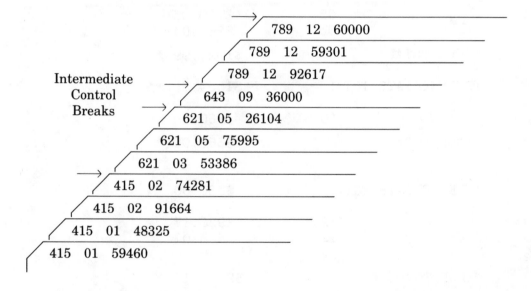

FIGURE 10-8

Intermediate Totals

TERRITORY	DEPARTMENT	SALES AMOUNT	
415	01	$594.60	
415	01	$483.25	
MINOR TOTAL		$1077.85	*
415	02	$916.64	
415	02	$742.81	
MINOR TOTAL		$1659.45	*
INTERMEDIATE TOTAL		$2737.30	**
621	03	$533.86	
MINOR TOTAL		$533.86	*
621	05	$759.95	
621	05	$261.04	
MINOR TOTAL		$1020.99	*
INTERMEDIATE TOTAL		$1554.85	**
643	09	$360.00	
MINOR TOTAL		$360.00	*
INTERMEDIATE TOTAL		$360.00	**
789	12	$926.17	
789	12	$593.01	
789	12	$600.00	
MINOR TOTAL		$2119.18	*
INTERMEDIATE TOTAL		$2119.18	**
FINAL TOTAL		$6771.33	

In modifying the previous program to take care of the possibility of both a minor and an intermediate break, we will have to expand our logic slightly. One important point is that we set up an OLD-TER-RITORY-NBR field in WORKING-STORAGE and move in the territory number from the first card (A100-OPENER). A second point is that after the last card has been processed and control returned to the CONTROL-MODULE, we will have to perform both the minor and intermediate break routines. Our testing statement in the A200-MAIN-PROCESSING routine will have to be expanded to take care of testing for changes in either or both the territory and department numbers. One easy way to do this is by means of a nested IF statement.

```
IF TERRITORY IS NOT EQUAL TO OLD-TERRITORY-NBR
    PERFORM B200-INTERMEDIATE-BREAK
ELSE
    IF DEPARTMENT IS NOT EQUAL TO OLD-DEPT-NBR
        PERFORM B100-MINOR-BREAK-ROUTINE.
    _____ .
    _____ .
    _____ .
```

With this arrangement, the program first tests for the intermediate level change, and if there is such a change, the second IF statement is ignored (false condition). The B200-INTERMEDIATE-BREAK paragraph will PERFORM the minor break routine since, by definition in the problem, every intermediate break automatically represents a minor break as well. If an intermediate break is not encountered, the second or nested IF is executed to see if a minor break is called for. If neither break is indicated, the Department and Territory numbers are moved to storage and regular detail line processing takes place. Figure 10-9 illustrates this logic.

The B100-MINOR-BREAK-ROUTINE will contain only one slight change: The MINOR-TOTAL value will be added to or rolled into the INTERME-DIATE-TOTAL field rather than into a final total as before. The B200-INTERMEDIATE-BREAK paragraph starts by PERFORMing the minor total routine; it then duplicates the actions of the minor break routine at a higher or intermediate level. Figure 10-10 illustrates this logic and Figure 10-11 shows the entire program.

FIGURE 10-9

Program Flowchart Main Processing

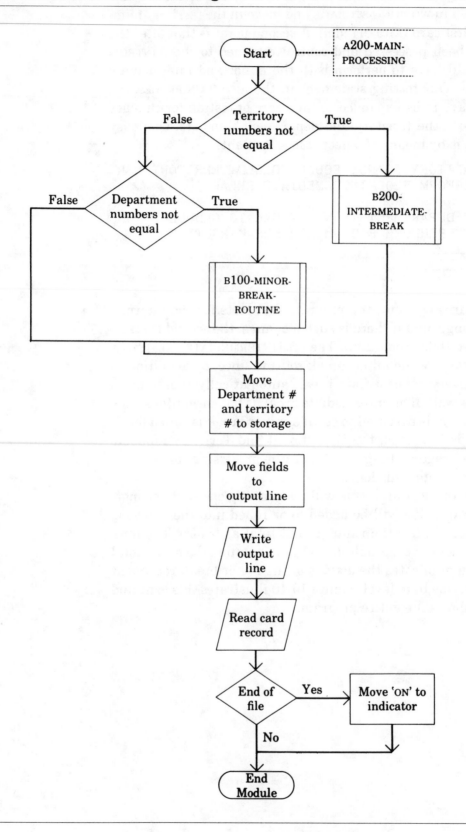

FIGURE 10-10

Program Flowchart Intermediate Break Logic

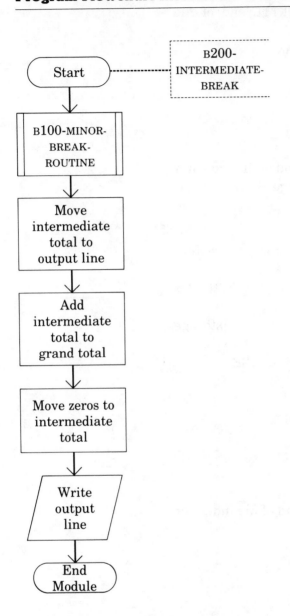

Pseudocode Specifications: INTERMEDIATE BREAK
```
CONTROL-MODULE
     PERFORM A100-OPENER
     PERFORM A200-MAIN-PROCESSING UNTIL end of file
          indicator = ON
     PERFORM B200-INTERMEDIATE-BREAK
     PERFORM A300-CLOSER
     STOP RUN

A100-OPENER
     Open the files
     Write a heading line
     Read a card record at end move ON to end of file indicator
     Move card department number to storage
     Move card territory number to storage

A200-MAIN-PROCESSING
     IF  card territory number is not = storage territory
         number
         PERFORM B200-INTERMEDIATE-BREAK-ROUTINE.
     ELSE
         IF card department number is not = storage
            department number
         PERFORM B100-MINOR-BREAK-ROUTINE
         ENDIF
     ENDIF
     Move card department number to storage
     Move card territory number to storage
     Add to minor total
     Move card fields to print area
     Write a report line on the printer
     Read a card record at end move ON to end of file indicator

B100-MINOR-BREAK-ROUTINE
     Move minor total to print area
     Add minor total to intermediate total
     Clear minor total area
     Write a minor total line on the printer

B200-INTERMEDIATE-BREAK
     PERFORM B100-MINOR-BREAK-ROUTINE
     Move intermediate total to print area
     Add intermediate total to grand total
     Clear intermediate total area
     Write an intermediate total on the printer

A300-CLOSER
     Move grand total to print area
     Write a grand total line
     Close the files
```

FIGURE 10-11

Intermediate Control Break

```
       IDENTIFICATION DIVISION.
       PROGRAM-ID. BREAK2.
      *******************************************
      *                                         *
      *  THIS PROGRAM DETAIL PRINTS A SALES     *
      *  REPORT WITH MINOR, INTERMEDIATE,       *
      *  AND FINAL TOTALS.                      *
      *                                         *
      *******************************************
       ENVIRONMENT DIVISION.
       CONFIGURATION SECTION.
       SOURCE-COMPUTER. IBM-360-F30.
       OBJECT-COMPUTER. IBM-360-F30.
       SPECIAL-NAMES.
           C01 IS TOP-OF-PAGE.
       INPUT-OUTPUT SECTION.
       FILE-CONTROL.
           SELECT CARD-FILE
               ASSIGN TO SYS007-UR-2540R-S.
           SELECT PRINT-FILE
               ASSIGN TO SYS009-UR-1403-S.
       DATA DIVISION.
       FILE SECTION.
       FD  CARD-FILE
           LABEL RECORDS ARE OMITTED
           DATA RECORD IS CARD-REC.
       01  CARD-REC                    PIC X(80).
       FD  PRINT-FILE
           LABEL RECORDS ARE OMITTED
           DATA RECORD IS PRINT-LINE.
       01  PRINT-LINE                  PIC X(121).
       WORKING-STORAGE SECTION.
       01  MISC-FIELDS.
           03  LAST-CARD-INDICATOR     PIC X(03) VALUE 'OFF'.
           03  OLD-DEPT-NBR            PIC 9(02).
           03  OLD-TERRITORY-NBR       PIC 9(03).
           03  MINOR-TOTAL             PIC 9(05)V99 VALUE ZERO.
           03  INTERMEDIATE-TOTAL      PIC 9(06)V99 VALUE ZERO.
           03  GRAND-TOTAL             PIC 9(06)V99 VALUE ZERO.
       01  CARD-REC-WS.
           03  TERRITORY               PIC 9(03).
           03  FILLER                  PIC X(02).
           03  DEPARTMENT              PIC 9(02).
           03  FILLER                  PIC X(02).
           03  SALES-AMT               PIC 999V99.
           03  FILLER                  PIC X(66).
```

```
01   HEAD-LINE.
     03   FILLER                    PIC X.
     03   FILLER                    PIC X(43) VALUE SPACES.
     03   FILLER                    PIC X(09) VALUE 'TERRITORY'.
     03   FILLER                    PIC X(10) VALUE SPACES.
     03   FILLER                    PIC X(10) VALUE 'DEPARTMENT'.
     03   FILLER                    PIC X(10) VALUE SPACES.
     03   FILLER                    PIC X(12) VALUE 'SALES AMOUNT'.
     03   FILLER                    PIC X(26) VALUE SPACES.
01   REPORT-LINE.
     03   FILLER                    PIC X.
     03   FILLER                    PIC X(46) VALUE SPACES.
     03   TERRITORY-PR              PIC 9(03).
     03   FILLER                    PIC X(17) VALUE SPACES.
     03   DEPARTMENT-PR             PIC 9(02).
     03   FILLER                    PIC X(16) VALUE SPACES.
     03   SALES-AMT-PR              PIC $$$$.99.
     03   FILLER                    PIC X(29) VALUE SPACES.
01   MINOR-TOTAL-LINE.
     03   FILLER                    PIC X.
     03   FILLER                    PIC X(54) VALUE SPACES.
     03   FILLER                    PIC X(11) VALUE 'MINOR TOTAL'.
     03   FILLER                    PIC X(17) VALUE SPACES.
     03   MINOR-TOTAL-PR            PIC $(6).99.
     03   FILLER                    PIC X VALUE SPACE.
     03   FILLER                    PIC X VALUE '*'.
     03   FILLER                    PIC X(27) VALUE SPACES.
01   INTERMEDIATE-TOTAL-LINE.
     03   FILLER                    PIC X.
     03   FILLER                    PIC X(54) VALUE SPACES.
     03   FILLER                    PIC X(18)
                         VALUE 'INTERMEDIATE TOTAL'.
     03   FILLER                    PIC X(9) VALUE SPACES.
     03   INT-TOTAL-PR              PIC $(07).99.
     03   FILLER                    PIC X VALUE SPACE.
     03   FILLER                    PIC X(02) VALUE '**'.
     03   FILLER                    PIC X(26) VALUE SPACES.
01   GRAND-TOTAL-LINE.
     03   FILLER                    PIC X.
     03   FILLER                    PIC X(54) VALUE SPACES.
     03   FILLER                    PIC X(11) VALUE 'FINAL TOTAL'.
     03   FILLER                    PIC X(16) VALUE SPACES.
     03   GRAND-TOTAL-PR            PIC $(7).99.
     03   FILLER                    PIC X(29) VALUE SPACES.
```

```
PROCEDURE DIVISION.
CONTROL-MODULE.
     PERFORM A100-OPENER.
     PERFORM A200-MAIN-PROCESSING
          UNTIL LAST-CARD-INDICATOR IS EQUAL TO ' ON'.
     PERFORM B200-INTERMEDIATE-BREAK.
     PERFORM A300-CLOSER.
     STOP RUN.
A100-OPENER.
     OPEN INPUT CARD-FILE OUTPUT PRINT-FILE.
     WRITE PRINT-LINE FROM HEAD-LINE
          AFTER ADVANCING TOP-OF-PAGE.
     MOVE SPACES TO PRINT-LINE.
     WRITE PRINT-LINE AFTER ADVANCING 2 LINES.
     READ CARD-FILE INTO CARD-REC-WS
          AT END MOVE ' ON' TO LAST-CARD-INDICATOR.
     MOVE DEPARTMENT TO OLD-DEPT-NBR.
     MOVE TERRITORY TO OLD-TERRITORY-NBR.
A200-MAIN-PROCESSING.
     IF TERRITORY IS NOT EQUAL TO OLD-TERRITORY-NBR
          PERFORM B200-INTERMEDIATE-BREAK
     ELSE
          IF DEPARTMENT IS NOT EQUAL TO OLD-DEPT-NBR
               PERFORM B100-MINOR-BREAK-ROUTINE.
     MOVE DEPARTMENT TO OLD-DEPT-NBR.
     MOVE TERRITORY TO OLD-TERRITORY-NBR.
     ADD SALES-AMT TO MINOR-TOTAL.
     MOVE DEPARTMENT TO DEPARTMENT-PR.
     MOVE TERRITORY TO TERRITORY-PR.
     MOVE SALES-AMT TO SALES-AMT-PR.
     WRITE PRINT-LINE FROM REPORT-LINE
          AFTER ADVANCING 1 LINES.
     READ CARD-FILE INTO CARD-REC-WS
          AT END MOVE ' ON' TO LAST-CARD-INDICATOR.
B100-MINOR-BREAK-ROUTINE.
     MOVE MINOR-TOTAL TO MINOR-TOTAL-PR.
     ADD MINOR-TOTAL TO INTERMEDIATE-TOTAL.
     MOVE ZEROS TO MINOR-TOTAL.
     WRITE PRINT-LINE FROM MINOR-TOTAL-LINE
          AFTER ADVANCING 2 LINES.
     MOVE SPACES TO PRINT-LINE.
     WRITE PRINT-LINE AFTER ADVANCING 2 LINES.
B200-INTERMEDIATE-BREAK.
     PERFORM B100-MINOR-BREAK-ROUTINE.
     MOVE INTERMEDIATE-TOTAL TO INT-TOTAL-PR.
     ADD INTERMEDIATE-TOTAL TO GRAND-TOTAL.
     MOVE ZEROS TO INTERMEDIATE-TOTAL.
     WRITE PRINT-LINE FROM INTERMEDIATE-TOTAL-LINE
          AFTER ADVANCING 2 LINES.
     MOVE SPACES TO PRINT-LINE.
     WRITE PRINT-LINE AFTER ADVANCING 2 LINES.
A300-CLOSER.
     MOVE GRAND-TOTAL TO GRAND-TOTAL-PR.
     WRITE PRINT-LINE FROM GRAND-TOTAL-LINE
          AFTER ADVANCING 3 LINES.
     CLOSE CARD-FILE PRINT-FILE.
```

Summary printing

Both program examples used in this chapter have produced detail printed reports—that is, one line for each record plus whatever total lines were required. Reports of this kind are very common, but management may not wish to see all the line-by-line details. Since a manager's time is valuable, he or she may wish to see only a group or summary printed report. Instead of one line per record, we would produce a report with one line per group or, in our case, one line for each of the totals. Two immediate advantages of this procedure are that the report is faster to print and that it takes less paper. Then, if the manager notices some numbers that seem out of the ordinary, a detail printed report may be requested for a closer look at particular sales areas.

The main difference between this program and the previous one (Figure 10-11) is that we will omit the detail printing statements although the record-by-record totaling activities must still be included. Figure 10-12 illustrates the logic by means of a Warnier/Orr diagram and Figures 10-13a and 10-13b show the output and the complete program.

FIGURE 10-12

Warnier/Orr Diagram Group Printing

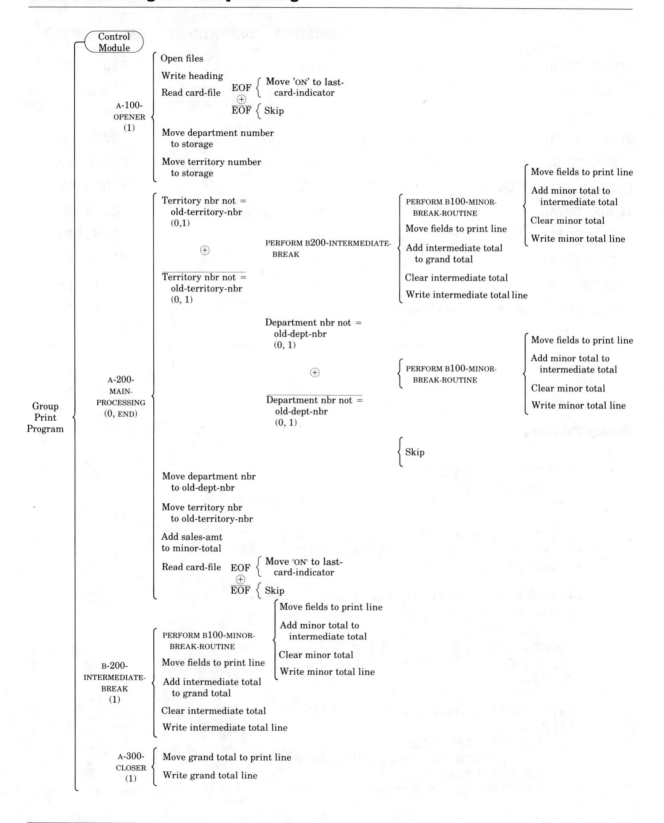

FIGURE 10-13a

Group Printed Output

	TERRITORY	DEPARTMENT	SALES AMOUNT
MINOR TOTAL	415	01	$1077.85
MINOR TOTAL	415	02	$1659.45
INTERMEDIATE TOTAL	415		$2737.30
MINOR TOTAL	621	03	$533.86
MINOR TOTAL	621	05	$1020.99
INTERMEDIATE TOTAL	621		$1554.85
MINOR TOTAL	643	09	$360.00
INTERMEDIATE TOTAL	643		$360.00
MINOR TOTAL	789	12	$2119.18
INTERMEDIATE TOTAL	789		$2119.18
FINAL TOTAL OF ALL TERRITORIES			$6771.33

FIGURE 10-13b

Group Printing

```
      IDENTIFICATION DIVISION.
          PROGRAM-ID. GRP-PR.
  ******************************************
  *                                        *
  *    THIS PROGRAM GROUP PRINTS A SALES    *
  *    REPORT WITH MINOR, INTERMEDIATE,     *
  *    AND FINAL TOTALS.                    *
  *                                        *
  ******************************************
      ENVIRONMENT DIVISION.
      CONFIGURATION SECTION.
      SOURCE-COMPUTER. IBM-360-F30.
      OBJECT-COMPUTER. IBM-360-F30.
      SPECIAL-NAMES.
          C01 IS TOP-OF-PAGE.
      INPUT-OUTPUT SECTION.
      FILE-CONTROL.
          SELECT CARD-FILE
              ASSIGN TO SYS007-UR-2540R-S.
          SELECT PRINT-FILE
              ASSIGN TO SYS009-UR-1403-S.
```

```
DATA DIVISION.
FILE SECTION.
FD   CARD-FILE
     LABEL RECORDS ARE OMITTED
     DATA RECORD IS CARD-REC.
01   CARD-REC                      PIC X(80).
FD   PRINT-FILE
     LABEL RECORDS ARE OMITTED
     DATA RECORD IS PRINT-LINE.
01   PRINT-LINE                    PIC X(121).
WORKING-STORAGE SECTION.
01   MISC-FIELDS.
     03   LAST-CARD-INDICATOR      PIC X(03) VALUE 'OFF'.
     03   OLD-DEPT-NBR             PIC 9(02).
     03   OLD-TERRITORY-NBR        PIC 9(03).
     03   MINOR-TOTAL              PIC 9(05)V99 VALUE ZERO.
     03   INTERMEDIATE-TOTAL       PIC 9(06)V99 VALUE ZERO.
     03   GRAND-TOTAL              PIC 9(06)V99 VALUE ZERO.
01   CARD-REC-WS.
     03   TERRITORY                PIC 9(03).
     03   FILLER                   PIC X(02).
     03   DEPARTMENT               PIC 9(02).
     03   FILLER                   PIC X(02).
     03   SALES-AMT                PIC 999V99.
     03   FILLER                   PIC X(64).
01   HEAD-LINE.
     03   FILLER                   PIC X.
     03   FILLER                   PIC X(43) VALUE SPACES.
     03   FILLER                   PIC X(09) VALUE 'TERRITORY'.
     03   FILLER                   PIC X(10) VALUE SPACES.
     03   FILLER                   PIC X(10) VALUE 'DEPARTMENT'.
     03   FILLER                   PIC X(10) VALUE SPACES.
     03   FILLER                   PIC X(12) VALUE 'SALES AMOUNT'.
     03   FILLER                   PIC X(26) VALUE SPACES.
01   MINOR-TOTAL-LINE.
     03   FILLER                   PIC X.
     03   FILLER                   PIC X(10) VALUE SPACES.
     03   FILLER                   PIC X(11) VALUE 'MINOR TOTAL'.
     03   FILLER                   PIC X(25) VALUE SPACES.
     03   TERRITORY-PR-M           PIC 9(03).
     03   FILLER                   PIC X(17) VALUE SPACES.
     03   DEPARTMENT-PR-M          PIC 9(02).
     03   FILLER                   PIC X(16) VALUE SPACES.
     03   MINOR-TOTAL-PR           PIC $(6).99.
     03   FILLER                   PIC X(27) VALUE SPACES.
01   INTERMEDIATE-TOTAL-LINE.
     03   FILLER                   PIC X.
     03   FILLER                   PIC X(10) VALUE SPACES.
     03   FILLER                   PIC X(18)
                        VALUE 'INTERMEDIATE TOTAL'.
```

```
            03   FILLER                    PIC X(18) VALUE SPACES.
            03   TERRITORY-PR-I            PIC 9(03).
            03   FILLER                    PIC X(34) VALUE SPACES.
            03   INT-TOTAL-PR              PIC $(07).99.
            03   FILLER                    PIC X(27) VALUE SPACES.
        01  GRAND-TOTAL-LINE.
            03   FILLER                    PIC X.
            03   FILLER                    PIC X(10) VALUE SPACES.
            03   FILLER                    PIC X(30) VALUE
                              'FINAL TOTAL OF ALL TERRITORIES'.
            03   FILLER                    PIC X(42) VALUE SPACES.
            03   GRAND-TOTAL-PR            PIC $(7).99.
            03   FILLER                    PIC X(27) VALUE SPACES.
    PROCEDURE DIVISION.
    CONTROL-MODULE.
        PERFORM A100-OPENER.
        PERFORM A200-MAIN-PROCESSING
            UNTIL LAST-CARD-INDICATOR IS EQUAL TO ' ON'.
        PERFORM B200-INTERMEDIATE-BREAK.
        PERFORM A300-CLOSER.
        STOP RUN.
    A100-OPENER.
        OPEN INPUT CARD-FILE OUTPUT PRINT-FILE.
        WRITE PRINT-LINE FROM HEAD-LINE
            AFTER ADVANCING TOP-OF-PAGE.
        MOVE SPACES TO PRINT-LINE.
        WRITE PRINT-LINE AFTER ADVANCING 2 LINES.
        READ CARD-FILE INTO CARD-REC-WS
            AT END MOVE ' ON' TO LAST-CARD-INDICATOR.
        MOVE DEPARTMENT TO OLD-DEPT-NBR.
        MOVE TERRITORY TO OLD-TERRITORY-NBR.
    A200-MAIN-PROCESSING.
        IF TERRITORY IS NOT EQUAL TO OLD-TERRITORY-NBR
            PERFORM B200-INTERMEDIATE-BREAK
        ELSE
            IF DEPARTMENT IS NOT EQUAL TO OLD-DEPT-NBR
                PERFORM B100-MINOR-BREAK-ROUTINE.
        MOVE DEPARTMENT TO OLD-DEPT-NBR.
        MOVE TERRITORY TO OLD-TERRITORY-NBR.
        ADD SALES-AMT TO MINOR-TOTAL.
        READ CARD-FILE INTO CARD-REC-WS
            AT END MOVE ' ON' TO LAST-CARD-INDICATOR.
```

```
B100-MINOR-BREAK-ROUTINE.
    MOVE OLD-DEPT-NBR TO DEPARTMENT-PR-M.
    MOVE OLD-TERRITORY-NBR TO TERRITORY-PR-M.
    MOVE MINOR-TOTAL TO MINOR-TOTAL-PR.
    ADD MINOR-TOTAL TO INTERMEDIATE-TOTAL.
    MOVE ZEROS TO MINOR-TOTAL.
    WRITE PRINT-LINE FROM MINOR-TOTAL-LINE
        AFTER ADVANCING 2 LINES.
    MOVE SPACES TO PRINT-LINE.
    WRITE PRINT-LINE AFTER ADVANCING 2 LINES.
B200-INTERMEDIATE-BREAK.
    PERFORM B100-MINOR-BREAK-ROUTINE.
    MOVE OLD-TERRITORY-NBR TO TERRITORY-PR-I.
    MOVE INTERMEDIATE-TOTAL TO INT-TOTAL-PR.
    ADD INTERMEDIATE-TOTAL TO GRAND-TOTAL.
    MOVE ZEROS TO INTERMEDIATE-TOTAL.
    WRITE PRINT-LINE FROM INTERMEDIATE-TOTAL-LINE
        AFTER ADVANCING 2 LINES.
    MOVE SPACES TO PRINT-LINE.
    WRITE PRINT-LINE AFTER ADVANCING 2 LINES.
A300-CLOSER.
    MOVE GRAND-TOTAL TO GRAND-TOTAL-PR.
    WRITE PRINT-LINE FROM GRAND-TOTAL-LINE
        AFTER ADVANCING 3 LINES.
    CLOSE CARD-FILE PRINT-FILE.
```

Programmed switches or indicators

By definition, a switch is any field that is used to convey control information within the program. In the text switches have been used extensively with the UNTIL version of the PERFORM statement to execute a block of code until a particular condition is met. For the sake of illustration the switches have been given various names— INDICATOR, EOF-INDICATOR, CARD-SWITCH, OLD-MSTR-SWITCH—that would help to identify these fields as switches. Since switches are used so frequently, a good habit to get into is that of naming and handling them in a standard, or preset, way. For example, you can always include the letters SW or the name SWITCH attached to the main characters as in OLD-MSTR-SWITCH or CARD-SW. For numerically defined switch fields, 0 normally indicates the OFF condition while 1 indicates ON. For those switches defined as X or A, YES (or Y) should indicate ON while NO (or N) should indicate OFF. It is also very likely that the shop where you work will have a standard way of handling switches.

Alphabetic or x defined switches have the advantage of providing for better documentation than would numeric switches. Note the following example:

```
77  TAPE-EOF-SW          PIC X(3) VALUE 'NO'.

    PERFORM 020-READ-MODULE
        UNTIL TAPE-EOF-SW IS EQUAL TO 'YES'.
```

The example shown above is better than using a numeric switch, but can be improved upon by using level 88s, which are condition name entries that define the values in a more meaningful way.

```
03  TAPE-EOF-SW   PIC X(3) VALUE 'NO'.
    88 OUT-OF-TAPE-RECORDS VALUE 'YES'.

    PERFORM 030-READ-MODULE
        UNTIL OUT-OF-TAPE-RECORDS.
```

Switches, however, are not limited to use with PERFORM. You can use them anytime you wish for whatever needs you have. One common use of a programmed switch is to set it to a particular value in one part of the program and then test that value in another part of the same program. In effect, a programmed switch (also known as a "flag") is a method of communicating or passing information from one part of the program to another. A simple example will illustrate this point. Recall that the first program in this chapter printed a minor total whenever a control break in the department number was detected. The key to *not* generating a control break on the first card was that in the A100-OPENER routine we read a card and moved the department number from the incoming card to OLD-DEPT-NBR. Then, when the department number from the first card record was tested in the A200-MAIN-PROCESSING paragraph, we knew that a minor break would not be generated. We can do the same thing, however, by means of a programmed switch. To make the change we will set up a switch in WORKING-STORAGE (appropriately called SWITCH since this is not a reserved word) and give it a beginning value of ON.

```
03  SWITCH        PIC X(03) VALUE 'ON'.
```

Then, we will remove the MOVE DEPARTMENT TO OLD-DEPAT-NBR statement from the A100-OPENER paragraph since it will no longer be needed. The value of the switch will then be tested in a nested IF statement when we come through the main processing routine.

```
IF  SWITCH IS NOT EQUAL TO 'ON'
    IF DEPARTMENT IS NOT EQUAL TO OLD-DEPT-NBR
    PERFORM B100-MINOR-BREAK-ROUTINE.
```

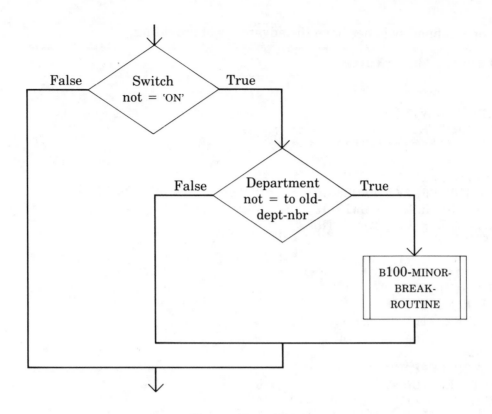

Since SWITCH was initially set to ON in WORKING-STORAGE, the test IF SWITCH IS NOT EQUAL TO 'ON' will be false and the department comparison will be ignored. So far so good; but if we leave SWITCH in the ON condition, the department number test will never be made and minor breaks will never be detected. To take care of this we will turn the switch off right after the IF statement by moving 'OFF' TO SWITCH.

Pseudocode for the revised A200-MAIN-PROCESSING module is shown below. The complete program and output is shown in Figures 10-14 and 10-15.

```
A200-MAIN-PROCESSING
    IF switch is not = ON
        IF card department number is not = storage depart-
        ment number
            PERFORM B100-MINOR-BREAK-ROUTINE
        ENDIF
    ENDIF
    Move OFF to switch
    Move card department number to storage
    Add to minor total
    Move card fields to print area
    Write a report line on the printer
    Read a card record at end move ON to end of file indicator
```

FIGURE 10-14

Programmed Switch Minor Totals

```
      IDENTIFICATION DIVISION.
      PROGRAM-ID. SWITCH1.
      ************************************
      *                                  *
      *   THIS PROGRAM PRINTS THE SAME   *
      *   OUTPUT AS THE BREAK1 PROGRAM   *
      *   BUT USES A PROGRAMMED SWITCH   *
      *   TO BY-PASS THE PROBLEM OF THE  *
      *   FIRST CARD.                    *
      *                                  *
      ************************************
      ENVIRONMENT DIVISION.
      CONFIGURATION SECTION.
      SOURCE-COMPUTER. IBM-360-F30.
      OBJECT-COMPUTER. IBM-360-F30.
      SPECIAL-NAMES.
          C01 IS TOP-OF-PAGE.
      INPUT-OUTPUT SECTION.
      FILE-CONTROL.
          SELECT CARD-FILE
              ASSIGN TO SYS007-UR-2540R-S.
          SELECT PRINT-FILE
              ASSIGN TO SYS009-UR-1403-S.
```

```
DATA DIVISION.
FILE SECTION.
FD   CARD-FILE
     LABEL RECORDS ARE OMITTED
     DATA RECORD IS CARD-REC.
01   CARD-REC                        PIC X(80).
FD   PRINT-FILE
     LABEL RECORDS ARE OMITTED
     DATA RECORD IS PRINT-LINE.
01   PRINT-LINE                      PIC X(121).
WORKING-STORAGE SECTION.
01   MISC-FIELDS.
     03   SWITCH                      PIC X(03) VALUE ' ON'.
     03   LAST-CARD-INDICATOR         PIC X(03) VALUE 'OFF'.
     03   OLD-DEPT-NBR                PIC 9(02).
     03   MINOR-TOTAL                 PIC 9(05)V99 VALUE ZERO.
     03   GRAND-TOTAL                 PIC 9(06)V99 VALUE ZERO.
01   CARD-REC-WS.
     03   FILLER                      PIC X(05).
     03   DEPARTMENT                  PIC 9(02).
     03   FILLER                      PIC X(02).
     03   SALES-AMT                   PIC 999V99.
     03   FILLER                      PIC X(66).
01   HEAD-LINE.
     03   FILLER                      PIC X.
     03   FILLER                      PIC X(31) VALUE SPACES.
     03   FILLER                      PIC X(10) VALUE 'DEPARTMENT'.
     03   FILLER                      PIC X(10) VALUE SPACES.
     03   FILLER                      PIC X(12) VALUE 'SALES AMOUNT'.
     03   FILLER                      PIC X(57) VALUE SPACES.
01   REPORT-LINE.
     03   FILLER                      PIC X.
     03   FILLER                      PIC X(35) VALUE SPACES.
     03   DEPARTMENT-PR               PIC 9(02).
     03   FILLER                      PIC X(17) VALUE SPACES.
     03   SALES-AMT-PR                PIC $$$$.99.
     03   FILLER                      PIC X(59) VALUE SPACES.
01   MINOR-TOTAL-LINE.
     03   FILLER                      PIC X.
     03   FILLER                      PIC X(31) VALUE SPACES.
     03   FILLER                      PIC X(11) VALUE 'MINOR TOTAL'.
     03   FILLER                      PIC X(10) VALUE SPACES.
     03   MINOR-TOTAL-PR              PIC $(6).99.
     03   FILLER                      PIC X(59) VALUE SPACES.
01   GRAND-TOTAL-LINE.
     03   FILLER                      PIC X.
     03   FILLER                      PIC X(31) VALUE SPACES.
     03   FILLER                      PIC X(11) VALUE 'FINAL TOTAL'.
     03   FILLER                      PIC X(9) VALUE SPACES.
     03   GRAND-TOTAL-PR              PIC $(7).99.
     03   FILLER                      PIC X(59) VALUE SPACES.
```

```
PROCEDURE DIVISION.
CONTROL-MODULE.
    PERFORM A100-OPENER.
    PERFORM A200-MAIN-PROCESSING
        UNTIL LAST-CARD-INDICATOR IS EQUAL TO ' ON'.
    PERFORM B100-MINOR-BREAK-ROUTINE.
    PERFORM A300-CLOSER.
    STOP RUN.
A100-OPENER.
    OPEN INPUT CARD-FILE OUTPUT PRINT-FILE.
    WRITE PRINT-LINE FROM HEAD-LINE
        AFTER ADVANCING TOP-OF-PAGE.
    MOVE SPACES TO PRINT-LINE.
    WRITE PRINT-LINE AFTER ADVANCING 2 LINES.
    READ CARD-FILE INTO CARD-REC-WS
        AT END MOVE ' ON' TO LAST-CARD-INDICATOR.
A200-MAIN-PROCESSING.
    IF SWITCH IS NOT EQUAL TO ' ON'
        IF DEPARTMENT IS NOT EQUAL TO OLD-DEPT-NBR
            PERFORM B100-MINOR-BREAK-ROUTINE.
    MOVE 'OFF' TO SWITCH.
    MOVE DEPARTMENT TO OLD-DEPT-NBR.
    ADD SALES-AMT TO MINOR-TOTAL.
    MOVE DEPARTMENT TO DEPARTMENT-PR.
    MOVE SALES-AMT TO SALES-AMT-PR.
    WRITE PRINT-LINE FROM REPORT-LINE
        AFTER ADVANCING 1 LINES.
    READ CARD-FILE INTO CARD-REC-WS
        AT END MOVE ' ON' TO LAST-CARD-INDICATOR.
B100-MINOR-BREAK-ROUTINE.
    MOVE MINOR-TOTAL TO MINOR-TOTAL-PR.
    ADD MINOR-TOTAL TO GRAND-TOTAL.
    MOVE ZEROS TO MINOR-TOTAL.
    WRITE PRINT-LINE FROM MINOR-TOTAL-LINE
        AFTER ADVANCING 2 LINES.
    MOVE SPACES TO PRINT-LINE.
    WRITE PRINT-LINE AFTER ADVANCING 2 LINES.
A300-CLOSER.
    MOVE GRAND-TOTAL TO GRAND-TOTAL-PR.
    WRITE PRINT-LINE FROM GRAND-TOTAL-LINE
        AFTER ADVANCING 3 LINES.
    CLOSE CARD-FILE PRINT-FILE.
```

FIGURE 10-15

Output: Minor Break Switch Program

DEPARTMENT	SALES AMOUNT
01	$594.60
01	$483.25
MINOR TOTAL	$1077.85
02	$916.64
02	$742.81
MINOR TOTAL	$1659.45
03	$533.86
MINOR TOTAL	$533.86
05	$759.95
05	$261.04
MINOR TOTAL	$1020.99
09	$360.00
MINOR TOTAL	$360.00
12	$926.17
12	$593.01
12	$600.00
MINOR TOTAL	$2119.18
FINAL TOTAL	$6771.33

Group indication

"Group indication" is the term used to describe a detail printed report in which a *complete* output line is printed only for the first record of each group. The output from the previous program (Figure 10-15) was *not* group indicated because we printed the department number each time a record was processed. For our example we will again use card records containing the department number (card columns 1 and 2) and a sales amount (card columns 5–9), but there will be fewer department numbers so you can get a better idea of how the output looks. Managers often request group indicated reports because detail reports have a "cluttered" look.

The SWITCH1 program can be modified for this purpose by using a second switch that will "tell" the program when to print the department number and when not to. Naturally, we will want to print the department number for the first card record that is read, but after that we only want to print the number for the first card of a new group. The first step is to set up our switch in WORKING-STORAGE.

```
03  GRP-INDICATE-SWITCH    PIC X(03) VALUE ' ON'.
```

The REPORT-LINE contains the field DEPARTMENT-PR and we will use the GRP-INDICATE-SWITCH to move either the department number or spaces to that area depending upon whether it is ON or OFF. To do this we will remove the MOVE DEPARTMENT TO DEPARTMENT-PR statement from the A200-MAIN-PROCESSING module and replace it with the following:

```
IF GRP-INDICATE-SWITCH IS EQUAL TO 'ON'
    MOVE DEPARTMENT TO DEPARTMENT-PR
ELSE
    MOVE SPACES TO DEPARTMENT-PR.
MOVE 'OFF' TO GRP-INDICATE-SWITCH.
```

The logic is as follows. First, the switch was set to ON in WORKING-STORAGE so the first time through the department number will be moved to the output area and printed. Immediately after that we will turn off the switch so that succeeding card records will not have the department number printed. Those statements take care of the first card and all succeeding cards of that group, but after a minor break is detected we will want to repeat the ON-for-one-card process. This is accomplished by turning the switch on again at the end of the minor break routine.

Although the logic expressed above is correct, there is still one small problem. Remember that we wanted to move either the department number or spaces to DEPARTMENT-PR depending upon a switch setting. The problem is that DEPARTMENT-PR is defined as PIC 9(02) and spaces cannot be moved to a numeric field. The solution is to use the REDEFINES clause to give a different name and format to the same area.

```
03  DEPARTMENT      PIC 9(02).
03  DEPT-SPACE-PR REDEFINES DEPARTMENT
                    PIC X(02).
```

The rules for using REDEFINES are simple. The entry containing REDEFINES must immediately follow the area being redefined and the level numbers must be the same. REDEFINES can be used at the group level, as the following example shows. Note that the total number of characters in each definition must be the same.

```
03   SENIOR-STUDENT.
     05   GRADE-AVERAGE          PIC 9V99.
     05   CAMPUS                 PIC X(10).
     05   COLLEGE-MAJOR          PIC 99.
03   GRAD-STUDENT REDEFINES SENIOR-STUDENT.
     05   ADVISOR-NAME           PIC X(15).
```

The original field may contain a VALUE entry, but the redefining field cannot. Of the following examples, the first one is permissible, but the second is *not*.

Examples

```
03   SWITCH-THREE      PIC 9 VALUE 1.
03   INDICATOR REDEFINES SWITCH-THREE    PIC X.
```

(Incorrect)

```
03   SWITCH-THREE      PIC 9 VALUE 1.
03   EOF-FLAG REDEFINES SWITCH-THREE     PIC X VALUE 'N'.
```

The revised IF statement and pseudocode for the A100-MAIN-PROCESSING and B100-MINOR-BREAK-ROUTINE are illustrated below. The flowchart of the A200-MAIN-PROCESSING module is shown in Figure 10-16 and the program and output are shown in Figures 10-17 and 10-18, respectively.

```
IF GRP-INDICATE-SWITCH IS EQUAL TO 'ON'
     MOVE DEPARTMENT TO DEPARTMENT-PR
ELSE
     MOVE SPACES TO DEPT-SPACE-PR.
```

Pseudocode Specifications: GROUP INDICATE

```
A200-MAIN-PROCESSING
     IF switch is not = to ON
          IF card department number is not = storage depart-
          ment number
               PERFORM B100-MINOR-BREAK-ROUTINE
          ENDIF
     ENDIF
     Move OFF to switch
     Move card department number to storage
     Add to minor total
     IF group indicate switch is = ON
          Move card department to print area
     ELSE
          Move spaces to department number print area
     ENDIF
     Move OFF to group indicate switch
     Move card fields to print area
     Write a report line on the printer
     Read a card record at end move ON to end of file switch

B100-MINOR-BREAK-ROUTINE
     Move minor total to print area
     Add minor total to grand total
     Clear minor total
     Write a minor total line on the printer
     MOVE ON to group indicate switch
```

FIGURE 10-16

Program Flowchart Group Indication

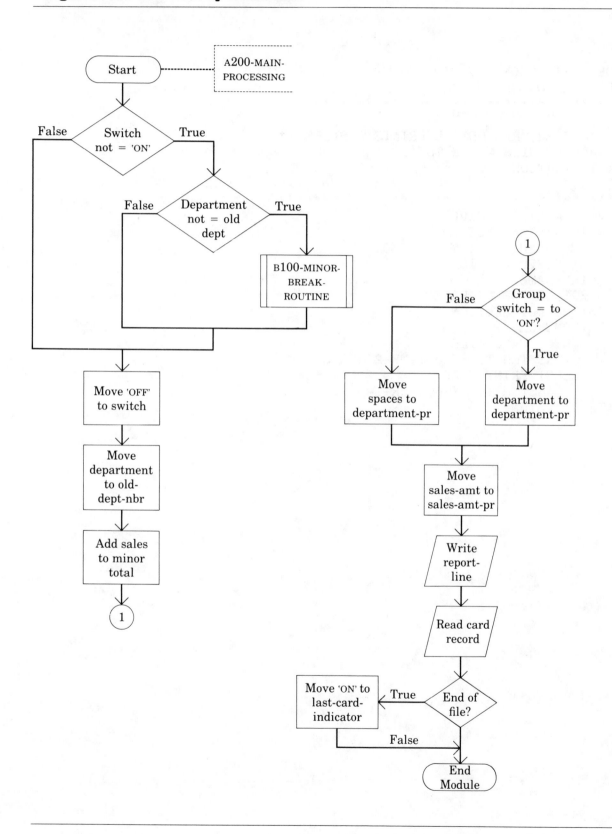

FIGURE 10-17

Group Indication

```
IDENTIFICATION DIVISION.
PROGRAM-ID. GRPIND.
*******************************************
*                                         *
*   THIS PROGRAM DETAIL PRINTS A SALES    *
*   REPORT WITH MINOR TOTALS AND GROUP    *
*   INDICATION.                           *
*                                         *
*******************************************
ENVIRONMENT DIVISION.
CONFIGURATION SECTION.
SOURCE-COMPUTER. IBM-360-F30.
OBJECT-COMPUTER. IBM-360-F30.
SPECIAL-NAMES.
    C01 IS TOP-OF-PAGE.
INPUT-OUTPUT SECTION.
FILE-CONTROL.
    SELECT CARD-FILE
        ASSIGN TO SYS007-UR-2540R-S.
    SELECT PRINT-FILE
        ASSIGN TO SYS009-UR-1403-S.
DATA DIVISION.
```

```
FILE SECTION.
FD   CARD-FILE
     LABEL RECORDS ARE OMITTED
     DATA RECORD IS CARD-REC.
01   CARD-REC                      PIC X(80).
FD   PRINT-FILE
     LABEL RECORDS ARE OMITTED
     DATA RECORD IS PRINT-LINE.
01   PRINT-LINE                     PIC X(121).
WORKING-STORAGE SECTION.
01   MISC-FIELDS.
     03   SWITCH                    PIC X(03) VALUE ' ON'.
     03   GRP-INDICATE-SWITCH       PIC X(03) VALUE ' ON'.
     03   LAST-CARD-INDICATOR       PIC X(03) VALUE 'OFF'.
     03   OLD-DEPT-NBR              PIC 9(02).
     03   MINOR-TOTAL               PIC 9(05)V99 VALUE ZERO.
     03   GRAND-TOTAL               PIC 9(06)V99 VALUE ZERO.
01   CARD-REC-WS.
     03   DEPARTMENT                PIC 9(02).
     03   FILLER                    PIC X(02).
     03   SALES-AMT                 PIC 999V99.
     03   FILLER                    PIC X(71).
01   HEAD-LINE.
     03   FILLER                    PIC X.
     03   FILLER                    PIC X(31) VALUE SPACES.
     03   FILLER                    PIC X(10) VALUE 'DEPARTMENT'.
     03   FILLER                    PIC X(10) VALUE SPACES.
     03   FILLER                    PIC X(12) VALUE 'SALES AMOUNT'.
     03   FILLER                    PIC X(57) VALUE SPACES.
01   REPORT-LINE.
     03   FILLER                    PIC X.
     03   FILLER                    PIC X(35) VALUE SPACES.
     03   DEPARTMENT-PR             PIC 9(02).
     03   DEPT-SPACE-PR REDEFINES   DEPARTMENT-PR
                                    PIC X(02).
     03   FILLER                    PIC X(17) VALUE SPACES.
     03   SALES-AMT-PR              PIC $$$$.99.
     03   FILLER                    PIC X(59) VALUE SPACES.
01   MINOR-TOTAL-LINE.
     03   FILLER                    PIC X.
     03   FILLER                    PIC X(31) VALUE SPACES.
     03   FILLER                    PIC X(11) VALUE 'MINOR TOTAL'.
     03   FILLER                    PIC X(10) VALUE SPACES.
     03   MINOR-TOTAL-PR            PIC $(6).99.
     03   FILLER                    PIC X(59) VALUE SPACES.
01   GRAND-TOTAL-LINE.
     03   FILLER                    PIC X.
     03   FILLER                    PIC X(31) VALUE SPACES.
     03   FILLER                    PIC X(11) VALUE 'FINAL TOTAL'.
     03   FILLER                    PIC X(9)
     03   GRAND-TOTAL-PR            PIC $(7).99.
     03   FILLER                    PIC X(59) VALUE SPACES.
```

```
PROCEDURE DIVISION.
CONTROL-MODULE.
    PERFORM A100-OPENER.
    PERFORM A200-MAIN-PROCESSING
        UNTIL LAST-CARD-INDICATOR IS EQUAL TO ' ON'.
    PERFORM B100-MINOR-BREAK-ROUTINE.
    PERFORM A300-CLOSER.
    STOP RUN.
A100-OPENER.
    OPEN INPUT CARD-FILE OUTPUT PRINT-FILE.
    WRITE PRINT-LINE FROM HEAD-LINE
        AFTER ADVANCING TOP-OF-PAGE.
    MOVE SPACES TO PRINT-LINE.
    WRITE PRINT-LINE AFTER ADVANCING 2 LINES.
    READ CARD-FILE INTO CARD-REC-WS
        AT END MOVE ' ON' TO LAST-CARD-INDICATOR.
A200-MAIN-PROCESSING.
    IF SWITCH IS NOT EQUAL TO ' ON'
        IF DEPARTMENT IS NOT EQUAL TO OLD-DEPT-NBR
            PERFORM B100-MINOR-BREAK-ROUTINE.
    MOVE 'OFF' TO SWITCH.
    MOVE DEPARTMENT TO OLD-DEPT-NBR.
    ADD SALES-AMT TO MINOR-TOTAL.
    IF GRP-INDICATE-SWITCH IS EQUAL TO ' ON'
        MOVE DEPARTMENT TO DEPARTMENT-PR
    ELSE
        MOVE SPACES TO DEPT-SPACE-PR.
    MOVE 'OFF' TO GRP-INDICATE-SWITCH.
    MOVE SALES-AMT TO SALES-AMT-PR.
    WRITE PRINT-LINE FROM REPORT-LINE
        AFTER ADVANCING 1 LINES.
    READ CARD-FILE INTO CARD-REC-WS
        AT END MOVE ' ON' TO LAST-CARD-INDICATOR.
B100-MINOR-BREAK-ROUTINE.
    MOVE MINOR-TOTAL TO MINOR-TOTAL-PR.
    ADD MINOR-TOTAL TO GRAND-TOTAL.
    MOVE ZEROS TO MINOR-TOTAL.
    WRITE PRINT-LINE FROM MINOR-TOTAL-LINE
        AFTER ADVANCING 2 LINES.
    MOVE SPACES TO PRINT-LINE.
    WRITE PRINT-LINE AFTER ADVANCING 2 LINES.
    MOVE ' ON' TO GRP-INDICATE-SWITCH.
A300-CLOSER.
    MOVE GRAND-TOTAL TO GRAND-TOTAL-PR.
    WRITE PRINT-LINE FROM GRAND-TOTAL-LINE
        AFTER ADVANCING 3 LINES.
    CLOSE CARD-FILE PRINT-FILE.
```

FIGURE 10-18

Group Indication

```
       DEPARTMENT          SALES AMOUNT
          01                   $95.16
                             $231.42
                             $533.00
                             $795.00
                             $462.91

     MINOR TOTAL            $2117.49
          02                 $803.77
                             $659.83
                             $428.05
                             $714.55
                             $988.09
                             $613.12

     MINOR TOTAL            $4207.41
          03                 $794.68
                             $865.97
                             $903.64
                             $456.89
                             $681.92

     MINOR TOTAL            $3703.10


     FINAL TOTAL           $10028.00
```

Common errors

We have already mentioned one common error when working with control breaks: forgetting to process the first record of a new group. The control field is used to trigger the break; but after the printing of minor totals the program must return to process the data from the record that caused the break.

Another common error involves the totaling process in the control break paragraph(s). Most beginners have no difficulty with the idea of rolling a minor total into an intermediate or final total. What they tend to forget, however, is to clear the minor total area in preparation for the next data group.

A third opportunity for error occurs after the last data record has been processed. Usually the programmer is quite aware that a final total must be printed, but he or she will often forget that the ending process requires the performance of all lesser control breaks. Both the BREAK1 and BREAK2 programs show this process.

Problem-Solving Techniques

When working with control breaks it is important for the programmer to have a clear idea as to the setup of the control break fields and their contents. A simple diagram containing representative values can be made up to help in the design process. This mock-up must contain all the control break possibilities, even if you are assured that some possibilities cannot occur.

For example, does your logic take care of the one-record group? Would a one-record group be processed correctly if it were the first record? Would it be processed correctly if it were the last record in the file? "Walk" your program through the sample data to see if the breaks are handled properly. Actually, this is not as bad as it sounds. Although it would be nice to do this "desk check" or "walk through" statement by statement, you can concentrate your efforts on the really important statements that set up, change, or test various switches or control fields.

Programmed switches are a very valuable programming tool and should be studied until they are thoroughly understood. Once their importance and use are grasped, they can be used anywhere in the program. As mentioned earlier, a standard format for the switch ON and OFF condition should be developed and used consistently.

Self-Study: Questions and Answers

1. How many levels of totals can you have?

    Answer
    Technically there is no limit to the number of totals one could have in a particular problem. However, three levels (minor, intermediate, major) plus a final one are all you are likely to run across.

2. Instead of looking for a change in department numbers, couldn't we check either for a blank card between each group or for a particular value, such as all 9s?

    Answer
    Yes, you could do this, and the blank card technique was used extensively with the punched-card operations years ago. The problem is that, even though the technique is entirely logical, its success is dependent upon the dummy record being placed between the control groups *every* time. To do so is both time-consuming and prone to error. If the dummy record were omitted, the control break would not be detected. Therefore, the more certain method is to compare the values in the control break fields.

3. The chapter programs to detail print and group print are very similar. Could they be combined into a single program and triggered by an entry when the program is executed?

    Answer
    Yes they could, and a problem of that type is included in the exercises at the end of the chapter.

4. Much like the previous question, since detail printing and detail printing with group indication are so similar, I assume they also could be combined into a single program.

    Answer
    Exactly right. Several types of control break and printing programs might be combined into one complex program.

5. Is there any limit to the number of programmed switches I may have in one program?

Answer
No there isn't. But regardless of the number, be sure to label them for ease of understanding and follow a set pattern of values to represent ON and OFF.

6. Is it possible to have an intermediate break and yet not have a minor break?

Answer
Theoretically it would be possible, although it would not be a very common occurrence. Depending upon the situation, it might be legitimate or it might be an error condition. You could have a situation as follows.

TERRITORY	DEPARTMENT	AMOUNT
500	01	_____
500	01	_____
	MINOR TOTAL	_____
500	02	_____
500	02	_____
	MINOR TOTAL	_____
	INTERMEDIATE TOTAL	_____
600	01	_____
600	01	_____
	MINOR TOTAL	_____
	INTERMEDIATE TOTAL	_____
700	01	_____
700	01	_____

Normally the intermediate break (700 vs. 600) would be used to force a minor level control break even though the department numbers had not changed.

Exercises

1. Define or explain what the term "control break" means. What is meant by "rolling" a total?

2. When working with control breaks what is the problem concerning the first data record? Explain and/or draw diagrams to show how the control break field is handled.

3. How does an intermediate break differ from a minor level break? How does a major level break differ from an intermediate level break?

4. What is the difference between a detail printed report and a group or summary printed report?

5. What is meant by the term "group indication"? Can a summary report be group indicated? If so, explain or diagram your answer.

6. What is a programmed switch? How does it differ from the end-of-file indicator you have been using so far?

7. For the next few problems you will need to punch data cards with the following format.

| cc 1–2 | cc 3–5 | cc 6–7 | cc 8–12 |
Region	Territory	Department	Sales Amount
01	415	01	59460
01	415	01	48325
01	415	02	91664
01	415	02	74281
01	621	03	53386
01	621	05	75995
01	621	05	26104
02	643	09	36000
02	789	12	92617
02	789	12	59301
02	789	12	60000

Write a program that detail prints a sales report with minor, intermediate, major, and final totals. Use the Department field for the minor break, Territory for the intermediate break, and Region for the major break. Edit your output for floating dollar signs, commas, and one asterisk for the minor total, two for intermediate, and three for the major level total.

8. Modify your program from the previous exercise to include an ending routine that verifies that the lower level totals correspond to the grand total figure. If they do not, print an appropriate error message.

9. Use the data from Exercise 7 to group print a report with a total for each Region group and each Territory. Output will be as follows.

```
                      SALES REPORT

  REGION        TERRITORY       DEPARTMENT     SALES AMOUNT

    01             415              01          _____
    01             415              02          _____
              TOTAL:  TERRITORY     415         _____
    01             621              03          _____
    01             621              05          _____
              TOTAL:  TERRITORY     621         _____
    02             643              09          _____
                     etc.


  FINAL         FINAL TOTAL:  ALL REGIONS       _____
```

10. Modify the program you wrote for Exercise 7 to group indicate the Region and Territory numbers. In addition, group indicate the dollar sign in the Sales Amount field so that it prints only for the first sales figure of each group.

11. Modify the program you wrote for Exercise 9 so that the Region and Territory values are group indicated. Also, group indicate the dollar sign in the Sales Amount field.

12. For this problem you will have to punch cards with the following format.

cc 1–20 Customer Name	cc 21–25 Purchase Amount	cc 26–29 Purchase Date
Johnson, Rex	02980	1012
Johnson, Rex	00641	1130
Johnson, Rex	12365	1201
Lambert, Ted	04495	1003
Lambert, Ted	00162	1015
Lambert, Ted	43897	1125
Lambert, Ted	01535	1128
Miller, Susan	00921	1222
Razo, Luisa	01489	1104
Razo, Luisa	06360	1128
Razo, Luisa	07105	1213

This problem is simple but illustrates the point that the control break field does not necessarily have to be numeric. Write a program that detail prints a purchase list with group indication of the customer name and minor and final totals. Output will be as follows.

```
                      PURCHASE LIST

CUSTOMER NAME            AMOUNT       PURCHASE DATE

JOHNSON, REX           $ 29.80          10/12
                          6.41          11/30
                        123.65          12/01
             TOTAL     $159.86
LAMBERT, TED
   etc.
```

13. For this problem you are to use the data from the GRP-IND program shown in the chapter. Modify that program so that a single card inserted before the regular data deck will trigger the printing of a detail printed report (a D in card column 1) or a summary printed report (an S in card column 1).

Chapter 11

Data in Tables

Until now, all the examples and problems have followed the same basic pattern of read-calculate-print. Data records have been read-in from files (cards or magnetic tape) and processed one record at a time. The critical point in each of these problems has been that each record of data can be processed *completely* by one execution of the COBOL program. A payroll program that reads a record, processes the data to produce a paycheck, and then branches back to read another record is a classic example of this type of program logic.

The need for tables

Some problems, however, either cannot or, for efficiency, should not be handled in this manner. One of the problems in an earlier chapter illustrated the "brute force" approach to programming. In that problem (Exercise 12, Chapter 8) you opened the tape file and read through the records looking for a particular department number (103). Everytime a match was found, your program printed a line of output. When the end of the file was detected, you wrote totals and then CLOSEd and OPENed the file in order to go through the data a second time to look for another department number.

This approach is reasonable as long as the file is relatively short and if you are going through the data only a few times. If the file were long, or if you were looking for many departments, that original approach would be extremely inefficient in terms of computer usage. Here is the situation where tables allow us to program far more efficiently. In general, a statistical program, or any program that requires repeated searching through the data, is a prime candidate for tables.

Creating tables

The idea of a table is very simple. A table is nothing more than a series of contiguous memory positions into which data are placed for quick and easy access. For example, suppose we have seven stores and wish to store the sales data for the month of January. We could create contiguous storage of this data by giving a separate name to each of the seven fields needed.

```
03   SALES-1      PIC 9(4)V99
03   SALES-2      PIC 9(4)V99
03   SALES-3      PIC 9(4)V99
03   SALES-4      PIC 9(4)V99
03   SALES-5      PIC 9(4)V99
03   SALES-6      PIC 9(4)V99
03   SALES-7      PIC 9(4)V99
```

Although this method would work, it would be very awkward to deal with whenever we wished to access a particular data record in our program. A far easier way is to create a table and to refer to the individual *elements* within it. The OCCURS clause in COBOL allows us to reserve the appropriate table area.

```
01   TABLE-DATA.
     03 SALES  PIC 9(4)V99 OCCURS 7 TIMES.
```

We have now reserved room for seven, 6-digit fields, each with the name SALES. To refer to a specific element within the table we use what is known as a *subscript*. In the entry SALES (3), (3) is the subscript, and refers to the third field in the table. Schematically, our SALES table would look as follows.

```
SALES (1) [      ]
SALES (2) [      ]
SALES (3) [      ]
SALES (4) [      ]
SALES (5) [      ]
SALES (6) [      ]
SALES (7) [      ]
```

Several rules must be followed when working with tables.

1. The OCCURS clause cannot be written at the 01 level.
2. Once a table is created with the OCCURS clause, any future reference to the table must be with a subscript.
3. The subscript value may be a constant value such as SALES (5), or it may be a variable such as SALES (COUNT). In this case, if COUNT had a value of 4, reference would be made to the fourth element in the table called SALES.
4. It is incorrect to try to access a position that is outside the range of the table. The entries SALES (0); SALES (8)—when there are only seven elements in the table—or SALES (3.5) are errors. (*Note:* In the case of the last example, the system will drop the fractional portion and go to the third element of the SALES table.) Obviously, you are not likely to make such an error if you are using real values in the subscripts. In actual practice you will be using variables almost all the time and the same rule holds true: The value of the subscript variable must meet the rules discussed above.
5. The OCCURS clause names the table and reserves an area for table data. It does *not* put any data into that area. Instead, we can enter data into a table in two ways: by bringing it in from a file and moving into the elements in the table, or by creating the table values by means of the VALUE entry.
6. On most computer systems there must be a space between the table name and the subscript. Check your system on this point.

Reading data into a table

Although there is one exception to the rule, generally you do not read data directly into a table. Instead, you READ in a record just as you have done before and then move the appropriate field(s) to your table(s). As an example, let's suppose we have seven cards that contain the sales data described earlier. Our FD entry for the incoming card file (SALES-INFO) is extremely simple.

```
FD   SALES-INFO
     LABEL RECORDS ARE OMITTED
     DATA RECORD IS SALES-RECORD.

01   SALES-RECORD.
     03 SALES-IN        PIC 9(4)V99.
     03 FILLER          PIC X(74).
```

We will set up our table in WORKING-STORAGE as shown before, but we will also have need for a variable to use as subscript.

```
WORKING-STORAGE SECTION.

01   TABLE-DATA.
     03   SALES  PIC 9(4)V99  OCCURS 7 TIMES.

01   MISC-FIELDS.
     03 COUNTER  PIC 9 VALUE 1.
     03 EOF-INDICATOR  PIC 9 VALUE ZERO.
```

The general logic of our program that actually places data into the table is shown below.

> Read in a card record.
> Move the SALES-IN field to SALES (COUNTER)
> Add 1 to the COUNTER
> Repeat the process until all the data fields have been moved into the SALES table.

The actual PROCEDURE DIVISION entries to accomplish this process are shown in structured format. Note that *all* the data are read-in and placed into the table *before* processing of that data begins.

```
PROCEDURE DIVISION.

CONTROL-ROUTINE.
    PERFORM 010-OPEN-ROUTINE.
    PERFORM 020-LOAD-TABLE
        UNTIL EOF-INDICATOR = 1.
        .
        .
        .

010-OPEN-ROUTINE.
    OPEN INPUT SALES-INFO.
    READ SALES-INFO
        AT END MOVE 1 TO EOF-INDICATOR.

020-LOAD-TABLE.
    MOVE SALES-IN TO SALES (COUNTER).
    ADD 1 TO COUNTER.
    READ SALES-INFO
        AT END MOVE 1 TO EOF-INDICATOR.
030-PROCESSING-ROUTINE.
        .
        .
        .
```

Note that we established our subscript field (COUNTER) with a beginning value of 1. Then, each time through the loop we increment this value by 1 so that we can access the next element of the table. Figures 11-1*a* and 11-1*b* illustrate the operation.

FIGURE 11-1*a*

Moving Data into a Table

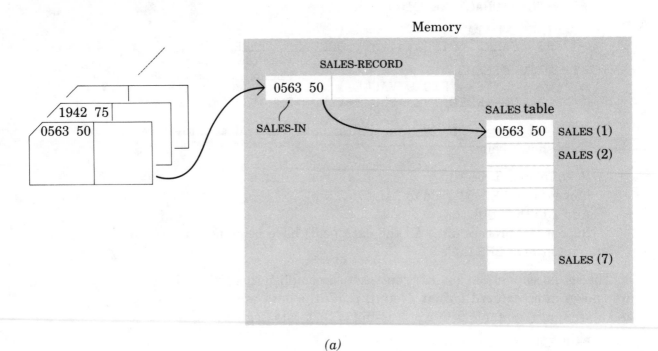

(*a*)

FIGURE 11-1*b*

Moving Data into a Table

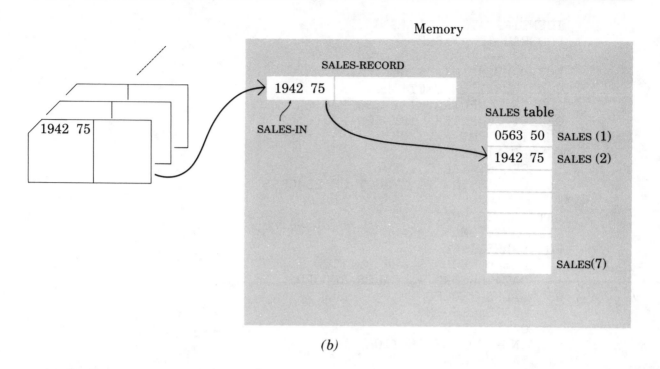

(b)

The next illustration, Figure 11-2, shows the complete program and illustrates the point that once data have been entered into a table, they can be processed the same way as before. The most important point to remember is that you must always use a subscript when referencing table data.

After coming out of the read loop, the program DISPLAYS several of the table values and then it shows how a simple loop can be used to sum all the values from the SALES table. For this we need to establish a TOTALS field in WORKING-STORAGE. Also note that once data are in the table, we do *not* READ them again. The data are now inside memory to be manipulated, but the programmer does not READ them again.

FIGURE 11-2

Moving Data into a Table

```
        IDENTIFICATION DIVISION.
        PROGRAM-ID. TABLE.
*
        ENVIRONMENT DIVISION.
        CONFIGURATION SECTION.
        SOURCE-COMPUTER. IBM-360-F30.
        OBJECT-COMPUTER. IBM-360-F30.
        INPUT-OUTPUT SECTION.
        FILE-CONTROL.
            SELECT SALES-INFO
                ASSIGN TO SYS007-UR-2540R-S.
*
        DATA DIVISION.
        FILE SECTION.
        FD  SALES-INFO
            LABEL RECORDS ARE OMITTED
            DATA RECORD IS SALES-RECORD.
        01  SALES-RECORD.
            03   SALES-IN                PIC 9(4)V99.
            03   FILLER                  PIC X(74).
        WORKING-STORAGE SECTION.
        01  TABLE-DATA.
            03   SALES                   PIC 9(4)V99 OCCURS 7 TIMES.
        01  OTHER-FIELDS.
            03   COUNTER                 PIC 9 VALUE 1.
            03   EOF-INDICATOR           PIC 9 VALUE ZERO.
            03   TOTALS                  PIC 9(6)V99 VALUE ZEROS.
            03   TOTALS-ED               PIC ZZZZZZ.99.
*
```

```
PROCEDURE DIVISION.
CONTROL-ROUTINE.
    PERFORM 010-OPEN-ROUTINE.
    PERFORM 020-LOAD-TABLE
        UNTIL EOF-INDICATOR = 1.
    PERFORM 030-PROCESSING-ROUTINE.
    PERFORM 040-ADD-ROUTINE
        UNTIL COUNTER = 8.
    PERFORM 050-PRINT-TOTAL.
    STOP RUN.
010-OPEN-ROUTINE.
    OPEN INPUT SALES-INFO.
    READ SALES-INFO
        AT END MOVE 1 TO EOF-INDICATOR.
020-LOAD-TABLE.
    MOVE SALES-IN TO SALES (COUNTER).
    ADD 1 TO COUNTER.
    READ SALES-INFO
        AT END MOVE 1 TO EOF-INDICATOR.
030-PROCESSING-ROUTINE.
    DISPLAY SALES (1).
    DISPLAY SALES (2).
    DISPLAY SALES (7).
    MOVE 1 TO COUNTER.
040-ADD-ROUTINE.
    ADD SALES (COUNTER) TO TOTALS.
    ADD 1 TO COUNTER.
050-PRINT-TOTAL.
    MOVE TOTALS TO TOTALS-ED.
    DISPLAY TOTALS-ED.
```

```
056350
194275
876552
 26380.72
```

Creating table data internally

The second method of getting data into a table is by creating the data internally within the program. This technique involves a slight refinement in the use of the VALUE clause you have used previously. We will start by defining or creating seven data values in the WORK-ING-STORAGE SECTION.

```
WORKING-STORAGE SECTION.
01   SALES-VALUES.
     03   FILLER        PIC 9(4)V99 VALUE 0563.50.
     03   FILLER        PIC 9(4)V99 VALUE 1942.75.
     03   FILLER        PIC 9(4)V99 VALUE 6873.00.
     03   FILLER        PIC 9(4)V99 VALUE 0045.21.
     03   FILLER        PIC 9(4)V99 VALUE 4976.58.
     03   FILLER        PIC 9(4)V99 VALUE 3214.16.
     03   FILLER        PIC 9(4)V99 VALUE 8765.52.
```

Unfortunately, just defining these values won't put them into a table. It would seem that we should be able to work in the OCCURS clause with the above entry. However, the rule is that "VALUE cannot be used with OCCURS." This rule is entirely logical since VALUE defines a *single* value while OCCURS sets aside room for multiple elements. We can get around this problem by using the REDEFINES clause. Right below our last entry we will do the following:

```
                .
                .
                .
     03   FILLER        PIC 9(4)V99 VALUE 8765.52.
01   TABLE-DATA REDEFINES SALES-VALUES.
     03   SALES         PIC 9(4)V99 OCCURS 7 TIMES.
```

Note that REDEFINES can only be used to redefine something that has been defined previously. As before, we had to abide by the rule that OCCURS cannot be at the 01 level. Our revised program (Figure 11-3) prints the same answers as before without reading the data from cards.

FIGURE 11-3

Creating a Table Internally

```
WORKING-STORAGE SECTION.
01   SALES-VALUES.
     03   FILLER                          PIC 9(4)V99 VALUE 0563.50.
     03   FILLER                          PIC 9(4)V99 VALUE 1942.75.
     03   FILLER                          PIC 9(4)V99 VALUE 6873.00.
     03   FILLER                          PIC 9(4)V99 VALUE 0045.21.
     03   FILLER                          PIC 9(4)V99 VALUE 4976.58.
     03   FILLER                          PIC 9(4)V99 VALUE 3214.16.
     03   FILLER                          PIC 9(4)V99 VALUE 8765.52.
01   TABLE-DATA REDEFINES SALES-VALUES.
     03   SALES                           PIC 9(4)V99 OCCURS 7 TIMES.
01   OTHER-FIELDS.
     03   COUNTER                         PIC 9 VALUE 1.
     03   TOTALS                          PIC 9(6)V99 VALUE ZEROS.
     03   TOTALS-ED                       PIC ZZZZZZ.99.
*
PROCEDURE DIVISION.
CONTROL-ROUTINE.
     PERFORM 030-PROCESSING-ROUTINE.
     PERFORM 040-ADD-ROUTINE
         UNTIL COUNTER = 8.
     PERFORM 050-PRINT-TOTAL.
     STOP RUN.
030-PROCESSING-ROUTINE.
     DISPLAY SALES (1).
     DISPLAY SALES (2).
     DISPLAY SALES (7).
     MOVE 1 TO COUNTER.
040-ADD-ROUTINE.
     ADD SALES (COUNTER) TO TOTALS.
     ADD 1 TO COUNTER.
050-PRINT-TOTAL.
     MOVE TOTALS TO TOTALS-ED.
     DISPLAY TOTALS-ED.
```

Using PERFORM with tables

In a previous chapter you saw that the PERFORM statement was a vital part of structured programming. The three forms of the statement—PERFORM, PERFORM THRU (used in conjunction with the EXIT verb), and PERFORM UNTIL—gave you several different methods of handling program loops. In the sample programs shown in Figures 11-2 and 11-3, note that the looping for handling tables is a little awkward because the programmer has to set the counter to an initial value of 1 and then add 1 to it each time through the loop. Other variations of PERFORM are particularly suited to working with tables.

The PERFORM TIMES format

The TIMES variation of the PERFORM statement is extremely simple and has the following format:

$$\text{PERFORM paragraph name} \left\{ \begin{array}{l} \text{identifier} \\ \text{integer} \end{array} \right\} \text{TIMES} .$$

Examples

```
PERFORM 090-PROCESSING X TIMES.
```

The 090-PROCESSING paragraph is performed a specific number of times depending upon the current value of the variable X. A statement of this type is very valuable when we wish to execute a loop a different number of times each time the program is run.

```
PERFORM 020-LOAD-TABLE 7 TIMES.
```

This version of PERFORM could be used in our sample programs in this chapter only if we knew in advance the exact number of repetitions, or loops, that would be required. If we were certain of seven loops, we could simplify the program considerably, as the following sequence shows:

```
CONTROL-ROUTINE.
    PERFORM 010-OPEN-ROUTINE.
    PERFORM 020-LOAD-TABLE 7 TIMES.
    PERFORM 030-PROCESSING-ROUTINE.

010-OPEN-ROUTINE.
    OPEN INPUT SALES-INFO.

020-LOAD-TABLE.
    READ SALES-INFO
        AT END MOVE 1 TO EOF-INDICATOR.
    MOVE SALES-IN TO SALES (COUNTER).
    ADD 1 TO COUNTER.
        .
        .
        .
```

The PERFORM VARYING format

Perhaps the most useful format of PERFORM with tables is the version that uses VARYING. A simplified format is shown below. (*Note:* In a text of this type it is not possible to cover all the complex variations that can be made with the PERFORM statement. Check the manufacturer's manual for the formats that are permitted on your machine.)

```
PERFORM paragraph name VARYING
    identifier-1 FROM literal-1 BY literal-2
    UNTIL test condition.
```

Example

```
PERFORM 020-LOAD-TABLE VARYING COUNTER
    FROM 1 BY 1 UNTIL COUNTER
    IS GREATER THAN 7.
```

Identifier-1 (our COUNTER field) must be established in the DATA DIVISION by the programmer. The "FROM 1" part of the statement sets COUNTER to this initial value by moving a 1 value into the field. The "BY 1" portion automatically adds 1 to COUNTER *after* the loop has been executed. The test condition may be any test the programmer wishes, but here we wish to stop executing the loop when COUNTER is greater than 7. The value of COUNTER is 1 *during* the first execution of the loop, but is automatically incremented by 1 at the end of the first pass through the loop. The software then tests the value of COUNTER against the test condition to see if the paragraph should be PERFORMed again. At the *conclusion* of the seventh pass through the loop, COUNTER is automatically incremented by 1. Again the software tests COUNTER against the test condition, and, since 8 is greater than 7, exits from the PERFORM to the next statement in sequence. If we had said "UNTIL COUNTER IS EQUAL TO 7," the loop would only have been executed six times. Figure 11-4 is a further revision of our program to show how PERFORM VARYING is used.

FIGURE 11-4

Tables with PERFORM VARYING

```
IDENTIFICATION DIVISION.
PROGRAM-ID. TABLE.
*
ENVIRONMENT DIVISION.
CONFIGURATION SECTION.
SOURCE-COMPUTER. IBM-360-F30.
OBJECT-COMPUTER. IBM-360-F30.
INPUT-OUTPUT SECTION.
FILE-CONTROL.
    SELECT SALES-INFO
        ASSIGN TO SYS007-UR-2540R-S.
*
```

```
        DATA DIVISION.
        FILE SECTION.
        FD  SALES-INFO
            LABEL RECORDS ARE OMITTED
            DATA RECORD IS SALES-RECORD.
        01  SALES-RECORD.
            03   SALES-IN                      PIC 9(4)V99.
            03   FILLER                        PIC X(74).
        WORKING-STORAGE SECTION.
        01  TABLE-DATA.
            03   SALES                         PIC 9(4)V99 OCCURS 7 TIMES.
        01  OTHER-FIELDS.
            03   COUNTER                       PIC 9 VALUE ZERO.
            03   EOF-INDICATOR                 PIC 9 VALUE ZERO.
            03   TOTALS                        PIC 9(6)V99 VALUE ZEROS.
            03   TOTALS-ED                     PIC ZZZZZZ.99.
*
        PROCEDURE DIVISION.
        CONTROL-ROUTINE.
            PERFORM 010-OPEN-ROUTINE.
            PERFORM 020-LOAD-TABLE
                VARYING COUNTER FROM 1 BY 1 UNTIL
                    COUNTER IS GREATER THAN 7.
            PERFORM 030-PROCESSING-ROUTINE.
            PERFORM 040-ADD-ROUTINE
                UNTIL COUNTER = 8.
            PERFORM 050-PRINT-TOTAL.
            STOP RUN.
        010-OPEN-ROUTINE.
            OPEN INPUT SALES-INFO.
            READ SALES-INFO
                AT END MOVE 1 TO EOF-INDICATOR.
        020-LOAD-TABLE.
            MOVE SALES-IN TO SALES (COUNTER).
            READ SALES-INFO
                AT END MOVE 1 TO EOF-INDICATOR.
        030-PROCESSING-ROUTINE.
            DISPLAY SALES (1).
            DISPLAY SALES (2).
            DISPLAY SALES (7).
            MOVE 1 TO COUNTER.
        040-ADD-ROUTINE.
            ADD SALES (COUNTER) TO TOTALS.
            ADD 1 TO COUNTER.
        050-PRINT-TOTAL.
            MOVE TOTALS TO TOTALS-ED.
            DISPLAY TOTALS-ED.


        056350
        194275
        876552
         26380.72
```

More about tables

So far we have been discussing how you can create and use one-dimensional tables. The term "one-dimensional" refers to the fact that you can reach a particular element in the table by means of a single subscript such as SALES (4). Unlike many other languages, COBOL has the interesting capability of allowing you to have multiple fields in a one-dimensional table. For example, suppose our data deck has the following format:

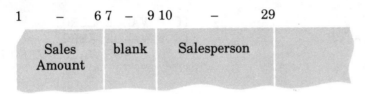

If our problem required that both the sales data and the name data be placed into table format, we would have two choices. First, we could set-up two *separate* tables and store the data accordingly, as the following schematic and partial program indicate:

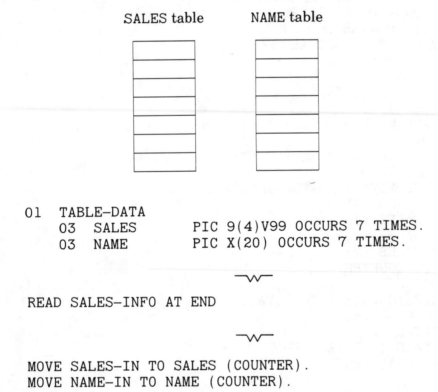

```
01   TABLE-DATA
     03   SALES       PIC 9(4)V99 OCCURS 7 TIMES.
     03   NAME        PIC X(20) OCCURS 7 TIMES.

                    -~w~-

     READ SALES-INFO AT END

                    -~w~-

     MOVE SALES-IN TO SALES (COUNTER).
     MOVE NAME-IN TO NAME (COUNTER).
```

The DATA DIVISION entries shown above set up two separate tables and the PROCEDURE DIVISION entries move the data as before.

A second possibility, however, is that the programmer can create a single-dimension table that contains *multiple* fields. Note the following DATA DIVISION entry:

```
01   TABLE-DATA.
     03   TABLES OCCURS 7 TIMES.
          05   SALES        PIC 9(4)V99.
          05   NAME         PIC X(20).
```

Since the OCCURS entry was written at the 03 level and both the 05 level entries are subordinate to it, the single table now contains room for seven SALES values and seven NAME entries. Schematically, our table looks as follows:

← TABLES (1) →	
SALES (1)	NAME (1)
← TABLES (2) →	
SALES (2)	NAME (2)
← TABLES (7) →	
SALES (7)	NAME (7)

The interesting point about this arrangement is that we can access the various parts of the table separately. As you can see from the diagram, SALES (2) accesses only the sales data from the second "slot" in the table. NAME (2) accesses only the name portion of the data in the second "slot." However, the entry TABLE (2) accesses *both* the SALES data and the NAME data in the second slot. Figure 11-5 is a further revision of our sample program to illustrate this idea.

FIGURE 11-5

Multi-Field Table Data

```
      IDENTIFICATION DIVISION.
      PROGRAM-ID. TABLE.
*
      ENVIRONMENT DIVISION.
      CONFIGURATION SECTION.
      SOURCE-COMPUTER. IBM-360-F30.
      OBJECT-COMPUTER. IBM-360-F30.
      INPUT-OUTPUT SECTION.
      FILE-CONTROL.
          SELECT SALES-INFO
              ASSIGN TO SYS007-UR-2540R-S.
*
      DATA DIVISION.
      FILE SECTION.
      FD   SALES-INFO
           LABEL RECORDS ARE OMITTED
           DATA RECORD IS SALES-RECORD.
      01   SALES-RECORD.
           03   SALES-IN                 PIC 9(4)V99.
           03   FILLER                   PIC X(3).
           03   NAME-IN                  PIC X(20).
           03   FILLER                   PIC X(51).
      WORKING-STORAGE SECTION.
      01   TABLE-DATA.
           03   TABLES OCCURS 7 TIMES.
                05   SALES               PIC 9(4)V99.
                05   NAME                PIC X(20).
      01   OTHER-FIELDS.
           03   COUNTER                  PIC 9 VALUE ZERO.
           03   EOF-INDICATOR            PIC 9 VALUE ZERO.
*
```

```
PROCEDURE DIVISION.
CONTROL-ROUTINE.
    PERFORM 010-OPEN-ROUTINE.
    PERFORM 020-LOAD-TABLE
        VARYING COUNTER FROM 1 BY 1
        UNTIL COUNTER IS GREATER THAN 7.
    PERFORM 030-PROCESSING-ROUTINE.
    STOP RUN.
010-OPEN-ROUTINE.
    OPEN INPUT SALES-INFO.
    READ SALES-INFO
        AT END MOVE 1 TO EOF-INDICATOR.
020-LOAD-TABLE.
    MOVE SALES-IN TO SALES (COUNTER).
    MOVE NAME-IN TO NAME (COUNTER).
    READ SALES-INFO
        AT END MOVE 1 TO EOF-INDICATOR.
030-PROCESSING-ROUTINE.
    DISPLAY SALES (1).
    DISPLAY NAME (1).
    DISPLAY SALES (4).
    DISPLAY NAME (4).
    DISPLAY TABLES (4).


056350
PEARSON
004521
ATWEILER
004521ATWEILER
```

Two-dimensional tables

At first glance two-dimensional tables appear to be the same as a single-dimensional table that contains multiple fields. However, there are two important differences. First, two OCCURS entries are needed and they must be at different levels. Second, to get to a given position, two subscripts are required. Let's expand our original SALES data so that each of the seven cards contains the sales for three months.

| 0563 50 | 0788 12 | 0795 00 |

We will create a two-dimensional table to store this data, as shown below.

```
01  TABLE-DATA.
    03  SALES OCCURS 7 TIMES.
        05 MONTH OCCURS 3 TIMES   PIC 9(4)V99.
```

Reference to the positions within the two-dimensional table is made by using the field name with the highest level number—MONTH in this case. Since this is the most subordinate, or lowest ranking, entry and since there is an OCCURS above it, reference to MONTH requires a double subscript such as MONTH (5, 2). The first value in the subscript refers to the position _down_ the table and the second number refers to the position _across_ the table. (COBOL also allows the use of three-dimensional tables that use three subscripts—down, across, and in—to reference the data elements. This type of table will not be covered in the text.) Note the following schematic and sample program (Figure 11-6) that illustrate a two-dimensional table.

MONTH (1,1)	MONTH (1,2)	MONTH (1,3)
MONTH (2,1)	MONTH (2,2)	MONTH (2,3)
MONTH (7,1)	MONTH (7,2)	MONTH (7,3)

FIGURE 11-6

Two-Dimensional Table

```
      IDENTIFICATION DIVISION.
      PROGRAM-ID. TWO-D-TABLE.
*
      ENVIRONMENT DIVISION.
      CONFIGURATION SECTION.
      SOURCE-COMPUTER.  IBM-360-F30.
      OBJECT-COMPUTER.  IBM-360-F30.
      INPUT-OUTPUT SECTION.
      FILE-CONTROL.
          SELECT SALES-INFO
              ASSIGN TO SYS007-UR-2540R-S.
*
```

```
DATA DIVISION.
FILE SECTION.
FD   SALES-INFO
     LABEL RECORDS ARE OMITTED
     DATA RECORD IS SALES-RECORD.
01   SALES-RECORD.
     03   SALES-IN-ONE              PIC 9(4)V99.
     03   SALES-IN-TWO              PIC 9(4)V99.
     03   SALES-IN-THREE            PIC 9(4)V99.
WORKING-STORAGE SECTION.
01   TABLE-DATA.
     03   SALES OCCURS 7 TIMES.
          05   MONTH OCCURS 3 TIMES PIC 9(4)V99.
01   OTHER-FIELDS.
     03   EOF-INDICATOR             PIC 9 VALUE ZERO.
     03   TOTALS                    PIC 9(6)V99 VALUE ZEROS.
     03   TOTALS-ED                 PIC ZZZZZZ.99.
     03   COUNTER                   PIC 9 VALUE 1.
     03   DOWN-T                    PIC 9 VALUE ZERO.
     03   ACROSS                    PIC 9 VALUE ZERO.
*
PROCEDURE DIVISION.
CONTROL-ROUTINE.
     PERFORM 010-OPEN-ROUTINE.
     PERFORM 020-LOAD-TABLE 7 TIMES.
     PERFORM 030-PROOF-ROUTINE.
     PERFORM 040-ADD-ROUTINE
          VARYING COUNTER FROM 1 BY 1
          UNTIL COUNTER IS EQUAL TO 8.
     PERFORM 050-PRINT-TOTAL.
     STOP RUN.
010-OPEN-ROUTINE.
     OPEN INPUT SALES-INFO.
     READ SALES-INFO
          AT END MOVE 1 TO EOF-INDICATOR.
020-LOAD-TABLE.
     ADD 1 TO DOWN-T.
     PERFORM 025-LOAD-ROUTINE.
     READ SALES-INFO
          AT END MOVE 1 TO EOF-INDICATOR.
     MOVE ZERO TO ACROSS.
025-LOAD-ROUTINE.
     ADD 1 TO ACROSS.
     MOVE SALES-IN-ONE TO MONTH (DOWN-T,ACROSS).
     ADD 1 TO ACROSS.
     MOVE SALES-IN-TWO TO MONTH (DOWN-T,ACROSS).
     ADD 1 TO ACROSS.
     MOVE SALES-IN-THREE TO MONTH (DOWN-T,ACROSS).
030-PROOF-ROUTINE.
     DISPLAY MONTH (1,1).
     DISPLAY MONTH (3,3).
     DISPLAY MONTH (7,1).
     DISPLAY MONTH (7,2).
     DISPLAY MONTH (7,3).
     DISPLAY SALES (7).
```

```
040-ADD-ROUTINE.
    ADD MONTH (COUNTER,1) TO TOTALS.
050-PRINT-TOTAL.
    MOVE TOTALS TO TOTALS-ED.
    DISPLAY TOTALS-ED.
```

```
056350
859744
876552
645367
718600
876552645367718600
 26380.72
```

A few extra points about the program should be noted.

1. All references to *individual* elements within the table were to MONTH and always included a double subscript.
2. The first value of the subscript referenced the down position while the second value referenced the across position.
3. In loading the table we had to progress across to move the individual sales values into table positions 1-1, 1-2, and 1-3. In order to place the second set of sales figures into the proper positions, we had to increment the first subscript (DOWN) by 1 *and* reset the second subscript (ACROSS) back to 1. By doing so the second set of values was moved into the correct table positions of 2-1, 2-2, and 2-3. This process continued until the last set of values was moved into 7-1, 7-2, and 7-3.
4. In the program a final reference was made to SALES with a *single* subscript. This is a correct reference because SALES, as set up in the DATA DIVISION, has only one OCCURS associated with it. MONTH, on the other hand, must always be referenced with a double subscript because it has two OCCURS associated with it.

Special COBOL statements for tables

As you know, table data can be referenced or accessed only by means of a subscript; previous examples illustrated how the programmer can manipulate this subscript value. The text further explained that the main reason for having tables is that we can search to find particular information quickly and easily. Since this searching operation is such a common task, COBOL has some special statements that permit us to perform searching with a little more ease and grace. When these special statements are used to do the searching, the subscript is usually referred to as an *index,* although it serves exactly the same purpose as before. Actually, the use of the COBOL SEARCH verb involves three separate components: an INDEXED BY entry and the use of the SET and the SEARCH statements.

As before, the process starts by establishing a table with the OCCURS entry. In this case, assume we have need for a 10-element, multi-field table called STUDENT-RECORDS that contains the fields S-NUMBER, S-NAME, S-MAJOR, and S-GRADE-AVE. The table will be set up the same as it was before with one minor addition—an INDEXED BY entry.

```
03   STUDENT-RECORDS OCCURS 10 TIMES
                          INDEXED BY TABLE-INDEX.
     05   S-NUMBER        PIC 9(9).
     05   S-NAME          PIC A(30).
     05   S-MAJOR         PIC A(20).
     05   S-GRADE-AVE     PIC 9V99.
```

This table contains unsorted data fields; that is, they are not in alphabetic or numeric sequence. The point is important, as COBOL has different search techniques depending on whether the table data is or is not in sorted order. The INDEXED BY entry alerts the system that the variable TABLE-INDEX will be used as the index when we reference the STUDENT-RECORD table. However, the programmer does *NOT* set up TABLE-INDEX in the DATA DIVISION. To do so would result in an error, because the software system does this on its own. Furthermore, the programmer is restricted to the use of certain special COBOL statements that can be used with this index variable.

The SET statement

The SET statement is used to control the value of the index variable. Two general formats are used: one to establish the initial value of the index and one to change that value. Abbreviated versions of the SET statement formats are shown below.

$$\text{SET index-name-1 TO} \begin{Bmatrix} \text{index-name-2} \\ \text{integer-1} \end{Bmatrix}$$

$$\text{SET index-name-1} \begin{Bmatrix} \text{UP BY} \\ \text{DOWN BY} \end{Bmatrix} \text{integer-1}$$

Examples

```
SET X TO COUNT.
```

```
SET TAG TO 1.
```

```
SET INDEX-VALUE UP BY 1.
```

```
SET COUNT DOWN BY 1.
```

In the examples above, the fields called X, TAG, INDEX-VALUE, and COUNT would have to be defined to the system as index values. Thus, SET cannot be used with fields that you might normally describe in the DATA DIVISION.

The SEARCH statement

The COBOL SEARCH verb has two general formats: one involving unsorted tables and one involving sorted tables. Let's work with the unsorted format first. As you would suspect, SEARCH can only be used with a table entry that contains INDEXED BY. At this point we will assume that the STUDENT-RECORDS table has been loaded with data. Now, we want to read in a card containing a student identification number and search the table to find the matching record. The program in skeletal form is shown below.

```
          .
          .
          .
     READ CARD-FILE           (To read in the value for which you are searching)
          AT END _____ .
          .
          .
          .
     PERFORM SEARCH-ROUTINE.
          .
          .
          .
SEARCH-ROUTINE.
     SET TABLE-INDEX TO 1.
     SEARCH STUDENT-RECORDS
          AT END
               MOVE 'MATCH NOT FOUND' TO _____
               MOVE CARD-NUMBER TO _____
          WHEN S-NUMBER (TABLE-INDEX)
               IS EQUAL TO CARD-NUMBER
          MOVE S-NAME (TABLE-INDEX) TO _____
          MOVE S-MAJOR (TABLE-INDEX) TO _____
          MOVE S-GRADE-AVE (TABLE-INDEX) TO _____ .
     WRITE OUTPUT-LINE FROM _____ .
```

The search operation involves the following steps:

1. The SET statement is used to establish the initial value of the index *before* entering the search routine.

2. Execution of the SEARCH statement causes the system to begin a *sequential* search through the table starting with the first element.

3. The condition set by WHEN is evaluated. (It should be apparent that WHEN is really an IF statement that has been adapted for use with SEARCH.)

   a. If the condition is *not* met, the index is *automatically* incremented and the search is repeated.

   b. If the condition is met, the statements following WHEN, down to the ending period, are executed; the index is *not* incremented; and the search is ended.

4. The AT END is optional, although it is usually included. If omitted, control passes to the next statement after the SEARCH. If AT END is included, the statements following AT END up to WHEN are executed and control then passes to the next statement after SEARCH. Note that in this example the SEARCH statement ends with the period ending the MOVE S-GRADE-AVE TO _____ .

5. The AT END condition is signalled when the value of the index exceeds the size of the table as set up with the OCCURS entry. The general logic of the SEARCH operation is shown on the next page.

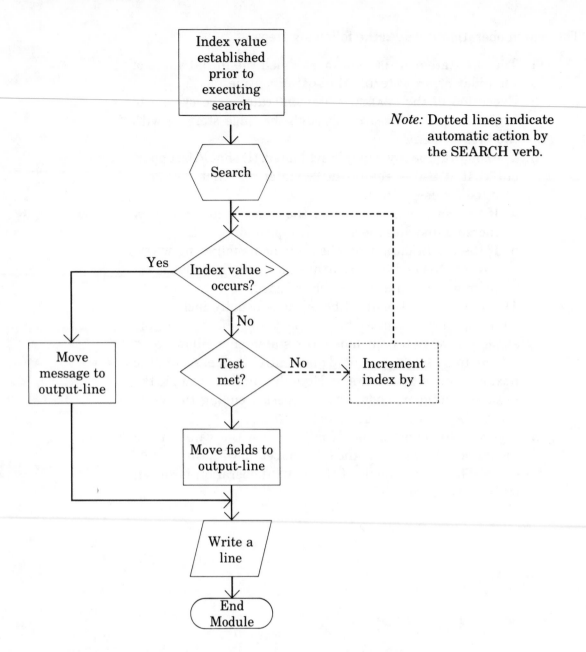

Note: Dotted lines indicate automatic action by the SEARCH verb.

Our example only searched the table once because we read in only one student search card. However, the logic of the search operation holds true no matter how many cards are used.

```
        .
        .
        .
    READ CARD-FILE                  (This is our priming read)
        AT END MOVE 'DONE' TO CARD-EOF.
        .
        .
        .
    PERFORM SEARCH-ROUTINE
        UNTIL CARD-EOF = 'DONE'.
        .
        .
        .
    SEARCH-ROUTINE.
        SET TABLE-INDEX TO 1.
        SEARCH STUDENT-RECORDS
            AT END
                MOVE 'MATCH NOT FOUND' TO _____
                MOVE CARD-NUMBER TO _____
            WHEN S-NUMBER (TABLE-INDEX)
                IS EQUAL TO CARD-NUMBER
                MOVE S-NAME (TABLE-INDEX) TO _____
                MOVE S-MAJOR (TABLE-INDEX) TO _____
                MOVE S-GRADE-AVE (TABLE-INDEX) TO _____ .
        WRITE OUTPUT-LINE FROM _____ .
        READ CARD-FILE
            AT END MOVE 'DONE' TO CARD-EOF.
```

The key element that makes the repetitive execution of the SEARCH-ROUTINE work is that the value of the index is reset to one each time a new search operation is initiated. A point worth noting, although you may not have need for it now, is that the index can be set to any beginning value you desire, not just one. Thus it is possible to begin the search at the fourth position by saying:

```
    SET TABLE-INDEX TO 4.
```

Another variation on the SEARCH verb is that multiple WHEN conditions are permitted.

```
        .
        .
        .
    SEARCH STUDENT-RECORDS
        AT END
            MOVE _____
            MOVE _____
        WHEN S-NUMBER (TABLE-INDEX)
            IS EQUAL TO CARD-NUMBER
            MOVE _____
            MOVE _____
            MOVE _____
        WHEN S-NUMBER (TABLE-INDEX)
            IS EQUAL TO ZERO
            MOVE 'ZERO STUDENT NUMBER' TO _____ .
    WRITE _____ .
    READ CARD-FILE _____ .
```

If multiple tests are used, the action is equivalent to the execution of OR in that the search will stop if *either* condition is met. The flowchart of this operation is illustrated below.

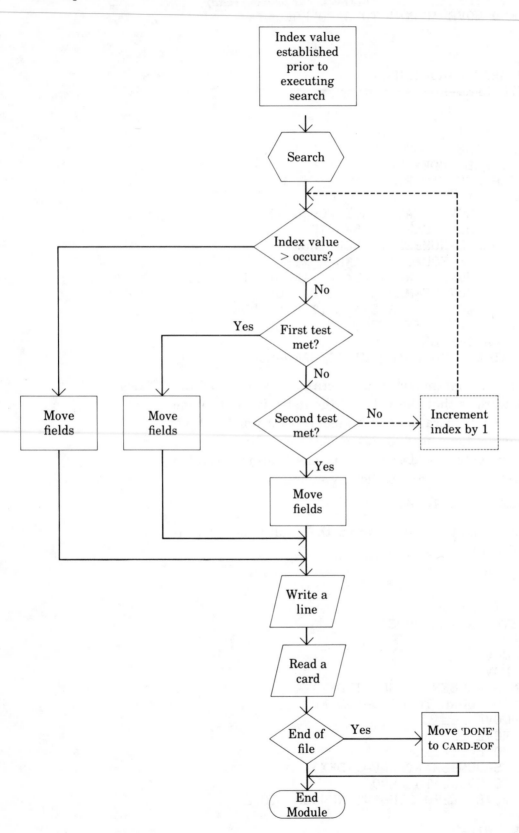

Multiple conditions *within* a WHEN may be tested by use of AND or OR as shown below. Remember that AND means that both conditions must be true while OR means that either condition may be true.

```
01 _____
    03   TEMPERATURE-TABLE
              OCCURS 365 TIMES
              INDEXED BY I-FIELD.
       05   TEMP   PIC 999.
       05   DATE-T PIC 9(6).
      .
      .
      .

SEARCH TEMPERATURE-TABLE
    WHEN TEMP (I-FIELD) IS LESS THAN 32

    OR TEMP (I-FIELD) IS GREATER THAN 100
    DISPLAY TEMP (I-FIELD).
```

If you have been following all of this, one question may have come to mind: What if I want to search through a table to find multiple occurrences of an item? The SEARCH statement as used so far will not work, as it stops the first time the condition is met. We can get around the problem and, for our illustration, we will go back to the SALES table that was used in the beginning of the chapter. Suppose we wish to search through the table and print a listing of those sales that exceed $3000. We could do this by simple subscripting, but SEARCH can be manipulated to do the same thing. The program segment that will do this for us is outlined below. (We will assume that data has been loaded into the table.)

```
    03   SALES    PIC 9(4)V99 OCCURS 7 TIMES
                  INDEXED BY X.
         .
         .
         .

    PERFORM  030-RESET-INDEX.
    PERFORM  040-TABLE-SEARCH
       UNTIL X IS GREATER THAN 7.
         .
         .
         .

030-RESET-INDEX.
    SET X TO 1.

040-TABLE-SEARCH.

    SEARCH SALES
        WHEN SALES (X) IS GREATER THAN 3000.00
        DISPLAY SALES (X)
        SET X UP BY 1.
```

Note that in this case a SET statement is included *within* the SEARCH so that the index will be incremented to the next table position after a match has been found. Another key point is that the index value is set, or initialized, to 1 *prior* to entering 040-TABLE-SEARCH. Finally, since the 040-TABLE-SEARCH paragraph is controlled by a PERFORM UNTIL, the system will continue to execute the paragraph until the index is greater than 7. Figure 11-7 and Figure 11-8 show the flow-chart and the complete program.

FIGURE 11-7

Continued Searching through a Table

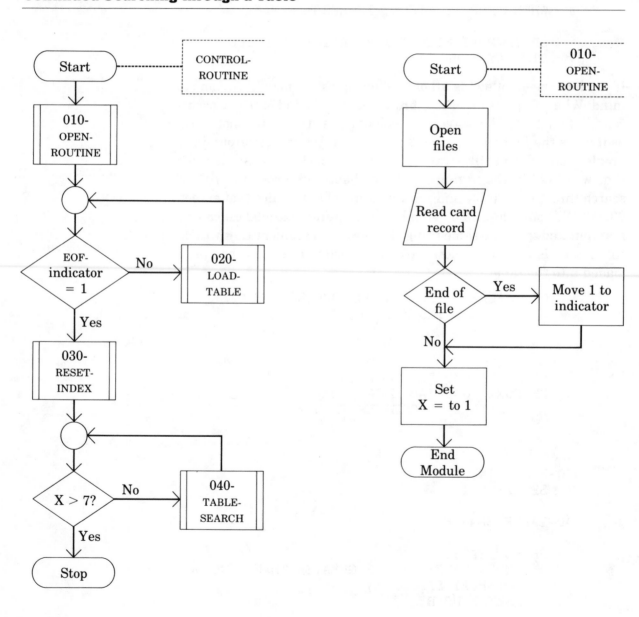

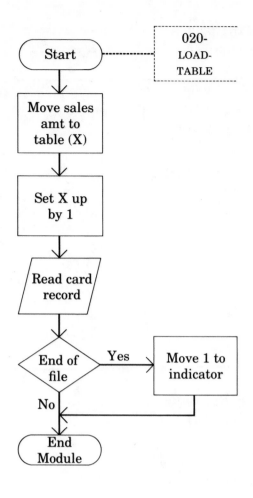

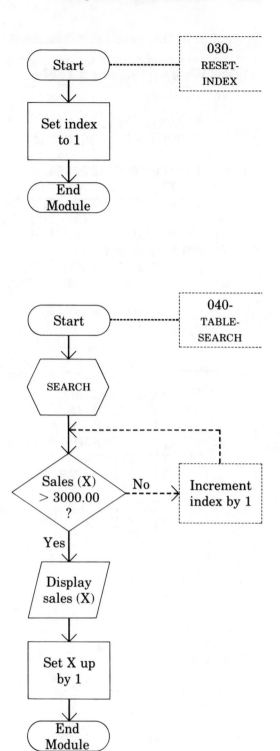

FIGURE 11-8

SEARCHing an Unsorted Table

```
      IDENTIFICATION DIVISION.
      PROGRAM-ID. SEARCHING.
*
      ENVIRONMENT DIVISION.
      CONFIGURATION SECTION.
      SOURCE-COMPUTER. IBM-360-F30.
      OBJECT-COMPUTER. IBM-360-F30.
      INPUT-OUTPUT SECTION.
      FILE-CONTROL.
          SELECT SALES-INFO
              ASSIGN TO SYS007-UR-2540R-S.
*
      DATA DIVISION.
      FILE SECTION.
      FD  SALES-INFO
          LABEL RECORDS ARE OMITTED
          DATA RECORD IS SALES-RECORD.
      01  SALES-RECORD.
          03  SALES-IN              PIC 9(4)V99.
          03  FILLER               PIC X(74).
      WORKING-STORAGE SECTION.
      01  TABLE-DATA.
          03  SALES-TABLE OCCURS 7 TIMES INDEXED BY X.
              05  SALES            PIC 9(4)V99.
      01  OTHER-FIELDS.
          03  EOF-INDICATOR        PIC 9 VALUE ZERO.
*
```

```
PROCEDURE DIVISION.
CONTROL-ROUTINE.
    PERFORM 010-OPEN-ROUTINE.
    PERFORM 020-LOAD-TABLE
        UNTIL EOF-INDICATOR = 1.
    PERFORM 030-RESET-INDEX.
    PERFORM 040-TABLE-SEARCH
        UNTIL X IS GREATER THAN 7.
    STOP RUN.
010-OPEN-ROUTINE.
    OPEN INPUT SALES-INFO.
    READ SALES-INFO
        AT END MOVE 1 TO EOF-INDICATOR.
    SET X TO 1.
020-LOAD-TABLE.
    MOVE SALES-IN TO SALES (X).
    SET X UP BY 1.
    READ SALES-INFO
        AT END MOVE 1 TO EOF-INDICATOR.
030-RESET-INDEX.
    SET X TO 1.
040-TABLE-SEARCH.
    SEARCH SALES-TABLE
        WHEN SALES (X) IS GREATER THAN 3000.00
            DISPLAY SALES (X)
            SET X UP BY 1.

687300
497658
321416
876552
```

As you know, the SEARCH statement is used with tables whose contents are *unordered;* that is, the data items are not in any sequence. Since the search process involves a straight sequential search of the table items beginning with the first element, efficiency would indicate that the most frequently needed items should appear early in the table. If all table items are likely to be needed with the same frequency, then our straight sequential search to find a particular element may become very inefficient. A solution to our problem lies in the use of the SEARCH ALL statement.

The SEARCH ALL statement *must* be used on sorted tables—that is, tables whose values have been sorted into ascending or descending sequence. (The topic of sorting will be covered in a later chapter.) Normal procedure would be to use it on large tables where the frequency of use of the elements is evenly distributed throughout the table.

With SEARCH ALL the system performs a "binary search" rather than a straight sequential search. In a binary search the system first goes to the middle entry in the table and compares the value found there against the test value. It is important for you to note here that the comparison can only be for equality; testing for greater than or less than is not permitted. The result of the test "tells" the system whether the desired element is now in the first half or second half of the table. Knowing this, the system then goes to the middle of that half and performs another comparison, and so on until the item is located.

As an example, suppose our SALES-TABLE includes multiple fields— SALES, REGION, and TABLE-ID. The ASCENDING KEY entry tells the system the name of the field on which the table data were sorted. As you can see from the example, SALES-TABLE is in ascending order according to the TABLE-ID field. Note that this is a single-dimension table consisting of three fields. Each field may be accessed by a single subscript.

```
WORKING-STORAGE SECTION.
01   TABLE-DATA.
     03   SALES-TABLE    OCCURS 1000 TIMES
                         INDEXED BY X
                         ASCENDING KEY IS TABLE-ID.
          05   SALES     PIC 9(4)V99.
          05   REGION    PIC 999.
          05   TABLE-ID  PIC 9(4).
```

SALES-TABLE

SALES (1)	REGION (1)	TABLE-ID (1)
SALES (2)	REGION (2)	TABLE-ID (2)
. . .	. . .	. . .
SALES (1000)	REGION (1000)	TABLE-ID (1000)

The SEARCH ALL statement has the following format with AT END being an optional entry:

```
SEARCH ALL   identifier-1
     AT END   imperative-statement-1
     WHEN _____IS EQUAL TO _____
     imperative statement-2.
```

To perform a binary search on the SALES-TABLE we would program as follows:

```
SEARCH ALL SALES-TABLE
     WHEN ID-NBR-INPUT IS EQUAL TO TABLE-ID (X)
     DISPLAY SALES (X)
     DISPLAY REGION (X).
```

Now, let's see how the binary search works. Suppose that we in some way input a value for ID-NBR-INPUT. We further assume that the TABLE-ID entry that matches this value is in the 743rd position of the table. Using a straight sequential search, the system would have to make 742 comparisons before coming to the matching element in the table. A binary comparison, however, is far more efficient as you will see by the following outline.

1. The system goes to the middle of the table and compares the ID-NBR-INPUT value against the value found in TABLE-ID (500). The comparison will show that ID-NBR-INPUT is greater than the value in TABLE-ID so the system now goes to the *middle* (position 750) of the *second half* of the table (positions 501 to 1000) to continue the comparison.

2. The value at TABLE-ID (750) is compared with the ID-NBR-INPUT value and the comparison now shows that ID-NBR-INPUT (743) is less than the value in TABLE-ID (750). The system now goes to the middle of the table elements between 500 and 750— that is, TABLE-ID (625).

3. Comparisons continue in this manner until the system gets to TABLE-ID (743), which contains a value equal to the value of ID-NBR-INPUT. Using this method, it will take a maximum of ten comparisons to find any matching value in the table.

4. As indicated in the SEARCH ALL statement, the system will then display the values found at SALES (743) and REGION (743). Unless otherwise specified by the AT END option or by PER-FORM or GO TO, the system will automatically go to the next statement.

5. The AT END part of a SEARCH ALL statement will be activated when a matching condition is not found—that is, when none of the comparisons is equal.

Common errors

There are very few errors that one can make with tables and most of these are relatively easy to detect. Perhaps the single most common error involves the subscript value. Certain commonsense rules apply to the subscript when referencing table data.

1. The subscript cannot be zero since there is no zeroth position in the table.

2. The same rule applies to the other end of the table data: The subscript cannot exceed the maximum number of elements as established by the OCCURS clause.

3. Negative subscripts are also forbidden, as are fractional subscript values such as 3.5. In the latter case some systems simply truncate the fractional part and, in this case, would go to the third element in the table.

Errors of the type described above will not be detected during the compilation of your program. Instead, they are execution, or run-time, errors that depend upon the value you have given to the subscript. It is up to the programmer to establish the beginning value of the subscript, to increment it properly, and to reset it when necessary. One very common error is forgetting to reset the subscript value after exiting from one loop and before entering into the next loop. In the same manner the programmer must remember to increment the subscript value when working within the loop. Even the SEARCH statement does not take care of this chore under all conditions, so be careful with the subscript.

Another type of error is really one of understanding exactly how tables work. Most beginners have no problem with reading-in a record and moving the data to appropriate tables, as shown in various examples throughout this chapter. After the data are in tables, however, many programmers try to READ the data "out" of the table so that they can be manipulated. This idea, of course, is entirely wrong since the data have already been read-in and placed in the table. READ implies the idea of bringing data into memory from some outside source such as cards, tape, or disk. Therefore, you do not READ the data "out" of tables; instead, you access them in the same general way you have always accessed data that are in memory. The only difference now is that the reference to the data must contain a subscript.

The last advice to the users of tables is to be careful by which name the table data are referenced, particularly in the case of multi-field single-dimensional tables or for two-dimensional tables.

Problem-Solving Techniques

There seems to be a tendency on the part of many beginning programmers to feel that the use of tables somehow falls outside of any known programming techniques. Just the opposite is true since tables fit with everything you have learned so far, plus they offer you the opportunity of developing additional programming techniques. Tables open a whole new way of thinking about how a problem can be solved.

In the traditional approaches to problem solving on the computer, you were obligated to perform all actions on the data record during the one time it was in memory. Thus the sequential nature of file handling forced you into a relatively narrow set of techniques. Tables free you from this limitation by allowing you to access table elements in a multitude of ways. Professional programmers make extensive use of tables to save time and effort, and so should you.

Self-Study: Questions and Answers

1. I don't understand when one is supposed to use tables and when one is not.

   Answer
   This answer may sound as though the question is being evaded, but it really isn't. The answer is that you have to determine when or when not to use tables. The general rule is that if you can completely process a record by accessing it once—as in a read-calculate-print loop—then tables are not needed. If an analysis of the problem shows that you cannot do all of the processing on a record at one time, then tables would seem to be a likely method. Another way of looking at this is for you to decide which is the most efficient method in terms of machine time and programmer time.

      Another reason for using tables is that your computer system may not have enough tape or disk units to do what you want. If that is so, you may be able to process the data in tables rather than writing them out temporarily to auxiliary storage.

2. What are the limitations on the use of tables?

   Answer
   The first and most obvious limitation is the size of memory. You would be amazed how fast memory can be used up by tables, particularly by table data in DISPLAY format. This is why we will store in tables only the pertinent data fields from the incoming record. It would be a total waste of your time and of computer memory to store unneeded or FILLER fields.

3. What do I do when I want to use a table but don't know how many elements there will be?

   Answer
   Well, you have hit upon one of the major problems concerning tables. Assuming you have a rough idea of the number of items, you can make that table larger than necessary. For example, if you think there may be 80 or 90 elements to deal with, you could play it safe by saying OCCURS 100 times. This is a perfectly acceptable way of programming since you are under no obligation to use all the space allotted. During the read-in phase of your program you can set up a counter and actually count the elements as they

come in. Then, future loops in your pattern can be executed "counter" times. This method is not as strange as it may seem because you might have a situation where the number of elements within the table vary with each execution of the program.

The problem with making the OCCURS entry too large is that it allocates memory that might be used for more important reasons. You can guess fairly close on the OCCURS and then, if your guess was too small, make the table larger. The fact that the table was too small will be detected by a run-time error; it will not be detected during compilation of your program.

4. Must I use SEARCH and SEARCH ALL with tables?

Answer
The answer to your question is both yes and no. No, you don't have to use the SEARCH statement because it is very easy to implement the SEARCH and SET actions by other simple COBOL statements such as MOVE, ADD, SUBTRACT, and IF.

The second part of the answer is that since SEARCH ALL is a binary rather than a sequential search, it would be very much to your benefit to take advantage of the actions of the SEARCH ALL verb.

5. Can you give me another example of the use of two-dimensional tables?

Answer
Certainly. One of the most common uses of tables is the calculation of payroll. Probably, the master payroll file will *not* contain an employee's actual salary amount. Instead, as in the case of many governmental workers, we will store the employee's job class and job step. For example, we may have five salary steps within the Clerk I category and another five steps for Clerk II, Supervisor I, and so on. The weekly or monthly payroll calculations are made by getting the employee job class and job step from the master record and using this information to access a salary amount in a two-dimensional salary table. The nice feature about this method is that across-the-board pay changes can be made on the relatively few elements in the pay table rather than on the individual employee master pay record.

Exercises

1. Write the COBOL entries to set up the following *one-dimensional* tables.
   a. A table called RETURNS that consists of 50, 4-digit numeric values in DISPLAY format.
   b. A table called SALES-AMT consisting of 50 packed numeric values in the format 9999V99.
   c. A 70-element alphabetic table consisting of EMPLOYEE-NAMES PIC A(20).
   d. A 60-element table called TABLE-INFO that consists of two fields: AMOUNT-IN PIC 9(4) and ITEM-DESCRIPTION PIC X(30).
   e. Same as d above, but AMOUNT-IN is to be in packed format.
   f. A 10-element table called TABLE-DATA that consists of four fields: SS-NBR PIC 9(9) packed format, E-NAME PIC X(30), RATE PIC S99V999 packed format, and HOURS PIC S99.

2. Write the COBOL entries to do the following. Use the table names you set up in the previous exercise. Assume that a field called COUNTER has been established with a beginning value of 1.
   a. Clear the RETURNS table to zero.
   b. Fill the RETURNS table with nines.
   c. Move zeros to the numeric fields in the tables you set up in Exercise 1f above.

3. Write the statements to do the following calculations.
   a. Calculate and place the answer to the following in the location ANS (5) (use COMPUTE): $A^2 + B^2$
   b. Calculate the answer to the above formula and place the answer in the Jth element of the ANS table (use COMPUTE).
   c. Sum the values found in the first three elements of the SALES table and place the answer in TOTAL.
   d. Add 6 to the value found in ANS (7) (use ADD).
   e. Add 1.3 to the value found in the xth element of the table called AMOUNT (use the COMPUTE statement).

4. Create a 4-element table called TABLE-1 that contains the following values (use REDEFINES): 6.75, 9.42, 8.56, and 1.49.

5. Assume that incoming card records have the following format:

Card Column	Field Description
1–40	Blank
41–45	Part number PIC 9(5)
46–48	Bin number PIC 9(3)
49–60	Blank
61–66	Cost price PIC 9(4)V99
67–70	Quantity on hand 9(4)
71–74	Orders 9(4)
75–80	Blank

    a. Write the program segment to set up the above numeric fields in five separate, one-dimensional tables. Assuming that there are 40 card records, place the numeric values in the tables.

    b. Change 5a above so that the table consists of five fields.

6. Using the tables from 5a above, write the PROCEDURE DIVISION entries to sum the ORDERS amounts from the table. Do not use PERFORM VARYING.

7. Change Exercise 6 so you *do* use PERFORM VARYING.

8. Set up the following two-dimensional tables.

    a. A ten-year temperature table consisting of 365 elements down by 10 elements across—PIC 999V9.

    b. DISPLAY the temperature for the 312th day of the 7th year.

    c. DISPLAY the temperature for the xth day of the Rth year.

    d. Change the temperature table so that it consists of 10 elements down and 365 elements across.

9. In the previous chapter you wrote a program in which you searched through a tape file several times looking for a particular department number. At the time it was pointed out that this was an inefficient way to do things. Now, you are to use one-dimensional tables in the solution to that problem. You may assume that Data File B contains 25 records of data. Do not use the SEARCH capabilities of COBOL.

10. For this problem you are to use Data File A (25 records on tape, blocked 5). The record format for this problem is as follows.

Field	Characters	Type
Filler	8	——
Name	20	Alphabetic
YTD Sales	7	Numeric dollars and cents, display format
Filler	7	——

Write a program that stores the above data in appropriate tables. Then, using IF, go through the table and print out the names of those salespeople whose YTD sales are greater than $6000.

11. Modify Exercise 10 to use the SEARCH, SET, and INDEXED BY statements. (*Note:* This table is not in sorted order.)

Chapter 12

Sorting

One of the most common operations performed in any data processing installation is sorting. By sorting, of course, we mean changing the order of the data records (as they now exist) to a different order that will make further processing more efficient. For example, it may be desirable to take an unordered student enrollment file and put it into ascending order based on the student identification number field or student name field. Sorting can be either numeric or alphabetic, and can place a file into descending order if that is appropriate to the application.

As indicated above, we can base our sort operation upon a single field (known as the key field), but multiple fields can be used as well. Customer charge amounts that had been accumulated for the past week might have to be sorted into ascending customer number order *within* the date-charged field. Sorting can be as simple or as complex as you wish, but it is a very common programming task with which you should be familiar. Before getting to the sorting capabilities of COBOL, let's consider a few more aspects of this operation.

Some sorting techniques

In general, sorting can be done internally or externally. Internal sorting is done by placing the data into a table (as discussed in Chapter 11) and then processing through them repeatedly until the data records are in the desired order. Some of the techniques involve what is known as "bubble sorts" or "pair exchange sorts," but are generally limited to very small files (perhaps under a hundred items) because of the great amount of computer time required for the job. The process involves the comparison of two table values and the movement of the lower (or higher) value through the other elements until all elements within the table are in order. Obviously, the size of available memory is a major determinant of the size of the data file that can be accommodated.

Larger files are said to be sorted externally because the process makes extensive use of disk or tape files. Different methods may be used, but the technique often involves building "strings" of sorted records. For example, two records are read into memory, sorted into order, and then written onto an output tape or disk file. In turn, these strings of two records are sorted and merged into a string of four. The process continues until the entire file is sorted and the elements merged together, a task that normally involves the use of three or more tape or disk files.

Fortunately, you will not have to worry about the various sorting techniques since COBOL has a special SORT feature to do the job.

Sorting in COBOL

The SORT statement in COBOL is extremely powerful, but very easy to use. The programmer indicates the name of the (input) file to be sorted, the file where the sorting will take place (the sort work file), and the name of the (result) file that will contain the new, sorted records. In addition to identifying the files as outlined above, the programmer also specifies the key field or fields on which the sort will take place. For our example we will use the PAY-DATA file (Data File A). The file actually is in ascending order according to the employee identification number field (positions 1 through 9). However, in this case we will assume that we wish the file to be in alphabetic order based on the name field (positions 10 through 29). Figure 12-1 shows the file in its original condition—in order by the identification number field.

FIGURE 12-1

PAY-DATA File Listing

```
        ID NUMBER                    NAME

        010114101              SMITH ELBERT
        010116104              BARNHART STANLEY
        050124101              WALSH JUDITH
        050125395              PEARSON SAMUEL
        060443916              LEE KIMBERLY
        140133010              CHICANE HERB
        190456301              HARKELRODE CLARA
        220133512              KOCHINIS ANGELO
        230965777              RUSE WAYNE
        270134109              MOORE SAMUEL
        304165298              BILBERRY DALTON
        320135004              MARTIN SUSAN
        346945678              FUJIMOTO KEN
        350214101              STOLL GEORGE
        365593864              EVANS ROBERT
        410954321              GARCIA FRAN
        555438619              DEE ELLIS
        666666666              BRONSON PATTY
        684836197              ROSSI JACK
        745678432              JOHNSON PAM
   END OF FILE
```

To set up the sort operation we have to specify the various input, sort, and result files that will be needed.

```
    SELECT INPUT-FILE
        ASSIGN TO SYS010-UT-2400-S.
```

This is our payroll data file that is on tape and that will be used as the input data to the COBOL sort routine. Sorting, however, does not in any way hurt or destroy the INPUT-FILE. The SORT facility will copy the contents of the file onto the sort work file prior to starting the sort operation.

```
    SELECT SORT-FILE
        ASSIGN TO SYS001-DA-2314-S-SORTWK1
        ACCESS IS SEQUENTIAL.
```

This is a disk file onto which a copy of the INPUT-FILE will be written. The SORT verb will then cause this file to be sorted in accordance with instructions specified in the PROCEDURE DIVISION. After the sorting is complete, the newly sorted records will be written onto a tape file (RESULT-FILE). And, of course, we will need a printer file to print the results of the sort process.

```
SELECT RESULT-FILE
    ASSIGN TO SYS011-UT-2400-S.
SELECT PRINTER-FILE
    ASSIGN TO SYS009-UR-1403-S.
```

The DATA DIVISION entries are just what you would expect for the INPUT-FILE.

```
FD  INPUT-FILE
    LABEL RECORDS ARE STANDARD
    DATA RECORD IS PAY-DATA-IN.
01  PAY-DATA-IN.
    03  ID-NBR      PIC 9(9).
    03  NAME        PIC X(20).
    03  FILLER      PIC X(51).
```

The entry for SORT-FILE, however, has one small but very important change. Instead of the "FD" entry, we will now show it not as FD (File Description) but as SD for sort Description. This designation alerts the software that this is the file that will be acted upon by the SORT statement.

```
SD  SORT-FILE
    LABEL RECORDS ARE STANDARD
    DATA RECORD IS SORT-RECORD.
01  SORT-RECORD.
    03  ID-NBR-SORT-FILE     PIC 9(9).
    03  NAME-SORT-FILE       PIC X(20).
    03  FILLER               PIC X(51).
```

The sorted records will be written automatically to the RESULT-FILE, which is described with an FD entry.

```
FD  RESULT-FILE
    LABEL RECORDS ARE STANDARD
    DATA RECORD IS SORTED-RECORDS.
01  SORTED-RECORDS.
    03  ID-NBR-RESULT-FILE     PIC 9(9).
    03  NAME-RESULT-FILE       PIC X(20).
    03  FILLER                 PIC X(51).
```

The SORT statement

The basic format of the SORT statement (in which file-name-1 must be a file identified with an SD entry) is outlined below.

$$\underline{\text{SORT}} \text{ file-name-1 } \underline{\text{ON}} \left\{ \frac{\text{ASCENDING}}{\text{DESCENDING}} \right\} \underline{\text{KEY}} \text{ data-name-1}$$
$$\underline{\text{USING}} \text{ file-name-2}$$
$$\underline{\text{GIVING}} \text{ file-name-3.}$$

In the example we have set up, file-name-1 is our SORT-FILE as described with an SD entry; file-name-2 is the INPUT-FILE; and file-name-3 is the RESULT-FILE that will contain the data records in sorted order. The sort itself will take place on the NAME-SORT-FILE field and the results are to be in ASCENDING order based on this key (field).

```
SORT SORT-FILE ON ASCENDING KEY NAME-SORT-FILE
    USING INPUT-FILE
    GIVING RESULT-FILE.
```

The complete program to sort our payroll data is shown in Figure 12-2. Note that, as compared to Figure 12-1, the names are now in alphabetic order from A to Z. If we had specified DESCENDING in the SORT statement, the order would have been reversed (Figure 12-3).

Pseudocode Specifications: SORT ASCENDING

```
CONTROL-ROUTINE
    PERFORM SORT-ROUTINE
    PERFORM 010-STARTING-PROCEDURE
    PERFORM 020-READ-AND-WRITE UNTIL end of file
    indicator = 1
    PERFORM 030-END-ROUTINE
    STOP RUN

SORT-ROUTINE
    Sort ascending name field
    Open the files

010-STARTING-PROCEDURE
    Write heading line
    Read sorted record at end move 1 to end of file indicator

020-READ-AND-WRITE
    Move fields to print area
    Write report line on printer
    Read sorted record at end move 1 to end of file indicator

030-END-ROUTINE
    Close the files
```

FIGURE 12-2

SORT ASCENDING

```
IDENTIFICATION DIVISION.
PROGRAM-ID. SORTING.
ENVIRONMENT DIVISION.
CONFIGURATION SECTION.
SOURCE-COMPUTER. IBM-360-F30.
OBJECT-COMPUTER. IBM-360-F30.
SPECIAL-NAMES.
    C01 IS TOP-OF-PAGE.
INPUT-OUTPUT SECTION.
FILE-CONTROL.
    SELECT INPUT-FILE ASSIGN TO SYS010-UT-2400-S.
    SELECT SORT-FILE ASSIGN TO SYS001-DA-2314-S-SORTWK1
        ACCESS IS SEQUENTIAL.
    SELECT RESULT-FILE ASSIGN TO SYS011-UT-2400-S.
    SELECT PRINTER-FILE ASSIGN TO SYS009-UR-1403-S.
```

```
DATA DIVISION.
FILE SECTION.
FD  INPUT-FILE
    LABEL RECORDS ARE STANDARD
    DATA RECORD IS PAY-DATA-IN.
01  PAY-DATA-IN.
    03  ID-NBR                      PIC 9(9).
    03  NAME                        PIC X(20).
    03  FILLER                      PIC X(51).
SD  SORT-FILE
    LABEL RECORDS ARE STANDARD
    DATA RECORD IS SORT-RECORD.
01  SORT-RECORD.
    03  ID-NBR-SORT-FILE            PIC 9(9).
    03  NAME-SORT-FILE              PIC X(20).
    03  FILLER                      PIC X(51).
FD  RESULT-FILE
    LABEL RECORDS ARE STANDARD.
    DATA RECORD IS SORTED-RECORDS.
01  SORTED-RECORDS.
    03  ID-NBR-RESULT-FILE          PIC 9(9).
    03  NAME-RESULT-FILE            PIC X(20).
    03  FILLER                      PIC X(51).
FD  PRINTER-FILE
    LABEL RECORDS ARE OMITTED
    DATA RECORD IS OUTPUT-LINE.
01  OUTPUT-LINE                     PIC X(121).
WORKING-STORAGE SECTION.
77  EOF-INDICATOR                   PIC 9 VALUE ZERO.
01  HEADING-LINE.
    03  FILLER                      PIC X.
    03  FILLER                      PIC X(10) VALUE SPACES.
    03  FILLER                      PIC X(9) VALUE 'ID NUMBER'.
    03  FILLER                      PIC X(14) VALUE SPACES.
    03  FILLER                      PIC X(4) VALUE 'NAME'.
    03  FILLER                      PIC X(83) VALUE SPACES.
01  DATA-OUT.
    03  FILLER                      PIC X.
    03  FILLER                      PIC X(10) VALUE SPACES.
    03  ID-NBR-OUT                  PIC 9(9).
    03  FILLER                      PIC X(10) VALUE SPACES.
    03  NAME-OUT                    PIC X(20).
    03  FILLER                      PIC X(71) VALUE SPACES.
```

```
PROCEDURE DIVISION.
CONTROL-ROUTINE.
    PERFORM SORT-ROUTINE.
    PERFORM 010-STARTING-PROCEDURE.
    PERFORM 020-READ-AND-WRITE
        UNTIL EOF-INDICATOR = 1.
    PERFORM 030-END-ROUTINE.
    STOP RUN.
SORT-ROUTINE.
    SORT SORT-FILE ON ASCENDING KEY
        NAME-SORT-FILE
            USING INPUT-FILE
            GIVING RESULT-FILE.
    OPEN INPUT RESULT-FILE
        OUTPUT PRINTER-FILE.
010-STARTING-PROCEDURE.
    WRITE OUTPUT-LINE
        FROM HEADING-LINE
            AFTER ADVANCING TOP-OF-PAGE.
    MOVE SPACES TO OUTPUT-LINE.
    WRITE OUTPUT-LINE AFTER ADVANCING 2 LINES.
    READ RESULT-FILE
        AT END MOVE 1 TO EOF-INDICATOR.
020-READ-AND-WRITE.
    MOVE ID-NBR-RESULT-FILE TO ID-NBR-OUT.
    MOVE NAME-RESULT-FILE TO NAME-OUT.
    WRITE OUTPUT-LINE FROM DATA-OUT
        AFTER ADVANCING 1 LINES.
    READ RESULT-FILE
        AT END MOVE 1 TO EOF-INDICATOR.
030-END-ROUTINE.
    CLOSE RESULT-FILE, PRINTER-FILE.
```

ID NUMBER	NAME
010116104	BARNHART STANLEY
304165298	BILBERRY DALTON
666666666	BRONSON PATTY
140133010	CHICANE HERB
555438619	DEE ELLIS
365593864	EVANS ROBERT
346945678	FUJIMOTO KEN
410954321	GARCIA FRAN
190456301	HARKELRODE CLARA
745678432	JOHNSON PAM
220133512	KOCHINIS ANGELO
060443916	LEE KIMBERLY
320135004	MARTIN SUSAN
270134109	MOORE SAMUEL
050125395	PEARSON SAMUEL
684836197	ROSSI JACK
230965777	RUSE WAYNE
010114101	SMITH ELBERT
350214101	STOLL GEORGE
050124101	WALSH JUDITH

FIGURE 12-3

SORT DESCENDING

```
      PROCEDURE DIVISION.
      CONTROL-ROUTINE.
          PERFORM SORT-ROUTINE.
          PERFORM 010-STARTING-PROCEDURE.
          PERFORM 020-READ-AND-WRITE
              UNTIL EOF-INDICATOR = 1.
          PERFORM 030-END-ROUTINE.
          STOP RUN.
      SORT-ROUTINE.
          SORT SORT-FILE ON DESCENDING KEY
              NAME-SORT-FILE
                  USING INPUT-FILE
                  GIVING RESULT-FILE.
```

ID NUMBER	NAME
050124101	WALSH JUDITH
350214101	STOLL GEORGE
010114101	SMITH ELBERT
230965777	RUSE WAYNE
684836197	ROSSI JACK
050125395	PEARSON SAMUEL
270134109	MOORE SAMUEL
320135004	MARTIN SUSAN
060443916	LEE KIMBERLY
220133512	KOCHINIS ANGELO
745678432	JOHNSON PAM
190456301	HARKELRODE CLARA
410954321	GARCIA FRAN
346945678	FUJIMOTO KEN
365593864	EVANS ROBERT
555438619	DEE ELLIS
140133010	CHICANE HERB
666666666	BRONSON PATTY
304165298	BILBERRY DALTON
010116104	BARNHART STANLEY

Sort operations

If you haven't already done so, take a close look at the sorting operation that was just shown in Figures 12-2 and 12-3. We "triggered" into the operation by setting up the appropriate files and by using the SORT verb. Notice what the system does for us.

1. The SORT software *automatically* OPENs the input file, the sort work file, and the result file. As a matter of fact, we *cannot* open these files—to do so would be an error.
2. The contents of the input file—that is, the file to be sorted—are copied onto the sort work file.
3. The sort work file is sorted according to the specifications given in the SORT statement (ASCENDING KEY or DESCENDING KEY).
4. The sorted contents of the sort work file are copied onto the result file.
5. All three files are automatically CLOSEd at the end of the SORT operation.

Figure 12-4 diagrams the basic SORT operation as described above. Note that after the SORT statement was executed, the RESULT-FILE was OPENed in the same way that you would handle any regular input file.

FIGURE 12-4

SORT Operation Physical Data Flow

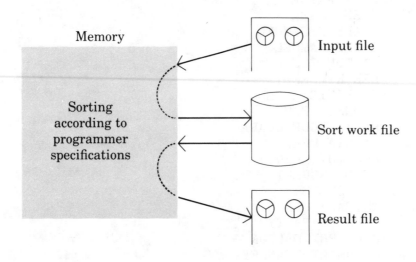

However, there is one additional point you should be aware of. We specified a single sort work file (SORT-FILE) for the sort operation. But, as described earlier in the chapter, the process of sorting commonly requires the use of *several* files. The sort software takes care of this by perhaps using several files for the actual sort process, but usually requires you to set up only one file as we did in this program.

As indicated earlier, it is possible to have records sorted on the basis of multiple fields simply by specifying these fields in the SORT statement. The fields must be listed according to the desired order of sorting. For example, to sort customer charge records into ascending date order *within* ascending customer number order, we would specify the following:

```
SORT
    ON ASCENDING KEY CUSTOMER-NBR
        ASCENDING KEY DATE-FIELD
    USING _____
    GIVING _____ .
```

A more complex version of SORT is also available to COBOL users. Its use is beyond the scope of this text, but at least you should be aware that it exists. The SORT operations described so far are very simple for the programmer to use, but are very inflexible in that the data records cannot be manipulated either on the way into memory from the input file or on the way out to the result file. The INPUT and OUTPUT PROCEDURE options of the SORT statement allow the programmer to manipulate data fields within the records before or after the sort operation.

Common errors

Since the basic SORT operation in COBOL is so straightforward, there is little chance of making an error. The one area that may cause some concern is the proper SELECT entry for the sort work file. On many systems there may be a very specific name and entry required for the file on which the sort will take place, so check your machine to be certain. Also, be sure to check the job control cards your system requires for a sort operation. In some cases you may have to inform the system of the size of the file to be sorted and the length of the records used.

The sample sort programs shown in Figures 12-2 and 12-3 used magnetic tape input and output files that were in unblocked format—that is, one record per block. Either or both of these files could be in blocked format and still be processed by the SORT software. For example, the INPUT-FILE could have been blocked 3 and RESULT-FILE might have been blocked something other than 3 without any change in the SORT operation. Also, we could have had any combination of magnetic disk and/or magnetic tape files for input, sorting, or output, although a disk would be more appropriate for the sort work file.

Problem-Solving Techniques

At various places in the past chapters you were told about some techniques that could be used if your program wouldn't work. Reevaluation of the design logic and disk checking the program statements are two methods you may have had to use already. Beyond this, however, there are some other problem-solving aids that are available and that depend more on the computer system software than on your abilities to locate errors.

Most computer systems have either specific diagnostic software for a particular language such as COBOL, or generalized software to help locate program errors. In COBOL one such software aid is called READY TRACE, and when this statement is inserted in your program, it will print a listing of the modules that were executed and the sequence of the execution. (Check with your instructor or the operator of your computer system to see exactly how this or a similar routine should be used on your system.)

If you wanted to check the flow of control throughout your entire program, the READY TRACE statement could be inserted in the CONTROL-MODULE paragraph.

```
PROCEDURE DIVISION.
CONTROL-MODULE.
    READY TRACE.
    PERFORM 010-OPENER.
    .
    .
    .
```

If you are concerned about the action of a particular module rather than the entire program, the READY TRACE statement can be inserted wherever you wish. Obviously the execution of READY TRACE takes valuable computer time, so its use should not be abused. In addition, you may not wish to continue the trace action beyond a particular point in the program. If this is so, the RESET TRACE entry will terminate the tracking action. One common practice is to insert READY TRACE just before entering the suspected paragraph and to use RESET TRACE immediately afterward.

```
    .
    .
    .

    READY TRACE.
    PERFORM CALCULATION-ROUTINE
        UNTIL _____
    RESET TRACE.
    .
    .
    .
```

Self-Study: Questions and Answers

1. The text talks about the constant need for sorting, but I don't understand why it is so important.

Answer

Data records that are in a random or unsorted order are difficult and inefficient to work with. You saw examples of this in an earlier chapter when we tried to match weekly payroll records with the corresponding record on the master tape file. If either or both files are in random order, we have to use a "brute force" approach to finding the matching record. By "brute force" we mean that you read through the master file until the matching record is found. Then, the master file must be closed and reopened in order to find the match to the next detail record. This approach may be feasible for small files, but the repeated opening and closing of files—particularly tape files—is very time consuming.

The alternative—sorting both files and then performing a sophisticated matching operation based on sorted files—is also expensive in that the sort operation does take computer time. However, it is usually far more efficient to work with sorted rather than with unsorted files, and in the "real world" most files are sorted prior to being processed.

2. How will I know when to do an internal sort as opposed to an external sort?

Answer

The text gave a rough rule-of-thumb that files with more than 100 records should be sorted externally. Under 100, it may be worthwhile to sort the records within a table. The most practical answer to the question is that a rule on this—based upon the strengths and weaknesses of your computer system—probably will have been established wherever you work.

Also, remember that when we say "external" sorting we actually mean that the sorting itself takes place in memory, but that the sorted records are ultimately stored on the sort work file. When sorting in tables, the data records remain inside memory.

Another point you may wish to consider is that the external SORT software, as shown in the chapter, already exists. If you wish to do an internal table sort, you will have to develop your own algorithm for the job.

3. Do I have to use the file names of SORT-FILE, INPUT-FILE, and RESULT-FILE? You seem to have used these names throughout the chapter.

Answer

Normally, you can use any names you want for the input, sort work, and result files. The only limitation is that your particular computer system may require a specific file name for the sort work file. The most likely situation is that you may choose any names you wish for the files, but may have to have a specific entry for the ASSIGN part of the sort work file entry.

Exercises

1. Explain the difference between internal and external sorting.

2. Under what conditions would you want to sort internally? When would you want to sort externally? Give an example of each use.

3. Assume you have three data values coming in from cards. Design the program and draw the flowchart for the steps necessary to put these values into ascending order. You are not to use a table, and each value is to be considered and tested as it enters from the card reader. Use the fields called LARGEST, SECOND-LARGEST, and THIRD-LARGEST for the sorted values. If necessary, use the fields HOLD-1 and HOLD-2 for temporary data storage.

4. Modify the previous exercise so that all the values are read into a table before sorting begins.

5. Modify Exercise 4 so that the values are placed in descending rather than ascending order.

6. If you did both Exercises 4 and 5, you are aware of the slight difference between the plans. Now, modify the plan still further so that the sort sequence (ascending or descending) can be determined just before the process is executed. (*Hint:* Try using a programmed switch.)

7. Although the text did not cover it in any detail, reference was made to an internal sorting technique called a bubble sort. Design a plan and flowchart that first reads five values into a table and then sorts these values into ascending order by "bubbling" the highest number up to the top. Multiple tables may be used in this exercise.

8. Describe in general terms the action of the computer system during an external sort operation.

9. Data File A (PAY-DATA) is stored on tape, blocked 5, and contains the following data fields:

Field	Length
ID Number	9 digits
Employee Name	20 characters
Filler	1 character
Rate of Pay	4 digits, dollars and cents
Number of Dependents	2 digits
Filler	19 characters

Write a program to list the contents of the file in ascending order based on the Rate of Pay field. Note that you will have to total the rates of pay and calculate the average pay rate. Output will be as follows:

```
                EMPLOYEE PAY RATES

   NAME    ID NUMBER    RATE    NUMBER OF DEPENDENTS




        TOTAL NUMBER OF EMPLOYEES   _____
        AVERAGE HOURLY PAY RATE     _____
```

10. Assume that Data File B (SALES-DATA) is on tape, is blocked 2, and contains the following data fields:

Field	Length
Sales Territory	3 digits
ID Number	5 digits
Name	20 characters
YTD Sales	7 digits, dollars and cents
UTD Sales Returns	6 digits, dollars and cents

Write a program to sort the file into ascending order based on the 3-digit sales territory field. After the file has been sorted, provide for printer output of those employees who have net year-to-date sales of over 1000 dollars. Output will have the following format:

```
                EMPLOYEE LISTING

   SALES TERRITORY    NAME  ID NUMBER  NET YTD SALES




   NUMBER OF RECORDS PROCESSED _____
```

11. Modify Exercise 9 so that the output records are in ascending order by Number of Dependents within the Rate of Pay field. The output format will be the same.

12. Modify Exercise 10 so that the data records are sorted into descending order of YTD Sales within ascending Sales Territory number. The output format will be the same.

Chapter 13

Magnetic Disk Processing

You are now ready to move on to a new storage medium—magnetic disk. Most large computer installations are likely to have both magnetic tape and disk drives attached to the computer system because the combination provides for operational flexibility. This chapter will not cover all aspects of disk usage, but will allow you to do simple disk operations.

Introduction to magnetic disk

In many ways, a magnetic disk is very similar to a magnetic tape. Data are recorded in the form of tiny magnetized spots on the surface of the disk. The reading part of the read/write heads detects the presence of spots, while the writing portion of the units records the spots on the thin iron-oxide coating. As with tape, reading does not harm the data in any way, but writing onto a disk is destructive since the new material is written over the old disk data.

Disk characteristics

Many varieties of disk storage units are available today, but they generally share similar characteristics. The disks resemble phonograph records and often are arranged in a stacked order, as shown in Figure 13-1. The metal disks are extremely smooth and are coated with a very thin layer of iron oxide. The figure also shows that read/write heads on the end of access arms can read or record data on both sides of the platters.

FIGURE 13-1

Stacked Disks

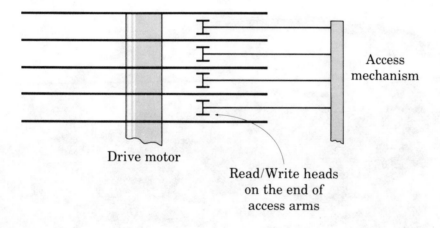

Drive motor

Access
mechanism

Read/Write heads
on the end of
access arms

Figure 13-2 shows a slightly different disk arrangement in which storage consists of a single platter. Usually the platter or set of platters that makes up disk storage is called a *disk pack* and can be removed from the *disk drive* and replaced in less than a minute (Figure 13-3). Magnetic tape, of course, has the same advantage so that auxiliary tape and disk storage is almost unlimited in size.

FIGURE 13-2

Single Disk Platter

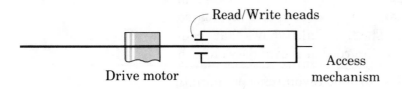

Read/Write heads

Drive motor

Access mechanism

FIGURE 13-3. *Removable Disk Pack.* (Courtesy of International Business Machines Corporation.)

From the previous figures you can see that the access arms all move in or out across the disk surfaces together. However, only one read/write head is activated at any one moment so that reading or writing takes place on only one part of the disk surface at any time.

On "hard" disks (as opposed to what are known as "soft," or "floppy," disks), the read/write heads do not touch the disk but are extremely close to the surface. A disk drive is a precision instrument—a point particularly evident when you realize that the platter is rotating at a constant speed of close to 3000 revolutions per minute while the access arms are going in and out to read or write information. A dreaded "head crash" occurs when the read/write heads actually make contact with the surface. When this happens not only are the data lost, but part of the disk drive electronics may be destroyed as well.

Soft, or "Floppy," Disks

A relative newcomer to auxiliary storage media are the soft or "floppy" disks brought out in 1972. Called Diskettes by IBM, the flexible disks are enclosed in a hard plastic cover that has openings for the drive spindle and access mechanism (Figure 13-4). After their introduction, they began to be used as a cheap auxiliary storage medium for intelligent terminals, office word processing systems, and microcomputers. The original floppies could record data on one side only, but the newer version, called "flippies," can record on both sides. Technical improvements over the years have pushed storage capacity to over one million characters per floppy disk.

FIGURE 13-4. *Small Computer System with Floppy Disk.*
(Courtesy of International Business Machines Corporation.)

The soft disks differ from the traditional hard disks in one very important aspect. On soft disks the read/write heads actually touch the disk surface. The contact point is lubricated, but after a specific number of revolutions the disk becomes worn and must be discarded (after copying the data onto a new floppy). The disks are relatively cheap (about $5–$6) but not particularly usable for large data files or files that have a great amount of read/write activity.

Disk addressing

So far, a magnetic disk has been very similar to magnetic tape, but we now come to the major point of difference. Tape, as you will recall from an earlier chapter, is a sequential access device in that access to a particular record is accomplished only by a sequential search through tape. Disk, on the other hand, is said to be a direct access device because we can go directly to a given location on the disk.

Much like the groove in a phonograph record, the surface of a disk consists of a series of smaller and smaller concentric circles called *tracks*. Each of these tracks has an address and can be directly referenced or accessed by the programmer. When reading or writing takes place, the access arms position the read/write heads directly above or below the track that the programmer addressed. Again, the precision of a disk unit may be appreciated when you realize that a track is thinner than the width of a pencil line and each track nearly touches the tracks on either side. The surface of a disk may contain anywhere from 100 to 800 tracks depending upon the size and type of disk. Also, each track holds the same amount of data with the data bits on the outer tracks being written slightly farther apart.

Figure 13-5 shows the general addressing structure of a single disk track. The track itself is identified by a series of bits that indicate the Home Address of that particular track. In a way, it is much like the numbering system used where you live—it indicates your street and house number. On a disk, the Home Address is coded to indicate the specific surface and track number, which means that each Home Address is unique to the disk addressing scheme. The diagram also illustrates the fact that many data records could be (and usually are) stored on one track. If this is done, then each record on the track is identified by means of some identifying bits written prior to the data bits. Just as with magnetic tape, gaps are used to separate the disk material.

FIGURE 13-5

Disk Track Format

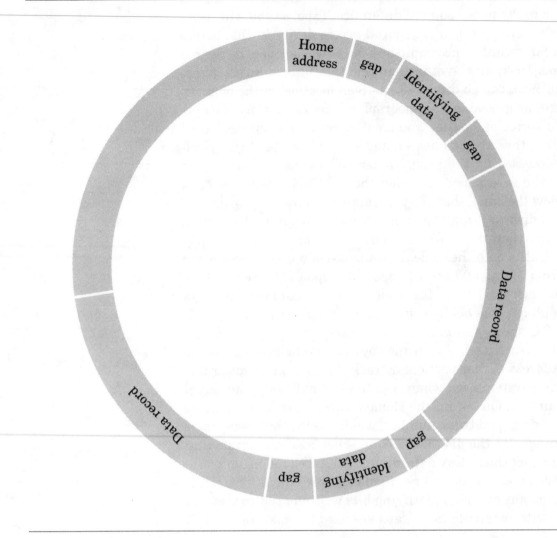

Another important disk concept is the idea of *cylinders*. Figure 13-3 showed that data records are written around the track surface. On first thought, it would seem that after filling one track area, you would then go to the next adjacent track for the storage of additional data records. Normally, this is not done because it would require a movement of the access arms. Instead, the programmer tries to avoid this time delay (called "access time") by using the "cylinder concept."

By definition, the same track on each disk surface is known as a cylinder. Thus, track 67 on each of the disk surfaces comprises cylinder 67. When writing the data onto a disk, the programmer will fill track 67 on disk surface 1, then go to track 67 on disk surface 2, and so on. The access arms will only be moved when cylinder 67 is full (Figure 13-6).

FIGURE 13-6

Disk Cylinders

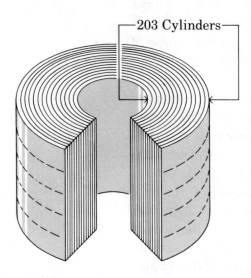

Many of the newer disk drives have much faster access times because they have eliminated some of the time delay associated with the reading or writing of disk records. Disk access time is comprised of two parts: access arm movement time and rotational delay time. Other than speeding up the disk drive motor, we cannot do much to cut down on the time it takes for the home address and the data record to come under the read/write heads. However, manufacturers have done something about the time it takes to move the access arms in or out.

As opposed to the traditional "moving head disk," some new disks have "fixed heads" positioned over every track on every surface. Arm movement delay has been eliminated entirely at the cost of a much more expensive disk pack. The fixed heads are contained within the removable pack and are carefully matched to the characteristics of the disk platter. In addition to the time savings, one added bonus is the considerable reduction (if not total elimination) of disk head crashes.

Using magnetic disk

Earlier we said that a disk is a direct access storage medium. Although this statement is correct, the nature of a disk is such that the programmer has the choice of using a disk as either a direct access or as a sequential access device.

Sequential access

When a disk is used in a purely sequential manner, the programming is almost identical to that shown in the chapter on magnetic tape. However, there is one important difference between disk and tape that should be apparent by now. When creating a *tape* file, the system automatically begins writing the records/blocks at the beginning of the tape. On a disk you can start anywhere on a particular cylinder, although the normal procedure would be to start at the beginning of the cylinder. The choice of the starting point of the file and the number of cylinders the file will occupy is often communicated to the system software by means of specific disk job control cards or operator console actions. As before, the new file is given a file name and the software will record the file name, beginning cylinder number, and file extent. Depending upon the sophistication of the system software, the *user* of a sequential disk file need only know the file name, not its actual disk location. As with tape, disk records may or may not be blocked depending upon the requirements of the problem. A program to create a sequential disk file is shown in skeletal form in Figure 13-7. Regular 80-column card records are read in and written onto the disk in unblocked form.

FIGURE 13-7

Creating a Sequential Disk File

```
      SELECT INPUT-CARD-FILE ASSIGN TO _____ .
      SELECT DISK-FILE ASSIGN TO _____ .
          ACCESS IS SEQUENTIAL.
  FD  DISK-FILE
      LABEL RECORDS ARE STANDARD
      DATA RECORD IS DISK-DATA.
        .
        .
        .
```

```
PROCEDURE DIVISION.
CONTROL-MODULE.
    PERFORM 010-OPENER.
    PERFORM 020-WRITE-ROUTINE
        UNTIL EOF-INDICATOR = 1.
        .
        .
        .
010-OPENER.
    OPEN INPUT INPUT-CARD-FILE
        OUTPUT DISK-FILE.
    READ INPUT-CARD-FILE
        AT END MOVE 1 TO EOF-INDICATOR.
020-WRITE-ROUTINE.
    MOVE  Card fields to disk record area
    WRITE DISK-DATA
        INVALID KEY
            DISPLAY 'DISK AREA FULL' UPON CONSOLE
            CLOSE FILES
            STOP RUN.
    READ INPUT-CARD-FILE
        AT END MOVE 1 TO EOF-INDICATOR.
```

Two new entries appear in the sample program. The first—ACCESS IS SEQUENTIAL or ACCESS MODE IS SEQUENTIAL—is simply informing the system of the method of access. The 1968 version of ANS COBOL provided for an additional entry of PROCESSING MODE IS SEQUENTIAL while 1974 ANS COBOL changed the entry to ORGANIZATION IS SEQUENTIAL. Disk applications have undergone many changes through the various versions of COBOL and you should check the manual for the acceptable or required entries for disk processing on your machine.

Remember that in this example we are creating a straight sequential file on magnetic disk. Therefore, the system-name part of the ASSIGN entry must reflect this sequential format. A typical IBM system name entry for this type of file would be as follows:

```
SYSXXX-UT-2314-S.
```

Note that it is described as a UT or Utility device that is used Sequentially (S).

The next change is in the PROCEDURE DIVISION WRITE statement, which has the additional entry of INVALID KEY. ANS 68 COBOL required this entry, but it has been deleted from the 1974 version. If used, the INVALID KEY clause is executed when the programmer attempts to write beyond the disk space allocated. The most usual response to this situation would be to display an appropriate message or to PERFORM the statements within an error routine. At the discretion of the programmer, the program may or may not be terminated.

The user of this sequential disk file READs the file data, and the READ statement, as with all sequential files, must contain the AT END clause. Just as with magnetic tape, the AT END part of the statement will be activated when your sequential READ encounters an end of file mark that was written by the system when the disk file was created.

The SELECT entry will contain the same ACCESS IS SEQUENTIAL entry, as shown in Figure 13-7. Although the example showed that the data records were unblocked, blocking would be far more efficient and would be accomplished by the usual BLOCK CONTAINS entry in the FD file description. Also, as indicated earlier, the user of the file would have to know the disk file name and possibly the cylinders used before being able to use the file.

Indexed sequential files

The sequential use of a disk file is necessary, but has its limitations in that you are not making use of the major advantage of a disk, which is its capability for random access. The best of both worlds would be to have an auxiliary storage device that offers both sequential and random access capability, and this is exactly what an Indexed Sequential file does.

The term "indexed" means that an index to the contents of the file will be built as the file itself is created. Fortunately, the programmer is not bothered with details of creating the index since it is "triggered" into by means of an entry in the SELECT statement. The entry itself may vary depending upon the level of the COBOL software and the machine being used. In some systems, the system name is sufficient to indicate an indexed file as the following example shows:

```
SELECT INDEXED-FILE
    ASSIGN TO SYSXXX-DA-2314-I
```

The DA letters establish it as a Direct Access file while the I indicates that the file will have an index. On some systems another entry—ORGANIZATION IS INDEXED—is also used. Our examples will show it in brackets to indicate that this entry may not be necessary on your system.

```
SELECT INDEXED-FILE
    ASSIGN TO SYSXXX-DA-2314-I
    [ORGANIZATION IS INDEXED]
```

We said earlier that the above entries will trigger into the software that will create an index to the records in the file you are creating. This index is based upon a KEY field within the data record. This field normally is something like Part Number, Customer Number, Social Security Number, and so on, and is chosen by the programmer. The programmer names and establishes the field within the DATA DIVISION and communicates this name to the software through the RECORD KEY entry in the SELECT statement.

```
SELECT INDEXED-FILE
    ASSIGN TO SYSXXX-DA-2314-I
    [ORGANIZATION IS INDEXED]
    RECORD KEY IS DISK-REC-ID.
```

Note that DISK-REC-ID is a field *within the disk* record. The value stored in that field is the key by which that data record will be stored, indexed, and retrieved. The COBOL software that creates the index to the disk data will go to this field (DISK-REC-ID) and use the value it contains to build the index. In general, the index contains the record key data and the disk area on which the record is stored. Schematically, the index will look as follows:

Record Key (Part Number)	Disk Location
0356	2001
1236	2002
2462	2003
3788	2004
5610	2005

The index itself is created in memory, but usually it is stored on the same disk as the data although large files may require that the index be stored on another direct access device. As with the disk *data* area, the disk index area usually is specified by means of job control cards. The illustration below shows this idea. However, remember that disk storage is always in terms of cylinders.

The data records being written to the disk file will be in sequential order, and writing onto specific disk areas is done sequentially from the starting disk location. This sequential mode of writing onto a disk is communicated to the software through another entry—ACCESS IS SEQUENTIAL—in the SELECT statement. Our complete SELECT now looks as follows:

```
SELECT INDEXED-FILE
    ASSIGN TO SYSXXX-DA-2314-I
    [ORGANIZATION IS INDEXED]
    RECORD KEY IS DISK-REC-ID
    ACCESS IS SEQUENTIAL.
```

Figure 13-8 is a skeletal COBOL program that creates an indexed sequential file from a file of 80-column IBM card records. We will assume that the card records contain inventory data and have the following format:

Part Name	Part Number	Quantity on Hand	Cost Price	Selling Price	etc.

The INVALID KEY part of the disk WRITE statement will be activated under three conditions.

1. Where the allocated disk space has been filled.
2. If there is a duplicate RECORD KEY value.
3. If the RECORD KEY value is out of sequence.

FIGURE 13-8

Creating an Indexed Sequential File

```
        SELECT INPUT-CARD FILE ASSIGN TO _____ .
        SELECT INDEXED-FILE
            ASSIGN TO SYSXXX-DA-2314-I
            [ORGANIZATION IS INDEXED]
            RECORD KEY IS DISK-REC-ID
            ACCESS IS SEQUENTIAL.
        .
        .
        .

    FD  INPUT-CARD FILE
        .
        .
        .
```

```
01  CARD-IN.
    03  PART-NAME    _____
    03  PART-NUMBER  _____
    .
    .
    .

FD  INDEXED-FILE
    .
    .
    .

01  DISK-RECORD.
    03  PART-NAME-DISK
    03  DISK-REC-ID
    03
    .
    .
    .

PROCEDURE DIVISION.
CONTROL-MODULE.
    PERFORM 010-OPENER.
    PERFORM 020-WRITE-INDEXED-FILE
        UNTIL EOF-INDICATOR = 1.
    .
    .
    .

010-OPENER.
    OPEN INPUT INPUT-CARD-FILE
        OUTPUT INDEXED-FILE.
    READ INPUT-CARD-FILE
        AT END MOVE 1 TO EOF-INDICATOR.
020-WRITE-INDEXED-FILE.
    Move card fields to disk record area
    (PART-NUMBER will be moved to DISK-REC-ID).
    WRITE DISK-RECORD
        INVALID KEY
            PERFORM DISK-ERROR-ROUTINE.
    READ INPUT-CARD-FILE
        AT END MOVE 1 TO EOF-INDICATOR.
    .
    .
    .
```

Sequential retrieval   Programming for *sequential* retrieval of data records in an indexed sequential file is essentially the same as that shown in Figure 13-8. The steps in the process are outlined below.

1. The disk file name and the locations of the disk index and disk data area are communicated to the software through control cards or operator entries.
2. The SELECT statement contains the same entries as before:

```
SELECT INDEXED-FILE
   ASSIGN TO SYSXXX-DA-2314-I
   [ORGANIZATION IS INDEXED]
   RECORD KEY IS DISK-REC-ID
   ACCESS IS SEQUENTIAL.
```

3. Since the file is being accessed sequentially, the disk READ statement must contain the AT END entry.
4. In the absence of any entry to the contrary, READing of the disk file records will begin with the first record in the file. When the disk file is OPENed, the software consults the index to find the disk location of the beginning record on the file.
5. During the READ loop operation, the system automatically goes to the next data record each time the READ statement is executed. As with magnetic tape, blocked records would be handled by the appropriate software called by the BLOCK CONTAINS entry.

Figure 13-9 is an example of sequential access of an indexed sequential disk file. Note that the RECORD KEY field is DISK-EMPLOYEE-NUMBER and that the READ DISK-FILE statement must contain the AT END entry.

FIGURE 13-9

Sequential Access: Indexed Sequential File

```
IDENTIFICATION DIVISION.
PROGRAM-ID. DISK-SEQ.
ENVIRONMENT DIVISION.
CONFIGURATION SECTION.
SOURCE-COMPUTER. IBM-360-F30.
OBJECT-COMPUTER. IBM-360-F30.
SPECIAL-NAMES.
    C01 IS TOP-OF-PAGE.
INPUT-OUTPUT SECTION.
FILE-CONTROL.
    SELECT DISK-FILE
        ASSIGN TO SYS080-DA-2314-I
        ACCESS IS SEQUENTIAL
        RECORD KEY IS DISK-EMPLOYEE-NUMBER.
    SELECT PRINT-FILE ASSIGN TO SYS009-UR-1403-S.
DATA DIVISION.
FILE SECTION.
FD  DISK-FILE
    LABEL RECORDS ARE STANDARD
    DATA RECORD IS DISK-RECORD.
01  DISK-RECORD.
    03  DISK-EMPLOYEE-NAME          PIC X(22).
    03  DISK-EMPLOYEE-NUMBER        PIC 9(8).
    03  FILLER                      PIC X(50).
FD  PRINT-FILE
    LABEL RECORDS ARE OMITTED
    DATA RECORD IS OUTPUT-RECORD.
01  OUTPUT-RECORD                   PIC X(121).
WORKING-STORAGE SECTION.
77  DISK-EOF-SWITCH                 PIC X(03) VALUE 'OFF'.
01  HEAD-LINE.
    03  FILLER                      PIC X.
    03  FILLER                      PIC X(17) VALUE SPACES.
    03  FILLER                      PIC X(04) VALUE 'NAME'.
    03  FILLER                      PIC X(21) VALUE SPACES.
    03  FILLER                      PIC X(06) VALUE 'NUMBER'.
    03  FILLER                      PIC X(72) VALUE SPACES.
01  MAIN-LINE.
    03  FILLER                      PIC X.
    03  FILLER                      PIC X(08) VALUE SPACES.
    03  EMP-NAME-PR                 PIC X(22).
    03  FILLER                      PIC X(11) VALUE SPACES.
    03  EMP-NBR-PR                  PIC 9(08).
    03  FILLER                      PIC X(71) VALUE SPACES.
```

```
PROCEDURE DIVISION.
CONTROL-MODULE.
    PERFORM 010-OPENER.
    PERFORM 020-PROCESS-DISK-DATA
        UNTIL DISK-EOF-SWITCH IS EQUAL TO ' ON'.
    PERFORM 030-CLOSER.
    STOP RUN.
010-OPENER.
    OPEN INPUT DISK-FILE OUTPUT PRINT-FILE.
    WRITE OUTPUT-RECORD FROM HEAD-LINE
        AFTER ADVANCING TOP-OF-PAGE.
    MOVE SPACES TO OUTPUT-RECORD.
    WRITE OUTPUT-RECORD AFTER ADVANCING 2 LINES.
    READ DISK-FILE
        AT END MOVE ' ON' TO DISK-EOF-SWITCH.
020-PROCESS-DISK-DATA.
    MOVE DISK-EMPLOYEE-NAME TO EMP-NAME-PR.
    MOVE DISK-EMPLOYEE-NUMBER TO EMP-NBR-PR.
    WRITE OUTPUT-RECORD FROM MAIN-LINE
        AFTER ADVANCING 1 LINES.
    READ DISK-FILE
        AT END MOVE ' ON' TO DISK-EOF-SWITCH.
030-CLOSER.
    CLOSE DISK-FILE PRINT-FILE.
```

```
        NAME                              NUMBER


    JONES,  JOHN                          12345600
    SMITH,  EDWARD                        12345601
    ANDERSON,  JEB                        12345602
    PERRY,  ALMA                          12345603
    ABERCROMBIE,  HARRY                   12345604
    THOMAS,  LORRAINE                     12345605
    CAESAR,  ANTHONY                      12345606
    REB,  JOHNNY                          12345607
    ABLE,  CHARLES                        12345608
    BAKER,  SIDNEY                        12345609
    JUAN,  DON                            12345610
    WATERLOO,  NAP                        12345611
    CRACKER,  GEORGE                      12345612
    WEEMS,  WANDA                         12345613
    PERCIVAL,  PERCIVAL                   12345614
    WONG,  SUSIE                          12345615
    CRUZ,  A.                             12345616
    BROWN,  TED                           12345617
    PLASTER,  JAMES                       12345618
    REED,  ROBERT                         12345619
    RATTER,  KENNETH                      12345620
    FOX,  ALBERT                          12345621
    COLE,  REX                            12345622
    JOHNSON,  CLAUDIA                     12345623
    ZINS,  NED                            12345624
```

Because the index contains the location of each disk record, the programmer has an additional option at his or her disposal when sequentially accessing an indexed sequential file. The system software assumes sequential retrieval to start at the beginning of the file only if not told otherwise. Instead, the NOMINAL KEY entry in the SELECT statement can cause sequential retrieval to start at any specified record. This entry simply names a field that will contain the key value at which the retrieval will begin. Normally this would be a field set up in WORKING-STORAGE to ACCEPT the value from the console, or it could come from any input device or be established by means of a VALUE entry. ACCEPTING the beginning key from the console would be the most flexible way of entering the starting record key, but any method will do.

A START statement is used to initialize the system to begin retrieval at a particular record in the disk file. (*Note:* START only positions the file for retrieval—it does not read in the data.) The INVALID KEY entry is executed if the system cannot find the start key in the index to the disk file. The format is

<u>START</u> file-name
       <u>INVALID</u> <u>KEY</u> imperative statements.

Figure 13-10 uses the same indexed file that was accessed in the previous program. In this problem the NOMINAL KEY field is called START-KEY and is set to the key value at which sequential retrieval will start.

FIGURE 13-10

Sequential Access: Indexed Sequential File—Different Starting Key

```
        IDENTIFICATION DIVISION.
        PROGRAM-ID. S-START.
        ****************************************
        *                                      *
        *    THIS PROGRAM USES THE START VERB  *
        *    TO BEGIN SEQUENTIAL RETRIEVAL AT  *
        *    A DIFFERENT STARTING POINT IN     *
        *    THE FILE.                         *
        *                                      *
        ****************************************
```

```
ENVIRONMENT DIVISION.
CONFIGURATION SECTION.
SOURCE-COMPUTER. IBM-360-F30.
OBJECT-COMPUTER. IBM-360-F30.
SPECIAL-NAMES
    C01 IS TOP-OF-PAGE.
INPUT-OUTPUT SECTION.
FILE-CONTROL.
    SELECT DISK-FILE
        ASSIGN TO SYS080-DA-2314-I
        ACCESS IS SEQUENTIAL
        NOMINAL KEY IS START-KEY
        RECORD KEY IS DISK-EMPLOYEE-NUMBER.
    SELECT PRINT-FILE ASSIGN TO SYS009-UR-1403-S.
DATA DIVISION.
FILE SECTION.
FD  DISK-FILE
    LABEL RECORDS ARE STANDARD
    DATA RECORD IS DISK-RECORD.
01  DISK-RECORD.
    03   DISK-EMPLOYEE-NAME          PIC X(22).
    03   DISK-EMPLOYEE-NUMBER        PIC 9(8).
    03   FILLER                      PIC X(50).
FD  PRINT-FILE
    LABEL RECORDS ARE OMITTED
    DATA RECORD IS OUTPUT-RECORD.
01  OUTPUT-RECORD                    PIC X(121).
WORKING-STORAGE SECTION.
77  START-KEY                        PIC 9(08) VALUE 12345608.
77  DISK-EOF-SWITCH                  PIC X(03) VALUE 'OFF'.
01  HEAD-LINE.
    03   FILLER                      PIC X.
    03   FILLER                      PIC X(17) VALUE SPACES.
    03   FILLER                      PIC X(04) VALUE 'NAME'.
    03   FILLER                      PIC X(21) VALUE SPACES.
    03   FILLER                      PIC X(06) VALUE 'NUMBER .
    03   FILLER                      PIC X(72) VALUE SPACES.
01  MAIN-LINE.
    03   FILLER                      PIC X.
    03   FILLER                      PIC X(08) VALUE SPACES.
    03   EMP-NAME-PR                  PIC X(22).
    03   FILLER                      PIC X(11) VALUE SPACES.
    03   EMP-NBR-PR                   PIC 9(08).
    03   FILLER                      PIC X(71) VALUE SPACES.
```

```
PROCEDURE DIVISION.
CONTROL-MODULE.
    PERFORM 010-OPENER.
    PERFORM 020-PROCESS-DISK-DATA
        UNTIL DISK-EOF-SWITCH IS EQUAL TO ' ON'.
    PERFORM 030-CLOSER.
    STOP RUN.
010-OPENER.
    OPEN INPUT DISK-FILE OUTPUT PRINT-FILE.
    WRITE OUTPUT-RECORD FROM HEAD-LINE
        AFTER ADVANCING TOP-OF-PAGE.
    MOVE SPACES TO OUTPUT-RECORD.
    WRITE OUTPUT-RECORD AFTER ADVANCING 2 LINES.
    START DISK-FILE
        INVALID KEY PERFORM ERROR-ROUTINE.
    READ DISK-FILE
        AT END MOVE ' ON' TO DISK-EOF-SWITCH.
020-PROCESS-DISK-DATA.
    MOVE DISK-EMPLOYEE-NAME TO EMP-NAME-PR.
    MOVE DISK-EMPLOYEE-NUMBER TO EMP-NBR-PR.
    WRITE OUTPUT-RECORD FROM MAIN-LINE
        AFTER ADVANCING 1 LINES.
    READ DISK-FILE
        AT END MOVE ' ON' TO DISK-EOF-SWITCH.
030-CLOSER.
    CLOSE DISK-FILE PRINT-FILE.
ERROR-ROUTINE.
    DISPLAY 'EMPLOYEE KEY NUMBER ' START-KEY
        'IS INCORRECT'.
    CLOSE DISK-FILE PRINT-FILE.
    STOP RUN.
```

NAME	NUMBER
ABLE, CHARLES	12345608
BAKER, SIDNEY	12345609
JUAN, DON	12345610
WATERLOO, NAP	12345611
CRACKER, GEORGE	12345612
WEEMS, WANDA	12345613
PERCIVAL, PERCIVAL	12345614
WONG, SUSIE	12345615
CRUZ, A.	12345616
BROWN, TED	12345617
PLASTER, JAMES	12345618
REED, ROBERT	12345619
RATTER, KENNETH	12345620
FOX, ALBERT	12345621
COLE, REX	12345622
JOHNSON, CLAUDIA	12345623
ZINS, NED	12345624

Random retrieval   You already know that the COBOL software establishes an index based on the record key field, and that the data record is stored on disk. The action of the software is very complex and beyond the scope of this text to explain, but a few additional points are in order at this time.

Although the actual terminology may vary from system to system, the indexes set up by the system generally are multilayered. For example, a Track Index records the record key and location of the data records stored on a particular disk surface of a particular disk track. When all the surfaces of a track (Track 45, for example) are filled, an entry is made in a Cylinder Index. When files get extremely large, it may be necessary to create an even higher level of index in order to reduce the time it takes to find the disk address of a specific data record.

In addition to specifying Data and Index Areas, the programmer may also have to specify an Overflow area. This point becomes important when you consider the nature and use of an indexed file as compared to a sequential file. A sequential file really cannot be updated. By that we mean new data records cannot be placed into their proper location in that file. For example, one cannot just slip record #25 into position between records #24 and #26. Instead, the sequential nature of the file dictates that a whole new sequential file be created just to add one more record.

With an indexed sequential file it is unnecessary to create a new file in order to include additional records. The index is changed to accommodate the addition or deletion of records from the file. The new record is inserted in its correct place and all following records are moved forward on the disk. An overflow area is used to take care of the storage and indexing of these added records. Again, the details of the software indexing method are beyond the scope of this book. Figure 13-11a shows the program logic in the form of a Warnier/Orr diagram and Figure 13-11b shows a traditional flowchart. Figure 13-12 is the complete program to randomly retrieve disk records from an indexed sequential file. In this example, data cards contain the NOMINAL KEY field that will trigger the disk retrieval of the data record having the matching RECORD KEY.

FIGURE 13-11a

Warnier/Orr Diagram: Random Disk Retrieval

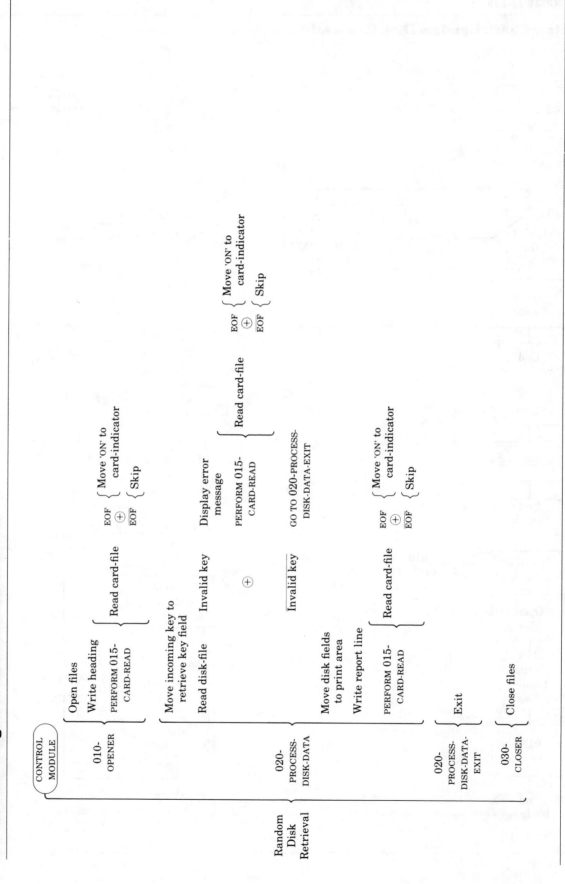

FIGURE 13-11*b*

Flow Chart: Random Disk Retrieval

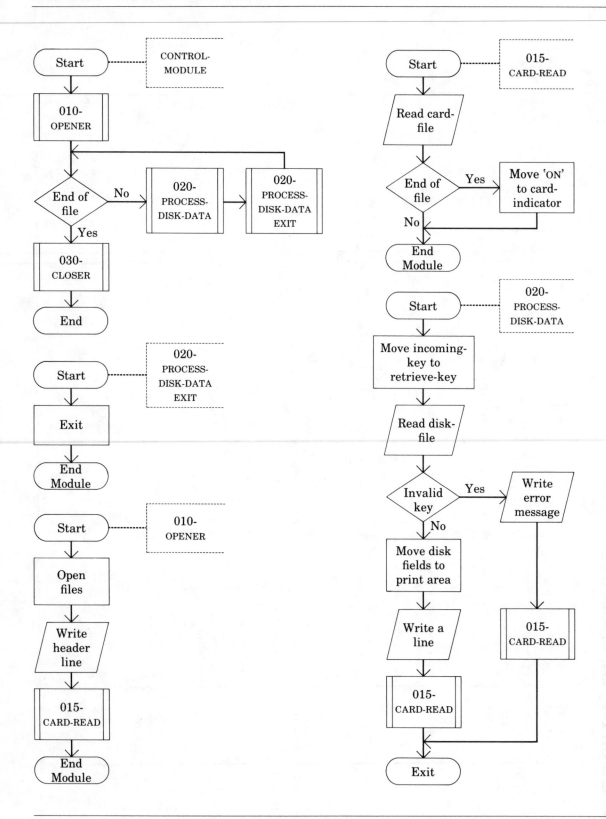

FIGURE 13-12

Indexed Sequential File: Random Retrieval

```
IDENTIFICATION DIVISION.
PROGRAM-ID. RANDOM-DISK.
ENVIRONMENT DIVISION.
CONFIGURATION SECTION.
SOURCE-COMPUTER. IBM-360-F30.
OBJECT-COMPUTER. IBM-360-F30.
SPECIAL-NAMES.
    C01 IS TOP-OF-PAGE.
INPUT-OUTPUT SECTION.
FILE-CONTROL.
    SELECT DISK-FILE
        ASSIGN TO SYS080-DA-2314-I
        ACCESS IS RANDOM
        NOMINAL KEY IS RETRIEVE-KEY
        RECORD KEY IS DISK-EMPLOYEE-NUMBER.
    SELECT PRINT-FILE ASSIGN TO SYS009-UR-1403-S.
    SELECT CARD-FILE
        ASSIGN TO SYS007-UR-2540R-S.
DATA DIVISION.
FILE SECTION.
FD  DISK-FILE
    LABEL RECORDS ARE STANDARD
    DATA RECORD IS DISK-RECORD.
01  DISK-RECORD.
    03  DISK-EMPLOYEE-NAME              PIC X(22).
    03  DISK-EMPLOYEE-NUMBER            PIC 9(8).
    03  FILLER                          PIC X(50).
FD  PRINT-FILE
    LABEL RECORDS ARE OMITTED
    DATA RECORD IS OUTPUT-RECORD.
01  OUTPUT-RECORD                       PIC X(121).
FD  CARD-FILE
    LABEL RECORDS ARE OMITTED
    DATA RECORD IS CARD-RECORD.
01  CARD-RECORD.
    03  INCOMING-KEY        PIC 9(08).
    03  FILLER              PIC X(72).
```

```
WORKING-STORAGE SECTION.
77   CARD-INDICATOR                      PIC X(03) VALUE 'OFF'.
77   RETRIEVE-KEY                        PIC 9(08).
01   HEAD-LINE.
     03   FILLER                         PIC X.
     03   FILLER                         PIC X(17) VALUE SPACES.
     03   FILLER                         PIC X(04) VALUE 'NAME'.
     03   FILLER                         PIC X(21) VALUE SPACES.
     03   FILLER                         PIC X(06) VALUE 'NUMBER'.
     03   FILLER                         PIC X(72) VALUE SPACES.
01   MAIN-LINE.
     03   FILLER                         PIC X.
     03   FILLER                         PIC X(08) VALUE SPACES.
     03   EMP-NAME-PR                     PIC X(22).
     03   FILLER                         PIC X(11) VALUE SPACES.
     03   EMP-NBR-PR                      PIC 9(08).
     03   FILLER                         PIC X(71) VALUE SPACES.
PROCEDURE DIVISION.
CONTROL-MODULE.
     PERFORM 010-OPENER.
     PERFORM 020-PROCESS-DISK-DATA THRU
             020-PROCESS-DISK-DATA-EXIT
             UNTIL CARD-INDICATOR IS EQUAL TO ' ON'.
     PERFORM 030-CLOSER.
     STOP RUN.
010-OPENER.
     OPEN INPUT DISK-FILE CARD-FILE OUTPUT PRINT-FILE.
     WRITE OUTPUT-RECORD FROM HEAD-LINE
         AFTER ADVANCING TOP-OF-PAGE.
     MOVE SPACES TO OUTPUT-RECORD.
     WRITE OUTPUT-RECORD AFTER ADVANCING 2 LINES.
     PERFORM 015-CARD-READ.
```

```
015-CARD-READ.
    READ CARD-FILE
        AT END MOVE ' ON' TO CARD-INDICATOR.
020-PROCESS-DISK-DATA.
    MOVE INCOMING-KEY TO RETRIEVE-KEY.
    READ DISK-FILE INVALID KEY
        DISPLAY 'EMPLOYEE KEY NUMBER ' RETRIEVE-KEY
            ' IS INCORRECT'
        PERFORM 015-CARD-READ
        GO TO 020-PROCESS-DISK-DATA-EXIT.
    MOVE DISK-EMPLOYEE-NAME TO EMP-NAME-PR.
    MOVE DISK-EMPLOYEE-NUMBER TO EMP-NBR-PR.
    WRITE OUTPUT-RECORD FROM MAIN-LINE
        AFTER ADVANCING 1 LINES.
    PERFORM 015-CARD-READ.
020-PROCESS-DISK-DATA-EXIT.
    EXIT.
030-CLOSER.
    CLOSE DISK-FILE CARD-FILE PRINT-FILE.
```

```
                    NAME                              NUMBER


                BAKER, SIDNEY                       12345609
                WEEMS, WANDA                        12345613
         EMPLOYEE KEY NUMBER  44444444      IS INCORRECT
                ANDERSON, JEB                       12345602
                FOX, ALBERT                         12345621
```

There are several important points to understand about the program.

1. A card is read-in that contains the key of the data record we want to retrieve.

2. Some computer systems require that the NOMINAL KEY field be a field in WORKING-STORAGE rather than in the FILE SECTION. Therefore, the CARD-KEY field is moved to START-KEY, which is the field named in the NOMINAL KEY entry.

3. When the READ DISK-FILE statement is executed, the system takes the value from the NOMINAL KEY field (START-KEY) and uses this to search the disk index. When a match is found on the index, the system then "knows" where that particular record is stored on disk.

4. The disk record is read-in and the value in the DISK-EMPLOYEE-NUMBER field is compared with the value in the START-KEY field. If they are equal, the record is released to the programmer. If they are not equal, the INVALID KEY routine is activated.

5. Note that the programmer does *not* test to see if the correct record has been retrieved since the software does this automatically.

6. In the example, if an invalid key is detected during the disk read operation, an ERROR-message is written and the program continues. This is not the only alternative since you may wish to terminate the processing at that point.

Common errors

Beginning programmers seem to make relatively few errors when working with disk files. Those errors that are made can be summarized as follows.

1. Not differentiating between a straight sequential disk file and an indexed sequential file that is handled sequentially. The difference, of course, is that a straight sequential disk file is identical to a regular tape file and should be thought of in that way. Therefore, the SELECT statement will *not* include the ORGANIZATION IS INDEXED entry but *will* indicate that ACCESS IS SEQUENTIAL.

2. Not recognizing that an indexed sequential file can be treated in either a sequential or random manner. In either case, the file access mode determines whether ACCESS IS SEQUENTIAL or ACCESS IS RANDOM will be used.

3. Perhaps the most serious error results when the programmer attempts to begin sequential retrieval of data records at a point other than the beginning of the file. On most systems it is imperative that the NOMINAL KEY *value* be placed in the NOMINAL KEY field *before* the file is OPENed. Traditionally, the programmer is so used to opening all the files first that he or she will forget to place the starting key value in the field. The use of the VALUE clause eliminates this problem but does not allow for the flexibility of entering the value from an outside source.

   Also, some systems do not permit this field to be in the FILE SECTION and some do not allow it to be at the 77 level. The best solution is to check the appropriate manual for your machine. Generally, an 02–49 level entry for the NOMINAL KEY field will be acceptable.

4. Finally, the last type of error is that of using an IF statement to test whether or not the disk system retrieved the correct record during random retrieval. As mentioned earlier, there is no need for the programmer to do this checking since it is done automatically by the system software. An incorrect match will be detected and invoke the INVALID KEY part of the statement.

Problem-Solving Techniques

One of the convenient features of top-down program design is that your *general* program logic can be tested without getting bogged down in the details of lesser or lower modules. Suppose we have the example of a payroll application where we are interested in overtime pay calculations. At this point in our coding we are concerned about the calculations in module B200 and reach the point where we will test to see if overtime pay should be included. Should we stop work on module B300 and code the overtime module A400 and then come back to the higher level module? Should we even be concerned about A400 now? The answer is probably not, and we can take care of the situation by using a *stub* module. Note that in the following example we will PERFORM a module that has not yet been written fully. The module will really be a stub of the real module and will contain only a DISPLAY statement.

```
B300-PAY-CALCULATIONS.

    _____

    _____
    IF HOURS-WORKED IS GREATER THAN 40
        PERFORM A-400-OVERTIME-PAY
    ELSE

        _____

        _____
    .
    .
    .
A-400-OVERTIME-PAY.
    DISPLAY 'A-400 OVERTIME PAY MODULE EXECUTED'.
```

With this arrangement, and knowing our sample data, we can verify our program logic—that we have entered the lower level module whenever HOURS-WORKED was greater than 40. After we are satisfied that the B-300-PAY-CALCULATIONS module is working, then we can drop down to code the A-400 module.

Self-Study: Questions and Answers

1. How many different kinds of magnetic disks are there?

    Answer
    Perhaps the best way to answer the question is to say that disks
    are either "hard" or "soft" with the soft disk being used mainly
    on the microcomputer and word processing systems. The so-called
    "hard" disks can be categorized as of the "moving head" or "fixed
    head" variety according to how data are accessed. After that, the
    distinction becomes less clear since we have removable and non-
    removable hard disks as well as disks of different diameters.
    After many years of little change, disk technology is undergoing
    a revolution in size, storage capacity, and access methods.

2. Disk terminology seems to bother me. Explain again about a
    track and a cylinder since I am not sure I understand the differ-
    ence.

    Answer
    By definition, a "track" is an area on a disk surface that is, in
    many ways, very much like a train track. The area, although
    smaller in width than a pencil mark, goes around the surface of
    the disk and returns to its starting point. It would be the equiv-
    alent of using a pencil and compass to draw a circle on paper.
    Other tracks are located on both sides, but each track is unique
    in that it has an address. Typically, the first track on the outside
    of the disk is numbered 000, the next 001, 002, and so forth until
    the inside track is reached.

    Since a disk drive usually has multiple disks or platters, the
    tracks are also identified by the disk surface on which they are
    located. Thus, track 27 on disk surface 3 might be numbered
    3-027, and track 27 on disk surface 4 will be numbered 4-027. By
    definition, all track 27's on all the disk surfaces are known as
    Cylinder 27.

One important point about a disk is that the programmer must always think in terms of a cylinder rather than tracks. When writing data to disk the programmer wants to avoid moving the access arms from one track to another since this essentially is "wasted" time. By thinking in terms of cylinders the programmer will be sure to fill up track 27 on surface 1, then track 27 on surface 2, surface 3, and so on until the whole cylinder is filled. Using this method the access arms will move only when going from one cylinder to another.

3. Since the inner tracks are smaller than the outer tracks, you must not be able to store as much data. Is that correct?

Answer

No. Even though your thinking is entirely logical, the outer and inner tracks both store the same amount of data. The reason for this is that the outer track is moving faster than the inner track so the data are spread out more.

4. None of the example programs showed blocked data on a disk. Is there something particularly difficult about this?

Answer

No, just the opposite. Blocked disk data are extremely simple in that you "trigger" into them by means of the BLOCK CONTAINS entry in the disk FILE Description. The system software takes care of all the blocking and unblocking of data records just as it did on magnetic tape.

5. You discussed "straight sequential" disk access and sequential access of an indexed sequential disk file. Why would you ever use straight sequential disk access if you have the possibility of using indexed sequential access?

Answer

Good question. The answer is that if you had a lot of disk files you were going to access sequentially *from the first record,* it would be better to set up those files on a straight sequential basis. The reason for this is that doing the same operation on an indexed sequential file is not quite as efficient since the system is obligated to check the index first to determine the location of the first record. On the other hand, if you were taking advantage of the ability to start sequential retrieval at a specific record, then it would be worth the expenditure of extra time to start straight sequential retrieval.

Exercises

1. Define or explain the following terms as they pertain to a magnetic disk.
   a. "Hard" disk
   b. "Soft" disk
   c. "Floppy" disk
   d. Tracks
   e. Cylinders
   f. Read/Write heads
   g. Access arms
   h. Moving head disk
   i. Fixed head disk
   j. Disk pack
   k. Disk drive
   l. Key field
   m. Index

2. What is the function of the ACCESS IS SEQUENTIAL entry? Explain in detail.

3. What is the function of the ORGANIZATION IS INDEXED entry? Explain in detail.

4. What is the purpose of the RECORD KEY entry? Give an example of it in use.

5. What is the general purpose of the NOMINAL KEY entry?
   a. Give an example of it as used with sequential access on an indexed sequential file.
   b. Give an example of it as used with random access on an indexed sequential file.

6. Explain why AT END is not used with READ in a random-access situation.

7. What is the purpose of the INVALID KEY entry when randomly accessing an indexed sequential file?

8. Write a program to create a straight sequential disk file called SEQ-SALES using Data File B (see appendix) coming in from cards. The card record format is as follows.

Field	Characters	Type
Sales Territory	3	Numeric
ID Number	5	Numeric
Salesperson's Name	20	Alphabetic
Year to Date Sales	7	Numeric
Year to Date Sales Returns	6	Numeric

The disk data record is to contain the same fields except that the Year to Date Sales and Year to Date Sales Returns are to be written to disk in packed format. Provide for a blocking factor of 4. (Check with your instructor concerning job control cards, disk parameters, etc.)

9. Modify Exercise 8 to create an indexed sequential file called IS-FILE. (Again, check with your instructor concerning the required job control entries for disk and the correct system name for the disk device.)

10. Use the file created in Exercise 8 to provide for the following.
    a. Sequential retrieval and printout of the data records starting with the beginning of the file.
    b. Sequential retrieval and printout of the data records starting with some record number other than the beginning record.

11. Use the file created in Exercise 9 to provide for random retrieval. Consult Appendix B and pick out six identification numbers. Punch each of these numbers on a separate card and write a program to randomly retrieve the matching disk record and print an appropriate line of output.

Appendix

Programming Tips

A great amount of programming can be learned from textbooks, but mistakes often can serve as excellent teachers and they have been used throughout the book precisely for that reason. A second source of programming wisdom can be found in the sayings attributed to the mysterious and omnipotent Murphy of Murphy's Law fame. Before getting into some COBOL programming tips we might look at a few of Murphy's sayings that apply particularly to programming. Of course, the general law postulated by Murphy is that "If anything can go wrong it *will* go wrong." Some further refinements of this law are listed for your consideration.

1. Murphy was an optimist. (True!)

2. There is always one more bug.

    This is another way of saying that just because your program works "correctly," don't be surprised if it does not work correctly at a later date. A lengthy and involved program may not be able to be tested for every possible combination of events, and of course the bug will appear when that "one-in-a-million" set of circumstances arises. Thus, a "working" program is one that has only unobserved bugs.

3. There is never time to do it right, but there is time to do it over.
    Moral to the story: Do it right the first time.

4. A hardware failure will cause the system software to crash and the Customer Engineer will blame the programmers.

5. A system software crash will cause the hardware to act strangely and the programmers will blame the Customer Engineer.

6. An error always exists in that part of the program you are sure cannot possibly contain a mistake because it is so simple a process.
    Corollary A: No one you ask will see the error.
    Corollary B: Everyone who stops by with unsolicited advice will see it immediately.

7. It takes more time to find where to change a program than to make the change itself.

    Many of the programming tips mentioned in this section were discussed or illustrated throughout the text. Others are added here for those of you who have been brave enough to read this far.

1. Plan first. Code later.

    Actually, this statement should be the first three rules of programming. Resist the urge to program! Much like the old saying that one picture is worth a thousand words, a few minutes of planning are certainly worth hours of coding, logic errors, and debugging. The particular planning method you use (flowcharts, HIPO charts, etc.) is not as important as the fact that you *have* planned. Understand the problem *completely* before coding!

2. Collect documentation material right away.

    Don't wait until the program is running—documentation will be hard to find then.

3. Program in a "top-down" manner.

This means that you must think in terms of levels of programming modules in the PROCEDURE DIVISION. The main advantage of this approach is that it allows the programmer to think in terms of the action of the program rather than getting bogged down in the semantics of COBOL.

4. Program in modular form.

The basic rule here is that each paragraph in the PROCEDURE DIVISION must have only one entry and one exit point. Unless so authorized where you work, GO TO statements are not permitted. (Note, however, that some shops allow downward GO TOs in conjunction with the EXIT statement.)

5. Avoid GO TO—use PERFORM.

As discussed earlier, the GO TO statement is not necessarily wrong, but its use can often get out of hand. A better approach is to use PERFORM because it tends to preserve the integrity of top-down design. Many shops still permit the use of GO TO, but generally restrict it to situations where the one-entry-one-exit rule can be maintained.

6. Use comments throughout the program.

This rule can be expanded to include extra spacing before paragraphs, starting each COBOL DIVISION on a new page, and inserting comments so they are visible. An excellent way to do this is by means of a box made up of asterisks.

```
* * * * * * * * * * * * * * * * * * * * * * * * * * * * *

*   THE NEXT PARAGRAPH CALCULATES THE OVER-TIME PAY        *

*   AMOUNT AND ADDS IT TO THE REGULAR PAY CALCULATED       *

*   PREVIOUSLY IN THE 050-REGULAR-PAY ROUTINE              *

* * * * * * * * * * * * * * * * * * * * * * * * * * * * *
```

7. For greater clarity and future ease of maintenance, place READ and WRITE statements in separate paragraphs that are PERFORMed when needed. Later, if the input/output file has to be changed, only a single correction in the program need be made as opposed to making a change in each and every place where the READ or WRITE is used. In theory, each file would have only one READ or WRITE statement associated with it in the entire program. Note the following examples:

```
020-BEGINNING-MODULE
    OPEN _____
    READ CUSTOMER-CARD-FILE
        AT END _____ .

030-PROCESSING-LOOP.
    _____
    _____
    WRITE CUSTOMER-PRINTER-FILE
        AFTER ADVANCING _____ .
    READ CUSTOMER-CARD-FILE
        AT END _____ .
```

A better arrangement is as follows:

```
020-BEGINNING-MODULE.
    OPEN _____ .
    PERFORM CARD-READ.

030-PROCESSING-LOOP.
    _____ .

    _____ .
    PERFORM PRINTER-OUTPUT.
    PERFORM CARD-READ.
_____

CARD-READ.
    READ CUSTOMER-CARD-FILE
        AT END _____ .


PRINTER-OUTPUT.
    WRITE CUSTOMER-PRINT-FILE
        AFTER ADVANCING _____ .
```

8. Beware of efficiency.

Efficiency can be defined in at least two ways: programmer efficiency and machine efficiency. Computers are fast; we humans are not. And in the long run it may be more "efficient" to produce an inefficient program (inefficient in terms of the machine) that is done quickly.

Now the intention of the last sentence is not to have you forget machine efficiency entirely, but it is important for the programmer and the supervisor to weigh the two kinds of efficiency. From a practical standpoint, however, there is a middle position that can be taken. First, write the program as you normally would. Then look at it to find the main loop(s) (probably the main processing loop) that will be executed most frequently in the program. If you do decide to spend some time optimizing your program for machine efficiency, this is the place at which to devote your time. In other words, don't spend your time trying to optimize the whole program as it usually is not worth the effort.

9. Every program can be improved.

A corollary to this rule is that every program can be made one statement shorter. The question is: Is it worth the time to do so?

10. Program for generality.

The rule here, of course, is that the more general your program the greater its value. Note the following example that uses the pay-raise rate in a COMPUTE statement:

```
COMPUTE NEW-RATE = OLD-RATE * .07
```

A better approach is to use a variable whose value is defined by a VALUE entry in the DATA DIVISION. Under this method the maintenance programmer will not have to search through the PROCEDURE DIVISION statements to locate every numeric literal that exists in the program. When the next pay rate change is authorized, the programmer need change only the VALUE entry.

```
WORKING-STORAGE SECTION.
01   CONSTANT-FIELDS.
     03   RATE-INCREASE   PIC V99 VALUE .07.

     COMPUTE NEW-RATE = OLD-RATE * RATE-INCREASE.
```

11. Programming productivity is not just output per man-hour; it is a function of usefulness.

    Three lines of code per hour that work are far better than 30 lines that do not work.

12. Keep it simple.

    Take the normal, straightforward approach to the problem. Don't try to get "cute" and use obscure statements or fancy techniques. Remember that somewhere between 50% to 80% of the total cost of a program comes *after* the program has been completed and run successfully. Think and program in terms of the effort that will be required to make changes to the program later.

13. Don't change "constant" values within the program.

    As the term indicates, a constant is an unchanging value. The rule here is that constants should be defined in the DATA DIVISION and then left alone. Non-numeric literals such as messages are perhaps the most frequent recipient of this abuse. Note the following example.

```
PROCEDURE DIVISION.
     _____
     _____

     DISPLAY 'SEQUENCE ERROR IN TRANSACTION CARD FILE'.
```

    A better way to do this is to define the message as a constant in the DATA DIVISION so that all such messages can be seen or located by the reader at one glance. (Incidentally, on IBM machines it is usually more machine efficient if the message is defined in the DATA DIVISION.)

```
DATA DIVISION.
     _____
     _____

WORKING-STORAGE SECTION.
01   MESSAGES.
     03   SEQUENCE-ERROR-TRANS PIC X(39) VALUE
          'SEQUENCE ERROR IN TRANSACTION CARD FILE'.
     03   SEQUENCE-ERROR-MASTER PIC X(34)
          'SEQUENCE ERROR IN MASTER TAPE FILE'.


PROCEDURE DIVISION.
     _____
     _____

     DISPLAY SEQUENCE-ERROR-TRANS.
```

14. Use meaningful names.

    One of the major advantages of COBOL is that you can use names up to 30 characters long to name data fields or paragraphs. Again and again we see beginning students use data names such as A1, A2, A3, and so on. It is true that this reduces the number of key-entry strokes required in a program, but the ultimate penalty is far too great: A program of this type becomes impossible for an outsider to follow.

Thus, the programmer has negated the self-documenting advantage of COBOL. Note the following examples of data names:

Horrible: C1, FIELD-1

Bad: ~~C-NAME, A-FIELD~~

Fair: CUST-NAME, AMOUNT

Good: CUSTOMER-NAME, NET-PAY-AMOUNT

Thus the statement

```
    MOVE C1 TO OUT-1
```

is almost meaningless. But the statement

```
    MOVE CUSTOMER-NAME TO
        CUSTOMER-NAME-OUT
```

is better.

15. Identify the source or nature of data fields, records, and files.

    We discussed this point earlier by saying that one frequently used technique is to identify WORKING-STORAGE fields with a WS prefix or suffix. The same holds true for input/output records and fields. For example, CUSTOMER-NAME is not as meaningful as CUSTOMER-NAME-WS or CUSTOMER-NAME-TAPE-IN or CUSTOMER-NAME-PR.

    Using the words FILE and RECORD serves the same purpose of further identifying the nature of the data element with which you are dealing. For example, CARD-INPUT-FILE is better than INPUT-FILE, but ACC-REC-CARD-INPUT-FILE is even better.

16. Indent for clarity and ease of reading, but be consistent. Set up rules for indenting and follow these rules.

    The statement

```
    WRITE AR-PRINTER-FILE AFTER ADVANCING 2 LINES
```

is more readable if indenting is used.

```
    WRITE AR-PRINTER-FILE
        AFTER ADVANCING 2 LINES.
```

Indenting is particularly important when using nested IF-ELSE statements so that the reader can properly associate the test options.

```
    IF _____
        IF _____
            IF _____
                _____
                _____
                _____
        ELSE
            _____
            _____
            _____
    ELSE
        _____
        _____
        _____
ELSE
    _____
    _____
    _____
```

The same rule holds true for simple COBOL statements within a paragraph. The following example may execute correctly, but is difficult to follow.

```
030-CALCULATION-LOOP.
      MOVE _____ .
      MOVE _____ .
        ADD _____ .
   SUBTRACT _____ .
          MOVE _____ .
   MOVE _____ .
          DIVIDE _____ .
```

Since all the COBOL statements are of the same general level, they all should start in the same relative position.

```
030-CALCULATION-LOOP.
      MOVE _____ .
      MOVE _____ .
      ADD _____ .
      SUBTRACT _____ .
      MOVE _____ .
      MOVE _____ .
      DIVIDE _____ .
```

When IF (testing) statements are used in the normal sequence of statements, they should be indented as indicated earlier and ELSE should appear on a line by itself.

```
030-CALCULATION-LOOP.
      MOVE _____ .
      MOVE _____ .
      ADD _____ .
      IF (test)
            _____
            _____
      ELSE
            _____
            _____
      SUBTRACT _____ .
      MOVE _____ .
```

17. Line up the PICTURE (or PIC) entries to make it easier to detect key-punching/key entry errors.

Poor:

```
03   NAME PIC X(20).
03   CUSTOMER-ID-NBR PIC 9(5).
03   FILLER PIC X(10).
03   DATE FIELD PIC 9(6).
```

Good:

```
03   NAME                 PIC X(20).
03   CUSTOMER-ID-NBR      PIC 9(5).
03   FILLER               PIC X(10).
03   DATE-FIELD           PIC 9(6).
```

Make all PICs two digits for clarity.

```
03   NAME                      PIC X(20).
03   CUSTOMER-ID-NBR           PIC 9(05).
03   FILLER                    PIC X(10).
03   DATE-FIELD                PIC 9(06).
```

18. When setting up data fields within a record, allow room for insertion of sub-fields by skipping level numbers.

    The sequence 01-02-03-04 and so on means that it is impossible to go back at a later date and sub-divide an 02-level field without the high probability of having to change most of the other entries. A level numbering sequence of 01-03-05 or 01-05-10 and so on allows for easy breakdown at a later date.

19. Specify COMP (binary) for subscript items or for fields involving extensive arithmetic operations. Also, include S in the PICTURE entry. Make binary items less than five digits if possible—if not, make them less than nine, as this is a more efficient format on IBM or byte-oriented machines.

20. When using VALUE with numeric fields, indicate positive numbers with a plus sign and include the S in the PICTURE entry.

    ```
    EX: 03 PI PIC S9V99 VALUE +3.14 COMP.
    ```

21. Except where COMP is desired, numeric fields should be specified as COMP-3 and include S in the PIC entry. In addition, it is more efficient to specify an odd number of digits when using COMP-3.

22. Use PIC X for switches—such as End of File switches—instead of numeric fields as it saves extra computer instructions during compare operations.

23. Whenever possible, specify the same USAGE for items involved in moves, comparisons, and arithmetic operations.

24. When using large sequential files on magnetic storage media, specify fairly large data blocks. Check your system to find the optimum blocking factor.

25. Avoid clearing a large table unless it is absolutely necessary.

26. Generally, indexing is more efficient than subscripting.

27. When using tables, there may be relatively few values that are needed over and over. If possible, place these at the beginning of the table so that they are found quickly by the SEARCH statement.

28. Use SEARCH if a table has fewer than 50 entries. If the table is sorted and contains over 50 entries, use SEARCH ALL.

29. Use OPEN and CLOSE sparingly. In addition, it is far more efficient to use a single OPEN rather than multiple OPENs to achieve the same result.

30. The IF NUMERIC and IF ALPHABETIC instructions are costly in terms of machine operation and should be used only when needed.

31. The ROUNDED option is costly, and you can round by hard coding rather than by using ROUNDED.

COBOL Reserved Words

The following list of COBOL reserved words includes those in general usage plus those used by IBM. Although the list is fairly complete, some computers have additional reserved words and you are advised to check the COBOL manual for your machine.

ACCEPT	CLOSE	C08	EGI
ACCESS	COBOL	C09	EJECT
ACTUAL	CODE	C10	ELSE
ADD	COLUMN	C11	EMI
ADDRESS	COM-REG	C12	ENABLE
ADVANCING	COMMA		END
AFTER	COMP	DATA	END-OF-PAGE
ALL	COMP-1	DATE	ENDING
ALPHABETIC	COMP-2	DATE-WRITTEN	ENTER
ALPHANUMERIC	COMP-3	DAY	ENTRY
ALPHANUMERIC-EDITED	COMP-4	DE	ENVIRONMENT
ALTER	COMPUTATIONAL	DEBUG	EOP
ALTERNATE	COMPUTATIONAL-1	DEBUG-CONTENTS	EQUAL
AND	COMPUTATIONAL-2	DEBUG-ITEM	EQUALS
APPLY	COMPUTATIONAL-3	DEBUG-SUB-1	ERROR
ARE	COMPUTATIONAL-4	DEBUG-SUB-2	ESI
AREA	COMPUTE	DEBUG-SUB-3	EVERY
AREAS	CONFIGURATION	DEBUG-NAME	EXAMINE
ASCENDING	CONSOLE	DEBUGGING	EXCEEDS
ASSIGN	CONSTANT	DECIMAL-POINT	EXHIBIT
AT	CONTAINS	DECLARATIVES	EXIT
AUTHOR	CONTROL	DELETE	EXTENDED-SEARCH
	CONTROLS	DELIMITED	
BASIS	COPY	DELIMITER	FD
BEFORE	CORE-INDEX	DEPENDING	FILE
BEGINNING	CORR	DEPTH	FILE-CONTROL
BLANK	CORRESPONDING	DESCENDING	FILE-LIMIT
BLOCK	COUNT	DESTINATION	FILE-LIMITS
BY	CSP	DETAIL	FILLER
	CURRENCY	DISABLE	FINAL
CALL	CURRENT-DATE	DISP	FIRST
CANCEL	CYL-INDEX	DISPLAY	FOOTING
CBL	CYL-OVERFLOW	DISPLAY-ST	FOR
CD	C01	DISPLAY-n	FROM
CF	C02	DIVIDE	
CH	C03	DIVISION	GENERATE
CHANGED	C04	DOWN	GIVING
CHARACTER	C05	DYNAMIC	GO
CHARACTERS	C06		GOBACK
CLOCK-UNITS	C07		

GREATER	LINES	PF	RESERVE
GROUP	LINKAGE	PH	RESET
	LOCK	PIC	RETURN
HEADING	LOW-VALUE	PICTURE	RETURN-CODE
HIGH-VALUE	LOW-VALUES	PLUS	REVERSED
HIGH-VALUES	LOWER-BOUND	POINTER	REWIND
HOLD	LOWER-BOUNDS	POSITION	REWRITE
		POSITIONING	RF
I-O	MASTER-INDEX	POSITIVE	RH
I-O-CONTROL	MEMORY	PREPARED	RIGHT
ID	MERGE	PRINT-SWITCH	ROUNDED
IDENTIFICATION	MESSAGE	PRINTING	RUN
IF	MODE	PRIORITY	
IN	MODULES	PROCEDURE	SA
INDEX	MORE-LABELS	PROCEDURES	SAME
INDEX-n	MOVE	PROCEED	SD
INDEXED	MULTIPLE	PROCESS	SEARCH
INDICATE	MULTIPLY	PROCESSING	SECTION
INITIAL		PROGRAM	SECURITY
INITIATE	NAMED	PROGRAM-ID	SEEK
INPUT	NEGATIVE		SEGMENT
INPUT-OUTPUT	NEXT	QUEUE	SEGMENT-LIMIT
INSERT	NO	QUOTE	SELECT
INSPECT	NOMINAL	QUOTES	SELECTED
INSTALLATION	NOT		SEND
INTO	NOTE	RANDOM	SENTENCE
INVALID	NSTD-REELS	RANGE	SEPARATE
IS	NUMBER	RD	SEQUENTIAL
	NUMERIC	READ	SERVICE
JUST	NUMERIC-EDITED	READY	SET
JUSTIFIED		RECEIVE	SIGN
	OBJECT-COMPUTER	RECORD	SIZE
KEY	OBJECT-PROGRAM	RECORD-OVERFLOW	SKIP1
KEYS	OCCURS	RECORDING	SKIP2
	OF	RECORDS	SKIP3
LABEL	OFF	REDEFINES	SORT
LABEL-RETURN	OH	REEL	SORT-CORE-SIZE
LAST	OMITTED	REFERENCES	SORT-FILE-SIZE
LEADING	ON	RELEASE	SORT-MODE-SIZE
LEAVE	OPEN	RELOAD	SORT-RETURN
LEFT	OPTIONAL	REMAINDER	SOURCE
LENGTH	OR	REMARKS	SOURCE-COMPUTER
LESS	OTHERWISE	RENAMES	SPACE
LIBRARY	OUTPUT	REORG-CRITERIA	SPACES
LIMIT	OV	REPLACING	SPECIAL-NAMES
LIMITS	OVERFLOW	REPORT	STANDARD
LINAGE		REPORTING	START
LINAGE-COUNTER	PAGE	REPORTS	STATUS
LINE	PAGE-COUNTER	REREAD	STOP
LINE-COUNTER	PERFORM	RERUN	STRING

SUB-QUEUE-1	TABLE	TRACK-LIMIT	UPSI-7
SUB-QUEUE-2	TALLY	TRACKS	USAGE
SUB-QUEUE-3	TALLYING	TRAILING	USE
SUBTRACT	TAPE	TRANSFORM	USING
SUM	TERMINAL	TYPE	
SUPERVISOR	TERMINATE		VALUE
SUPPRESS	TEXT	UNEQUAL	VALUES
SUSPEND	THAN	UNIT	VARYING
SYMBOLIC	THEN	UNSTRING	
SYNC	THROUGH	UNTIL	WHEN
SYNCHRONIZED	THRU	UP	WITH
SYSIN	TIME	UPON	WORDS
SYSIPT	TIME-OF-DAY	UPPER-BOUND	WORKING-STORAGE
SYSLST	TIMES	UPPER-BOUNDS	WRITE
SYSOUT	TO	UPSI-1	WRITE-ONLY
SYSPCH	TOTALED	UPSI-2	WRITE-VERIFY
SYSPUNCH	TOTALING	UPSI-3	
S01	TRACE	UPSI-4	ZERO
S02	TRACK	UPSI-5	ZEROES
	TRACK-AREA	UPSI-6	ZEROS

COBOL Format Summary

This appendix contains a general format summary of the valid statements in COBOL. It is not intended to be a complete list of all COBOL entries, but it does include the most commonly used features of the language. For a complete list of the valid entries on a particular machine you should check the appropriate COBOL specification manual.

The notation for the reference formats is as follows:
1. Words printed in capital letters are reserved words.
2. Underlined reserved words are required unless that portion of the entry is optional.
3. Lowercase words are terms supplied by the programmer.
4. Brackets [ ] indicate optional entries.
5. Braces { } indicate alternative features, one of which may be chosen.
6. Ellipses (. . .) indicate repetition of part of the entry.

Formats for the IDENTIFICATION DIVISION

```
IDENTIFICATION DIVISION.
PROGRAM-ID. program-name.
[AUTHOR. [comment-entry] . . . ]
[INSTALLATION. [comment-entry] . . . ]
[DATE-WRITTEN. [comment-entry] . . . ]
[DATE-COMPILED. [comment-entry] . . . ]
[SECURITY. [comment-entry] . . . ]
```

Formats for the ENVIRONMENT DIVISION

```
ENVIRONMENT DIVISION.
CONFIGURATION SECTION.
SOURCE-COMPUTER. computer-name [WITH DEBUGGING MODE] .
OBJECT-COMPUTER. computer-name
SPECIAL-NAMES. implementor-name is mnemonic-name
INPUT-OUTPUT SECTION.
FILE-CONTROL.
```

FORMAT 1:

```
SELECT [OPTIONAL] file-name
    ASSIGN TO implementor-name-1 [, implementor-name-2] . . .

    [; RESERVE integer-1 [ AREA  ]]
                        [ AREAS ]

    [; ORGANIZATION is SEQUENTIAL]
    [; ACCESS MODE IS SEQUENTIAL].
```

FORMAT 2:

```
SELECT file-name
    ASSIGN TO implementor-name-1 [, implementor-name-2] . . .

    [; RESERVE integer-1 [ AREA  ]]
                        [ AREAS ]

    ; ORGANIZATION IS RELATIVE

    [; ACCESS MODE IS  { SEQUENTIAL  [, RELATIVE KEY IS data-name-1] }]
                       { { RANDOM  }                                 }
                       { { DYNAMIC }  , RELATIVE KEY IS data-name-1   } .
```

FORMAT 3:

```
SELECT file-name
    ASSIGN TO implementor-name-1 [, implementor-name-2] . . .

    [; RESERVE integer-1 [ AREA  ]]
                        [ AREAS ]

    ; ORGANIZATION IS INDEXED

    [; ACCESS MODE IS { SEQUENTIAL }]
                      { RANDOM     }
                      { DYNAMIC    }

    ; RECORD KEY IS data-name-1
    [; ALTERNATE RECORD KEY IS data-name-2 [WITH DUPLICATES]] . . .
```

Formats for the **DATA DIVISION**

```
DATA DIVISION.
FILE SECTION.
FD  file-name

    [; BLOCK CONTAINS [integer-1 TO] integer-2 {RECORDS  }]
                                              {CHARACTERS}

    [; RECORD CONTAINS [integer-3 TO] integer-4 CHARACTERS]

    ; LABEL {RECORD IS  } {STANDARD}
            {RECORDS ARE } {OMITTED }

    [; VALUE OF implementor-name-1 IS {data-name-1}
                                      {literal-1  }

        [, implementor-name-2 IS {data-name-2}] . . . ]
                                 {literal-2  }

    [; DATA {RECORD IS  } data-name-3 [, data-name-4] . . . ]
            {RECORDS ARE }

        record description entry
SD  file-name

    [; RECORD CONTAINS [integer-1 TO] integer-2 CHARACTERS]

    [; DATA {RECORD IS  } data-name-1 [, data-name-2] . . . ] .
            {RECORDS ARE }

        record description entry

01  record-name
[02-49 record description entry
 WORKING-STORAGE SECTION.

 [77-level-description-entry ] . . . ]
 [record-description-entry  ]
```

Formats for data description entries

FORMAT 1:

```
level-number {data-name-1}
             {FILLER     }

    [; REDEFINES data-name-2]

    [  {PICTURE}                    ]
    [; {PIC    } IS character-string]

    [           {COMPUTATIONAL}     ]
    [           {COMP         }     ]
    [; [USAGE IS]{DISPLAY      }     ]
    [           {INDEX        }     ]

    [              {LEADING }                      ]
    [; [SIGN IS]   {TRAILING} [SEPARATE CHARACTER] ]

    [         {integer-1 TO integer-2 TIMES DEPENDING ON data-name-3}
    [; OCCURS {integer-2 TIMES                                       }
    [         {                                                      }

         [{ASCENDING }                                    ]
         [{DESCENDING} KEY IS data-name-4 [, data-name-5] . . . ] . . .

         [INDEXED BY index-name-1 [, index-name-2] . . . ]  ]

    [  {SYNCHRONIZED}{LEFT }  ]
    [; {SYNC        }{RIGHT} ]

    [  {JUSTIFIED}       ]
    [; {JUST     } RIGHT ]

    [; BLANK WHEN ZERO]

    [; VALUE IS literal].
```

FORMAT 2:

```
66 data-name-1; RENAMES data-name-2 [ {THROUGH / THRU} data-name-3 ].
```

FORMAT 3:

```
88 condition-name; {VALUE IS / VALUES ARE} literal-1 [ {THROUGH / THRU} literal-2 ]

    [ , literal-3 [ {THROUGH / THRU} literal-4 ] ] . . . .
```

Formats for the PROCEDURE DIVISION

```
ACCEPT identifier [FROM mnemonic-name]

ADD {identifier-1 / literal-1} [ , identifier-2 / , literal-2] . . . TO identifier-m [ROUNDED]

    [, identifier-n [ROUNDED]] . . . [; ON SIZE ERROR imperative-statement]

ADD {identifier-1 / literal-1} , {identifier-2 / literal-2} [ , identifier-3 / , literal-3] . . .

    GIVING identifier-m [ROUNDED] [, identifier-n [ROUNDED]] . . .

    [; ON SIZE ERROR imperative-statement]

ADD {CORRESPONDING / CORR} identifier-1 TO identifier-2 [ROUNDED]

    [; ON SIZE ERROR imperative-statement]

CLOSE file-name-1 {REEL / UNIT} [ WITH {NO REWIND / LOCK} ] . . .

COMPUTE identifier-1 [ROUNDED] [, identifier-2 [ROUNDED]] . . .

    = arithmetic-expression [; ON SIZE ERROR imperative-statement]

DISPLAY {identifier-1 / literal-1} [ , identifier-2 / , literal-2 ] . . . [UPON mnemonic-name]

DIVIDE {identifier-1 / literal-1} INTO identifier-2 [ROUNDED]

    [, identifier-3 [ROUNDED]] . . . [; ON SIZE ERROR imperative-statement]
```

$$\underline{\text{DIVIDE}} \left\{ \begin{array}{l} \text{identifier-1} \\ \text{literal-1} \end{array} \right\} \underline{\text{INTO}} \left\{ \begin{array}{l} \text{identifier-2} \\ \text{literal-2} \end{array} \right\} \underline{\text{GIVING}} \text{ identifier-3} [\underline{\text{ROUNDED}}]$$

[, identifier-4 [ROUNDED]] . . . [; ON SIZE ERROR imperative-statement]

$$\underline{\text{DIVIDE}} \left\{ \begin{array}{l} \text{identifier-1} \\ \text{literal-1} \end{array} \right\} \underline{\text{BY}} \left\{ \begin{array}{l} \text{identifier-2} \\ \text{literal-2} \end{array} \right\} \underline{\text{GIVING}} \text{ identifier-3} [\underline{\text{ROUNDED}}]$$

[, identifier-4 [ROUNDED]] . . . [; on SIZE ERROR imperative-statement]

$$\underline{\text{DIVIDE}} \left\{ \begin{array}{l} \text{identifier-1} \\ \text{literal-1} \end{array} \right\} \underline{\text{INTO}} \left\{ \begin{array}{l} \text{identifier-2} \\ \text{literal-2} \end{array} \right\} \underline{\text{GIVING}} \text{ identifier-3} [\underline{\text{ROUNDED}}]$$

REMAINDER identifier-4 [; ON SIZE ERROR imperative-statement]

$$\underline{\text{DIVIDE}} \left\{ \begin{array}{l} \text{identifier-1} \\ \text{literal-1} \end{array} \right\} \underline{\text{BY}} \left\{ \begin{array}{l} \text{identifier-2} \\ \text{literal-2} \end{array} \right\} \underline{\text{GIVING}} \text{ identifier-3} [\underline{\text{ROUNDED}}]$$

REMAINDER identifier-4 [; ON SIZE ERROR imperative-statement]

EXIT [PROGRAM].

GO TO [procedure-name-1]

GO TO procedure-name-1 [, procedure-name-2] . . . , procedure-name-n

DEPENDING ON identifier

$$\underline{\text{IF}} \text{ condition}; \left\{ \begin{array}{l} \text{statement-1} \\ \underline{\text{NEXT}} \underline{\text{SENTENCE}} \end{array} \right\} \left\{ \begin{array}{l} ; \underline{\text{ELSE}} \text{ statement-2} \\ ; \underline{\text{ELSE}} \underline{\text{NEXT}} \underline{\text{SENTENCE}} \end{array} \right\}$$

INSPECT identifier-1 TALLYING

$$\left\{ , \text{identifier-2} \underline{\text{FOR}} \left\{ , \left\{ \begin{array}{l} \underline{\text{ALL}} \\ \underline{\text{LEADING}} \\ \underline{\text{CHARACTERS}} \end{array} \right\} \left\{ \begin{array}{l} \text{identifier-3} \\ \text{literal-1} \end{array} \right\} \right\} \left[\left\{ \begin{array}{l} \underline{\text{BEFORE}} \\ \underline{\text{AFTER}} \end{array} \right\} \text{INITIAL} \left\{ \begin{array}{l} \text{identifier-4} \\ \text{literal-2} \end{array} \right\} \right] \right\} . . . \right\} . . .$$

INSPECT identifier-1 REPLACING

$$\left\{ \begin{array}{l} \underline{\text{CHARACTERS}} \underline{\text{BY}} \left\{ \begin{array}{l} \text{identifier-6} \\ \text{literal-4} \end{array} \right\} \left[\left\{ \begin{array}{l} \underline{\text{BEFORE}} \\ \underline{\text{AFTER}} \end{array} \right\} \text{INITIAL} \left\{ \begin{array}{l} \text{identifier-7} \\ \text{literal-5} \end{array} \right\} \right] \\ \left\{ , \left\{ \begin{array}{l} \underline{\text{ALL}} \\ \underline{\text{LEADING}} \\ \underline{\text{FIRST}} \end{array} \right\} \right\} \left\{ , \left\{ \begin{array}{l} \text{identifier-5} \\ \text{literal-3} \end{array} \right\} \underline{\text{BY}} \left\{ \begin{array}{l} \text{identifier-6} \\ \text{literal-4} \end{array} \right\} \left[\left\{ \begin{array}{l} \underline{\text{BEFORE}} \\ \underline{\text{AFTER}} \end{array} \right\} \text{INITIAL} \left\{ \begin{array}{l} \text{identifier-7} \\ \text{literal-5} \end{array} \right\} \right] \right\} . . . \end{array} \right\} . . .$$

```
MOVE {identifier-1} TO identifier-2 [, identifier-3] . . .
     {literal     }
```

```
MOVE {CORRESPONDING} identifier-1 TO identifier-2
     {CORR         }
```

```
MULTIPLY {identifier-1} BY identifier-2 [ROUNDED]
         {literal-1   }
```

```
        [, identifier-3 [ROUNDED]] . . . [; ON SIZE ERROR imperative-statement]
```

```
MULTIPLY {identifier-1} BY {identifier-2} GIVING identifier-3 [ROUNDED]
         {literal-1   }    {literal-2   }
```

```
        [, identifier-4 [ROUNDED]] . . . [ ; ON SIZE ERROR imperative-statement]
```

```
      ⎧                 ⎡REVERSED       ⎤              ⎡REVERSED       ⎤ ⎫
      ⎪ INPUT file-name-1⎢WITH NO REWIND ⎥  [, file-name-2⎢WITH NO REWIND ⎥]⎪ . . .
      ⎪                 ⎣               ⎦              ⎣               ⎦ ⎪
      ⎪                                                                  ⎪
OPEN ⎨ OUTPUT file-name-3 [WITH NO REWIND] [, file-name-4 [WITH NO REWIND]] . . . ⎬ . . .
      ⎪                                                                  ⎪
      ⎪ I-O file-name-5 [, file-name-6] . . .                            ⎪
      ⎪ EXTEND file-name-7 [, file-name-8] . . .                         ⎪
      ⎩                                                                  ⎭
```

```
          ⎧ INPUT file-name-1 [, file-name-2] . . . ⎫
          ⎪                                          ⎪
OPEN     ⎨ OUTPUT file-name-3 [, file-name-4] . . . ⎬  . . .
          ⎪                                          ⎪
          ⎩ I-O file-name-5 [, file-name-6] . . .    ⎭
```

$$\underline{\text{PERFORM}}\text{ procedure-name-1}\left[\begin{Bmatrix}\underline{\text{THROUGH}}\\\underline{\text{THRU}}\end{Bmatrix}\text{procedure-name-2}\right]$$

$$\underline{\text{PERFORM}}\text{ procedure-name-1}\left[\begin{Bmatrix}\underline{\text{THROUGH}}\\\underline{\text{THRU}}\end{Bmatrix}\text{procedure-name-2}\right]\begin{Bmatrix}\text{identifier-1}\\\text{integer-1}\end{Bmatrix}\underline{\text{TIMES}}$$

$$\underline{\text{PERFORM}}\text{ procedure-name-1}\left[\begin{Bmatrix}\underline{\text{THROUGH}}\\\underline{\text{THRU}}\end{Bmatrix}\text{procedure-name-2}\right]\underline{\text{UNTIL}}\text{ condition-1}$$

$$\underline{\text{PERFORM}}\text{ procedure-name-1}\left[\begin{Bmatrix}\underline{\text{THROUGH}}\\\underline{\text{THRU}}\end{Bmatrix}\text{procedure-name-2}\right]$$

$$\underline{\text{VARYING}}\begin{Bmatrix}\text{identifier-2}\\\text{index-name-1}\end{Bmatrix}\underline{\text{FROM}}\begin{Bmatrix}\text{identifier-3}\\\text{index-name-2}\\\text{literal-1}\end{Bmatrix}$$

$$\underline{\text{BY}}\begin{Bmatrix}\text{identifier-4}\\\text{literal-3}\end{Bmatrix}\underline{\text{UNTIL}}\text{ condition-1}$$

$$\left[\underline{\text{AFTER}}\begin{Bmatrix}\text{identifier-5}\\\text{index-name-3}\end{Bmatrix}\underline{\text{FROM}}\begin{Bmatrix}\text{identifier-6}\\\text{index-name-4}\\\text{literal-3}\end{Bmatrix}\right.$$

$$\underline{\text{BY}}\begin{Bmatrix}\text{identifier-7}\\\text{literal-4}\end{Bmatrix}\underline{\text{UNTIL}}\text{ condition-2}$$

$$\left[\underline{\text{AFTER}}\begin{Bmatrix}\text{identifier-8}\\\text{index-name-5}\end{Bmatrix}\underline{\text{FROM}}\begin{Bmatrix}\text{identifier-9}\\\text{index-name-6}\\\text{literal-5}\end{Bmatrix}\right.$$

$$\left.\left.\underline{\text{BY}}\begin{Bmatrix}\text{identifier-10}\\\text{literal-6}\end{Bmatrix}\underline{\text{UNTIL}}\text{ condition-3}\right]\right]$$

READ file-name RECORD [INTO identifier] [; AT END imperative-statement]

READ file-name [NEXT] RECORD [INTO identifier]

[; AT END imperative-statement]

READ file-name RECORD [INTO identifier] [; INVALID KEY imperative-statement]

READ file-name RECORD [INTO identifier]

[; KEY IS data-name]

[; INVALID KEY imperative-statement]

$$\text{SEARCH identifier-1} \left[\underline{\text{VARYING}} \left\{ \begin{array}{l} \text{identifier-2} \\ \text{index-name-1} \end{array} \right\} \right] [; \text{AT } \underline{\text{END}} \text{ imperative-statement-1}]$$

$$; \underline{\text{WHEN}} \text{ condition-1} \left\{ \begin{array}{l} \text{imperative-statement-2} \\ \underline{\text{NEXT}} \underline{\text{SENTENCE}} \end{array} \right\}$$

$$\left[; \underline{\text{WHEN}} \text{ condition-2} \left\{ \begin{array}{l} \text{imperative-statement-3} \\ \underline{\text{NEXT}} \underline{\text{SENTENCE}} \end{array} \right\} \right] . . .$$

$$\underline{\text{SEARCH}} \underline{\text{ALL}} \text{ identifier-1} [; \text{AT } \underline{\text{END}} \text{ imperative-statement-1}]$$

$$; \underline{\text{WHEN}} \left\{ \begin{array}{l} \text{data-name-1} \\ \text{condition-name-1} \end{array} \right\} \left\{ \begin{array}{l} \text{IS } \underline{\text{EQUAL}} \text{ TO} \\ \text{IS} = \end{array} \right\} \left\{ \begin{array}{l} \text{identifier-3} \\ \text{literal-1} \\ \text{arithmetic-expression-1} \end{array} \right\} \right\}$$

$$\left[\underline{\text{AND}} \left\{ \begin{array}{l} \text{data-name-2} \\ \text{condition-name-2} \end{array} \right\} \left\{ \begin{array}{l} \text{IS } \underline{\text{EQUAL}} \text{ TO} \\ \text{IS} = \end{array} \right\} \left\{ \begin{array}{l} \text{identifier-4} \\ \text{literal-2} \\ \text{arithmetic-expression-2} \end{array} \right\} \right\} \right] . . .$$

$$\left\{ \begin{array}{l} \text{imperative-statement-2} \\ \underline{\text{NEXT}} \underline{\text{SENTENCE}} \end{array} \right\}$$

$$\underline{\text{SET}} \left\{ \begin{array}{l} \text{identifier-1} [, \text{identifier-2}] . . . \\ \text{index-name-1} [, \text{index-name-2}] . . . \end{array} \right\} \underline{\text{TO}} \left\{ \begin{array}{l} \text{identifier-3} \\ \text{index-name-3} \\ \text{integer-1} \end{array} \right\}$$

$$\underline{\text{SET}} \text{ index-name-4} [, \text{index-name-5}] . . . \left\{ \begin{array}{l} \underline{\text{UP}} \underline{\text{BY}} \\ \underline{\text{DOWN}} \underline{\text{BY}} \end{array} \right\} \left\{ \begin{array}{l} \text{identifier-4} \\ \text{integer-2} \end{array} \right\}$$

$$\underline{\text{SORT}} \text{ file-name-1 ON} \begin{Bmatrix} \underline{\text{ASCENDING}} \\ \underline{\text{DESCENDING}} \end{Bmatrix} \text{KEY data-name-1} [\text{, data-name-2}] \ . \ . \ .$$

$$\begin{Bmatrix} \underline{\text{INPUT}} \ \underline{\text{PROCEDURE}} \text{ IS section-name-1} \left[\begin{Bmatrix} \underline{\text{THROUGH}} \\ \underline{\text{THRU}} \end{Bmatrix} \text{section-name-2} \right] \\ \underline{\text{USING}} \text{ file-name-2 } [\text{, file-name-3}] \ . \ . \ . \end{Bmatrix}$$

$$\begin{Bmatrix} \underline{\text{OUTPUT}} \ \underline{\text{PROCEDURE}} \text{ IS section-name-3} \left[\begin{Bmatrix} \underline{\text{THROUGH}} \\ \underline{\text{THRU}} \end{Bmatrix} \text{section-name-4} \right] \\ \underline{\text{GIVING}} \text{ file-name-4} \end{Bmatrix}$$

$$\underline{\text{START}} \text{ file-name} \left[\underline{\text{KEY}} \begin{Bmatrix} \text{IS } \underline{\text{EQUAL}} \text{ TO} \\ \text{IS } = \\ \text{IS } \underline{\text{GREATER}} \text{ THAN} \\ \text{IS } > \\ \text{IS } \underline{\text{NOT}} \ \underline{\text{LESS}} \text{ THAN} \\ \text{IS } \underline{\text{NOT}} < \end{Bmatrix} \text{data-name} \right]$$

[; <u>INVALID</u> KEY imperative-statement]

$$\underline{\text{STOP}} \begin{Bmatrix} \underline{\text{RUN}} \\ \text{literal} \end{Bmatrix}$$

$$\underline{\text{SUBTRACT}} \begin{Bmatrix} \text{identifier-1} \\ \text{literal-1} \end{Bmatrix} \left[\begin{matrix} \text{, identifier-2} \\ \text{, literal-2} \end{matrix} \right] \ . \ . \ . \underline{\text{FROM}} \text{ identifier-m} [\underline{\text{ROUNDED}}]$$

$$\left[\text{, identifier-n} [\underline{\text{ROUNDED}}] \right] \ . \ . \ . \left[\text{; ON } \underline{\text{SIZE}} \ \underline{\text{ERROR}} \text{ imperative-statement} \right]$$

$$\underline{\text{SUBTRACT}} \begin{Bmatrix} \text{identifier-1} \\ \text{literal-1} \end{Bmatrix} \left[\begin{matrix} \text{, identifier-2} \\ \text{, literal-2} \end{matrix} \right] \ . \ . \ . \underline{\text{FROM}} \begin{Bmatrix} \text{identifier-m} \\ \text{literal-m} \end{Bmatrix}$$

$$\underline{\text{GIVING}} \text{ identifier-n} [\underline{\text{ROUNDED}}] \left[\text{, identifier-6} [\underline{\text{ROUNDED}}] \right] \ . \ . \ .$$

[; ON <u>SIZE</u> <u>ERROR</u> imperative-statement]

$$\underline{\text{SUBTRACT}} \begin{Bmatrix} \underline{\text{CORRESPONDING}} \\ \underline{\text{CORR}} \end{Bmatrix} \text{identifier-1} \ \underline{\text{FROM}} \text{ identifier-2} [\underline{\text{ROUNDED}}]$$

[; On <u>SIZE</u> <u>ERROR</u> imperative-statement]

WRITE record-name [FROM identifier-1]

$$\left[\left\{ \begin{matrix} \underline{BEFORE} \\ \underline{AFTER} \end{matrix} \right\} ADVANCING \left\{ \begin{matrix} \left\{ \begin{matrix} identifier-2 \\ integer \end{matrix} \right\} \left[\begin{matrix} LINE \\ LINES \end{matrix} \right] \\ \left\{ \begin{matrix} mnemonic-name \\ \underline{PAGE} \end{matrix} \right\} \end{matrix} \right\} \right]$$

$$\left[; AT \left\{ \begin{matrix} \underline{END-OF-PAGE} \\ \underline{EOP} \end{matrix} \right\} imperative-statement \right]$$

WRITE record-name [FROM identifier] [; INVALID KEY imperative-statement]

Miscellaneous formats: *Conditions*

RELATION CONDITION:

$$\left\{ \begin{matrix} identifier-1 \\ literal-1 \\ arithmetic-expression-1 \\ index-name-1 \end{matrix} \right\} \left\{ \begin{matrix} IS\ [\underline{NOT}]\ \underline{GREATER}\ THAN \\ IS\ [\underline{NOT}]\ \underline{LESS}\ THAN \\ IS\ [\underline{NOT}]\ \underline{EQUAL}\ TO \\ IS\ [\underline{NOT}]\ > \\ IS\ [\underline{NOT}]\ < \\ IS\ [\underline{NOT}]\ = \end{matrix} \right\} \left\{ \begin{matrix} identifier-2 \\ literal-2 \\ arithmetic-expression-2 \\ index-name-2 \end{matrix} \right\}$$

CLASS CONDITION:

$$identifier\ IS\ [\underline{NOT}] \left\{ \begin{matrix} \underline{NUMERIC} \\ \underline{ALPHABETIC} \end{matrix} \right\}$$

SIGN CONDITION:

$$arithmetic-expression\ is\ [\underline{NOT}] \left\{ \begin{matrix} \underline{POSITIVE} \\ \underline{NEGATIVE} \\ \underline{ZERO} \end{matrix} \right\}$$

PICTURE CLAUSE CHARACTERS

A	Alphabetic character
B	Blank space
P	Decimal scaling position
S	Sign
V	Assumed decimal point
Z	Zero suppression
9	Numeric character
0	Zero insertion character
.	Decimal point edit character
,	Comma edit character
+	Plus sign edit character
—	Minus sign edit character
CR	Credit symbol edit character
DB	Debit symbol edit character
*	Asterisk symbol edit character
$	Dollar sign

QUALIFICATION:

$$\begin{Bmatrix} \text{data-name-1} \\ \text{condition-name} \end{Bmatrix} \left[\begin{Bmatrix} \underline{OF} \\ \underline{IN} \end{Bmatrix} \text{data-name-2} \right] \dots$$

$$\text{paragraph-name} \left[\begin{Bmatrix} \underline{OF} \\ \underline{IN} \end{Bmatrix} \text{section-name} \right]$$

$$\text{text-name} \left[\begin{Bmatrix} \underline{OF} \\ \underline{IN} \end{Bmatrix} \text{library-name} \right]$$

Operating the IBM 029 Card Punch

Operating Features

The *Card Hopper,* with a capacity of approximately 500 cards, is on the upper right side of the machine. Cards are placed in the hopper face forward, 9-edge down. A sliding pressure plate insures uniform feeding. A card is fed from the hopper to the card bed automatically or when the operator depresses the Feed Key. The first two cards *must* be fed by key, but all others may be fed automatically by means of the Auto Feed Key.

Punching is performed at the first of two stations in the card bed through which the cards pass from right to left. Usually, to start an operation, two cards are fed into the card bed at the right of the punching station. As the second card is fed in, the first card is automatically registered for punching; that is, it is positioned at the punching station. While the first card is being punched, the second card is at the right in the card bed. When column 80 of the first card passes the punching station, the second card is registered at the punching station, and the next card in the hopper is fed into the right of the card bed. This method of card feeding minimizes the time required for feeding and ejecting.

In certain instances it is desirable to insert cards manually, one at a time, as in the case of making over a damaged card or correcting an error found while verifying. A card can be manually inserted in the card bed to the right of either the punching station or the reading station. Do not insert a single card in the hopper.

A card is read for duplicating at the *Reading Station,* just to the left of the Punching Station. Remember that the card at the Punching Station and the card at the Reading Station are always synchronized and move through the unit column by column.

The card stacker, with a capacity of approximately 500 cards, is on the upper left side of the machine on a level with the hopper. After each card passes the reading station, it feeds into the stacker automatically or by key. Cards stack at an angle, 12's down, face back, and are held in position by a card weight. When the cards are removed from the stacker, they are in their original sequence.

The red *Main-line Switch* is located underneath the work table on the right side. As soon as the switch is turned on the machine is ready for use.

The *Backspace Key* is located between the Reading and Punching Stations and holding down the key causes the Card Punch to backspace continually. At the same time, the program card, which controls skipping and duplicating, also backspaces.

The *Program Unit* controls automatic skipping, automatic duplicating, and shifting from numeric to alphabetic punching on all models of the 029 Card Punch. In addition, on Model B, the program unit controls left-zero insertion; on Model C, it controls the skipping of fields that are not to be interpreted, and the 11-12 elimination feature. The unit is accessible to the operator from the front of the machine. By lifting the middle portion of the top cover, the program drum can be removed for the installation of the program card.

Each of the operations performed under the control of the program unit is designated by a specific code recorded in a program card. The program card is punched with the program card codes to fit the application desired. The program card is mounted on the program drum, which is placed on the program unit of the 029 Card Punch. The program drum revolves in synchronism with the movement of the cards past the punching and reading stations so that the program card codes control the operations column by column.

The program control unit on the 029 Card Punch is equipped with two program levels, which give added flexibility to a program operation. Automatic skipping, duplicating, field definition, alphabetic shift, and additional controls of Models B and C can be performed through both levels of the program control.

The *Program Control Lever,* located below the program unit, controls operation of the program unit. Turn the control lever on, to the left, to lower the sensing mechanism. The sensing mechanism consists of up to 12 starwheels that, when the mechanism is lowered, ride along the surface of the program card to sense the program control punches in the card. When a punched hole is sensed by a starwheel, a signal goes to the controlling circuits of the machine. This signal initiates the particular function designated by the code punch detected in the program card.

Turn the control lever off, to the right, to raise the sensing mechanism. This lifts the starwheels off the program card; the program control punches will not be sensed. The control lever *must* be turned to the off position when no program drum is in the machine.

The *Column Indicator,* located at the base of the program drum holder, shows the next column to be punched. Refer to this indicator as a guide for spacing or backspacing to a particular column.

The *Pressure-roll Release Lever* is next to the column indicator. It is accessible by raising the center cover over the program unit. Press this lever to permit the manual removal of a card from the punching or reading station. Normally a card can be removed in one piece if it is pulled out with care. If torn pieces are caught at either station, push them out with another card or a smooth-edge metal blade while holding down the pressure-roll release lever. Do not use saw-edge metal blades.

Program Drum and Program Card

The Program Card Codes for the various models of the 029 Card Punch are given below.

Program One	Function	Where Punched	Used On
12	Field Definition	Each column except first	Models A, B, C
11	Start Auto-Skip	First column only	Models A, B, C
0	Start Auto-Duplicate	First column only	Models A, B Model C only when in punch mode
0	11/12 Elimination	Necessary column only	Model C only when in interpret mode
1	Alphabetic Shift	Each necessary column	Models A, B Model C only when in punch mode
2	8-Column Left-Zero Field	First column only	Model B only
3	7-Column Left-Zero Field	First column only	Model B only
2,3	6-Column Left-Zero Field	First column only	Model B only
1,2	5-Column Left-Zero Field	First column only	Model B only
1,3	4-Column Left-Zero Field	First column only	Model B only
1,2,3	3-Column Left-Zero Field	First column only	Model B only

The program drum is the part of the program unit that holds the program card. This part can be removed by the operator so that the program card can be inserted to set up the program operation for a specific application.

Drum removal

1. Raise the sensing mechanism by turning the program control lever to the right or off position.
2. Remove the program drum by pulling in a direction parallel to the sensing mechanism. The program card can then be removed from the drum.

Card removal

1. Turn the clamping strip handle to the center position and remove the column-1 end of the card from beneath the clamping strip.
2. Now turn the handle fully counterclockwise and remove the card from the drum.

Card insertion

1. With the clamping strip handle turned fully counterclockwise, insert the column-80 end of the card under the smooth edge of the clamping strip. Two alignment check holes in the card are flush with the metal edge under the strip. The card should be positioned so that the 9-edge of the card is against the rim of the drum.
2. Turn the handle to the center position. This tightens the smooth edge of the clamping strip and loosens the toothed edge.
3. Wrap the card tightly around the drum and insert the column-1 edge under the toothed edge of the clamping strip.
4. Turn the handle clockwise as far as it will go. This fastens the toothed edge of the clamping strip. The drum is ready to be inserted in the machine.

Drum insertion

1. With the program sensing mechanism raised, place the drum on the mounting shaft of the program unit, positioned so that the aligning pin falls in the aligning hole in the column indicator dial.
2. Turn the program control lever to the left or to the on position to lower the sensing mechanism to the program card. Press the release key.

Caution: An empty program drum should not be inserted in the program unit, and the sensing mechanism must never be lowered when no program drum is in place.

Other Keys and Switches

The *Auto Skip/Duplicate (Auto Skp/Dup)* switch must be set on to obtain automatic skipping and duplicating initiated by the program card 11 and zero punches, respectively. When the switch is off, these functions can be started only by the Skp and Dup keys.

Program Selection (Prog Sel): With a program card in place and the program control lever in the on position, the position of this switch determines whether program control starts in Program One (12-03) or Program Two (4–9). The switch setting selects the program level as a new card is registered for punching. The program level may be changed at will during punching by using the program selection keys. However, each time a card is registered, the switch setting selects the start program level.

When the *Auto Feed Switch* is turned on and column 80 of the card passes the punch station, a new card is fed automatically. At the same time, the card in the left of the card bed is stacked, the one in the center is registered at the read station, and the one at the right is registered at the punch station. This automatic feeding occurs after the card, completely processed, passes column 80.

When the switch is off, cards may be fed manually by pressing the feed key, program one key, or the program two key.

Clear: The clear switch is a spring-loaded, self-restoring switch used to clear all cards from the feed bed without feeding additional cards from the hopper. One operation of the switch initiates the multiple cycles necessary to complete the operation.

The *Numeric Shift* and *Alpha Shift* keys put the unit into the appropriate shift as long *as the key is held down.*

The *Duplicate Key* (DUP) is used to duplicate information from the card at the Reading Station into the card at the Punching Station. Under program control, one depression of the dup key initiates the operation. Duplication continues until the end of field definition.

Encountering a space during duplication of numeric fields locks the keyboard. The error reset key unlocks the keyboard and permits keying of the space, substitute data, or release. The alpha shift key can also be used to allow duplication of the space.

Without program control, duplication occurs at the rate of 9 or 10 columns per second and occurs only as long as the key is held down. This permits precise column control in a card correction or make-over application.

Duplication of characters other than the standard 64 can cause damage to the print mechanism on printing models of the 29 Card Punch.

The *Release Key* (REL) is used to advance the card in the Read or Punch Station through card column 80. Multiple release and register cycles are not required to clear the card transport area of cards. Use the Clear Key for this operation.

The *Feed Key,* if held depressed, moves two cards from the hopper into the punch station and pre-register station. It is inoperative when a card is registered at the punch station.

A skip can be initiated manually by operating the *Skip Key.* Skipping occurs at 80 columns per second and continues to the end of the field definition under program control, or, in the absence of field definition, each key operation results in a single space.

The *Multiple Punch Key* (Mult Pch) places the keyboard in numeric shift and suppresses spacing while individual codes are keyed and punched. (Duplicating these invalid characters should not be attempted on printing models of the 029 Card Punch.)

The *Error Reset Key* is used to unlock the keyboard.

Operating Suggestions

Removing a card from the punch or read station

If for any reason a card must be removed manually from the punch or read station, hold down the pressure-roll release lever while pulling out the card. If a card at the punch station does not move easily, press all the numeric keys; then, while holding down the lever, pull the card forward without tearing it.

Keyboard locking

The keyboard locks under any of the following conditions:

1. The main line switch is turned off and then on while a card is registered at the punch station. The clear switch should be operated to move the card to the stacker; however, the card at the punch station need not be removed. One depression of the feed key brings a second card down without advancing the first card, and restores the machine to operating condition.
2. On the combination keyboard, when either the A or Z key is pressed in a column programmed for numeric punching. Press the error reset key to unlock the keyboard.
3. A blank column is duplicated in a field programmed for numeric punching. This serves as a blank-column detection device to insure that a digit is punched in every column of a numeric field that is being duplicated. Unlock the keyboard by pressing the error reset key or the alphabetic shift key on the combination keyboard.
4. A card is not registered at the punch station. It is impossible to do any punching or spacing unless a card is registered at the punch station. To move a card into punching position, press the register, the feed, or (with the autofeed switch on) the release key.
5. The register key or the feed key is pressed when a card is already registered at the punch station. Press the error reset key to unlock the keyboard.

Answers to Selected Chapter Exercises

Chapter 2   Top-Down Design and Structured Programming

2b.

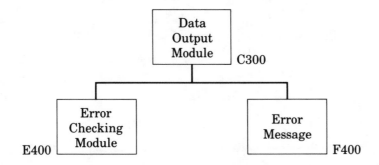

Note: The function of module F400 might be combined with module E400.

5.

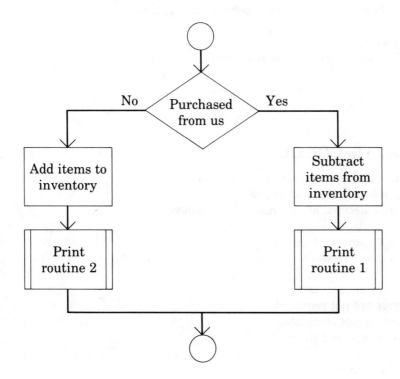

6.

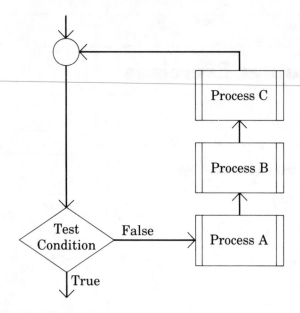

9. a. CARD-DATA
  b. LIST
  c. CONTROL-ROUTINE
     010-OPENER
     020-READER
     030-CLOSER
  d. To create the program loop by making this paragraph execute repeatedly.
  e. Get the files ready for processing.
  f. The loop is terminated when the INDICATOR field contains a value of 1.
11. The INDICATOR field serves as a signal to tell the system to stop executing the program loop.

Chapter 3   Getting Started in COBOL

2. The COBOL compiler is controlled by Supervisor, which, as the name indicates, is the major controlling piece of software.
4. Files are comprised of Records. Records are normally broken down into a series of fields of data.
6. Commas are not required in COBOL statements.
8. a. Incorrect: NUMBER is a reserved word.
  b. Incorrect: No period.
  c. Correct: But a poor choice of field names.
  d. Correct: But the commas are not required.
  e. Incorrect: The statement is not complete.
  f. Incorrect: OVERFLOW is a reserved word.
  g. Correct
  h. Incorrect: Used MORE instead of MOVE.
  i. Incorrect: There is a blank in the SS-NUMBER field instead of a hyphen.

9. **a.** Correct

   b. Correct

   c. Incorrect: No ending quote.

   d. Incorrect: You cannot work numerically with non-numeric literals.

   e. Correct

   f. Incorrect: You don't have to tell it how many SPACES.

   g. Incorrect: You can't do arithmetic on non-numeric literals.

   h. Correct

   i. Incorrect: You can't manipulate figurative constants.

11. **a.** Numeric constant

   b. Non-numeric literal

   c. Non-numeric literal

   d. Illegal numeric constant

   e. Non-numeric literal

   f. Numeric constant

   g. Figurative constant

   h. Numeric constant

   i. Figurative constant

   j. Non-numeric literal

Chapter 4 Setting up the Program

2. **a.** Incorrect: No period.

   b. Incorrect: Spaces are not allowed in a name.

   c. Incorrect: No hyphen.

   d. Correct

   e. Incorrect: Misspelled word ENVIRONMENT.

   f. The second and third lines cannot begin in the A area.

3. **a.** FD CARD-FILE

   LABEL RECORDS ARE OMITTED

   DATA RECORD IS _____ .

   b. FD PRINTER

   LABEL RECORDS ARE OMITTED

   DATA RECORD IS _____ .

4. **a.** SELECT PRINTED-DATA

   ASSIGN TO SYS003-UR-1403-S.

   b. SELECT INPUT-FILE

   ASSIGN TO SYS011-UR-1442R-S.

   c. SELECT OUTPUT-FILE-DATA

   ASSIGN TO SYSPRINT.

5.

01	INVENTORY-DATA.	
	03 PART-NBR	PIC 9(10).
	03 FILLER	PIC X(6).
	03 PART-NAME	PIC A(15).
	03 BIN-NBR	PIC 9(5).
	03 SHELF-NBR	PIC 9(5).
	03 FILLER	PIC X(39).
	03 CODE-FIELD	PIC X.

6.   01   EMPLOYEE-RECORD.

          03 FILLER   PIC X(20).

          03 SS-NBR   PIC 9(9).

          03 EMP-NAME   PIC A(21).

          03 ADDRESS   PIC X(20).

          03 CODE-FIELD   PIC 99.

          03 FILLER   PIC X(8).

7.   01   EMPLOYEE-RECORD.

          03 FILLER   PIC X(20).

          03 SS-NBR.

                05 SS-1   PIC 999.

                05 SS-2   PIC 99.

                05 SS-3   PIC 9999.

          03 EMP-NAME   PIC A(21).

          03 ADDRESS   PIC X(20).

          03 CODE-FIELD   PIC 99.

          03 FILLER   PIC X(8).

Chapter 5   The PROCEDURE DIVISION—Part I

1. a. Incorrect: You cannot PERFORM a COBOL statement. You can only PERFORM a PROCEDURE DIVISION paragraph.

   b. Correct, but foolish if you mean this as a paragraph name.

   c. Correct

   d. Incorrect: You always READ a file name, not a record name.

   e. Incorrect: You always WRITE a record name.

   f. Incorrect: You must specify whether the file is INPUT or OUTPUT.

   g. Incorrect: You must not specify either INPUT or OUTPUT with the CLOSE statement.

   h. Correct

2. a. Incorrect: You cannot move anything to a FILLER area.

   b. Correct: You may have as many statements as you wish after the AT END portion of the statement.

   c. Incorrect: If you once use the ADVANCING option with a file, you must always use it with that file.

   d. Correct: This series writes a blank line.

   e. Incorrect: You must write the record name.

6. a. 567 ∧ Truncation occurs

   b. 45 ∧ 50 Correct move

   c. 3 ∧ 000 Truncation occurs

   d. 0000 ∧ Truncation occurs

   e. 000000 Correct move

   f. Spaces are moved correctly.

9. Yes, you can PERFORM a single statement by PERFORMing a PROCEDURE DIVISION paragraph that contains one statement.

11. PERFORM READ-LOOP.

    PERFORM READ-LOOP.

12. a. PERFORM PROGRAM-LOOP

        UNTIL B IS GREATER THAN A.

   b. PERFORM PROGRAM-LOOP

        UNTIL C IS NOT EQUAL TO D.

   c. PERFORM PROGRAM-LOOP

        UNTIL AMOUNT IS LESS THAN TEST-AMT.

   d. PERFORM PROGRAM-LOOP

        UNTIL COUNTER IS EQUAL TO 50.

Chapter 6   Handling Data

1. The FILE SECTION is used exclusively for setting up the incoming and outgoing data file areas. The WORKING-STORAGE SECTION may contain items that are independent of the data files.

3. There is no point in naming fields that will not be referenced in the program, and that is why the reserved word FILLER was established.

7. If the VALUE entry had been omitted, there is no way of knowing what the initial value of the field would be. Normally it would be junk and the program would have aborted the first time the INDICATOR field was tested. If the field had contained a 5, the program would work because a valid 1-digit number in the INDICATOR field would permit correct testing.

9. **a.** NO-OF-SALES PIC 999 VALUE ZEROS.

   b. COUNTER-1 PIC 9(5) VALUE ZEROS.

   c. AREA-1 PIC 9(5)V99 COMP-3 VALUE ZEROS.

   d. AREA-1 PIC 9(4)V99 COMP VALUE ZEROS.

   e. AREA-1 PIC 9(6)V99 VALUE ZEROS.

   f. DATA-AREA PIC 9(4)V99 COMP-3.

   g. DATA-AREA PIC 9(4) COMP.

10. **a.** CONSTANT PIC 9(3)V9(3) VALUE 763.714.

   b. FUDGE-AMT PIC 99V99 VALUE 21.65 COMP.

   c. ONE-AMT PIC 9 VALUE 9 COMP-3.

   d. THREE-FIELD PIC 999 VALUE 6 COMP.

   e. MESSAGE PIC X(13) VALUE 'BAD CARD DATA'.

   f. TODAYS-DATE PIC X(16) VALUE '_____'.

   g. NAME-DATA PIC A(30) VALUE '_____'.

11. **a.** 01   HEAD-1.

```
        03 FILLER       PIC X.
        03 FILLER       PIC X(52) VALUE SPACES.
        03 FILLER       PIC X(16) VALUE 'INCOME STATEMENT'.
        03 FILLER       PIC X(52) VALUE SPACES.
```

   b. 01   HEAD-2.

```
        03 FILLER       PIC X.
        03 FILLER       PIC X(30) VALUE SPACES.
        03 FILLER       PIC X(23) VALUE 'FOR THE YEAR ENDED 1981'.
        03 FILLER       PIC X(79) VALUE SPACES.
```

   c. 01   HEAD-3.

```
        03 FILLER       PIC X.
        03 FILLER       PIC X(79) VALUE SPACES.
        03 FILLER       PIC X(23) VALUE 'FOR THE YEAR ENDED 1981'.
        03 FILLER       PIC X(30) VALUE SPACES.
```

12. **a.** EDIT-FIELD PIC ZZZ.99.

   b. EDIT-FIELD PIC $$$$.99.

   c. EDIT-FIELD PIC Z,ZZZ.99.

   d. EDIT-FIELD PIC $$,$$$.99.

   e. EDIT-FIELD PIC ZZZ.99CR.

   f. EDIT-FIELD PIC ZZZ.99 + .

   g. EDIT-FIELD PIC $99,999.99DB.

   h. EDIT-FIELD PIC 999B99B9999.

Chapter 7   The PROCEDURE DIVISION—Part II

1. a. Correct
   b. Incorrect: You cannot add to a literal.
   c. Incorrect: You cannot have TO and GIVING in the same ADD statement.
   d. Correct
   e. Correct
   f. Incorrect: AND is not permitted.
   g. Correct
   h. Incorrect: Improper use of ROUNDED.
   i. Correct
   j. Incorrect: You cannot use any symbols in arithmetic operations.
   k. Correct

2. a. Correct
   b. Correct
   c. Incorrect: You cannot subtract from a literal.
   d. Correct
   e. Incorrect: Format requires FROM.
   f. Correct
   g. Incorrect use of ROUNDED.
   h. Incorrect placement of period.
   i. Incorrect: LINES is a reserved word.
   j. Incorrect use of ROUNDED.

3. a. Correct
   b. Incorrect: A literal cannot be the second operand in a MULTIPLY statement.
   c. Correct
   d. Incorrect: Incorrect MULTIPLY format.
   e. Correct
   f. Correct
   g. Correct
   h. Incorrect: You cannot have more than one ROUNDED.
   i. Correct
   j. Correct

4. a. COMPUTE X = (A + B) / C.
   b. COMPUTE X = A / C + B.
   c. COMPUTE X = A ** 2 + B ** 3.
   d. COMPUTE X = 6 * A * B + 4 * R * Q * G.
   e. COMPUTE X = (6 * A * B) / (4 * Q * G).
   f. COMPUTE X ROUNDED = (6 * A * B) / (4 * Q * G).
   g. COMPUTE X = (A + A ** 2 + (A ** 3 − 15)) / T.
   h. COMPUTE X ROUNDED = (A + B) / C ON SIZE ERROR GO TO MESSAGE-
                              ROUTINE.
   i. COMPUTE R = R + 1.

5. a. 9(4)V9(4)
   b. 9(3)V9(5)
   c. 999V99 ; three
   d. V999 ; two

6. a. If A-FIELD IS NOT EQUAL TO ZERO GO TO ROUTINE-1.

   b. IF A-FIELD IS GREATER THAN LIMIT
       ADD 1 TO COUNTER-A
   ELSE
       SUBTRACT CONSTANT FROM COUNTER-B.

   c. IF NAME-FIELD IS NOT ALPHABETIC
       DISPLAY 'NAME FIELD NOT ALPHABETIC'
          UPON CONSOLE
       ADD 1 TO COUNT-B.
   ADD 1 TO COUNT-C.

   d. IF AMT-OF-PAY IS NOT NUMERIC
       DISPLAY 'DATA OF WRONG TYPE'
          UPON CONSOLE
   ELSE
       MOVE BODY-LINE TO OUTPUT-LINE
          AFTER ADVANCING 3 LINES.
   MULTIPLY SUB-TOTAL BY RATE
       GIVING ANSWER-1.

7. a. IF A > B
       COMPUTE X = A − B
       MOVE ZEROS TO
          TOTAL-3
   ELSE
       COMPUTE X = B − A
       COMPUTE Q = (R + Z) ** 2.
   MOVE MSG-2 TO
       OUTPUT-LINE.
   WRITE OUTPUT-LINE
       AFTER ADVANCING
          3 LINES.

   b. IF A > B
       COMPUTE X = A − B
       MOVE ZEROS TO
          TOTAL-3
   ELSE
       COMPUTE X = B − A
       COMPUTE Q = (R + Z) ** 2
       MOVE MSG-2 TO OUTPUT-LINE
       WRITE OUTPUT-LINE
          AFTER ADVANCING 3 LINES.

   c. IF A = B
       COMPUTE X = A + B
       ADD 1 TO TOTAL-X
   ELSE
       IF A > B
          SUBTRACT 1 FROM TOTAL-A
       ELSE
          ADD 1 TO TOTAL-A.
   MOVE ZEROS TO COUNTER-G.

Chapter 8   Magnetic Tape Processing

5. 03 W-CODE PIC 9(3) COMP-3.

FD

BLOCK CONTAINS 7 RECORDS

RECORD CONTAINS 75 CHARACTERS

6. COMP-3 applies only to numeric data.

7. a. $100,000 \times 80 = 8,000,000$ bytes.

$8,000,000 \div 6250 = 1280$ inches for data

$20,000$ blocks $\times .5 = 10,000$ inches for gaps

$11,280$ inches—Answer

b. $65,000 \times 35 = 2,275,000$ bytes.

$2,275,000 \div 6250 = 364$ inches for data

$65,000 \div 25 = 2600$ blocks $\times .5 = 1300$ inches for gaps

1664 inches—Answer

c. $65,000 \times 35 = 2,275,000$ bytes.

$2,275,000 \div 6250 = 364$ inches for data

$65,000$ blocks $\times .5 = 32,500$ inches for gaps

$32,864$ inches, which is larger than a tape spool.

d. $50,000 \times 70 = 3,500,000$ bytes.

$3,500,000 \div 6250 = 560$ inches for data

$25,000$ blocks $\times .5 = 12,500$ inches for gaps

$13,060$ inches—Answer

e. $50,000 \times 70 = 3,500,000$.

$3,500,000 \div 6250 = 560$ inches for data

$5,000$ blocks $\times .5 = 2500$ inches for gaps

$3,060$ inches—Answer

8. a. $8,000,000 \div 1600 = 5,000$ inches—data

$= 10,000$ inches—gap

Total $15,000$

b. $2,275,000 \div 1600 = 1,422$—data

$= 1,300$ inches—gap

Total $2,722$

c. $2,275,000 \div 1600 = 1,422$ inches—data

$= 32,500$ inches—gap

Total $33,922$ (too large for tape spool)

d. $3,500,000 \div 1600 = 2,188$ inches—data

$= 12,500$ inches—gap

Total $14,688$

e. $3,500,000 \div 1600 = 2,188$ inches—data

$= 2,500$ inches—gap

Total $4,688$

9. a. $8,000,000$ characters $\div 100,000 = 80$ seconds—data

$20,000$ gaps $\times .1 = 200$ seconds—gaps

Total 280

b. 2,275,000 characters ÷ 10,000 =   22.75 seconds—data
2600 gaps × .1   = 260 seconds—gaps
Total   282.75

c. 3,500,000 characters ÷ 100,000 =   35 seconds—data
25,000 gaps × .1   = 2500 seconds—gaps
Total   2535

d. 3,500,000 characters ÷ 100,000 =   35 seconds—data
5,000 gaps × .1   = 500 seconds—gaps
Total   535

10. a. 5 bytes   ØX XX XX XX XS
b. 1 byte   XS
c. 2 bytes   ØX XS
d. 2 bytes   XX XS
e. 6 bytes   XX XX XX XX XX XS

Chapter 9   Manipulating Data Files

1. a. A file that contains data of temporary value or likely to be used only once. Typical examples include *daily* charge transactions, *weekly* inventory adjustments, and so on.
b. See Detail File.
c. As opposed to a Detail or Transaction file, a Master File contains data that change relatively infrequently and which are likely to be used by many different application programs.
d. The existing Master File that is going through or has just gone through an up-dating process.
e. The latest version of the Master that is being developed from the processing of the Detail File and the old Master File.

2. a. M: 1   2   3   4   5   6
  D: 2   5   1
b. M: 1   2   3   4   5   6   7
  D1:   2   5   7
  D2:   1   3   4
c. M: 1   2   3   4   5   6
  D: 2   5   1   6
d. M: 1   2   3   4   5   6   7
  D1:   2   7   5
  D2:   1   3   4

4. a. M: 1   3   4   6   7   8
  D: 2   5
b. M: 1   3   4   7   8   10
  D: 2   6   5   9
c. M: 3   6   7   9   10
  D1:   1   4   8
  D2:   2   5

5. D1:   1   3   4   6   7
  D2:   2   4   5   6   9

Chapter 10   Control Breaks

1. A control break occurs when the value in a designated field of the first input record has a value different from that of the next or second input record. Rolling a total is the act of adding a total into a higher-level total. For example, a minor total will be rolled into an intermediate-level total, and so on.

2. The "first record" problem is that there is no valid number against which to compare it. Even if we assume that the computer system accepts the comparing process, the first card record will always trigger a minor break. The chapter showed two ways around the problem. One was by moving the control break value from the first record into a compare area; the second method was to use a switch to by-pass the comparing operation on the first record.

3. By definition, an intermediate-level break would always contain a lower-level break field (minor field). In the same manner a major-level break would always contain both an intermediate- and a minor-level break.

4. A detail printed report prints one line per record plus the appropriate total lines. A group or summary printed report prints one line for each control group.

5. Group indication occurs when the printing of the identifying material for a group occurs only for the first record of that group. One exception to this is if the group indicated report were to go onto a new page, the first line on the new page would print the complete line of identifying material.

   A summary report could be group indicated. Exercise 9 in this chapter showed a Sales Report in which the department sales amounts were summary printed. Group indication could take place on the territory and region numbers.

6. A programmed switch is any field that you designate as a switch and that is used to convey control information from one part of the program to another. It differs from the EOF switches used so far in that the testing of the EOF switch has been done automatically by the software of the PERFORM statement. However, any switch may be tested or reset at any point in the program.

Chapter 11   Data in Tables

1. **a.** 03 RETURNS PIC 9(4) OCCURS 50 TIMES.
   b. 03 SALES-AMT PIC 9(4)V99 OCCURS 50 TIMES
            USAGE IS COMP-3.
   c. 03 EMPLOYEE-NAMES PIC A(20) OCCURS 70 TIMES.
   d. 03 TABLE-INFO OCCURS 60 TIMES.
            05 AMOUNT-IN   PIC 9(4).
            05 ITEM-DESCRIPTION   PIC X(30).
   e. 05 AMOUNT-IN PIC 9(4) COMP-3.
   f. 03 TABLE-DATA OCCURS 10 TIMES.
            05 SS-NBR   PIC 9(9) COMP-3.
            05 E-NAME   PIC X(30).
            05 RATE   PIC S99V99 COMP-3.
            05 HOURS   PIC S99.

2. a.   PERFORM CLEAR-LOOP 50 TIMES.
    CLEAR-LOOP.
       MOVE ZEROS TO RETURNS (COUNTER).
       ADD 1 TO COUNTER.

b.   77 NINES PIC 9(4) VALUE 9999.
       .
       .
       .

       PERFORM FILL-TABLE 50 TIMES.
    FILL-TABLE.
       MOVE NINES TO RETURNS (COUNTER).
       ADD 1 TO COUNTER.

c.   PERFORM CLEAR-LOOP 10 TIMES.
       .
       .
       .

    CLEAR-LOOP.
       MOVE ZEROS TO SS-NBR (COUNTER).
       MOVE ZEROS TO RATE (COUNTER).
       MOVE ZEROS TO HOURS (COUNTER).
       ADD 1 TO COUNTER.

3. a. COMPUTE ANS (5) = A * A + B * B
  b. COMPUTE ANS (J) = A * + B * B
  c. COMPUTE TOTAL = SALES (1) + SALES (2) + SALES (3).
  d. ADD 6 TO ANS (7).
  e. COMPUTE AMOUNT (X) = AMOUNT (X) + 1.3.

4. 01   DATA-VALUES.
      03 FILLER   PIC 9V99 VALUE 6.75.
      03 FILLER   PIC 9V99 VALUE 9.42.
      03 FILLER   PIC 9V99 VALUE 8.56.
      03 FILLER   PIC 9V99 VALUE 1.49.
    01   TABLE-DATA REDEFINES DATA-VALUES.
      03 TABLE-L PIC 9V99 OCCURS 4 TIMES.

5. a. WORKING-STORAGE SECTION.
    77   COUNTER   PIC 99 VALUE 01.
    01   TABLES.

03 PART	PIC 9(5)	OCCURS 40 TIMES.
03 BIN	PIC 9(3)	OCCURS 40 TIMES.
03 QUANTITY	PIC 9(4)	OCCURS 40 TIMES.
03 ORDERS	PIC 9(4)	OCCURS 40 TIMES.

       .
       .
       .

       PERFORM TABLE-READ 40 TIMES
    TABLE-READ.
       READ CARD FILE AT END _____ .
       MOVE PART-IN   TO BIN (COUNTER).
       MOVE COST-IN   TO COST (COUNTER).
       MOVE QUANTITY-IN   TO QUANTITY (COUNTER).
       MOVE ORDERS-IN   TO ORDERS (COUNTER).

b. 01 _____ .

      03 TABLES OCCURS 40 TIMES.

05 PART	PIC 9(5).
05 BIN	PIC 9(3).
05 COST	PIC 9(4)V99.
05 QUANTITY	PIC 9(4).
05 ORDERS	PIC 9(4).

6. PERFORM ADD-LOOP 40 TIMES.

   MOVE 1 TO COUNTER.

       .

       .

       .

ADD-LOOP.

     ADD ORDERS (COUNTER) TO _____ .

     ADD 1 COUNTER.

7. PERFORM ADD-LOOP

    VARYING COUNTER FROM 1 BY 1

    UNTIL COUNTER IS GREATER THAN 40.

8. a. 01 TABLE-DATA.

     03 TEMP OCCURS 365 TIMES.

        05 YEARS OCCURS 10 TIMES PIC 999V9.

b. DISPLAY YEARS (312,7).

c. DISPLAY YEARS (X,R).

d. 01 TABLE-DATA.

     03 YEARS OCCURS 10 TIMES.

        05 TEMP OCCURS 365 TIMES PIC 999V9.

Chapter 12 Sorting

1. Internal sorting is done in memory and usually is limited to few values—perhaps fewer than 100. External sorting involves large volumes of data and requires the use of external storage such as disk or tape.

3. One possible plan and flowchart is shown below.

    Read in value A and place in storage area called LARGEST

    Read in value B into HOLD–1 and compare against value stored in LARGEST

      If HOLD–1 is greater than the value in LARGEST, move LARGEST to SECOND–LARGEST and move HOLD–1 to SECOND–LARGEST

     Else move HOLD–1 to SECOND–LARGEST

    Read C into HOLD–1 and compare against value stored in LARGEST

      If HOLD–1 is greater than the value in LARGEST, move the value in LARGEST to HOLD–2

      move SECOND–LARGEST to THIRD–LARGEST

      move HOLD–1 to LARGEST

      move HOLD–2 to SECOND–LARGEST

     Else compare HOLD–1 against the value stored in SECOND–LARGEST

      If HOLD–1 is greater than SECOND–LARGEST, move SECOND–LARGEST to THIRD–LARGEST and move HOLD–1 to SECOND–LARGEST

      If HOLD–1 is not greater than SECOND–LARGEST, move HOLD–1 to THIRD–LARGEST

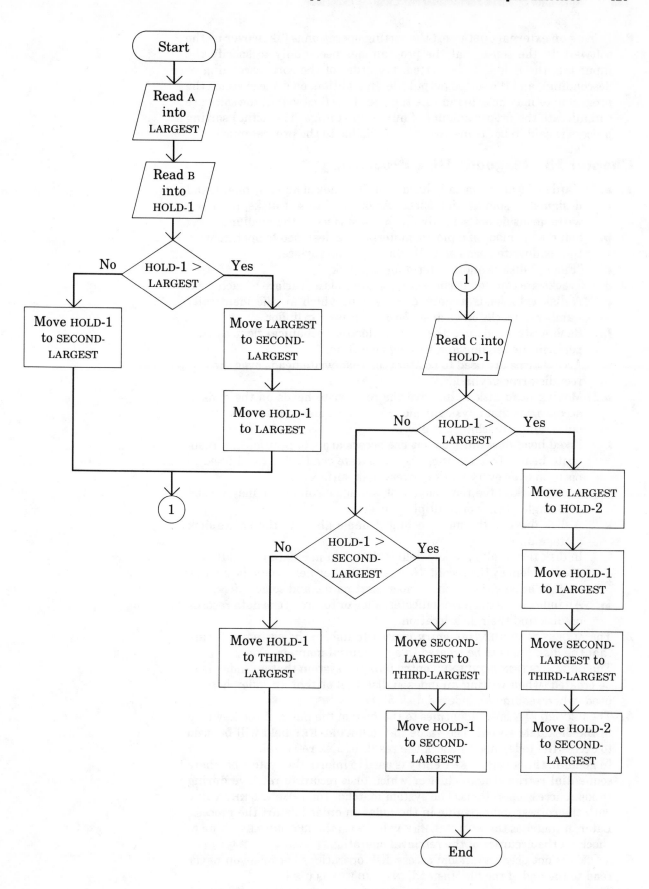

8. During an external COBOL sort the sorting operation is taken over by the software in the sense that the programmer needs only to specify the input file, the field(s) to be sorted, the order of the sort (ascending or descending), and the sorted output file. In addition, on some systems the programmer may have to indicate the size of the files so that the software can allocate the proper amount of auxiliary storage. The actual sorting process is said to be "transparent" or invisible to the programmer.

Chapter 13   Magnetic Disk Processing

1. a. Hard disks are physically hard, usually made of an alloy metal, and designed to spin at high speed. As opposed to soft disks, the read/write heads do not actually touch the surface of the medium.

b. Soft disk is made of a plastic material and designed to operate with the read/write heads actually touching the surface.

c. "Floppy" disk is another term for soft disk.

d. Tracks are concentric rings circling around the surface of each disk.

e. A disk cylinder is a storage concept in which all the identically numbered tracks on each surface comprise a cylinder.

f. Read/write heads are the actual electro/mechanical devices that perform the reading and writing operations.

g. Access arms are used to position the read/write heads over the correct disk track/cylinder.

h. Moving head disk units have the read/write heads on the ends of access arms that physically move across the disk surface area (without actually touching the disk).

i. Fixed head disk units do not use access arms to position the read/write heads. Instead, there is a separate read/write head fixed in position over every track of every disk surface.

j. A disk pack is the removable disk storage medium and may consist of a single platter or multiple platters.

k. A disk drive is the more technical name given to the entire disk storage unit.

l. In disk terminology, a key field is that field in a data record that is used to identify the record. Normally, the key field would be a value such as an identification number, part name, and so on.

m. An index is, as the term indicates, a log or record of the data records on disk and their disk location.

2. The ACCESS IS SEQUENTIAL entry is used to inform the system software that the disk file is to be treated in a sequential manner.

3. The ORGANIZATION IS INDEXED entry tells the system that an index is to be created (when writing an indexed disk file) or that an index is to be used (when reading an indexed disk file).

4. The RECORD KEY entry identifies to the system the name of the key field in the disk data record. The value in the RECORD KEY field will be used to access the index and to check the result of disk retrieval.

5. In general, the NOMINAL KEY entry is used to inform the system of where sequential retrieval is to start or which disk record to retrieve during random access operations. The system matches the NOMINAL KEY value with the corresponding value in the index in order to start the process. Later, it matches the NOMINAL KEY value with the RECORD KEY value to check on the accuracy of the retrieval operation.

6. AT END is not used in random access disk operations because you never read to the end of the file. Instead, INVALID KEY is used.

7. The INVALID KEY is used to trigger into a set of statements whenever an error has occurred in disk retrieval operations.

Data for Use in Problems

Data Set A

```
          1         2         3         4         5
1234567890123456789012345678901234567890123456789012345

1   010114101SMITH ELBERT        M0750031200050000100040036A
2   010116104BARNHART STANLEY    S1125010650100000000004019R
3   050124101WALSH JUDITH        M0655021200050000000004016A
4   050125395PEARSON SAMUEL      M0775051200000000025004036A
5   060443916LEE KIMBERLY        S0450010650025000000038A76
6   140133010CHICANE HERB        M0475011200000000015004036C
7   190456301HARKELRODE CLARA    M0525041200000000150040189
8   220133512KOCHINIS ANGELO     S0965010650000000200040194
9   230965777RUSE WAYNE          M0850021200050000000004236A
10  270134109MOORE SAMUEL        M0775031200025000000004036A
11  304165298BILBERRY DALTON     M0775011200000000005004036A
12  320135004MARTIN SUSAN        M0550081200025000000003919R
13  346945678FUJIMOTO KEN        S1130010650150000000004019R
14  350214101STOLL GEORGE        S0955021200050000000004119C
15  365593864EVANS ROBERT        M0655081200000000000004036C
16  410954321GARCIA FRAN         M0545051200000000015004236A
17  555438619DEE ELLIS           S0450010650000000000004027R
18  666666666BRONSON PATTY       M0750031200025000000003819R
19  684836197ROSSI JACK          M0650041200000000100040100
20  745678432JOHNSON PAM         S0850010650050000000004027R
```

Data Set B

```
                      1         2         3         4
         12345678901234567890123456789012345678901234567890
```

```
 1  10700415MARTIN PEARSON       0105080012027
 2  10300532JOE SMITH            0139055013615
 3  10400617MIKE GONZALES        0137017000000
 4  10701009GEORGE STOLL         0145626002584
 5  10701362SUSAN HASHIMOTO      0139581011559
 6  10401589ABBY JOHNSON         0131519000000
 7  10301666PATRICK JACKSON      0565265042617
 8  10501743JOHN BOSCH           0125554002125
 9  10701824OTTO EHRLIN          0468923001063
10  10302340SHARON HELM          0155581000000
11  10302785JORDAN HOTCHKISS     1032665468555
12  10402965ALVIN WALL           0146277195360
13  10603524PATRICK WONG         0190088000000
14  10703955WAYNE MOORE          0138000000961
15  10404876VERNA APPLEWHITE     0195091000000
16  10705291ANGELA CHANG         1176804001875
17  10505900LISA MOULTON         0132586132586
18  10506893DANIEL PARKER        0968427336597
19  10307444CURTIS HAHN          0660061271783
20  10608321RAYMOND BUTLER       0539609143268
21  10508965DIXIE RHINEHART      0773647051556
22  10709401SARA THOMAS          0131033000000
23  10609653LINDA HAYES          0139998086317
24  10610468FRED WILSON          1047752186537
25  10311639DICK HENNING         0865419256856
```

Index

431